Sorel: Reflections on Violence

Georges Sorel's *Reflections on Violence* is one of the most controversial books of the twentieth century: J. B. Priestley argued that if
one could grasp why a retired civil servant had written such a book
then the modern age could be understood. It heralded the political
turmoil of the decades that were to follow its publication and provided inspiration for Marxists and Fascists alike. Developing the
ideas of violence, myth and the general strike, Sorel celebrates the
heroic action of the proletariat as a means of saving the modern
world from decadence and of reinvigorating the capitalist spirit of
a timid bourgeoisie. This new edition of Sorel's classic text is
accompanied by an editor's introduction by Jeremy Jennings, a leading scholar in political thought, both setting the work in its context
and explaining its major themes. A chronology of Sorel's life and a
list of further reading are included.

JEREMY JENNINGS is professor of political theory at the University
of Birmingham. He is the author or editor of numerous books and
articles, including *Georges Sorel: The Character and Development of
his Thought* (1985), *Syndicalism in France: A Study of Ideas* (1990)
and *Intellectuals in Politics* (1997).

CAMBRIDGE TEXTS IN THE
HISTORY OF POLITICAL THOUGHT

Series editors

RAYMOND GEUSS

Reader in Philosophy, University of Cambridge

QUENTIN SKINNER

Regius Professor of Modern History, University of Cambridge

Cambridge Texts in the History of Political Thought is now firmly established as the major student textbook series in political theory. It aims to make available to students all the most important texts in the history of Western political thought, from ancient Greece to the early twentieth century. All the familiar classic texts will be included but the series seeks at the same time to enlarge the conventional canon by incorporating an extensive range of less well-known works, many of them never before available in a modern English edition. Wherever possible, texts are published in complete and unabridged form, and translations are specially commissioned for the series. Each volume contains a critical introduction together with chronologies, biographical sketches, a guide to further reading and any necessary glossaries and textual apparatus. When completed, the series will aim to offer an outline of the entire evolution of Western political thought.

For a list of titles published in the series, please see end of book.

GEORGES SOREL

Reflections on Violence

EDITED BY

JEREMY JENNINGS
University of Birmingham

CAMBRIDGE
UNIVERSITY PRESS

PUBLISHED BY THE PRESS SYNDICATE OF THE UNIVERSITY OF CAMBRIDGE
The Pitt Building, Trumpington Street, Cambridge, United Kingdom

CAMBRIDGE UNIVERSITY PRESS
The Edinburgh Building, Cambridge, CB2 2RU, UK
40 West 20th Street, New York, NY 10011–4211, USA
477 Williamstown Road, Port Melbourne, VIC 3207, Australia
Ruiz de Alarcón 13, 28014 Madrid, Spain
Dock House, The Waterfront, Cape Town 8001, South Africa

http://www.cambridge.org

First published 1999
Fourth printing 2006

Printed in the United Kingdom at the University Press, Cambridge

Typeset in Ehrhardt 9.5pt [WV]

A catalogue record for this book is available from the British Library

Library of Congress Cataloguing in Publication data

Sorel, Georges, 1847–1922.
[Réflexions sur la violence. English]
Sorel, reflections on violence / edited by Jeremy Jennings.
p.   cm. – (Cambridge texts in the history of political thought)
ISBN 0 521 55117 X (hardback) – 0 521 55910 3 (paperback)
1. Syndicalism. 2. Strikes and lockouts. 3. Social conflict. 4. Violence. I. Jennings, Jeremy,
1952–   . II. Title. III. Series.
HD6477.S523   1999   335′.82 – dc21   98-55975   CIP

ISBN 0 521 55117 X hardback
ISBN 0 521 55910 3 paperback

Contents

Acknowledgements

It is a pleasure to acknowledge my debt to my friends in the Société d'Etudes Soréliennes. To Christophe Prochasson and Sophie Coeuré (and, latterly, Aurélien) go my thanks (and much more) for being there. I also record my deep affection and appreciation for the late John L. Stanley: no one has done more than he to make Sorel available and intelligible to an English-reading audience. David Boucher provided typically helpful advice about the presentation of the manuscript, whilst Katy Cooper provided excellent and invaluable copy-editing. I thank my colleagues at the University of Birmingham for providing such a convivial and stimulating environment in which to work.

Finally, I thank Michel Prat for sharing with me his immense knowledge of Sorel's life and work. It is to him that I dedicate my Introduction.

Introduction

Sorel's early writings

Born in 1847, Georges Sorel came late to writing about politics. A provincial and bourgeois upbringing was completed by an education in Paris and then by over twenty years working as a civil engineer for the French State. Most of that time was spent in the southern town of Perpignan, far from the intellectual and political excitement of Paris. Yet it was here that Sorel began to write.

Sorel's first articles appeared in the mid-1880s. For the most part these were concerned with obscure scientific subjects, but many were devoted to studying the impact of the French Revolution upon the Pyrénées-Orientales region where he worked. Then, in 1889, came the publication of two books: *Contribution à l'étude profane de la Bible* and *Le Procès de Socrate*. Both dealt only indirectly with politics, but where they did so they conveyed a message of moral conservatism. The France of the Third Republic was thought to be in a state of moral decline. To reverse this process, Sorel recommended the values of hard work, the family and those of a rural society.

Sorel's retirement from government service in 1892 and move to the suburbs of Paris coincided with his first interest in Marxism. Upon the basis of a limited acquaintance with the texts of Marx, Sorel initially saw Marxism as a science. This, however, was quickly to change as he perceived the inadequacies of the economic determinism associated with Marxist orthodoxy. Accordingly, Sorel undertook a fundamental reinterpretation of Marxism, calling for a

vii

return to what he described as 'the Marxism of Marx'. Denying the veracity of the so-called 'laws of capitalist development', he deprived Marxism of the certitude of ultimate victory, replacing the idea of an economic catastrophe facing capitalism with that of a moral catastrophe facing bourgeois society. 'Socialism', Sorel wrote, 'is a moral question, in the sense that it brings to the world a new way of judging human actions and, to use a celebrated expression of Nietzsche, a new evaluation of all values.' This momentarily brought him close to an endorsement of political democracy and reformism, only for his allegiances to shift again with the new century.

The context of Sorel's *Reflections*

Two movements serve to explain this new stance and form the immediate backdrop to the argument of *Reflections on Violence*. The first is the rise of the French syndicalist movement, committed to the tactics of direct action by the working class. Sorel had been following these developments since the late 1890s, producing a series of texts that sketch out the potential of the *syndicats* or trade unions,[1] and he had been especially impressed by the efforts of his friend Fernand Pelloutier to forge the *bourses du travail*[2] into organizations of proletarian self-emancipation; but it was after 1902, when the Confédération Générale du Travail (CGT) launched a series of spectacular strikes, that syndicalism came to the forefront of Sorel's attention. In 1906 the CGT adopted the 'Charter of Amiens', announcing that it 'brings together, outside every political school of thought, all those workers conscious of the struggle necessary to obtain the disappearance of wage-earners and employers'. As such, syndicalism was 'le parti du travail'; it scorned politics, the Republic and patriotism, and, in its regular clashes with employers and the State, denounced what it termed the

---

[1] See especially 'L'Avenir socialiste des syndicats', *L'Humanité nouvelle* 2 (1898), pp. 294–307, 432–45; 'L'histoire du trade-unionisme anglais', *L'Ouvrier des deux mondes* 2 (1898), pp. 337–40; 'Les grèves', *La Science sociale* 30 (1900), pp. 311–32, 417–36; 'Les grèves de Montceau-les-mines et leur signification', *Pages libres* 9 (1901), pp. 169–73.
[2] The *bourses du travail* were originally conceived as labour exchanges but in Pelloutier's scheme figured as centres of working-class life and education.

'government of assassins'. Through strikes it intended to bring capitalism to an end, replacing it not by State socialism but by a society of producers. Sorel did not create or even inspire the syndicalist movement, nor was he ever fully in agreement with its ideas (he never endorsed its use of industrial sabotage, for example), but he did believe that it embodied what was 'truly true' in Marxism, giving substance to its central tenet of class struggle leading to a 'catastrophic' revolution. Moreover, observation of its activities revealed to Sorel that 'the normal development of strikes has included a significant number of acts of violence' (p. 39) and it was this that led him to conclude that 'if we wish to discuss socialism seriously, we must first of all investigate the functions of violence in present social conditions' (p. 39).

The Dreyfusard movement provides the second context for these reflections. In 1898 Sorel had rallied to the cause of the Jewish army officer Alfred Dreyfus, wrongly imprisoned for treason. In this he shared the conviction of many that more was at stake than the fate of Dreyfus himself. For Sorel, the defence of Dreyfus followed from what he regarded as the ethical impulse that defined socialism, an impulse that meant that the notions of 'morality and justice' informed socialist conduct. Sorel, like many of his friends who frequented the bookshop of Charles Péguy, was to feel deeply betrayed by the outcome of Dreyfusard agitation. On this view, with the victory of the Bloc des Gauches in 1902 the slogan of 'republican defence' was turned into an excuse for careerism and political advancement by politicians only too ready to abandon their principles and to adorn themselves with the privileges of power. Yet this alone cannot explain the sheer venom that is directed by Sorel against these Third Republic politicians, most of whom have been long since forgotten. From 1901, with the 'law of associations', the government passed a series of anticlerical laws, culminating in the separation of Church and State in 1905. These laws, to Sorel's disgust, were applied vindictively against the religious orders of the Catholic Church. This, however, was not all. Under Prime Minister Combes, the government began the process of purging the higher ranks of the army and in doing so used the Masonic Lodges to provide information about the religious and political loyalties of its officers. When the scandal broke, it provided damning evidence of an intricate system of spying and delation. For Sorel, this was final proof of the corruption of the Republic and of its politicians. This disgust is evident throughout Sorel's text.

Philosophical influences

If syndicalism and the Dreyfus affair provide the immediate political context for *Reflections on Violence*, then it is Sorel's immersion in the broader intellectual environment of his day that gives the text its vibrancy and its originality. Sorel received one of the best educations that the French State could offer, yet he regarded himself as self-educated. This was true to the extent that he was a voracious reader, consuming books on a daily basis, usually for review. He was, however, also a great listener (regularly attending Bergson's lectures in Paris), conversationalist (especially before his many young admirers) and letter writer (with correspondents all over Europe). No subject was out of bounds, and all were dissected by Sorel's penetrating intelligence. The footnotes of *Reflections on Violence* alone make for fascinating reading. What they show is the mind of a man who was equally at home with science, history, politics, philosophy and theology, who could move easily from discussing the early history of the Christian Church to contemporary tracts on psychology. In *Reflections on Violence*, references to the virtually unknown Giambattista Vico are found alongside those to Blaise Pascal, Ernest Renan, Friedrich Nietzsche, Eduard von Hartmann, Pierre-Joseph Proudhon, John Henry Newman, Karl Marx, Alexis de Tocqueville and countless other intellectual luminaries of the Third Republic, as part of an argument designed to focus our attention upon the possibility of attaining an 'ethics of sublimity'.

There are at least three of Sorel's conclusions or perspectives that need to be highlighted. To begin, Sorel was amongst the first in France to read Marx seriously. The interpretation that underpins much of the economic argument of *Reflections on Violence* is that Marxism is a form of 'Manchesterianism' (i.e. classical liberal economics). Marxism believed, therefore, that the capitalist economy should be allowed to operate unhindered, without interference from the State and without concern for the welfare of the workers. In this way not only would capitalism surmount all the obstacles before it but the workers would prepare themselves for the final struggle for emancipation. When capitalism did not follow this path – due, for example, to a concern to foster 'social peace' or class 'solidarity' – the result was 'economic decadence' and, as a consequence, the non-attainment of the intellectual, moral and technical education of the proletariat. This is why Sorel believed that the workers should respond with 'black ingratitude' to the benevolence of the employers and to the propagators of what he contemptuously refers to as 'civilized socialism'.

Secondly, as an assiduous reader of the works of Max Nordau, Théodule Ribot and Gustave le Bon, as well as Henri Bergson, Sorel became acutely aware of the non-rational sources of human motivation. This was a major preoccupation at the end of the nineteenth century. Human beings, Sorel tells us, 'do nothing great without the help of warmly coloured images which absorb the whole of our attention' (p. 140). It is this that informs Sorel's rejection of what he dubs the 'intellectualist philosophy' and which he associates most of all in this text with the great nineteenth-century critic and Biblical scholar, Ernest Renan. A sceptic such as Renan, like all those who believed that 'eventually everything will be explained rationally', could not understand why an individual, be it a Napoleonic soldier or a striking worker, would perform a selfless and heroic act.

Thirdly, Sorel dismissed the nineteenth-century 'illusion of progress', scorning its optimism in favour of an undisguised pessimism. This is a theme that can be found in Sorel's very earliest writings (where, like Nietzsche, he castigates the 'optimism' of Socrates), but in this text it owes much to his reading of Eduard von Hartmann and the seventeenth-century religious philosopher, Pascal. It is from the latter that he takes the idea that the 'march towards deliverance' is narrowly conditioned both by the immense obstacles that we face and by 'a profound conviction of our natural weakness' (p. 11). On this view, happiness will not be produced automatically for everybody; rather deliverance – if it is ever obtained – will be the outcome of heroic acts, secured with the help of 'a whole band of companions'. It is this emphasis upon the difficulties to be encountered on the journey ahead that allows Sorel to regard the wandering Jew, 'condemned to march forever without knowing rest', as 'the symbol of the highest aspiration of mankind'. Similarly, it encouraged him to believe that the pessimist is not 'subject to the bloodthirsty follies of the optimist driven mad by the unforeseen obstacles that his projects meet' (p. 11).

Style and methodology

If Sorel regarded himself as self-educated, so too he was acutely aware that the way he presented his argument in *Reflections on Violence* did not conform to 'the rules of the art of writing'. As the introductory 'Letter to Daniel Halévy' reveals, he was unapologetic about this, informing his readers that 'I write notebooks in which I set down my thoughts as they arise' (p. 5). Into those notebooks went only those things that he had not met elsewhere. There was, however, more to this than stylistic idiosyncrasy. As a methodology, it was suited to what Sorel described in one of his essays on syndicalism as 'the fluid character of reality' and, indeed, Sorel was appalled at the idea of producing a perfectly symmetrical and coherent body of knowledge. To do so would be to pander to those content with 'the impersonal, the socialized, the *ready-made*' and it is to avoid this that Sorel, in the appendix entitled 'Unity and multiplicity', outlines his concept of *diremption* as a method of investigation providing 'a symbolic knowledge' of what he characterizes as 'the chaos of social phenomena'.[3] The explanations disclosed by this process would be at best partial and incomplete.

Similarly, Sorel had no desire to provide a closed philosophical system that could readily be put to use by any disciples. Rather, he saw philosophy as 'only the recognition of the abysses which lie on each side of the path that the vulgar follow with the serenity of sleepwalkers' (p. 7). His aim, therefore, was to awaken 'within every man a metaphysical fire'. This commitment to 'the spirit of invention' impacts upon the argument of *Reflections on Violence* in a whole series of ways. If Sorel shared Bergson's hostility towards the prevailing scientism of their day, it is important to realize that Sorel believed that he himself was 'proceeding scientifically'. It was the opponents of syndicalism who were out of touch with the discoveries of modern science and philosophy. Thus, for example, it

---

[3] See G[eorges] Sorel, *Matériaux d'une théorie du prolétariat* (Paris, Rivière, 1921), pp. 6–7.

is central to Sorel's argument that he should dismiss the 'bourgeois conception of science' that sees the latter as 'a mill which produces solutions to all the problems we are faced with' (p. 132) . In the same way he constantly disparages the purveyors of the 'little science' who believed that the 'aim of science was to forecast the future with accuracy'. All confuse science with clarity of exposition.

Amongst those purveyors were the Intellectuals (a noun Sorel always capitalizes). These, Sorel tells us, 'are not, as is so often said, men who think: they are people who have adopted the profession of thinking' (p. 156). They have done so for an 'aristocratic salary' and also because they intend to exploit the proletariat. To that end they sketch out a utopia, an 'intellectual product' that as 'the work of theorists' directs 'men's minds towards reforms which can be brought about by patching up the system' (pp. 28–9).

Myths

This leads to the development of one of Sorel's most controversial ideas: the importance of myths. Myths, as 'expressions of a will to act', are the very antithesis of utopias. Again Sorel addresses this issue in his introductory 'Letter to Daniel Halévy', precisely because it informs so much of his subsequent argument. 'The mind of man', Sorel tells us, is so constituted that it cannot remain content with the mere observations of facts but wishes to understand the inner reason of things' (pp. 24–5). Moreover, it is Bergson's philosophy that helps us to understand this. Bergson, Sorel tells us, asks us to consider 'the inner depths of the mind and what happens during a creative moment' (p. 26). Acting freely, we recover ourselves, attaining the level of pure 'duration' that Bergson equates with 'integral knowledge'. This new form of comprehension was identified as 'intuition', a form of internal and empathetic understanding, and it was precisely this form of intuitive understanding that Sorel believed was encompassed by his category of myth. Sorel had been working towards this conclusion for sometime, concluding in his essay *La Décomposition du marxisme* (1908) that Marx had 'always described revolution in mythical form', but in the main body of *Reflections on Violence* it is the general strike that features as a myth, precisely because it provides an 'intuitive' understanding and 'picture' of the essence of socialism. More than this, those who live in the world of myths are 'secure from all refutation' and cannot be discouraged. It is therefore through myths that we understand 'the activity, the sentiments and the ideas of the masses as they prepare themselves to enter on a decisive struggle' (p. 28).

Class struggle and violence

What is the purpose of this decisive struggle? In the final chapter of his text Sorel describes what will be 'the ethic of the producers of the future' and in doing so he confirms that the 'great preoccupation' of his entire life was 'the historical genesis of morality'.[4] The particular morality described is an austere one, owing much to the severe moralism of Proudhon and not diverging substantially from that set out in Sorel's early pre-socialist writings. It is also a description couched in terms of Sorel's only extended discussion of the ideas of Nietzsche. Sexual fidelity, grounded upon the institution of the family, is at its heart. Having earlier told us that the world will become more 'just' to the extent that it becomes more 'chaste', Sorel now argues in this text that 'Love, by the enthusiasm it begets, can produce that sublimity without which there would be no effective morality' (p. 236).[5] But, at another level, it is to be a morality that rejects 'an ethics adapted to consumers', an ethics that devalued work and overvalued pleasure, an ethics that gave pride of place to the parasitic activities of the politician and the intellectual. In its place was to be a morality that turned 'the men of today into the free producers of tomorrow, working in workshops where there are no masters' (p. 238). A new morality of selfless dedication to one's work and one's colleagues would, in other words, be attained through participation in what amounted to a new set of self-governing industrial institutions. Yet there was more to this 'secret virtue' than a distinct proletarian morality. Work in the modern factory, Sorel believed, demanded constant innovation and improvement in the quantity and quality of production, and it was through this that 'indefinite progress' was achieved. This striving for perfection ensured not only that industrial work attained the

---

[4] 'Lettere di Georges Sorel a B. Croce', *La Critica* 26 (1928), p. 100.
[5] On this important theme, see F[rançoise] Blum, 'Images de "la Femme" chez Georges Sorel', *Cahiers Georges Sorel* 4 (1986), pp. 5–25.

status of art but also that the factory would become the site of an 'economic epic' to rival the Homeric epic of the battlefield. Sorel also makes it clear that this new morality will emerge at the expense of the 'total elimination' of the bourgeoisie. It will, moreover, be brought about by a class working 'subterraneously' within society, 'separating itself' from the modern world. Sorel locates the entire argument of *Reflections of Violence* in the context of a situation where the possibility and nearness of decline is ever present, thus again continuing a theme found in his earliest essays. The bourgeoisie, as the title of one chapter makes clear, are seen as being decadent, 'destined henceforth to live without morals'.[6] Their decadence, however, is also economic: no longer are they willing to function as the bold captains of industry, driving the economy forward to greater heights. Here, Sorel believed, history presented us with a clear historical precedent. By locating his argument within the framework of Vico's ideal history of *corsi* and *ricorsi* (see pp. xxxiii–xxxiv, below), he felt himself able to demonstrate the consequences of a social transformation carried out in a period of moral and economic decadence: the victory of Christianity over the Roman Empire showed that 'at least four centuries of barbarism had to be gone through before a progressive movement showed itself; society was compelled to descend to a state not far removed from its origins' (pp. 83–4). The same descent into barbarism would occur if the proletariat, itself corrupted, secured its ends by dispossessing a humanitarian and timorous bourgeoisie of its possession of a degenerate capitalism.

Sorel's conclusion was unambiguous: the workers must maintain divisions within society, distancing themselves from the corrupting processes of bourgeois democracy and forsaking social peace in favour of class struggle and confrontation: 'everything may be saved if the proletariat, by their use of violence, manage to re-establish the division into classes and so restore to the bourgeoisie something of its energy' (p. 85). This followed from Sorel's account of Marxism as a version of 'Manchesterianism': violence, 'carried on as a pure and simple manifestation of the sentiment of class struggle', would disabuse philanthropic employers of their paternal concern for their employees, teaching them to devote themselves to securing

---

[6] See also 'La Crise morale et religieuse', *Le Mouvement socialiste* 22 (1907), p. 35.

the progress of production and nothing more. This, in turn, would restore the *fatalité* of capitalist development, thereby allowing capitalism to attain its 'historical perfection' and to establish the material foundations of a future socialist society. On this account, proletarian violence appears 'a very fine and heroic thing', serving 'the immemorial interests of civilization'.

The revolutionary tradition

This, then, was Sorel's shocking conclusion: violence would save the world from barbarism. But what sort of violence was it to be? Here we come to the heart of so much of the subsequent misunderstanding (as well as misuse) of his ideas, for Sorel was adamant that a distinction had to be drawn between the violence of the revolutionary proletariat and the force deployed in the name of the State by politicians and intellectuals.

As Sorel made clear in his essay 'Mes raisons du syndicalisme',[7] he did not come to syndicalism via Jacobinism, nor did he share the 'veneration' for the men who made the French Revolution. Moreover, this distaste for the 'terrorists of 1793' can be traced back to his very earliest writings. A letter of 1872, for example, highlights his aversion to 'la jésuitière rouge',[8] whilst his writings prior to his conversion to Marxism in 1892 likewise detail his hatred of the Jacobin tradition, its bourgeois adherents and their passion for dictatorial State power.

In his mature writings – and especially in *Reflections on Violence* – his criticisms of the Revolution and its supporters can be distilled into three specific claims. Firstly, if Sorel recognized that Rousseau was not responsible for the Terror and the actions of Robespierre, he did believe that certain key Rousseauian notions had been passed on into democratic theory. Specifically, Sorel considered that the concept of the general will had been used to justify the idea of 'government by all the citizens', despite the fact that the whole thing was nothing but a 'fiction'. The reality had been that during the Revolution every *salon*, and then every Jacobin club, believed

---

[7] 'Mes raisons du syndicalisme', in *Matériaux d'une théorie du prolétariat*, p. 248.
[8] P[ierre] Andreu, 'Une lettre de Sorel en 1872', *Cahiers Georges Sorel* 2 (1894), pp. 93–107.

that it possessed the secret of the general will, thereby justifying
their limitless authority; passed down to the democrats of contemporary France, this conceit was now entertained by a class of intellectuals who had turned themselves into the people's masters.[9]

Secondly, Sorel believed that contemporary socialism had
embraced a whole set of the Revolution's most reprehensible attitudes. First among these was the idea of 'Parisian dictatorship'.
'Even today', Sorel wrote, 'many socialists believe that if power
were to fall into their hands it would be easy to impose their programme, their new morals and new ideas upon France.' More
damning still was Sorel's contention that the Revolution was fundamentally inegalitarian in inspiration. Thus, Sorel wrote, it was clear
that those socialist politicians 'imbued with the spirit of the Revolution' wished to preserve 'the principle of hierarchy'. So we find
that in *Reflections on Violence*, not only does Sorel endorse Tocqueville's conclusion that there was no radical break between the political structures of pre- and post-revolutionary France but he also
contends that, for contemporary socialists, revolution can be
reduced to a change of government personnel.[10]

It is the theme of continuity between the *ancien régime*, the Revolution and contemporary socialism that underpins Sorel's third
major criticism of the ideology and practice of 1789–93. 'One of the
fundamental ideas of the *ancien régime*'. Sorel writes in what is argu-
ably the key chapter of *Reflections on Violence* (chapter III, 'Prejudices against violence'), 'had been the employment of the penal
procedure to ruin any power which was an obstacle to the monarchy' (p. 96). The aim had been not to maintain justice but to
enhance the strength of the State and thus 'negligence, ill-will and
carelessness became revolt against authority, crime or treason'. The
Revolution, Sorel argued, 'piously inherited this tradition', giving
immense importance to imaginary crimes, guillotining those who
could not satisfy the expectations aroused by public opinion, and
producing in the classic piece of 'Robespierre's legislation', the law
of 22nd Prairial, a law whose definitions of 'political crime' were so
vague as to ensure that no 'enemy of the Revolution' could escape.

[9] See 'L'Avenir socialiste des syndicats', in *Matériaux d'une théorie du prolétariat*,
p. 118 and *Les Illusions du progrès* (Paris, Rivière, 1921), p. 106.
[10] See especially 'Le Socialisme et la Révolution française', *Le Pays de France* I
(1899), pp. 220–8.

Here, raised to pre-eminence, was the 'doctrine of the State'. Stripped of its prestige, therefore, all that remained of the Revolution were 'police operations, proscriptions and the sittings of servile courts of law'.

Little, Sorel indicates, has changed. 'By cruel experience', he tells us, 'we know now, alas! that the State still had its high priests and its fervent advocates among the Dreyfusards' (p. 101). No sooner was the Dreyfus case over than Combes and the government of 'republican defence' began another 'political prosecution'. Jaurès and his friends could not bring themselves to condemn the system of spying introduced into the army. Ultimately, however, one is led to conclude that for Sorel the key piece of evidence was provided by Jaurès' equivocation in his *Histoire socialiste de la Révolution française* when faced with the need to account for the Jacobins. Such people, Sorel tells us, 'are worthy successors of Robespierre', they 'preserve the old cult of the State; they are therefore prepared to commit all the misdeeds of the *ancien régime* and of the Revolution'.

The general strike

The point of all this is to establish that 'the abuses of the revolutionary bourgeois force of [17]93' should not be confused with 'the violence of our revolutionary syndicalists'. Syndicalism conceived the transmission of power not in terms of the replacement of one intellectual elite by another but as a process diffusing authority down into the workers' own organizations. Those organizations, unlike a system of political democracy replete with Rousseauian baggage, provided a pattern of genuine and effective representation. Most importantly, the violence employed by the proletariat in the course of the general strike bore no relationship to the ferocious and bloodthirsty acts of jealousy and revenge that characterized the massacres of the French Revolution.

Here, therefore, Sorel goes to great pains to define what he means by violence. If the object of State force was to impose a social order based upon inequality and exploitation, the purpose of proletarian violence was 'the destruction of that order'. Secondly, such violence would be inspired by a conception of war drawn from the ancient Greeks: it would be unselfish, heroic, disciplined, devoid of all material considerations. It would be informed by ethical values engendering 'an entirely epic state of mind'. The proletariat, Sorel writes, 'longs for the final conquest in which it will give proof of the whole measure of its valour. Pursuing no conquest, it has no need to make plans for utilizing its victories' (p. 161).

Sorel, in fact, pays little attention to the details of the general strike, preferring to emphasize that it will be 'a revolt pure and simple' in which the proletariat engages upon 'serious, formidable and sublime work'. On one point, however, he is clear: 'It may be conceded to those in favour of mild methods that violence may hamper economic progress and even, when it goes beyond a certain limit, that it may be a danger to morality' (pp. 177–8). Too much violence would be a threat to civilization. There is, though, little danger of this from the proletariat. Drawing again upon historical parallels, Sorel points out that although there were few Christians martyrs their martyrdom served to prove the absolute truth of the new religion; in the same way, for syndicalism there would in reality be 'conflicts that are short and few in number', yet these would be sufficient to evoke the idea of the general strike as being 'perfectly revolutionary'. It would be accomplished 'by means of incidents which would appear to bourgeois historians as of small importance'. 'We have the right to hope', Sorel therefore concludes, 'that a socialist revolution carried out by pure syndicalists would not be defiled by the abominations which sullied the bourgeois revolutions' (p. 108).

Lenin and the Russian Revolution

It was precisely because in the years after 1909 the syndicalist movement appeared to effect a compromise with the forces of parliamentary socialism that Sorel withdrew his support from it, engaging in a series of publishing enterprises with figures drawn from the antiparliamentary Right. The latter act has been seen as an indication of Sorel's support for the restoration of the monarchy. This was not so, although it is the case that Sorel's writings in the years immediately prior to the First World War consist almost totally of a series of unforgiving attacks upon virtually every aspect of France's republican political system: its decaying democracy, corrupt administration, superficial art, poor morals and shallow religion. Controversially, his loathing of politicians and bourgeois intellectuals now focused upon the form of the messianic and rootless Jew as the antithesis of everything that had brought greatness to France.[11] Given this shift of emphasis towards an unremitting attack upon the whole culture of the Third Republic, it is important to note that in his 'Foreword to the third edition', written in 1912, Sorel proclaims himself 'more than ever convinced of the value of this philosophy of violence'.

It was this scorn of the bourgeois and democratic Republic that ensured that Sorel could not rally to the *union sacrée* that brought France's political forces together in 1914. He poured scorn on pronouncements calling for the workers as 'citizens' to relive the days of 1793, to organize a 'levée en masse'. In time, he concluded, 'this war will be regarded as execrable above all because of the reawakening of the Jacobin spirit it promoted'. 'All socialist thought', he wrote to Mario Missiroli in August 1914, 'has become Jacobin', the recent dismal events showing that 'the old Jacobin tradition remained alive, a tradition formed of frenzied envy, pride and puerile imaginings'.[12]

There remained for Sorel, however, one final episode which seemed to indicate that socialism might be able to free itself of the State force of Jacobinism: the 'extraordinary events' of the October Revolution and Lenin's seizure of power. Sorel's enthusiasm for the Bolsheviks was such that he added a new section voicing his approval not just to *Reflections on Violence* but also to *Les Illusions du progrès* and *Matériaux d'une théorie du prolétariat*. He also wrote for *La Revue communiste*. What Sorel actually knew of Lenin and the Russian Revolution was slim indeed, but importantly he saw Lenin as the very antithesis of a Russian Jacobin and he believed that the Revolution itself had been carried out on syndicalist lines. Note, too, that Sorel again makes a distinction between different types of violence. If he admits that Lenin is not a candidate for a 'prize for virtue', he will succeed thanks to the 'heroic efforts' of the Russian proletariat rather than through 'a war of cowardice' that

[11] 'Quelques prétentions juives', *L'Indépendance* 3 (1912), pp. 217–36, 277–95, 317–36.
[12] 'Lettres à Mario Missiroli', in [Georges Sorel] *Da Proudhon a Lenin e L'Europa sotto la tormenta* [ed. Gabriele de Rosa] (Rome, Edizioni di storia e litteratura, 1974), pp. 500–14.

denies 'the true laws of war'. The workers obey not his political but his 'moral authority'.

For Sorel, therefore, the events in Russia marked the revolt of the producers against politicians, intellectuals and the bourgeoisie, with the *soviets* giving institutional form to a new productivist ethic. His hope was that Lenin's Russia of the *soviets* would provide a new myth capable of inspiring the proletariat across Europe to rise up against 'the arrogant bourgeois democracies, today shamelessly triumphant'. An old man, he summoned up all his moral fervour to call forth the destruction of New Carthages.

Conclusion

Reflections on Violence remains a profoundly disturbing book. This most obviously derives from the fact that Sorel not only takes violence as his subject but, more importantly, is prepared to equate it with life, creativity and virtue. Was this not Sorel's own illusion? And was it not, perhaps, one of the illusions that served most to disfigure the twentieth century? How, it might be asked, could the reality of violence have provided an escape from the 'total ruin of institutions and morals' Sorel described? Yet, whatever might have been made of his ideas by later enthusiasts, the fact remains that the violence endorsed by Sorel was not very violent at all; it amounts to little more than a few heroic gestures. This was so because Sorel was not a Jacobin socialist. Distancing himself from the 'Robespierrean tradition', at the centre of his thought was the distinction between the violence of the proletariat and that deployed by bourgeois politicians and their intellectual ideologues through the State. It was the politicians and ideologues, and not the proletariat, who resorted to wholesale acts of terror and repression in order to secure their own dominance. For his part, Sorel saw himself as nothing more than a 'disinterested servant of the proletariat'.

Select bibliography

A wide selection of Sorel's work is now available in English, mostly translated by the late John L. Stanley: see *The Illusions of Progress* (Berkeley and Los Angeles, University of California Press, 1969); *From Georges Sorel: Essays in Socialism and Philosophy* (New York, Oxford University Press, 1976); *Social Foundations of Contemporary Economics* (New Brunswick, NJ, Transaction Books, 1984) and *Hermeneutics and the Sciences* (New Brunswick, NJ, Transaction Books, 1990). Selections of Sorel's writings are also available in Richard Vernon, *Commitment and Change: Georges Sorel and the Idea of Revolution* (Toronto, University of Toronto Press, 1978).

Most of the early work on Sorel was undertaken by American scholars: see especially Michael Curtis, *Three against the Republic* (Princeton, University of Princeton Press, 1959); James Meisel, *The Genesis of Georges Sorel* (Ann Arbor, University of Michigan Press, 1953); Richard Humphrey, *Georges Sorel, Prophet without Honor: A Study in Anti-Intellectualism* (Cambridge, MA, Harvard University Press, 1951) and Irving L. Horowitz, *Radicalism and the Revolt Against Reason* (New York, Humanities Press, 1961). The latter also contains a translation of Sorel's important essay 'The Decomposition of Marxism'.

A revival of interest in Sorel took place from the mid-1970s onwards, broadening the picture of his intellectual output and producing new interpretations of his significance. For two detailed intellectual biographies see Jeremy Jennings, *Georges Sorel: The Character and Development of his Thought* (London, Macmillan, 1985) and John L. Stanley, *The Sociology of Virtue: The Political and Social Theories of Georges Sorel* (Berkeley and Los Angeles, University of California Press, 1982). The wider intellectual and political context in which Sorel worked is examined in Jack Roth, *The Cult of Violence: Sorel and the Sorelians* (Berkeley and Los Angeles, University of California Press, 1980) and Jeremy Jennings, *Syndicalism in France: A Study of Ideas* (London, Macmillan, 1990). Of less interest are Arthur L. Greil, *Georges Sorel and the Sociology of Virtue* (Washington DC, University Press of America, 1981) and Larry Portis, *Georges Sorel* (London, Pluto Press, 1980).

Of the many articles and chapters written in English on Sorel, see especially: Isaiah Berlin, 'Georges Sorel' in Henry Hardy (ed.), *Against the Current: Essays in the History of Ideas* (London, Hogarth Press, 1979), pp. 296–331; Leszek Kolakowski, 'Georges Sorel: A Jansenist Marxist', in his *Main Currents of Marxism* (Oxford, Oxford University Press, 1981), II, pp. 151–74; and K. Steven Vincent, 'Interpreting Georges Sorel: defender of virtue or apostle of violence', *History of European Ideas* 12 (1990), pp. 239–57. For Sorel's relationship with both the Left and the Right, see Larry Wilde, 'Sorel and the French Right', *History of Political Thought* 7 (1986), pp. 361–74 and Darrow Schecter, 'Two views of revolution: Gramsci and Sorel, 1916–1929', *History of European Ideas* 12 (1990), pp. 637–53. See also the special issue of *The European Legacy* 3(5) (1998), devoted to Sorel, with articles by John L. Stanley, Jeremy Jennings, Shlomo Sand, K. Steven Vincent and Cécile Laborde.

In France there has also been a revival of scholarly interest in Sorel's ideas. Of the early studies see Georges Goriely, *Le Pluralisme dramatique de Georges Sorel* (Paris, Marcel Rivière, 1962) and Pierre Andreu, *Notre Maître, M. Sorel* (Paris, Grasset 1953), reprinted as *Georges Sorel: Entre le noir et le rouge* (Paris, Syros, 1982). As examples of more recent work, see Shlomo Sand, *L'Illusion du politique: Georges Sorel et le débat intellectuel 1900* (Paris, La Découverte, 1985); Michel Charzat (ed.), *Georges Sorel* (Paris, Cahiers de l'Herne, 1986); and Jacques Julliard and Shlomo Sand (eds.), *Georges Sorel en son temps* (Paris, Seuil, 1985). The latter contains the most complete bibliography of Sorel's writings to date.

Mention must be made of the most valuable source of recent Sorel scholarship, the *Cahiers Georges Sorel*, published annually since 1983 and from 1987 onwards under the title *Mil neuf cent: Revue d'histoire intellectuelle*. In addition to numerous articles on

Sorel, these volumes have also made available previously unpublished material, especially Sorel's correspondence. Of greatest interest are Sorel's letters to his closest associate, Edouard Berth (3–6, 1985–8) and to Eduard Bernstein (11, 1993); but see also Sorel's correspondence to Henri Bergson, Roberto Michels, Daniel Halévy and Jean Bourdeau.

Finally, it should be pointed out that some of the very best Sorel scholarship comes from Italy. For a recent example see Marco Gervasoni, *Georges Sorel, una biografia intellettuale* (Milan, Edizioni Unicopli, 1997).

Chronology

1847	2 November; Georges Sorel born in Cherbourg, a cousin to Albert-Emile Sorel, one of the great historians of the French Third Republic.
1864	Moves to Paris and enters the Collège Rollin.
1865–7	Studies at the prestigious Ecole Polytechnique.
1867–70	Continues his studies as an engineer with the Ministère des Ponts et Chaussées.
1870	Secures first posting as government engineer to Corsica, where he remains during the Franco-Prussian war.
1871–3	Posted to Albi, in the south of France.
1875	Sorel meets Marie-Euphrasie David in Lyon, who will remain his companion and 'wife' until her death in 1897. It is to her that *Réflexions sur la violence* will be dedicated.
1876–9	Posted to Mostaganem (Algeria), then considered part of France.
1879–92	Posted to Perpignan, where he remains until his resignation from government service.
1886	Sorel publishes his first article, 'Sur les applications de la psychophysique', in *La Revue philosophique*.
1889	Sorel publishes his first two books: *Contribution à l'étude profane de la Bible* (*A Contribution to a Secular Study of the Bible*) and *Le Procès de Socrate* (*The Trial of Socrates*).
1891	Sorel made Chevalier of the Légion d'honneur, the

insignia of which he was always to wear on his lapel.

1892   Returns to Paris, before settling in the suburb of Boulogne-sur-Seine, where he is to remain until his death.

1893   'Science et socialisme', published in *La Revue philosophique*, indicates Sorel's enthusiasm for Marx.

1894   Sorel writes for the short-lived *L'Ere nouvelle*, one of the first Marxist journals in France.

1895   Sorel writes for *La Jeunesse socialiste*, the Toulouse-based journal of the young Hubert Lagardelle.

1895–8   With Paul Lafargue, Gabriel Deville and Alfred Bonnet, Sorel launches *Le Devenir social*.

1898   January; Sorel's name appears on the second petition in support of Alfred Dreyfus, calling for the Chamber of Deputies 'to defend the legal guarantees of citizens against arbitrary power'.

1898   Sorel publishes *L'Avenir socialiste des syndicats* (*The Socialist Future of the Trade Unions*). He also publishes in *L'Ouvrier des deux mondes*, the journal of Fernand Pelloutier.

1899   Sorel publishes his first article in Lagardelle's *Le Mouvement socialiste*.

1902   Publication of *La Ruine du monde antique. Conception matérialiste de l'histoire* (*The Downfall of the Ancient World: The Materialist Conception of History*).

1903   Publication of *Introduction à l'économie moderne* (*Introduction to the Modern Economy*).

1905   Sorel publishes 'Le syndicalisme révolutionnaire' in *Le Mouvement socialiste*.

1906   Sorel publishes 'Les illusions du progrès' in *Le Mouvement socialiste*.
        Publication of *Le Système historique de Renan* (*The Historical System of Renan*).

1908   Publication of *La Décomposition du marxisme* (*The Decomposition of Marxism*).

1909	Publication of *La Révolution dreyfusienne* (*The Dreyfusard Revolution*). Sorel breaks with Lagardelle and *Le Mouvement socialiste*, at the same time withdrawing his support from the syndicalist movement as it enters a period of 'crisis'.
1910	With Edouard Berth and monarchist Georges Valois, Sorel attempts to launch *La Cité française*.
1911–13	Along with an assortment of figures drawn from the antidemocratic Right, Sorel publishes in *L'Indépendance*, established by Jean Valois.
1914–18	Sorel remains silent during the First World War.
1919	Publication of *Matériaux d'une théorie du prolétariat* (*Materials for a Theory of the Proletariat*).
1920	Sorel publishes in *La Revue communiste*.
1921	Publication of *De l'Utilité du pragmatisme* (*The Utility of Pragmatism*), setting out Sorel's interest in the ideas of William James.
1922	March; Sorel dies and is buried in the same cemetery as Marie-Euphrasie David in Tenay (Ain).

Biographical synopses

Henri Bergson (1859–1941); philosopher; appointed professor at the Collège de France in 1900; his principal works included *Essai sur les données immédiates de la conscience* (1888), *Matière et mémoire* (1896), *L'Evolution créatrice* (1907) and *Les Deux Sources de la morale et de la religion* (1932).

In his day Bergson was the most well-known philosopher in the Western world, deeply influencing modern thought and literature. Bergson did much to rehabilitate the spiritual or 'inner' life by suggesting that we could go beyond time and space to what he described as 'duration', the pure flow of reality that could only be comprehended through intuition. It was this inner life that was the source of liberty and creativity. In 1907, however, Bergson added the notion of *élan vital*, a vital impulse that 'carried life, by more and more complex forms, to higher and higher destinies', to his philosophy, thereby falling foul of the monism he had done so much to repudiate.

Sorel attended Bergson's lectures every week and made frequent reference to him in his writings. Both shared a hostility to the all-encompassing positivism and scientism of their day, with Sorel using Bergson's concept of intuition to develop his theory of myths. Yet it is a mistake to see Sorel's views as a straightforward application of Bergson's theories. If Sorel believed that Bergson greatly extended our understanding of 'large-scale, popular, modern movements', he always remained extremely doubtful about the validity of Bergson's later vitalist evolutionary theory. Sorel increasingly came to see Bergson's philosophy as a fundamentally religious one, capable of encouraging a spiritual revival. For Sorel's most extended discussion of Bergson see 'L'Evolution créatrice', *Le Mouvement socialiste* 22 (1907), pp. 257–82, 478–94; 23 (1908), pp. 34–52, 184–94, 276–94.

Eduard Bernstein (1850–1932); a leading light in the German Social Democratic Party and the first of the so-called 'revisionists'.

Bernstein's argument that socialists should remove 'cant' from their doctrines and replace it with Kant caused immense controversy and effectively undermined the position of Marxist orthodoxy.

Sorel began corresponding with Bernstein in 1898 and, like him, believed that the official representatives of Marxism adhered to the most peripheral and out-of-date of Marx's doctrines. He therefore had considerable admiration for Bernstein's efforts to revise Marxism and to free it from utopianism. Initially Sorel also sympathised with Bernstein's attempt to formulate a practice of political reformism, but this changed with Sorel's support for revolutionary syndicalism, leaving Sorel to conclude that Bernstein's revisionism represented a 'decomposition' of the original 'Marxism of Marx'. See Sorel's essay 'Les Dissensions de la social-démocratie en Allemagne', *Revue politique et parlementaire* 25 (1900), pp. 35–66 and *La Décomposition du marxisme* (Paris, Rivière, 1908).

Daniel Halévy (1872–1962); essayist and writer, brother of Elie Halévy and a member of one of the great intellectual families of Paris.

Halévy made a rapid entry into the Parisian literary world and was one of the first to rally to the Dreyfusard cause. He was amongst those responsible for collecting the signatures for the 'petition of the intellectuals' in January 1898, the second of which was signed by Sorel.

Sorel and Halévy subsequently saw each other regularly at the office of Charles Péguy's *Cahiers de la Quinzaine* and worked together on two reviews, *Le Mouvement socialiste* and *Pages libres*. Halévy later described Sorel as the 'new Socrates, our Socrates', but the admiration was a mutual one. Both felt betrayed by the outcome of the Dreyfus affair, Sorel publishing his *La Révolution dreyfusienne* (1909) to Halévy's more famous *Apologie pour notre passé* (1910). Most importantly, it was Halévy who had the idea of publishing *Reflections on Violence* in book form, with the intention of making Sorel's ideas available to a wider readership. See 'Lettres de Georges Sorel à Daniel Halévy (1907–1920)', *Mil neuf cent* 12 (1994), pp. 151–223.

Eduard von Hartmann (1842–1906); German philosopher and author of the *Philosophie des Unbewussten* (1869), translated into English as *The Philosophy of the Unconscious* (1884).

Hartmann continued the tradition of philosophical pessimism associated with Schopenhauer, and did so by combining his ideas with those of Hegel and Schelling. His key idea was that there was an ultimate reality or force which had given rise to the course of world development and that this was 'the Unconscious'. It is a philosophy of pessimism precisely because it postulates as a final end a distant future where existence itself shall cease and where the world will return to its original state of unconsciousness. In the meantime, the process of consciousness is one where human beings believe, incorrectly, that pleasure and satisfaction can be gained from the world, thus producing a series of illusions (including religion) which shield them from an acknowledgement that they have a duty to suffer.

Hartmann's ideas were received with considerable success at the end of the nineteenth century but appealed to Sorel principally because of their unashamed pessimism. Like Sorel, Hartmann believed that Christianity rested upon a pessimistic conception of the world and therefore that liberal Protestantism was fundamentally irreligious. For Sorel, this provided a welcome contrast to the naive optimism of Ernest Renan.

Jean Jaurès (1859–1914); academic and one of the leaders of the French socialist movement.

In 1898 he lent his support to the Dreyfusard cause, playing a central role in convincing his socialist colleagues that they should defend a bourgeois army officer, and then in 1902 was instrumental in securing their support for the Bloc des Gauches in the name of the Republic and the principles of 1789. In 1904 he established the socialist newspaper *L'Humanité*, after which he spent much of his energies campaigning against the likelihood of war. He was assassinated in 1914.

In 1899, at the height of his enthusiasm for the Dreyfusard cause, Sorel wrote that 'the admirable conduct of Jaurès is the best proof that there exists a socialist ethic'. However, this admiration for the personal courage of Jaurès was soon to turn to hatred. Jaurès became for Sorel the embodiment of 'false socialism', the symbol of every-thing he despised about socialist politicians. Both Jaurès and his newspaper, therefore, are mercilessly pilloried in *Reflections on Violence*. For his part, Jaurès described Sorel as 'the metaphysician of syndicalism'.

Charles Péguy (1873–1914); essayist and editor.

Of humble origins, Péguy entered the Ecole Normale Supérieure, only in 1898 to open a socialist bookshop in the Latin Quarter. Two years later he established his review, the *Cahiers de la Quinzaine*. Sorel first met Péguy in 1899 and from the following year became a weekly visitor to Péguy's bookshop, holding court before his young admirers. Péguy's bookshop and journal were at the centre of the campaign to release Dreyfus, with both Sorel and Péguy bringing an intense moralism to this campaign. Each loathed politicians and praised Jaurès: each sought the moral renaissance of France. Like Sorel, however, he was quick to denounce the 'decomposition of *dreyfusisme*' and the corruption of the socialists, now denouncing Jaurès and the 'parti intellectuel'. It was Péguy who published Halé-vy's *Apologie pour notre passé* and it was this text that elicited Péguy's own *Notre jeunesse* (1910) in which he defended the 'mystique' of the Dreyfusard movement. Sorel took Halévy's side in the sub-sequent quarrel, leading to a cooling of his relationship with Péguy and an eventual break in 1912. As war approached, Péguy effected a public reconciliation with the Catholic Church, only to die in battle in 1914.

Fernand Pelloutier (1867–1901); journalist and activist in the French labour movement; as one of the earliest advocates of the general strike, he can be regarded, according to fellow syndicalist Pierre Monatte, as 'the father of revolutionary syndicalism'.

Pelloutier wrote first for *La Démocratie de l'Ouest* and then the anarchist *Les Temps nouveaux*, before being appointed secretary of the Fédération des Bourses du Travail. In 1897 (the year he met Sorel) he launched his journal *L'Ouvrier des deux mondes* (for which

Sorel wrote articles on trade unionism), published his empirical study *La Vie ouvrière en France* in 1900 and, posthumously, *Histoire des Bourses du travail* in 1902. In his preface to the latter, Sorel wrote that this 'great servant of the people' had spurned the role of socialist theoretician in order 'to convince the workers that they would easily find among themselves men capable of directing their own institutions'; in the *bourses du travail* he had created 'a conception of socialist life'. For Sorel, therefore, Pelloutier's life provided a model of revolutionary commitment that scorned the blandishments of politics, whilst his ideas provided the basis of Sorel's later syndicalism.

Frédéric Le Play (1806–82); sociologist and social reformer; author of numerous monographs, including *Les Ouvriers européens* (1855), *La Réforme sociale* (1864) and *L'Organisation de la famille* (1871).

A conservative by disposition, Le Play's concern to enhance social order was reflected in his emphasis on religion, the family and the utility of charity. Whilst critical of the works of Le Play (rejecting their paternalism, for example), Sorel was an attentive reader of the works of Le Play's followers, frequently citing their empirical studies. In 1899–1900 Sorel himself published a number of articles exploring the nature of strikes and the utility of cooperatives in one of the key journals of the Le Play school, *La Science sociale*. Sorel also made frequent use of Le Play's concept of 'social authorities' to describe the morally uplifting effects of the *syndicats* upon their members.

Pierre-Joseph Proudhon (1809–65); author of *Système des contradictions économiques, ou Philosophie de la misère* (1846), *L'Idée générale de la révolution au XIXe siècle* (1851) and *De la Justice dans la Révolution et dans l'Eglise* (1858).

The first self-proclaimed anarchist, Proudhon was a consistent opponent of Marx and of his emphasis upon political action. Starting from the individual, Proudhon rejected government by advocating economic equality and free contractual relationships between independent workers, grounded upon a conception of immanent justice. He believed that 'the proletariat must emancipate itself' and it was this that gave his ideas considerable influence in the French labour movement. A stern moralist, especially with regard to marriage, Proudhon also appealed to the antidemocratic Right.

Sorel refers extensively to Proudhon throughout his writings, making a variety of different uses of his ideas. Both shared a hatred of the French Revolution and of the statism from which politicians and intellectuals benefited. For each the coming revolution was to be an economic process in which the proletariat would figure as the bearer of a new conception of justice. Sorel also made much of Proudhon's picture of France as a country suffering from moral decline. See especially 'Essai sur la philosophie de Proudhon', *Revue philosophique* 33 (1892), pp. 622–38; 34 (1892), pp. 41–68.

Ernest Renan (1823–92); philologist and historian; one of the towering intellectual figures of the latter half of the nineteenth century. Educated for the priesthood, Renan subsequently became professor of Hebrew at the Collège de France, only to be dismissed the following year after the publication of his *Vie de Jésus*, a book in which he effectively denied the divinity of Christ. In the subsequent studies that were to comprise his *Les Origines du christianisme* (1863–83), he pursued this line further, using the critical methods of German Biblical scholarship to provide a purely secular account of the emergence of Christianity, thereby challenging the accuracy of the Scriptures and denying the miracles of Christ. The new religion was to be that of science and reason.

Renan is extensively cited in *Reflections on Violence*, as he is throughout Sorel's work. This is principally because Sorel shared Renan's fascination with the origins of Christianity. However, Sorel dismissed Renan's work as an example of an 'intellectualist philosophy' that was obliged to see Christianity solely in terms of 'illusions and accidents'. This was no idle dispute. The qualities of originality and purity which Renan denied to Christianity and which Sorel attributed to it were precisely those Sorel wished to accredit to the emerging syndicalist movement. See especially Sorel's *Le Système historique de Renan* (Paris, Jacques, 1906).

Giambattista Vico (1688–1744); Italian philosopher and jurist, author of *The New Science* (1725).

Vico develops the notion of what he describes as an 'ideal eternal history', a necessary process of social, cultural and political development followed by all nations. The first phase is 'poetic', dominated by mythical ways of seeing the world, whilst the final 'third' stage, the 'fully human', is an era where reason is presumed to have developed to the point when the true nature of things can be understood. Society then enters a period described as the 'barbarism of reflection', characterized by over-refinement and the beginning of decline, taking society back to its primitive beginnings, whence begins the whole process again. The *corsi* and *ricorsi* are therefore part of an eternally recurring cycle of human history.

Sorel came to this line of Vico's work via Marx, and from the mid-1890s onwards made great use of this and other of Vico's ideas: specifically, the notion and structure of the 'ideal eternal history' underpins much of the argument of *Reflections on Violence*. The syndicalist movement is located at its beginning, where everything is 'instinctive, creative and poetic'. Accordingly, 'each notable strike can become a partial *ricorso*', capable of rejuvenating the socialist idea and pushing society away from its state of decadence. See especially Sorel's 'Etude sur Vico', *Le Devenir social* 2 (1896), pp. 785–817, 906–41, 1013–46 and 'Le syndicalisme révolutionnaire', *Le Mouvement socialiste* 17 (1905), pp. 265–80.

Note on the text

The earliest version of the text that was to become *Reflections on Violence* first appeared in an Italian journal, *Il Divenire sociale*, edited by Enrico Leone. In a series of articles published during 1905 and 1906 – 'La lotta di classe e la violenza', 'La decadenza borghese e la violenza', 'I pregiudizi contro la violenza', 'Lo sciopero generale', 'Lo sciopero generale politico', 'Morale e violenza', 'Lo sciopero generale e la morale' and 'La morale dei produttori' – Sorel responded to debates within the Italian socialist movement about the utility of violence that had been taking place since 1903. These essays were brought together as *Lo sciopero generale e la violenza* (Rome, Il Divenire sociale, 1906).[1]

Revised and augmented, these articles were next published in Hubert Lagardelle's journal, *Le Mouvement socialiste*, during the first half of 1906, and this time under the general title of 'Réflexions sur la violence'. This would in all probability have been the end of their evolution had not Daniel Halévy convinced Sorel in May 1907 that they should be brought together in one single volume. The result was not only the publication of a further revised edition in book form by Pages Libres in 1908 but the addition of a thirty-page introduction entitled 'Lettre à Daniel Halévy' (also published the previous year in *Le Mouvement socialiste*).[2]

---

[1] See Willy Gianinazzi, 'Chez les "soréliens" italiens', in Michel Charzat (ed.), *Georges Sorel* (Paris, Cahiers de l'Herne, 1986), pp. 202–12.
[2] For the history of this collaboration see Michel Prat (ed.), 'Lettres de Georges Sorel à Daniel Halévy (1907–1920)', *Mil neuf cent: Revue d'histoire intellectuelle* 12 (1994), pp. 151–223.

Publication of *Réflexions sur la violence* proved an immediate success, bringing Sorel's name and ideas to the attention of a much wider audience and even providing him with an element of notoriety. A second edition, published by Marcel Rivière, quickly followed in 1910 (with the addition of the appendix entitled 'Unité et multiplicité') and then a third in 1912. The latter appeared with a short, but important, prefatory note indicating Sorel's belief in the continued relevance of the ideas expounded in his text. The fourth edition was published in 1920, complete with the famous 'Plaidoyer pour Lénine', written during September 1919 at the height of Sorel's enthusiasm for the Russian Revolution.

There was one subsequent edition of the text published during Sorel's lifetime, with a further twelve later published by Marcel Rivière. In French the most recent editions have been those published by Slatkine (Geneva–Paris, 1982) and Seuil (Paris, 1990). As with the latter, this translation of the text uses the eleventh edition published by Marcel Rivière (Paris, 1950).

If *Réflexions sur la violence* brought Sorel an element of fame, he also recognized that it quickly attained the status of his 'standard work'.[3] This is true not only because of its content but also because his text reveals all the idiosyncratic stylistic features of his writings. As we have already seen, Sorel was always loath to leave a text alone, forever adding new ideas gleaned from his voracious intellectual appetite. The result, for the reader, can often be one of apparent disorder. Yet Sorel felt no embarrassment at this. 'I write notebooks', he tells us in his 'Lettre à Daniel Halévy', 'in which I set down my thoughts as they arise; I return three or four times to the same question, adding points which amplify the original and sometimes even transform it completely; I only stop when I have exhausted the reserve of ideas stirred up by recent reading.' As a 'self-taught man', his aim was to discover what was 'personal' rather than express his 'intuitions' in a 'perfectly symmetrical form'. In this translation the character of Sorel's 'notebook' style has been respected.

Notoriety brought an international audience. The text was almost immediately translated into Russian and Italian, and then later into Spanish, Japanese, German as well as English. We know relatively

---

[3] See 'Lettere di Georges Sorel a B. Croce', *La Critica* 28 (1930), p. 194.

little about the process of its appearance in English. In an unpublished letter to Marcel Rivière, dated 19 April 1912, Sorel writes: 'You will find attached a letter from M. Hulme who is the translator who must undertake the metamorphosis into English of my *Réflexions sur la violence*. The English editors accept, he says, your conditions and there remains only the contract to sign; I think that it will be necessary to specify, as you have intended to do, that the royalties should be paid immediately.'[4] Four years later, presumably with the money paid, we find Sorel's only other reference to the English edition in a letter to Jean Bourdeau, dated 29 March 1916. 'I know' he writes, 'that the English translation of my *Réflexions sur la violence* has appeared; the translation has been done by M. Hulme, who has translated volumes of Bergson. He asked me to add a letter on the war. I did not dare write it; not knowing at all the true state of opinion in England I was worried about talking nonsense; it is probable, moreover, that I would have had great difficulty in finding something interesting to say'.[5]

Thomas Ernest Hulme (1883–1917) was, indeed, the translator of Henri Bergson, as well as being much else beside.[6] He was also (unlike Sorel) an enthusiastic supporter of the war, denouncing Bertrand Russell's pacifism at the same time as serving in the trenches. He was killed in battle in September 1917. In Sorel he felt that he had found someone who shared his hatred of the progressive sentiments of the age.

Hulme's translation was first published in the United States in November 1914 by W. B. Heubsch and then in March 1916 in England by George Allen and Unwin. The latter carried as a preface a slightly altered version of an article that Hulme had published in the *New Age*, designed to clarify the nature of Sorel's thought. 'Sorel', Hulme writes, 'is one of the most remarkable writers of the time, and certainly the most remarkable socialist since Marx.' Why was this so? Because, according to Hulme, Sorel was 'a revolutionary in economics, but classical in ethics'. It was, in short, the pessimism of Sorel, the view that the transformation of society and mor-

---

[4] Fonds M. Rivière, Internationaal Institut voor Sociale Geschiedenis, Amsterdam.
[5] 'Lettres de Georges Sorel à Jean Bourdeau, 2me partie, 1913–21', *Mil neuf cent: Revue d'histoire intellectuelle* 15 (1997), p. 176.
[6] See Karen Csengari (ed.), *The Collected Writings of T. E. Hulme* (Oxford, Clarendon Press, 1994).

ality would only be attained by dint of heroic effort, that appealed to Hulme, the indignant critic of Romanticism and of Rousseauism.[7] As with the original French edition, so the English language edition did not fail to evoke a response, being reviewed by such eminent figures as T. S. Eliot in *Mind*, Alfred Richard Orage and Herbert Read in the *New Age*, Arthur O. Lovejoy in the *American Political Science Review* as well as by Bernard Bosanquet.

Reflections on Violence was subsequently reprinted by Peter Smith (New York, 1941) and then by the Free Press (New York, 1950) and again by Collier Books (New York, 1961). The Collier edition was last reprinted in 1972, with the appendices 'Unité et multiplicité' and the 'Plaidoyer pour Lénine' translated into English for the first time. Unfortunately, during the 1950s and 1960s the text was habitually seen as one of those that had contributed most to the emergence of twentieth-century totalitarianism, the seeming admiration of both Lenin and Mussolini for Sorel's views doing much to foster this account. This, in the words of Jacob Laib Talmon, was 'the legacy of Georges Sorel'.

The revival of Sorel studies that has taken place since the mid-1970s in France, Britain, the United States, and elsewhere has done much to correct this impression. It is now possible, as should be done, to locate *Reflections on Violence* in the broader context of Sorel's work as a whole.

---

[7] *Ibid.*, pp. 246–52.

Note on the translation

The present text is a revised translation of that originally provided by Thomas Ernest Hulme. I had intended to use this translation in an unchanged form, but upon closer inspection decided that some, at times considerable, revision was necessary. To give just one important example, I have translated Sorel's *lutte de classe* not as class war but as class struggle.

I have also retained the French *syndicat* for trade union, principally because Sorel uses the English expression in his text, usually to denote the reformist unionism of which he disapproves. Hulme anglicized the French, producing the misnomer 'syndicate'.

I have not tried to eradicate Sorel's 'notebook' style and have preserved his own subsectioning of the text.

The edition of the French text I have used is that published by Seuil in 1990, edited by Michel Prat. This itself is a reproduction of the eleventh edition, published by Marcel Rivière in 1950.

Different editions of the text have changed the order of its presentation. I have adopted what seems the most logical pattern.

Wherever possible I have completed the bibliographical information required in the footnotes, the additions being contained within squared brackets. Sorel's own footnotes are numbered, whilst my editorial footnotes are lettered.

REFLECTIONS
ON VIOLENCE

A la mémoire
de la compagne de ma jeunesse
je dédie ce livre
tout inspiré par son esprit

Introduction: Letter to Daniel Halévy

My dear Halévy,

I would no doubt have left these studies buried in the bound volumes of a review if friends, whose judgement I greatly value, had not thought that it would be a good idea to bring to the attention of a wider public reflections which serve to make better known one of the most singular social phenomena that history records. But it seemed to be that this public deserves some explanations, since I cannot often expect to find judges as indulgent as you have been.

When in *Le Mouvement socialiste*[a] I published the articles that are now to be brought together in a volume, I did not have the intention of writing a book. I wrote these reflections as they came to my mind, knowing that the subscribers to that review would have no difficulty following me as they were already familiar with the theories that had there been developed by my friends over several years. But I am convinced that the readers of this book will be bewildered if I do not submit a kind of defence that will better enable them to

---

[a] *Le Mouvement socialiste* was established by Hubert Lagardelle (1874–1958) in 1899 and ceased publication in 1914. During its existence it was subject to considerable change in political position, but throughout managed to secure the participation of an impressive array of French and European writers of the Left. Initially Dreyfusard and supportive of what Lagardelle termed the 'humanitarian intervention of Jaurès', from 1904 the review became one of the principal advocates of revolutionary syndicalism, publishing most of Sorel's writings of the period as well as the articles of his most enthusiastic admirers in the so-called '*new school*'. As the syndicalist movement itself entered a period of crisis at the end of the decade, so too did *Le Mouvement socialiste*. After the departure of Sorel and his friends, the review lost much of its political and intellectual direction.

3

see things from my own point of view. In the course of our conversations you have made critical comments which fitted so well into the system of my own ideas that they have led me to investigate certain interesting questions more thoroughly. I am sure that the thoughts which I here submit to you, and which you have provoked, will be very useful to those who wish to read this book with profit.

There are perhaps few studies in which the defects of my method of writing are more evident; time and again I have been reproached for not respecting the rules of art followed by all our contemporaries and therefore of inconveniencing my readers by the disorder of my arguments. I have tried to render the text more clear by numerous minor corrections but I have not been able to make the disorder disappear. I do not, however, wish to defend myself by invoking the example of great writers who have been criticized for not knowing how to write. Arthur Chuquet,[b] speaking of J[ean-Jacques] Rousseau, said: 'His writings lack harmony, order, and that connection of the parts which constitutes a unity.'[1] The defects of famous men do not justify the faults of the obscure, and I think that it is better to explain frankly the origin of this incorrigible vice in my writings.

It is only relatively recently that the rules of the art of writing have imposed themselves in a genuinely imperative way; contemporary authors appear to have accepted them without too much difficulty because they wish to please a hurried and often very inattentive public which is, above all, concerned to avoid any personal investigation. These rules were first applied by the producers of academic books. Ever since we have wanted pupils to absorb an enormous amount of information, it has been necessary to put into their hands manuals suitable to this extra-rapid form of instruction; everything has had to be presented in a form so clear, so interconnected and so arranged to avoid uncertainty, such that beginners come to believe that science is much simpler that our fathers believed. In no time at all the mind is very richly furnished, but it is not provided with the instruments which facilitate individual effort. These methods have been imitated by popularizers of knowledge

---

[1] A[rthur] Chuquet, *Jean-Jacques Rousseau* [Paris, Hachette, 1893], p. 179.

[b] Arthur Chuquet (1853–1925); professor at the Collège de France.

and by political publicists.[2] Seeing these rules of art so widely adopted, people who reflect little have ended up believing that they were based upon the nature of things themselves.

I am neither a professor, a popularizer of knowledge nor a candidate for party leadership; I am a self-taught man exhibiting to other people the notebooks which have served for my own instruction. This is why the rules of the art of writing have never interested me very much.

For twenty years I strove to free myself from what I retained of my education; I indulged my curiosity by reading books less to learn than to efface from my memory the ideas that had been thrust upon it. It is only during the last ten years or so that I have really worked with the purpose of learning; but I have never found anyone to teach me what I wanted to know; I have had to be my own master and, in a way, to teach myself. I write notebooks in which I set down my thoughts as they arise; I return three or four times to the same question, adding points that amplify the original and sometimes even transform it completely; I only stop when I have exhausted the reserve of ideas stirred up by recent reading. This work is very difficult for me; it is for this reason that I like to take as my subject the discussion of a book by a good author; I can then more easily arrange my own thoughts than when I am left to my own efforts.

You will remember what Bergson has written about the impersonal, the socialized, the *ready-made*, all of which contains a lesson for students who need to acquire knowledge for practical life. The student has more confidence in the formulas that he is taught and consequently retains them more easily, especially when he imagines that they are accepted by the great majority; in this way he is distanced from all metaphysical concerns and gets used not to feeling the need for a personal conception of things; often he comes to regard the absence of any inventive spirit as a superiority.

My method of work is entirely opposite to this; I put before my readers the product of a mental effort which is endeavouring to break through the constraints of what has previously been constructed for common use and which seeks to discover what is

---

[2] I am here reminded of the sentence of Renan: 'In order to be of use reading must be an exercise involving some effort': *Feuilles détachées* [Paris, Calmann-Lévy, 1892], p. 231.

5

personal. The only things I find it truly interesting to enter into my notebooks are those that I have not come across elsewhere; I readily skip the points of transition because they nearly always fall into the category of commonplaces.

The communication of thought is always very difficult for someone who has strong metaphysical preoccupations: he thinks that speech will spoil the most fundamental parts of his thought, those which are very close to the motive power of the mind, those which appear so natural to him that he never seeks to express them. The reader has great difficulty in grasping the thought of an inventor because he can only understand it by finding again the path followed by the latter. Verbal communication is much easier than written communication because words act upon the feelings in a mysterious way and easily establish a bond of sympathy between people; it is for this reason that an orator is able to produce conviction by arguments which are not easily comprehensible to anyone who later reads the speech. You know yourself how useful it is to have heard Bergson if one wants to understand the drift of his argument and properly to understand his books; when one has followed his lectures one becomes familiar with the order of his ideas and gets one's bearings more easily amidst the novelties of his philosophy.

The defects of my manner of writing prevent me from gaining access to a wide public; but I think that we ought to be content with the place that nature and circumstances have assigned to each of us, without wishing to force our natural aptitude. There is a necessary division of functions in the world: it is good that some are content to work in order to submit their reflections to a few studious people whilst others prefer to address the great mass of busy humanity. All things considered, I do not consider my lot to be the worst, since I do not run the risk of becoming my own disciple, as has happened to the greatest philosophers when they have tried to give a perfectly symmetrical form to the intuitions that they have brought into the world. You will certainly not have forgotten with what smiling disdain Bergson has spoken of this fall from genius. I am so little capable of becoming my own disciple that I cannot take up an old work with a view to stating it better while completing it; it is easy enough for me to add corrections and to annotate it, but I have many times vainly tried to think the past over again.

Much more am I prevented from becoming the founder of a school;[3] but is that really a great misfortune? Disciples have nearly always exercised a pernicious influence upon the thought of him they call their master, and he in turn has often believed himself obliged to follow them. There is no doubt that for Marx it was a real disaster to have been transformed into the leader of a sect by his young enthusiasts; he would have produced much more useful work had he not become the slave of the Marxists.

People have often laughed at Hegel's belief that humanity, since its origins, had worked to give birth to the Hegelian philosophy and that with it the Spirit had at last completed its development. Similar illusions are found to a greater or lesser extent in all founders of schools: disciples expect their masters to close the era of doubt by providing definitive solutions. I have no aptitude for a role of that kind: every time that I have approached a question I have found that my enquiries have ended up by giving rise to new problems, the further I push my investigations the more disquieting the results. But perhaps, after all, philosophy is only a recognition of the abysses which lie on each side of the path that the vulgar follow with the serenity of sleepwalkers.

It is my ambition to be able occasionally to awaken a personal vocation. There is probably within every man a metaphysical fire which lies hidden beneath the ashes, and the greater the number of ready-made doctrines it has blindly received the more likely it is to be extinguished; the awakener is he who stirs the ashes and who thus makes the flames fly up. I do not think that I am unduly praising myself when I say that I have sometimes succeeded in liberating the spirit of invention in my readers; and it is this spirit of invention which it is, above all, necessary to arouse in the world. To achieve this result is far better than gaining the banal approval

---

[3] It may be interesting to quote here some reflections borrowed from the admirable book of Newman's: 'It will be our wisdom to avail ourselves of language, as far as it will go, but to aim mainly, by means of it, to stimulate in those to whom we address ourselves, a mode of thinking and trains of thought similar to our own, leading them to their own independent action, not by any syllogistic compulsion. Hence it is that an intellectual school will always have something of an esoteric character; for it is an assemblage of minds that think, their bond of unity is thought, and their words become a sort of *tessera*, not expressing thought but symbolizing it': [John Henry Newman,] *Grammaire de l'assentiment*, French trans. [Paris, Bloud, 1907], p. 250. [See John Henry Newman, *An Essay in aid of a Grammar of Assent* (London, Burns, Oates & Co., 1870).]

7

of people who repeat formulas and who subjugate their own thought to the disputes of schools.

I

My *Reflections on Violence* have annoyed many people because of the pessimistic conception upon which the whole study rests; but I know that you do not share this opinion; you have shown brilliantly in your *Histoire de quatre ans*[c] that you despise the deceptive hopes with which the weak console themselves. We can therefore speak freely about pessimism between ourselves, and I am happy to have in you a correspondent who does not rebel against a doctrine without which nothing of greatness has been accomplished in the world. I have felt for a long time that if Greek philosophy did not produce any great moral results it was because as a rule it was very optimistic. Socrates was at times optimistic to an unbearable degree.[d]

The aversion of our contemporaries to every pessimistic conception is doubtless derived to a great extent from our education. The Jesuits, who created nearly everything that the University still teaches, were optimists because they had to combat the pessimism which dominated Protestant theories, and because they popularized the ideas of the Renaissance; the latter interpreted antiquity by means of the philosophers, and consequently misunderstood the masterpieces of tragic art so badly that our contemporaries have had great difficulty in rediscovering their pessimistic significance.[4]

At the beginning of the nineteenth century there was a concert of groaning which greatly contributed to making pessimism odious.

---

[4] 'The sadness which, despite the sense of life they show, exists as a form of foreboding in all the masterpieces of Greek art shows that, even at that time, there were individuals of genius capable of peering beyond the illusions of life to which the spirit of their time surrendered without hesitation': E[duard] von Hartmann, *Philosophie de l'inconscient*, French trans. [Paris, Baillière, 1877], II, p. 436. I call attention to this view which sees in the genius of the Greeks an historical anticipation; there are few doctrines more important for the understanding of history than that of anticipations, a doctrine used by Newman in his research on the history of dogmas.

[c] Daniel Halévy, *Histoire de quatre ans, 1997–2001* (Paris, Cahiers de la Quinzaine, 1903).

[d] For an earlier expression of this view see Georges Sorel, *Le Procès de Socrate* (Paris, Alcan, 1889).

Poets, who in truth did not have much to complain about, claimed to be the victims of human wickedness, of fate and, worse, the stupidity of a world which had not been able to amuse them; they eagerly took on the attitudes of a Prometheus called upon to dethrone jealous gods; and with a pride equal to the fierce Nimrod of Victor Hugo (whose arrows, launched at the sky, returned bloodstained),[e] they imagined that their verses inflicted deadly wounds on the established powers who were daring enough not to bow down before them; never did the prophets of the Jews dream of so much destruction to avenge their Jehovah as these men of letters did to satisfy their vanity. When this fashion for complaining had passed, sensible people asked themselves if all this display of pretended pessimism had not been the result of a lack of mental balance.

The immense successes obtained by industrial civilization has created the belief that, in the near future, happiness will be produced automatically for everybody. 'The present century', wrote Hartmann almost forty years ago, 'has only entered the third period of illusion. In the enthusiasm and the enchantment of its hopes it rushes towards the realization of the promise of a new golden age. Providence does not allow that the anticipations of an isolated thinker should trouble the course of history by prematurely influencing too many adherents.' He also thinks that his readers will have some difficulty in accepting his criticism of the illusion of future happiness. The leaders of the contemporary world are pushed towards optimism by economic forces.[5]

So little are we prepared to understand pessimism that we generally employ the word quite incorrectly: we wrongly take pessimists to be disillusioned optimists. When we meet a man who, having been unfortunate in his enterprises, deceived in his most legitimate ambitions, humiliated in his affections, expresses his sorrow in the form of a violent revolt against the bad faith of his colleagues, the

---

[5] Hartmann, [*ibid.*], p. 462.

[e] A letter written by Sorel to Halévy (26 August 1907) explains this reference. Sorel had originally come across it in Ernest Renan's *Feuilles détachées*, believing its source to be the Bible, only to discover that Renan had taken it from Victor Hugo's *La Fin de Satan*. Both, however, were inspired by the image of Nimrod found in *Genesis* 10: 1–13. See 'Lettres de Georges Sorel à Daniel Halévy (1907–1920)', *Mil neuf cent* 12 (1994), pp. 162–3.

stupidity of society or the blindness of destiny, we are disposed to regard him as a pessimist – whereas we ought nearly always to regard him as a disheartened optimist who has not had the courage to rethink his ideas and who cannot understand why so many misfortunes have befallen him, in contrast to the general law governing the production of happiness.

The optimist in politics is an inconstant and even dangerous man, because he takes no account of the great difficulties presented by his projects; these projects seem to him to possess a force of their own which tends to bring about their realization all the more easily as, in his opinion, they are destined to produce more happiness.

He frequently thinks that small reforms of the political system and, above all, of government personnel will be sufficient to direct the movement of society in such a way as to mitigate those evils of the modern world which seem so hideous to sensitive souls. As soon as his friends come to power he declares that it is necessary to let things alone for a while, not to be too hasty, and to learn to be content with whatever their good intentions suggest; it is not always self-interest that dictates these expressions of satisfaction, as people have often believed: self-interest is strongly aided by vanity and by the illusions of poor-quality philosophy. The optimist moves with remarkable ease from revolutionary anger to the most ridiculous social pacifism.

If he possesses an excitable temperament and if unhappily he finds himself armed with great power, permitting him to realize an ideal he has fashioned, the optimist can lead his country to the worst disasters. He is not long in discovering that social transformations are not brought about with the ease he had counted on; he then blames these disappointments upon his contemporaries, instead of explaining what actually happens as the result of historical necessities; he is tempted to get rid of people whose ill will seems to him to be a danger to the happiness of all. During the Terror the men who spilt the most blood were precisely those who had the strongest desire to let their equals enjoy the golden age of which they dreamt and who had the greatest sympathy for human misery: optimistic, idealistic and sensitive, they showed themselves to be the more unyielding the greater their desire for universal happiness.

Pessimism is quite a different thing from the caricatures that are usually presented of it; it is a metaphysics of morals rather than a theory of the world; it is a conception of a *march towards deliverance* that is narrowly conditioned: on the one hand, by the experimental knowledge that we have acquired of the obstacles which oppose themselves to the satisfaction of our imaginations (or, if one prefers, by the feeling of social determinism) – on the other, by a profound conviction of our natural weakness. These three aspects of pessimism should never be separated, although as a rule little attention is paid to their close connection.

1) The concept of pessimism derives from the fact that literary historians have been very struck by the complaints of the great poets of antiquity about the sorrow and pain that constantly threaten mankind. There are few people who have not at least once experienced a piece of good fortune; but we are surrounded by evil forces which are always ready to spring an ambush and overwhelm us; from this are born the very real sufferings which arouse the sympathy of all men, even of those who have been treated most favourably by fortune; hence the literature of grief has had an appeal throughout almost all history.[6] But we would have a very imperfect idea of pessimism if we considered only this kind of literature; as a general rule, in order to understand a doctrine it is not sufficient to study it in an abstract manner, nor even as it occurs in isolated people: we need to find out how it is manifested in historical groups; it is for this reason that I am here led to add the two elements that were mentioned earlier.

2) The pessimist regards social conditions as forming a system bound together by an iron law which cannot be evaded, as something in the form of one block, and which can only disappear through a catastrophe which involves the whole. If this theory is admitted, it then becomes absurd to attribute the evils from which society suffers to a few wicked men; the pessimist is not subject to the bloodthirsty follies of the optimist driven mad by the unforeseen obstacles that his projects meet; he does not dream of bringing about the happiness of future generations by slaughtering existing egoists.

3) The most fundamental element of pessimism is its method of conceiving the path towards deliverance. A man would not go far in the examination either of the laws of his own wretchedness or of

---

[6] The false cries of despair which were heard at the beginning of the nineteenth century owed their success in part to the analogies of form which they presented to the real literature of pessimism.

fate, which so shock the ingenuousness of our pride, if he were not borne up by the hope of putting an end to these tyrannies by an effort to be attempted with a whole band of companions. The Christians would not have discussed original sin so much if they had not felt the necessity of justifying the deliverance (which was to result from the death of Jesus) by supposing that this sacrifice had been made necessary by a frightful crime attributable to humanity. If the people of the West were much more occupied with original sin than those of the East it was not solely, as Taine thought, due to the influence of Roman law,[7] but also because the Latin peoples, having a more elevated conception of imperial majesty than the Greeks, regarded the sacrifice of the Son of God as having realized an extraordinarily marvellous deliverance; from this proceeded the necessity of deepening the mysteries surrounding human wretchedness and destiny.

It seems to me that the optimism of the Greek philosophers depended to a great extent upon economic reasons; it probably arose in the rich and commercial urban populations who were able to regard the world as a gigantic shop full of excellent things that could satisfy their greed.[8] I imagine that Greek pessimism sprang from the poor warlike tribes living in the mountains who possessed an enormous aristocratic pride but whose material conditions were very modest; their poets charmed them by praising their ancestors and made them look forward to victorious expeditions led by superhuman heroes; they explained their present wretchedness to them by relating catastrophes in which semi-divine former chiefs had succumbed to fate or to the jealousy of the gods; the courage of the warriors might for the moment be unable to accomplish anything but it would not always be so; they had to remain faithful to the old customs so as to be ready for the great and victorious expeditions that might be near at hand.

Oriental asceticism has very often been considered the most remarkable manifestation of pessimism; Hartmann is certainly right when he regards it as having only the value of an anticipation whose utility was to remind men how much is illusory in vulgar riches; he

---

[7] H[ippolyte] Taine, *Le Régime moderne* [Paris, Hachette, 1894, II], pp. 121–2.
[8] The Athenian comic poets several times depicted a land of milk and honey where there was no longer the need to work: (A[lfred] and M[aurice] Croiset, *Histoire de la littérature grecque* [Paris, Thorin, 1895], III, pp. 472–4).

was wrong, however, in saying that asceticism taught men that 'the destined end of all their efforts' was the annihilation of the will;[9] for in the course of history deliverance has taken quite different forms from this.

In primitive Christianity we find a fully developed and completely armed pessimism: man is condemned to slavery from birth – Satan is the prince of the world; the Christian, already regenerated by baptism, can render himself capable of obtaining the resurrection of the body by means of the Eucharist;[10] he awaits the glorious second coming of Christ who will destroy the rule of Satan and call his comrades in the fight to a heavenly Jerusalem. This Christian life was dominated by the necessity of belonging to a holy army constantly beset by ambushes led by the accomplices of Satan; this conception produced many heroic acts, engendered a courageous propaganda and was the cause of considerable moral progress. Deliverance did not take place; but we know by innumerable testimonies from this time what great things the march towards deliverance can bring about.

Sixteenth-century Calvinism presents us with a spectacle which is perhaps even more instructive; but we must be very careful not to confuse it, as many authors have done, with contemporary Protestantism; these two doctrines are the very opposite of each other. I cannot understand how Hartmann can say that Protestantism 'is a halting place on the journey of true Christianity' and that it 'allied itself with the renaissance of ancient paganism';[11] these judgements apply only to recent Protestantism, which has abandoned its own principles in order to adopt those of the Renaissance. Pessimism, which formed no part of the current of ideas that characterized the Renaissance,[12] has never been so strongly affirmed as it was by the

---

[9] Hartmann, [*Philosophie de l'inconscient*], p. 492. 'Contempt for the world, combined with a transcendent life of the spirit, had been taught in India through the esoteric teachings of Buddhism. But this teaching was only accessible to a narrow circle of initiates living a celibate life. The outside world had only taken the letter which kills and its influence was only evident in the eccentric form of the lives of hermits and penitents' (p. 439).

[10] P[ierre] Batiffol, *Etudes d'histoire et de théologie positive* [Paris, Lecoffre, 1905], p. 162.

[11] E[duard] von Hartmann, *La Religion de l'avenir*, French trans. [Paris, Baillière, 1876], p. 27 and p. 21.

[12] 'At this epoch began the struggle between the pagan love of life and the Christian contempt of the world and flight from it': *ibid.*, p. 126. This pagan conception is

men of the Reformation. The dogmas of sin and of predestination – which correspond to the first two aspects of pessimism, the wretchedness of the human species and social determinism – were pushed to their most extreme consequences. Deliverance was conceived in a very different form from that which it had been given by primitive Christianity; Protestants organized themselves militarily wherever this was possible; they made expeditions into Catholic lands, expelled the priests, introduced their form of worship, and promulgated laws proscribing papists. They no longer borrowed from the books of the apocalypse the idea of a great final catastrophe in which their brothers in Christ, who had for so long defended themselves against the attacks of Satan, would only be spectators; the Protestants, nourished on the reading of the Old Testament, wanted to imitate the exploits of the earlier conquerors of the Holy Land; they therefore took the offensive and sought to establish the kingdom of God by force. In each locality that they conquered, the Calvinists brought about a real catastrophic revolution, changing everything from top to bottom.

Calvinism was finally vanquished by the Renaissance; it was full of theological concerns derived from medieval traditions and there came a time when it feared to be thought too far behind the times; it wished to be on the level of modern culture and finished by becoming simply a lax Christianity.[13] Today very few people have a sense of what the reformers of the sixteenth century meant by free examination; Protestants apply the same methods to the Bible as philologists apply to any secular text; Calvin's style of exegesis has been replaced by humanist criticism.

The chronicler of events who contents himself with recording facts is tempted to regard deliverance as either a dream or an error; but the true historian considers things from a different point of view: whenever he endeavours to find out what has been the influence of the Calvinist spirit upon morals, law or literature he is always led to examine how earlier Protestant thought was influenced by the conception of the path towards deliverance. The experience of this great epoch shows quite clearly that in the sentiment of battle

to be found in liberal Protestantism and this is why Hartmann rightly considers it to be irreligious; but the men of the sixteenth century saw things very differently.

[13] If socialism perishes it will obviously be in the same way, because it will have been frightened by its own barbarism.

that accompanies this *will to deliverance* the courageous man finds a satisfaction that is sufficient to keep up his ardour. I am convinced, therefore, that from this case one can draw excellent illustrations of the idea that you once expressed to me: that the legend of the wandering Jew, condemned to march forever without knowing rest, is the symbol of the highest aspirations of mankind.

II

My theses have shocked many people who are, to a certain extent, under the influence of ideas implanted in us by our education on the subject of natural law; very few educated people have been able to free themselves from these ideas. If this philosophy of natural law accords perfectly with that of force (understanding this word in the special sense I give it in chapter V, section IV) it cannot be reconciled with my conception of the historical role of violence. Scholastic doctrines of natural law amount to nothing but a simple tautology: what is just is good and what is unjust is bad; as if we had not always implicitly admitted that the just adapts itself to the natural order of events in the world. It was for this reason that economists for a long time asserted that the relations created under the capitalist regime of competition were perfectly just, because they resulted from the *natural course* of things; conversely utopians have always claimed that the actual state of the world is *not natural enough*. They have wished, consequently, to paint a picture of a society naturally better regulated and therefore more just.

I cannot resist the pleasure of quoting some of Pascal's *Pensées*, which terribly embarrassed his contemporaries and which have only been properly understood in our day. Pascal[f] had considerable difficulty in freeing himself from the ideas of natural law he found in the philosophers; he abandoned them because he did not think them sufficiently imbued with Christianity: 'I have passed a great part of my life', he writes, 'believing that there was justice; and in this I was mistaken, because it exists *only as God has willed to reveal it to us*. But I

---

[f] Blaise Pascal (1623–62); philosopher; he was closely associated with the Jansenist movement centred on the convent of Port-Royal outside Paris and condemned by Pope Innocent X in 1653. First published in 1670, the *Pensées* are a long set of fragmentary notes on the nature of religious faith, in part designed to show the impotence of reason in metaphysical matters.

did not take it so, and this is where I made the mistake; for I believed that our justice was essentially just and that I possessed the means by which I could know it and judge of it' (fragment 375 of the Brunschvicq edition); – 'Doubtless there are natural laws; but this good reason once corrupted,[14] has corrupted all' (fragment 294); – '*Veri juris.* We have it no longer' (fragment 297).

Moreover, mere observation showed Pascal the absurdity of the theory of natural law; if this theory was correct, we ought to find laws that are universally admitted; but actions which we regard as crimes have at other times been regarded as virtuous: 'Three degrees of elevation nearer the pole reverse all jurisprudence, a meridian decides what is truth; fundamental laws change after a few years of possession; right has its epochs, the entry of Saturn into the constellation of the Lion marks to us the origin of such and such a crime. What a strange justice it is that is bounded by a river! Truth on this side of the Pyrenees becomes error on the other . . . We must, we are told, get back to the fundamental and original laws of the State which an unjust custom has abolished. This is a game certain to result in the loss of all; nothing will be just on the balance' (fragment 294; cf. fragment 379).

As it is thus impossible to reason about justice, we ought to appeal to custom, and Pascal often falls back upon this axiom (fragments 294, 297, 299, 309, 312). He goes much further and shows how justice is practically dependent on force: 'Justice is subject to dispute; force is easily recognizable and beyond dispute. Thus it is not possible to attribute force to justice, because force has contradicted justice and has said that it itself was just. And therefore not being able to make what was just strong, what was strong has been made just' (fragment 298; fragments 302, 303, 306, 307, 311).

This criticism of natural law has not the perfect clarity that we could give it today, because we know that it is in economics that we must seek the type of force that has attained a fully automatic status and can thus be identified naturally with law – whilst Pascal confuses under one heading all the manifestations of force.[15]

---

[14] It seems to me that the editors of 1670 must have been alarmed at his Calvinism. I am astonished that Sainte-Beuve should have restricted himself to saying only that there 'was in Pascal's Christianity something that they could not understand . . . that Pascal had greater need of being a Christian than they had': C[harles-Augustin] Sainte-Beuve, *Port-Royal* [Paris, Hachette, 1888], III, p. 383.

[15] Cf. what I say about force in chapter V.

Pascal was vividly struck by the changes that justice has experienced over time and they still continue to embarrass philosophers; a well-organized social system is destroyed by a revolution and is replaced by another system which is considered perfectly fair; and what was before considered just becomes unjust. Any amount of sophisms have been provided to show that force has been placed at the service of justice during revolutions; on many occasions these arguments have been shown to be absurd; but the public is so accustomed to believe in natural law that it cannot make up its mind to abandon them!

There is nothing, including even war, that it has not been tried to bring inside the scope of natural law: they compare war to a process in which a people claims a right which a malevolent neighbour refuses to recognize. Our fathers readily acknowledged that God decided the outcome of battles in favour of those who had right on their side; the vanquished were to be treated as an unsuccessful litigant: they must pay the costs of the war and give guarantees to the victor in order that the latter might enjoy his restored rights. Today there is no shortage of people who propose that international conflicts should be submitted to arbitration; this would be a secularization of the ancient mythology.[16]

The supporters of natural law are not always implacable enemies of civil struggles, and certainly not of tumultuous rioting; that has been amply demonstrated during the course of the Dreyfus affair. When the authority of the law was in the hands of their opponents they accepted willingly enough that it was being employed to violate justice and they then proved that one could forego legality in order to make a return to right (to borrow a phrase of the Bonapartists); when they could not overthrow the government they tried at least to intimidate it. But when they attacked the upholders of the authority of the law, they did not at all seek to suppress that authority, because they wished one day to utilize it for their own ends; all the revolutionary disturbances of the nineteenth century ended by strengthening the State.

Proletarian violence entirely changes the appearance of all the conflicts in which it plays a part, since it disowns the force organized by

---

[16] I cannot succeed in finding the idea of international arbitration in fragment 296 of Pascal, where several people claim to have discovered it; Pascal here simply points out the ridiculous aspect of the claim made in his day by every belligerent to condemn the conduct of his adversary in the name of justice.

the bourgeoisie and wants to suppress the State which serves as its central nucleus. Under such conditions it is no longer possible to argue about the original rights of man; this is why our parliamentary socialists, who are the offspring of the bourgeoisie and who know nothing outside the ideology of the State, are so bewildered when they are confronted with proletarian violence; they cannot apply to it the commonplaces which ordinarily serve them when they speak about force, and they look with terror on movements which might lead to the ruin of the institutions by which they live: if revolutionary syndicalism triumphs there will be no more speeches on immanent Justice, no more parliamentary regime for the use of Intellectuals; – it is the abomination of desolation. We must not be astonished therefore that they speak about violence with so much anger.

Giving evidence on 5 June 1907 before the Assize Court of the Seine in the Bousquet–Lévy case,[g] Jaurès said: 'I have no superstitious belief about legality. It has already been subject to too many defeats! but I always advise the workers to have recourse to legal means; because *violence is a sign of temporary weakness.*' This is clearly a reference to the Dreyfus affair: Jaurès remembered that his friends were obliged to have recourse to revolutionary demonstrations and it is easy to understand from this affair that he did retain a very great respect for a legality that was in conflict with what he regarded to be right. He likened the position of the syndicalists to that of the former Dreyfusards: at the moment they are weak but they are destined one day to take possession of the State; it would therefore be unwise to destroy by violence a force which is destined to become theirs. Perhaps he may even regret at times that the State was so severely shaken by the Dreyfus agitation, just as Gambetta[h] regretted that the administration had lost its former prestige and discipline.

[g] Jean Bousquet (1867–1925) was secretary of the Fédération de l'Alimentation; Albert Lévy (1871–1926) was treasurer and one of the leaders of the Confédération Générale du Travail. Both were sentenced to eighteen months in prison for incitement to violence.
[h] Léon Gambetta (1838–82); one of the great republican politicians of the nineteenth century and a key figure in securing the existence of the Third Republic (1870–1940) after the disasters of the Franco-Prussian war. After his election in 1871, one of his principal concerns was to 'republicanize' the administrative personnel of the new Republic.

One of the most elegant ministers of the Republic[17] has made a speciality of high-sounding pronouncements against the upholders of violence: Viviani[i] charms deputies, senators and the employees assembled to hear his Excellency on his official tours by telling them that violence is a caricature or rather 'the fallen and degenerate daughter of force'. After boasting that by a magnificent gesture he has extinguished the lamps of heaven, he assumes the manner of a matador at whose feet a furious bull is about to fall.[18] If I were more vain about my literary efforts I would like to think that this *fine socialist* was thinking of me when he told the Senate on 16 November 1906 that 'one must not confuse a *fanatic* for a party nor a *rash statement* for a system of thought'. After the pleasure of being understood by intelligent people there is none greater than not being understood by muddleheads who are only capable of expressing in jargon what serves them in the place of thought; but I have every reason to imagine that in the brilliant entourage that surrounds this *tout*[19] there is not one who has ever heard of *Le Mouvement socialiste*. That the people may attempt an insurrection when they feel sufficiently well organized to take over the State is something that Viviani and his ministerial staff can understand; but proletarian violence, which has no such aim,

---

[17] *Le Petit Parisien*, that one always cites with pleasure as the monitor of bourgeois stupidity, tells us that today 'this scornful definition of the elegant and *immoral* M. de Morny – *Republicans are people who dress badly* – is completely without foundation'. I borrow this philosophical observation from the enthusiastic account of the marriage of the charming minister Clémental (22 October 1905). This well-informed newspaper has accused me of giving the workers the advice of an *apache*.

[18] 'I have myself seen violence', he told the Senate on 16 November 1906, 'face to face. I have been, day after day, in the midst of thousands of men who bore on their faces the marks of terrifying exaltation. I remained amongst them chest to chest, eye to eye.' He boasted that in the end he triumphed over the strikers in the Creusot workshops.

[19] In the course of the same speech, Viviani strongly insisted on his own socialism and declared that he intended 'to remain faithful to the ideals of his first years in public life'. If we are to judge from a pamphlet published by the Allemanistes in 1897 under the title of *La Vérité sur l'union socialiste* [Paris, J. Allemane], this ideal was opportunism. When he left Algiers for Paris, Viviani was transformed into a socialist and the pamphlet qualifies his new position as a lie. Obviously this text was written by fanatics who know nothing of the refinements of life.

[i] René Viviani (1863–1925); socialist deputy; minister of labour between 1906–10 and prime minister between 1914–15: it was whilst Viviani was minister of labour that there occurred frequent clashes between strikers and the State, with the latter deploying the army to quell industrial unrest. A famed orator, Viviani had taken elocution lessons at the bastion of French classical theatre, the Comédie Française.

seems to them only folly and an odious caricature of revolt. Do what you like, but don't kill the goose that lays the golden egg!

III

In the course of these studies one thing seemed so evident to me that I did not believe that I needed to lay much stress on it: men who are participating in great social movements always picture their coming action in the form of images of battle in which their cause is certain to triumph. I proposed to give the name of 'myths' to these constructions, knowledge of which is so important for historians:[20] the general strike of the syndicalists and Marx's catastrophic revolution are such myths. As remarkable examples of myths I have given those which were constructed by primitive Christianity, by the Reformation, by the Revolution, and by the followers of Mazzini.[j] I wanted to show that we should not attempt to analyse such groups of images in the way that we break down a thing into its elements, that they should be taken as a whole, as historical forces, and that we should be especially careful not to make any comparison between the outcomes and the pictures people had formed for themselves before the action.

I could have given one more example which is perhaps even more striking: Catholics have never been discouraged even in the hardest trials, because they have pictured the history of the Church as a series of battles between Satan and the hierarchy supported by Christ: every new difficulty that arises is an episode in this war which must finally end in the victory of Catholicism.

At the beginning of the nineteenth century the revolutionary persecutions revived this myth of the struggle with Satan, providing Joseph de Maistre[k] with so many eloquent words. This rejuvenation

[20] In my *Introduction à l'économie moderne* [Paris, Jacques, 1903] I gave to the word 'myth' a more general sense, which corresponds closely to the narrower meaning employed here. [In this text, Sorel defined as myths those theories of Marx that contained 'something of the essence of socialism'.]

[j] Guiseppe Mazzini (1805–72); Italian nationalist and leader of the militant *Risorgimento* movement for a united Italian republic.

[k] Joseph de Maistre (1753–1821); the most vociferous critic of the Revolution of 1789 and defender of the old order. In his *Considérations sur la France* (1796), he announced that 'There is a satanic quality to the French Revolution that distinguishes it from everything we have ever seen or anything that we are ever likely to see in the future.'

explains to a large extent the religious renewal which took place at that time. If Catholicism is so under threat today it is largely owing to the fact that the myth of the Church militant is tending to disappear. Ecclesiastical literature has greatly contributed to rendering it ridiculous; for example, in 1872 a Belgian writer recommended a revival of exorcisms as they seemed to him an effective way of combating the revolutionaries.[21] Many educated Catholics are horrified when they discover that the ideas of Joseph de Maistre have contributed to encouraging the ignorance of a clergy which avoided any attempt to gain an adequate knowledge of a science judged accursed; to them the myth of the struggle with Satan therefore appears dangerous and they point out its ridiculous aspects, but they in no way understand its historical significance. The gentle, sceptical and, above all, pacific habits of the present generation are, moreover, not favourable to its continued existence; and the enemies of the Church loudly proclaim that it does not wish to return to a regime of persecutions that might restore their former power to the images of war.

By employing the term 'myth' I believed that I had made a happy choice, because I thus put myself in a position of refusing all discussion with the people who wish to subject the general strike to detailed criticism and who accumulate objections against its practical possibility. It appears, on the contrary, that I had a very bad idea, since while some tell me that myths are only appropriate to a primitive society others imagine that I thought the modern world might be moved by dreams analogous to those which Renan thought might usefully replace religion;[22] but there has been a worse misunderstanding and it has been believed that my theory of myths was only a lawyer's plea, a falsification of the real opinions of the revolutionaries, *an intellectualist sophistry.*

---

[21] P[aul] Bureau, *La Crise morale des temps nouveaux* [Paris, Bloud, 1907], p. 213. The author, who teaches at the Institut Catholique de Paris, adds: 'This recommendation can only excite hilarity today. We are, however, obliged to believe that the author's curious proposition was then accepted by a large number of his co-religionists, when we remember the astonishing success of the writings of Léo Taxil after his alleged conversion.'

[22] These dreams seem to me to have the principal object of calming the anxieties that Renan had retained on the subject of the beyond (cf. an article by Mgr d'Hulst in *Le Correspondant* of 25 October 1892, pp. 210, 224–5).

If this were true I would have had very little luck, since I have wanted to escape the influence of that intellectualist philosophy which is, it seems to me, a great hindrance for the historian who accepts it. The contradiction that exists between this philosophy and a true understanding of events has often struck the readers of Renan: the latter is continually wavering between his own intuition, which was nearly always admirable, and a philosophy which cannot approach history without falling into platitudes; but, alas, he too often believed himself bound to argue in accordance with the *scientific opinion* of his contemporaries.

The sacrifice of his life made by the soldier of Napoleon in order to have had the honour of taking part in 'eternal' deeds and of living in the glory of France knowing that 'he would always remain a poor man';[23] the extraordinary virtues shown by the Romans who resigned themselves to an appalling inequality and yet who suffered so much to conquer the world;[24] 'the belief in glory [which was] a value without equal', created by Greece and as a result of which 'a selection was made from the swarming masses of humanity, life had a motive, and there was a recompense for those who had pursued the good and the beautiful';[25] – these are things that the intellectualist philosophy cannot explain. Rather it leads to an admiration, in the fifty-first chapter of the Book of Jeremiah,[1] of 'the lofty though profoundly sad feeling with which the peaceful man contemplates these falls [of empire], the pity excited in the heart of the *wise man* by the spectacle of peoples *labouring for nothing*, victims of the arrogance of the few'. Greece, according to Renan,[26] did not experience anything of that kind, and I do not think this is something to complain about! Moreover, he himself praises the Romans for not having acted in accordance with the conceptions of the Jewish thinker: 'They laboured, they wore themselves out – for nothing, says the Jewish thinker – yes, doubtless, but that is the virtue that history rewards.'[27]

---

[23] E[rnest] Renan, *Histoire du peuple d'Israël* [Paris, Calmann-Lévy, 1887–93], IV, p. 191.
[24] *Ibid.*, p. 267.
[25] *Ibid.*, pp. 199–200.
[26] *Ibid.*, III, pp. 458–9.
[27] *Ibid.*, IV, p. 267.

[1] This is the chapter in which God denounces the destruction of Babylon.

Religions constitute a particularly serious problem for the intellectualist, because he can neither regard them as being without historical importance nor can he explain them; Renan, for example, has written some very strange sentences on the subject: 'Religion is a necessary imposture. Even the most obvious ways of throwing dust in people's eyes cannot be neglected when you are dealing with a race as stupid as the human species, created for error and which, when it does admit the truth, never does so for the right reasons. It is necessary therefore to give it bad ones.'[28]

Comparing Giordano Bruno,[m] who 'allowed himself to be burnt at the Champ-de-Flore', with Galileo, who submitted to the Holy See, Renan sides with the second because, according to him, the scientist need not bring anything to support his discoveries beyond good arguments; he considered that the Italian philosopher wished to supplement his inadequate proofs by his sacrifice and he puts forward this scornful maxim: 'A man suffers martyrdom only for the sake of things about which he is not certain.'[29] Renan here confuses *conviction*, which must have been very powerful in Bruno's case, with that particular kind of *certitude* associated with accepted theories of science which teaching ultimately produces; it would be difficult to give a less exact idea of the forces which move men!

The whole of this philosophy can be summed up in this proposition of Renan's: 'Human affairs are an approximation lacking gravity and precision'; and, as a matter of fact, for the intellectualist whatever lacks precision must also lack gravity. But in Renan the conscience of the historian was never entirely asleep, and he at once adds this qualifying statement: 'To have recognized [this truth] is a great result obtained by philosophy; but it is an abdication of any

---

[28] *Ibid.*, V, pp. 105–6.

[29] E[rnest] Renan, *Nouvelles Etudes d'histoire religieuse* [Paris, Calmann-Lévy, 1884], p. VII. Previously he had said, speaking of the persecutions, 'People die for *opinions* and not for *certitudes*, for what one believes and not what one knows . . . whenever it is a case of beliefs the greatest testimony and the most effective demonstration is to die for them': E[rnest] Renan, *L'Eglise chrétienne* [Paris, Calmann-Lévy, 1879], p. 317. This thesis presupposes that martyrdom is a kind of ordeal, which was partly true in the Roman epoch because of special circumstances: G[eorges] Sorel, *Le Système historique de Renan* [Paris, Jacques, 1906], p. 335.

[m] Giordano Bruno (1548?–1600); Italian philosopher and champion of Copernican cosmology: he was arrested by the Inquisition in 1592 and burnt at the stake in 1600.

active role. The future lies in the hands of those who are not disillusioned.'[30] From this we can conclude that the intellectualist philosophy is entirely unable to explain great historical movements.

The intellectualist philosophy would have vainly endeavoured to convince ardent Catholics, who for so long struggled successfully against the revolutionary traditions, that the myth of the Church militant did not conform to the scientific theories formulated by the most learned authors according to the best rules of criticism; it would never have succeeded in persuading them. No argument would have been possible to shake the faith that these men had in the promises made to the Church; and as long as this certitude survived the myth was, in their eyes, uncontestable. Similarly, the objections raised by the philosopher against revolutionary myths would have only made an impression on those men who were happy to find a pretext for abandoning 'any active role' and who wanted to be revolutionaries in words alone.

I can understand that this myth of the general strike offends many *wise men* because of its infinite quality; the world of today is very inclined to return to the opinions of the ancients and to subordinate ethics to the smooth working of public affairs, which results in a definition of virtue as a happy medium. As long as socialism remains a *doctrine expressed entirely in words*, it is very easy to deflect it towards this happy medium; but this transformation is obviously impossible when the myth of the general strike is introduced, as this implies an absolute revolution. You know, as well as I, that all that is best in the modern mind is derived from the torment of the infinite; you are not one of those people who regard as happy discoveries those tricks by means of which readers can be deceived by words. That is why you will not condemn me for having attached great worth to a myth which gives socialism such high moral value and such great honesty. It is because the theory of myths produces such fine results that so many people seek to dispute it.

IV

The mind of man is so constituted that it cannot remain content with the mere observation of facts but wishes to understand the

---

[30] Renan, *Histoire du peuple d'Israël*, III, p. 497.

inner reason of things; I therefore ask myself whether it might not be desirable to study this theory of myths more thoroughly, utilizing the insights we owe to the philosophy of Bergson. The attempt that I am about to submit to you is doubtless very imperfect, but I think that it has been conceived in accordance with the method that must be followed to throw light on the problem.

Firstly, we should notice that moralists rarely ever discuss what is truly fundamental about our individuality; as a rule they try to appraise our already completed acts with the aid of judgements formulated in advance by society for different types of action most common in contemporary life. They say that in this way they are determining motives; but these motives are of the same nature as those of which jurists take account in criminal law: they are social evaluations of facts known to everybody. Many philosophers, especially those of antiquity, have believed it possible to reduce everything to a question of utility; and if any social evaluation does exist it is surely utility; – theologians estimate transgressions by the place they occupy on the road which, according to average human experience, leads to mortal sin; they are thus able to ascertain the degree of malice represented by sexual desire and therefore the appropriate punishment; – the moderns teach that we judge our will before acting, comparing our projected conduct with general principles which are, to a certain extent, analogous to declarations of the rights of man; and this theory is, very probably, inspired by the admiration engendered by the *Bills of Rights* placed at the head of each American constitution.[31]

We are all so extremely concerned to know what the world thinks of us that, sooner or later, considerations analogous to those moralists speak do pass through our mind; as a result of this the latter have been able to imagine that they have really made an appeal to experience so as to discover what exists at the bottom of the creative conscience, when, as a matter of fact, all they have done is to

---

[31] The constitution of Virginia dates from June 1776. The American constitutions were known in Europe by two French translations, in 1778 and 1789. Kant had published the *Foundations of the Metaphysics of Morals* in 1785 and the *Critique of Practical Reason* in 1788. One might say that the utilitarian system of the ancients has certain analogies with economics, that of the theologians with law, and that of Kant with the political theory of a nascent democracy. (cf. [Georg] Jellinek, *La Déclaration des droits de l'homme* [Paris, Fontemoing, 1902], pp. 18–25, 49–50, 89).

consider already accomplished acts from the point of view of their social effects.

Bergson, on the contrary, invites us to consider the inner depths of the mind and what happens during a creative moment: 'There are', he says,'two different selves, one of which is, as it were, the external projection of the other, its spatial and, so to speak, social representation. We reach the former by deep introspection, which leads us to grasp our inner states as living things, constantly in a process of becoming, as states not amenable to measure . . . But *the moments when we grasp ourselves are rare*, and this is why we are rarely free. The greater part of the time we live outside ourselves; we perceive only a colourless shadow . . . We live for the external world rather than ourselves; we speak more than we think; we are *acted upon* rather than act ourselves. To act freely is to recover possession of oneself, and to get back into pure duration.'[32]

In order to acquire a real understanding of this psychology we must 'carry ourselves back in thought to those moments of our life when we made some serious decision, moments unique of their kind, which will not be repeated any more than the past phases of the history of a people will come back again'.[33] It is very evident that we enjoy this liberty most of all when we are making an effort to create a new individuality within ourselves, thus endeavouring to break the bonds of habit which enclose us. It might at first be supposed that it would be sufficient to say that, at such moments, we are dominated by an overwhelming emotion; but everybody now recognizes that movement is the essence of emotional life and it is then in terms of movement that we must speak of creative consciousness.

Here is how it seems to me the psychology of the deeper life must be represented. We should abandon the idea that the soul can be compared to something moving, which, obeying a more or less mechanical law, is impelled in the direction of certain given motive forces. When we act we are creating a completely artificial world

[32] H[enri] Bergson, *Essai sur les données immédiates de la conscience* [Paris, Alcan, 1889], pp. 175–6. In this philosophy a distinction is made between *duration* which flows, in which our personality manifests itself, and mathematical *time* following the measure which science uses to space out accomplished facts.

[33] *Ibid.*, p. 181.

placed ahead of the present world and composed of movements which depend entirely on us. In this way our freedom becomes perfectly intelligible. Starting from these constructions, which cover everything that interests us, several philosophers, inspired by Bergsonian doctrines, have been led to formulate a rather startling theory. For example, Edouard Le Roy[n] says: 'Our real body is the entire universe as far as it is experienced by us. And what common sense more strictly calls our body is only the region of least unconsciousness and greatest free activity, the part which we most directly control and by means of which we are able to act on the rest.'[34] We must not, as this subtle philosopher constantly does, confuse a passing state of our willing activity with the stable affirmations of science.[35]

These artificial worlds generally disappear from our minds without leaving any trace in our memory; but when the masses are deeply moved it then becomes possible to describe a picture which constitutes a social myth.

The belief in glory, which Renan praised so much, quickly fades away into rhapsodies when it has not been supported by myths, which have themselves varied greatly in different epochs: the citizen of the Greek republics, the Roman legionary, the soldier of the wars of Liberty, and the artist of the Renaissance did not picture their conception of glory through the same set of images. Renan complained that 'faith in glory is compromised by the *limited historical outlook* that tends to be prevalent in our day'. 'Very few people', he wrote, 'act with eternity in mind ... Everyone wants to enjoy his own glory; they eat the unripened seed in their lifetime; and do not gather it in sheaves after death.'[36] In my opinion, this limited historical outlook is not a cause but a consequence; it results from the weakening of the heroic myths which enjoyed such great popularity at the beginning of the nineteenth century; the belief in glory

[34] E[douard] Le Roy, *Dogme et Critique* [Paris, Bloud, 1907], p. 239.
[35] It is easy to see here how the sophism creeps in: *the universe experienced by us* may be either the real world in which we live or the world invented by us for action.
[36] Renan, *Histoire du peuple d'Israël*, IV, p. 329.

[n] Edouard Le Roy (1871–1954); mathematician and Bergsonian philosopher; professor at the Collège de France; author of *Dogme et critique* (1907), a text condemned by the Papacy in its rejection of theological 'modernism' of that year.

perished and the limited historical outlook became predominant at the same time that these myths vanished.[37]

As long as there are no myths accepted by the masses, one may go on talking of revolts indefinitely without ever provoking any revolutionary movement; this is what gives such importance to the general strike and renders it so odious to socialists who are afraid of revolution; they do all they can to shake the confidence felt by the workers in the preparations they are making for the revolution; and in order to succeed in this they cast ridicule on the idea of the general strike, which alone has a value as a motive force. One of the chief means employed by them is to represent it as a utopia; this is easy enough, as there are very few myths which are perfectly free from any utopian element.

The revolutionary myths which exist at the present time are almost pure; they allow us to understand the activity, the sentiments and the ideas of the masses as they prepare themselves to enter on a decisive struggle; they are not descriptions of things but expressions of a will to act. A utopia is, on the contrary, an intellectual product; it is the work of theorists who, after observing and discussing the facts, seek to establish a model to which they can compare existing societies in order to estimate the amount of good and evil they contain;[38] it is a combination of imaginary institutions having sufficient analogies to real institutions for the jurist to be able to reason about them; it is a construction which can be broken into parts and of which certain pieces have been shaped in such a way that they can (with a few alterations) be fitted into future legislation. – Whilst contemporary myths lead men to prepare

---

[37] 'Assent', said Newman, 'however strong, and accorded to images however vivid, is not therefore necessarily practical. Strictly speaking, it is not imagination that causes action; but hope and fear, likes and dislikes, appetite, passion, the stirrings of selfishness and self-love. What imagination does for us is to find a means of stimulating these motive powers; and it does so by providing a supply of objects strong enough to stimulate them': [Newman, *Grammaire*,] p. 69. It may be seen that the famous thinker adopts a position very close to the theory of myths. It is impossible to read Newman without being struck by the analogies between his thought and that of Bergson: people who like to make the history of ideas depend on ethnic traditions will not fail to observe that Newman is descended from Israelites.

[38] It was evidently a method of this kind that was adopted by those Greek philosophers who wished to be able to argue about ethics without being obliged to accept the customs that historical necessity had imposed at Athens.

themselves for a combat which will destroy the existing state of things, the effect of utopias has always been to direct men's minds towards reforms which can be brought about by patching up the system; it is not surprising then that so many believers in utopias were able to develop into able statesmen when they had acquired greater experience of political life. – A myth cannot be refuted since it is, at bottom, identical to the convictions of a group, being the expression of these convictions in the language of movement; and it is, in consequence, unanalysable into parts which could be placed on the plane of historical descriptions. A utopia, on the other hand, can be discussed like any other social constitution; the spontaneous movements it presupposes can be compared with those actually observed in the course of history, and we can in this way evaluate their verisimilitude; it is possible to refute it by showing that the economic system on which it has been made to rest is incompatible with the necessary conditions of modern production.

Liberal political economy is one of the best examples of a utopia that could be given. A society was imagined where everything could be reduced to types produced by commerce and operating under the law of the fullest competition; it is recognized today that this kind of ideal society would be as difficult to realize as that of Plato; but several great statesmen of modern times have owed their fame to the efforts they made to introduce something of this ideal of commercial liberty into industrial legislation.

We have here a utopia free from any element of myth; the history of French democracy, however, offers us a very remarkable combination of utopias and myths. The theories that inspired the authors of our first constitutions are today regarded as extremely fanciful; indeed, often people are loath to concede them the value which they have been so long recognized to possess: that of an ideal on which legislators, magistrates and administrators should constantly fix their eyes in order to secure for men an element of justice. With these utopias were mixed myths which represented the struggle against the *ancien régime*; as long as the myths survived, all the refutations of liberal utopias could produce no effect; the myth safeguarded the utopia with which it was mixed.

For a long time socialism was scarcely anything but a utopia; and the Marxists were right in claiming for their master the honour of having changed the situation: socialism has now become the preparation of the masses employed in large-scale industry who wish to do away with the State and with property; it is no longer necessary therefore to discuss how men must organize themselves in order to enjoy future happiness; everything is reduced to the *revolutionary apprenticeship* of the proletariat. Unfortunately, Marx was not acquainted with the facts which have now become familiar to us; we know better than he did what strikes are, because we have been able to observe economic conflicts of considerable extent and duration: the myth of the general strike has now become popular and is now firmly established in the minds of the workers; we have ideas about violence that it would have been difficult for him to form; we can therefore complete his doctrine, instead of making commentaries on his texts as his unfortunate disciples have done for so long.

In this way utopianism tends to disappear completely from socialism; the latter has no longer any need to concern itself with the organization of industry since capitalism does this. I think, moreover, that I have shown that a general strike corresponds to sentiments which are closely related to those that are necessary to promote production in a very progressive form of industry, that a revolutionary apprenticeship may also be an apprenticeship as a producer.

People who are living in this world of myths are secure from all refutation; something which has led many to assert that socialism is a kind of religion. For a long time people have been struck by the fact that religious convictions are unaffected by criticism; and from this they have concluded that everything which claims to be beyond science must be a religion. It has also been observed that in our day Christianity tends to be less a system of dogmas than a Christian life, that is, a moral reform penetrating to the roots of one's being; consequently, a new analogy has been discovered between religion and a revolutionary socialism which aims at the apprenticeship, preparation and even reconstruction of the individual which takes place with this gigantic task in mind. But Bergson has taught us that it is not only religion which occupies the profounder region of our mental life; revolutionary myths have their place there equally with religion. The arguments which Yves Guyot[o] puts forward

---

[o] Yves Guyot (1843–1928); economist and politician; advocate of free trade and an opponent of socialism; minister of public works between 1889–92; author of many books including *La Comédie socialiste* (1897) and *Sophismes socialistes et faits économiques* (1908).

against socialism on the ground that it is a religion therefore seem to me to be founded on an imperfect knowledge of the new psychology. Renan was very surprised to discover that socialists were beyond discouragement: 'After each abortive experience they begin again; the solution has not been found, we will find it. The idea that no solution exists never occurs to them, and there lies their strength.'[39] The explanation given by Renan is superficial; it sees socialism as a utopia, as a thing comparable to observed realities; we can hardly understand how confidence can thus survive so many failures. But, by the side of utopias, there have always existed myths capable of leading the workers on to revolt. For a long time these myths were founded on the legends of the Revolution, and they preserved all of their value as long as these legends remained unshaken. Today the confidence of the socialists is much greater than it was in the past, now that the myth of the general strike dominates the true working-class movement in its entirety. No failure proves anything against socialism, as it has become a work of preparation; if it fails, it merely proves that the apprenticeship has been insufficient; they must set to work again with more courage, persistence and confidence than before; the experience of labour has taught the workers that it is by means of patient apprenticeship that one can become a true comrade at work; and it is also the only way of becoming a true revolutionary.[40]

V

The works of my friends have been treated with great contempt by the socialists who mix in politics, but at the same time with much sympathy by people who do not concern themselves with parliamentary affairs. We cannot be suspected of seeking to carry on a kind of *intellectual industry* and we protest every time that we are confused with the Intellectuals who are the very people who make the exploitation of thought their profession. The old stagers of democracy cannot understand why so much trouble should be taken

---

[39] Renan, *Histoire du peuple d'Israël*, III, p. 497.
[40] It is extremely important to observe the analogies which exist between the revolutionary state of mind and those which correspond to the *ethic of the producers*; I have indicated some remarkable resemblances at the end of these reflections, but there are many more analogies that could be pointed out.

unless one secretly aims at the leadership of the working class. However, we could not act in any other way.

The man who has constructed a utopia designed to make humanity happy is inclined to look upon his invention as his own personal property; he believes that no one is better placed than he is to apply his system; he finds it quite unreasonable that his writings should not secure for him a post in government. But we, on the contrary, have not invented anything at all, and even assert that there is nothing to be invented: we have limited ourselves to defining the historical significance of the idea of the general strike; we have tried to show that a new culture might spring from the struggle of the revolutionary trade unions against the employers and the State; our greatest claim to originality consists in having maintained that the proletariat can emancipate itself without needing to seek guidance from those members of the bourgeoisie who consider themselves experts in matters of the intellect. We have thus been led to regard as essential in contemporary affairs what had previously been seen as accessory: what is really educative for a revolutionary proletariat that is serving its apprenticeship in struggle. It would be impossible for us to exercise any direct influence on such a work of preparation.

We may play a useful role, but only if we limit ourselves to attacking bourgeois thought in such a way as to put the proletariat on guard against the invasion of ideas and morals from the hostile class.

Men who have received an elementary education are generally prone to a reverence for books and they readily attribute genius to people who attract the attention of the literary world to any great extent; they imagine that they must have much to learn from authors whose names are so often cited with praise in the newspapers; they listen with remarkable respect to the commentaries that these literary prize-winners present to them. It is not easy to combat these prejudices; but it is very useful work; we regard this task as being of fundamental importance and we can carry it to a successful conclusion without ever taking control of the working-class movement. The proletariat must be preserved from the experience of the Germans who conquered the Roman Empire; they were ashamed of their barbarism and put themselves to school with the rhetoricians of Latin decadence; they had no reason to congratulate themselves for having wished to be civilized!

In the course of my career I have touched on many subjects that might be considered outside the proper range of a socialist writer. I have endeavoured to show my readers that the science whose marvellous results the bourgeoisie constantly boasts of is not as infallible as those who live by its exploitation would have us believe; and that often a study of the phenomena of the socialist world would furnish philosophers with an enlightenment that they do not often find in the works of the learned. I do not believe then that I am labouring in vain; because I am helping to ruin the prestige of bourgeois culture which up to now has been opposed to the complete development of the principle of class struggle.

In the last chapter of my book I have said that art is an anticipation of the kind of work that ought to be performed in a highly productive state of society. This observation, it seems, has been very much misunderstood by some of my critics, who have been under the impression that I wished to propose the aesthetic education of the proletariat under the tutelage of modern artists as the answer of socialism. This would have been a singular paradox on my part, for the art that we possess today is a *residue* left to us by aristocratic society, a residue which has, moreover, been greatly corrupted by the bourgeoisie. According to the most enlightened minds, it is greatly to be desired that contemporary art should renew itself by a more intimate contact with craftsmen; academic art has used up the greatest geniuses without succeeding in producing anything which equals what has been given us by generations of craftsmen. I had in mind something altogether different from such an imitation when I spoke of an anticipation; I wished to show how one finds in art (practised by its best representatives and, above all, in its best periods) analogies which allow us to understand what would be the qualities of the worker of the future. Moreover, so little did I think of asking the schools of fine art to provide a teaching suitable for the proletariat that I based the ethic of the producers not on an aesthetic education transmitted by the bourgeoisie but on the feelings developed by the struggles of the workers against their masters.

These observations lead us to recognize the enormous difference that exists between the *new school*[p] and the anarchism that flourished twenty years ago in Paris. The bourgeoisie itself had much less admiration for its literary men and its artists than the anarchists of that time felt for them; their enthusiasm for the passing celebrities of the day often surpassed that felt by disciples for the greatest masters of the past; we need not then be astonished if by a kind of compensation the novelists and poets, thus adulated, showed a sympathy for the anarchists which has often surprised people who do not appreciate the role of vanity in the artistic world.

This anarchism was then *intellectually entirely bourgeois* and it was for this reason that the Guesdists attacked it; they said that their adversaries, while proclaiming themselves the irreconcilable enemies of the past, were themselves the servile pupils of this detestable past; they noted, moreover, that the most eloquent dissertations of revolt could produce nothing and that literature cannot change the course of history. The anarchists replied by showing that their opponents had entered on a road which could not lead to the revolution they had announced; by taking part in political debate, they argued, the socialists will become merely reformers of a more or less radical kind and will lose the sense of their revolutionary formulas. Experience was not slow in showing that the anarchists were right about this, and that, in entering into bourgeois institutions, revolutionaries have been transformed by adopting the spirit of these institutions: all the parliamentary deputies agree that there is very little difference between a representative of the bourgeoisie and a representative of the proletariat.

[p] The '*nouvelle école*' comprised Sorel himself as well as his close associates Edouard Berth, Hubert Lagardelle, Paul Delesalle and others who participated in the publication of *Le Mouvement socialiste*. As described by Sorel, its goal was to purge Marxism of all that was not properly Marxist, in order to return to the 'heart' of the doctrine: the notion of class struggle. In *La Décomposition du marxisme* (Paris, Rivière, 1908), pp. 63-4, Sorel writes: 'the *new school* was able slowly to gain a clear idea of its independence from the old socialist parties; it did not claim to form a new party ... its ambition was completely different, to understand the nature of the movement which seemed unintelligible to everyone. It proceeded completely differently from Bernstein: little by little, it rejected all the formulas which came from either utopianism or Blanquism; it thus purged Marxism of all that was not specifically Marxist and it intended to preserve only what, according to it, was the core of the doctrine.' A clear statement of the new school's position can be found in Sorel's 'Le syndicalisme révolutionaire', *Le Mouvement socialiste* 17 (1905), pp. 267–80.

Many anarchists finished up by getting tired of always reading the same grandiloquent denunciations hurled at the capitalist system and set themselves to find a way which would lead them to acts which were really revolutionary; they entered the *syndicats* which, thanks to violent strikes, somehow realized the social war they had so often spoken of. Historians will one day see in this entry of the anarchists into the *syndicats* one of the greatest events that has been produced in our time; and then the name of my poor friend, Fernand Pelloutier, will be as well known as it ought to be.[41]

The anarchist writers who remained faithful to their former revolutionary literature do not seem to have looked with much favour upon the passage of their friends into the *syndicats*; their attitude proves that the anarchists who became syndicalists showed real originality and that they did not apply theories which had been fabricated in philosophical coteries. Above all, they taught the workers that they need not be ashamed of acts of violence. Up to that point it had been usual in the socialist world to attenuate or to excuse the violence of strikers; the new members of the *syndicats* regarded these acts of violence as normal manifestations of the struggle and, as a result, the tendencies pushing them towards trade unionism[q] were abandoned. It was their revolutionary temperament which led them to this conception of violence; it would be a gross error to suppose that these former anarchists carried over into the workers' associations any of the ideas associated with propaganda by the deed.

Revolutionary syndicalism is not, therefore, as many believe, the first confused form of the working-class movement, which is bound in the end to free itself from this youthful error. It has been, on the contrary, the product of an improvement brought about by men who had just arrested a deviation towards bourgeois ideas. It might, therefore, be compared to the Reformation, which wished to prevent Christianity submitting to the influence of the humanists; like the Reformation, revolutionary syndicalism may prove abortive if it

---

[41] I believe that Léon de Seilhac [1861–1920] was the first to render justice to the high qualities of Fernand Pelloutier: *Les Congrès ouvriers en France* [Paris, Colin, 1899], p. 272.

[q] Sorel here uses the English.

35

loses, as did the latter, the sense of its own originality; it is this which gives such great interest to enquiries on revolutionary violence.

15 July 1907

Foreword to the third edition

I have often been asked lately if since 1906 I have observed any facts that invalidate some of the arguments set forth in this book. On the contrary, I am more than ever convinced of the value of this philosophy of violence. I have even thought it useful to add to this reprint an 'apology for violence' that I published in *Le Matin* on 18 May 1908, at the time when the first edition appeared.

This is one of the books that public opinion does not allow an author to improve; I have only allowed myself to change a few words here and there in order to make certain phrases clearer.

February 1912

Introduction to the first publication[1]

The reflections that I submit to the readers of *Le Mouvement socialiste* on the subject of violence have been inspired by very simple observations about evident facts which play an increasingly marked role in the history of contemporary classes.

For a long time I have been struck by the fact that the *normal development* of strikes has included a significant number of acts of violence;[2] but certain learned sociologists seek to disguise a phenomenon that everyone who cares to use his eyes must have noticed. Revolutionary syndicalism keeps alive the desire to strike in the masses and only prospers when important strikes, accompanied by violence, take place. Socialism tends to appear more and more as a theory of revolutionary syndicalism – or rather as a philosophy of modern history, in so far as it is under the influence of syndicalism. It follows from these incontestable data that, if we wish to discuss socialism seriously, we must first of all investigate the functions of violence in present social conditions.[3]

I do not believe that this question has yet been approached with the attention it deserves; I hope that these reflections will lead a few

---

[1] First publication was in *Le Mouvement socialiste* during the first six months of 1906.

[2] Cf. 'Les Grèves', *La Science sociale* [30] (1900), [pp. 395–413].

[3] In the *Insegnamenti sociali della economia contemporanea* [Palermo, Sandron, 1907], written in 1903 but not published until 1906, I had already pointed out, but in a very inadequate manner, what seemed to me to be the function of violence in maintaining the division between the *proletariat* and the *bourgeoisie* (pp. 53–5). [Still not available in French, this text has been translated into English as *Social Foundations of Contemporary Economics* (New Brunswick, NJ, Transaction Books, 1984); see pp. 74–5.]

thinkers to examine the problems associated with proletarian violence more closely; I cannot too strongly recommend these studies to the *new school* which, inspired by the principles of Marx rather than the formulas taught by the official proprietors of Marxism, is in the process of giving socialist doctrines a sense of reality and a seriousness which they have certainly lacked for several years. Since the *new school* calls itself Marxist, syndicalist and revolutionary it should have nothing more at heart than understanding the exact historical significance of the spontaneous movements which are being produced in the working classes and which may ensure that the future direction of social development will conform to the ideas of its master.

Socialism is a philosophy of the history of contemporary institutions, and Marx always argued as a philosopher of history when he was not led by personal polemics to write about matters outside his own system.

The socialist imagines, then, that he has been transported into the very distant future, so that he can consider actual events as elements of a long and completed development and that he can attribute to them the colour that they might take for the future philosopher. Such a procedure certainly presupposes a considerable use of hypotheses; but there would be no social philosophy, no reflection about the process of evolution and even no important action in the present without certain hypotheses about the future. The object of this study is to deepen our understanding of moral conduct and not to discuss the merits or faults of prominent people; we need to find out how the feelings which move the masses form into groups; all the discussions by moralists about the motives for the actions of prominent men and the psychological analyses of character are therefore of quite secondary and even negligible importance.

It seems, however, that it is more difficult to reason in this way when we are concerned with acts of violence than with any other set of circumstances. This is due to our habit of regarding conspiracy as the typical example of violence or as an *anticipation of a revolution*; we are thus led to ask ourselves if certain criminal acts could not be considered heroic, or at least meritorious, because of the consequences envisaged by their authors for the happiness of their fellow citizens. Certain individual attacks have rendered such great services to democracy that democracy has consecrated as great men those who, at the risk of their lives, have tried to rid it of its enemies. It has done this the more readily since these great men were no longer living when the hour for dividing the spoils of victory arrived; and we know that the dead obtain admiration more easily than the living.

Each time, therefore, that an attack takes place, the doctors of the ethico-social sciences, who are found in profusion in journalism, indulge in high-minded discussions about whether a criminal act can ever be excused, or even justified, from the point of view of the highest standards of justice. There is then an irruption in the democratic press of that casuistry for which the Jesuits have so many times been reproached.

Here it seems to me not unuseful to mention a note on the assassination of the Grand Duke Sergius which appeared in *L'Humanité*[a] on 18 February 1905; the author was not one of those vulgar members of the Bloc[b] whose intelligence is hardly superior to that of a Negrito but rather one of the leading lights of the university system: Lucien Herr[c] is one of those who ought to know what he is talking about. The title, *Les Justes représailles*, warns us that the question is to be treated from a high ethical standpoint: it is the *judgement of the world*[4] which is about to be pronounced. The author scrupulously endeavours to assign the responsibility, calculates the equivalence which ought to exist between the crime and its expiation, goes back to the original misdeeds which have engendered

---

[4] This expression is not too strong, as the author has devoted most of his studies to Hegel.

[a] *L'Humanité* was founded in 1904, jointly by Jaurès, Léon Blum, Lucien Herr and Lucien Lévy-Bruhl. It was very much a paper run by intellectuals for the workers, and hence attracted Sorel's criticism.

[b] The Bloc had its origin in the so-called 'délégation des gauches', which represented the four political groupings that spanned the radical and socialist positions. A loose coalition, it came into its own after the elections of 1902 when it effectively sustained the premiership of Emile Combes in his anticlerical policies. The coalition came to an end in 1905 when the socialists were required to withdraw from a bourgeois government by the Second International. 'Combisme' came to be known for its unscrupulous political partisanship and it was this that led to the disillusionment of so many former Dreyfusards, including Sorel.

[c] Lucien Herr (1864–1926); librarian at the Ecole Normale Supérieure and one of the leading members of the 'parti intellectuel' that Sorel came to detest. A socialist and a Dreyfusard, he wrote a regular column on foreign affairs for *L'Humanité*.

these acts of violence in Russia; all of this is a philosophy of history in accordance with the pure principles of Corsican banditry. Carried away by the lyricism of his subject, Lucien Herr concludes in the style of a prophet: 'The battle will go on in this way, in suffering and in blood, abominable and odious, until that *inescapable day* not far off, when the throne itself, the murderous throne, the throne which heaps up so many crimes, will fall down into the ditch that has today been dug for it.' This prophecy has not yet been realized; but it is the true character of great prophecies never to be realized: the *murderous throne* is much more secure than the cash box of *L'Humanité*. But, after all, what can we learn from this?

It is not the business of historians to award prizes for virtue, to propose the erection of statues, or to establish any catechism whatever; his role is *to understand what is least individual* in the course of events; the questions which interest chroniclers and excite novelists are those which he most willingly leaves on one side. And so I am not concerned to justify the *perpetrators of violence* but to enquire into the function of *the violence of the working classes* in contemporary socialism.

It seems to me that the question of violence has been very badly formulated by socialists. As proof of this I can cite the article by Rappoport[d] that appeared in *Le Socialiste* on 21 October 1905: the author, who has written a book on the philosophy of history,[5] ought, it seems to me, to have discussed the question by examining the long-term consequences of these events; but, on the contrary, he considers them from their most immediate, most trivial and, consequently, least historical aspect. According to him, syndicalism leads necessarily to opportunism; and as this law does not seem to be verified in France, he adds: 'If in some Latin countries it assumes revolutionary attitudes, that is pure appearance. It shouts louder but that is always for the purpose of demanding reforms inside the framework of existing society. It is reformism by blows, but it is always reformism.'

[5] C[harles] Rappoport, *La Philosophie de l'histoire comme science de l'évolution* [Paris, Jacques, 1903].

[d] Charles Rappoport (1865–1941); writer and socialist activist; a forthright opponent of both 'reformism' and the tactics of direct action that he associated with anarchism and syndicalism.

Thus there would be two types of reformism: the one, patronized by the Musée Social,^c the Direction du Travail^f and Jaurès, which would work with the aid of pleas to eternal justice, maxims and half-lies; the other proceeds by blows; the latter being the only one that is within the scope of uneducated people who have not yet been touched by the grace of advanced social economics. The *wise men*, the democrats devoted to the cause of the rights of man and the duties of the informer, the sociologist members of the Bloc, all think that violence will disappear when popular education becomes more advanced; they recommend, therefore, a great increase in the number of courses and lectures; they hope to drown revolutionary syndicalism in the saliva of professors. It is very strange that a revolutionary such as Rappoport should agree with these *wise men* and their acolytes in their estimation of the meaning of syndicalism; this can only be explained by admitting that even for the best-informed socialists the problems connected with violence have, until now, remained very obscure.

To examine the effects of violence it is necessary to start from its long-term consequences and not from its immediate results. We should not ask whether it is more or less directly advantageous for contemporary workers than skilful diplomacy, but rather ask ourselves what will result from the introduction of violence into the relations of the proletariat with society. We are not comparing two kinds of reformism, but want to know what contemporary violence is in relation to future social revolution.

Many will reproach me for not having given information that might be useful with regard to tactics: no formulas, no recipes! What then was the use of writing at all? Shrewd people will say that these studies are addressed to men who live outside the realities of every-day life and outside the true movement, that is, outside editors'

---

^c The Musée Social was established in 1894, with the specific intent, through empirical investigation, of 'improving the material and moral conditions of the workers'. Funded by the Comte de Chambrun, it was heavily influenced by the Le Play school and counted amongst its early collaborators both Paul de Rousiers and Paul Bureau. Sorel was a frequent visitor to its library, which still exists today in the Rue Las Cases.

^f The Direction du Travail was a late nineteenth-century forerunner of the Ministère du Travail, itself established in 1906. It was principally responsible for gathering statistics about labour conditions.

officers, parliamentary lobbies and the antechambers of socialist financiers. Those who have become scientists by coming into contact with Belgian sociology will accuse me of having a metaphysical rather than a scientific turn of mind.[6] These are opinions which scarcely touch me, since I have never paid attention to the views of people who think vulgar stupidity the height of wisdom and who admire, above all, men who speak and write without thinking.

Marx was also accused by the grandees of positivism of having treated economics metaphysically in *Capital*; they were astonished 'that he had confined himself to a mere critical analysis of actual facts, instead of formulating recipes'.[7] This criticism does not seem to have moved him very much; moreover, in the preface to his book he had warned the reader that he would not determine the social position of any country and that he would confine himself to an investigation of the laws of capitalist production, 'the tendencies working with iron necessity'.[8]

One does not need a great knowledge of history to perceive that the mystery of historical development is only intelligible to men who are far removed from superficial disturbances: the chroniclers and the actors of the drama do not see at all what later on will be regarded as fundamental; so that one might formulate this apparently paradoxical rule: 'It is necessary to be outside in order to see the inside.' When we apply these principles to contemporary events one runs the risk of being taken for a metaphysician, but that is of no importance because we are not in Brussels, you know.[9] If we are

---

[6] This expectation has already been realized; for in a speech to the Chamber of Deputies on 11 May 1907 Jaurès, doubtless ironically, called me 'the metaphysician of syndicalism'.

[7] K[arl] Marx, *Le Capital* [Paris, Librairie du Progrès, 1875], I, p. 349, col. 2. [Karl Marx, *Capital* (Harmondsworth, Penguin, 1976), I, p. 99. The accusation is that Marx was unprepared to provide 'recipes . . . for the cook-shops of the future'.]

[8] *Ibid.*, p. 10. [The quotation in the original English edition reads as 'these tendencies working with iron necessity towards inevitable results': see *Capital* (New York, Charles H. Kerr, 1906), p. 13.]

[9] Some Belgian comrades have been offended by these innocent jokes, which nevertheless I retain here: Belgian socialism is best known in France through Vandervelde, one of the most useless creatures that ever existed, who not being able to console himself for having been born in a country too small to give scope to his genius, came to Paris and gave lectures on all kinds of subjects, and who can be reproached, amongst other things, for having made an enormous profit on a very small intellectual capital. I have already said what I think of him in the *Introduction à l'économie moderne*, [Paris, Jacques, 1903], pp. 42–9.

dissatisfied with the unsystematic views formed by common sense, we must follow methods altogether opposed to those of the sociologists, who found their reputation amongst stupid people by means of dull and confused prattle; we must firmly resolve to disregard immediate applications and to think only of elaborating concepts and ideas; we must set aside all the favourite preoccupations of the politicians. I hope that it will be recognized that I have not broken this rule.

Although they may lack other qualities, these reflections possess a merit that cannot be questioned; it is clear that they are inspired by a passionate love of truth. Love of truth is becoming a quite rare quality; the members of the Bloc despise it profoundly; official socialists regard it as having anarchical tendencies; politicians and their hangers-on cannot sufficiently insult the wretched people who prefer the truth to the delights of power. But there are still honest people in France and it is for them alone that I have always written.

The more I have gained experience the more I have recognized that in the study of historical questions a passion for truth is worth more than the most learned methodologies; it enables one to break through conventional wrappings, to penetrate to the bottom of things, and to grasp reality. There has never been a great historian who has not been carried away by this passion; and when we look at it closely we see that it is this that has given rise to so many fruitful intuitions.

*   *   *

I do not claim to present here everything that can be said about violence, and still less to have produced a systematic theory of violence. I have merely reunited and revised a series of articles that appeared in an Italian review, *Il Divenire sociale*,[10] which maintains, on the other side of the Alps, the good fight against the exploiters of popular credulity. These articles have been written without any

---

[10] The last four chapters have been very much more developed than they were in the Italian text. I have thus been able to give more space to philosophical considerations. The Italian articles have been collected together in a book under the title *Lo Sciopero generale e la Violenza* [Rome, Il Divenire sociale, 1906] and with a preface by Enrico Leone. [*Il Divenire sociale* (1905–9) was established by Enrico Leone (1875–1940). Sorel was one of its principal contributors.]

coherent plan; I have not tried to rewrite them because I did not know how to set about giving a didactic appearance to such an exposition; it even seemed to me better to preserve their untidy arrangement, because in that form they will perhaps more easily provoke thought. We should always be careful when approaching a little-known subject not to trace its boundaries too rigorously, for in this way we run the risk of closing the door to new facts that arise from unforeseen circumstances. Time and time again have not the theoreticians of socialism been embarrassed by contemporary history? They have constructed magnificent clear-cut and symmetrical formulas; but they could not make them fit the facts; rather than abandon their theories, they have preferred to declare that the most important facts were simple anomalies which science must ignore if it is to obtain a real understanding of the whole!

I Class struggle and violence

I. The struggle of poorer groups against rich ones. – The opposition
of democracy to the division into classes. – Methods of buying social
peace. – The corporative mind.
II. Illusions relating to the disappearance of violence. – The mechanisms of conciliation and the encouragement which it gives to strikers. – Influence of fear on social legislation and its consequences.

I

Everyone explains that discussions about socialism are exceedingly
obscure; this obscurity is due, to a large extent, to the fact that
contemporary socialists use a terminology which no longer corresponds to their ideas. The best known of the people who call themselves *reformists* do not wish to appear to be abandoning certain
phrases which have for a long time served to characterize socialist
literature. When Bernstein, perceiving the enormous contradiction
that existed between the language of social democracy and the true
nature of its activity, urged his German comrades to have the courage to appear to be the way that they were in reality[1] and to revise
a doctrine that had become false, there was a universal outcry at his
audacity; and the reformists were not in the least eager to defend

---

[1] Bernstein complains of the chicanery and *cant* that reigns amongst the social
democrats: E[duard] Bernstein, *Socialisme théorique et social-démocratie pratique*
[Paris, Stock, 1900], p. 277. He addresses these words taken from Schiller to social
democracy: 'Let it dare to appear what it is': p. 238.

the old formulas; I remember hearing well-known French socialists say that they found it easier to accept the tactics of Millerand[a] than the theses of Bernstein.

This idolatry of words plays a significant role in the history of all ideologies; the preservation of a Marxist vocabulary by people who have become estranged from the thought of Marx constitutes a great misfortune for socialism. The expression 'class struggle' is, for example, employed in the most improper manner; and until a precise meaning has been given to it we must give up all hope of providing an accurate account of socialism.

A. – To most people the class struggle is *the principle of socialist tactics*. This means that the socialist party bases its electoral successes upon the clashing of interests that exists in an acute state between certain groups and that, if need be, it would undertake to make this hostility more acute; their candidates ask the most numerous and the poorest class to look upon themselves as forming a corporation and they offer to become the advocates of this corporation; thanks to the influence they gain from their position as representatives, they promise to seek to improve the lot of the disinherited. Thus we are not very far from what happened in the Greek city-states: the parliamentary socialists are similar to the demagogues who constantly called for the annulment of debts and the division of landed property, who piled all public taxation upon the rich and who invented conspiracies in order to have large fortunes confiscated. 'In the democracies where the crowd is above the law,' says Aristotle, 'the demagogues, by their continual attacks upon the rich, always divide the city into two camps . . . The oligarchs should abandon all swearing of oaths like those they swear today; for there are cities which have taken this oath: "I will be the constant enemy of the people and I will do them all the evil that lies in my

---

[a] Etienne-Alexandre Millerand (1859–1943); socialist deputy and president of the Republic from 1920–4; a leading advocate of reformist socialism in the mid-1890s, before joining Waldeck-Rousseau's government of 'republican defence' in 1899 as minister of commerce. The first socialist to enter a 'bourgeois' government, this act was the subject of controversy across Europe, especially as the minister of war, Gallifet, had participated in the repression of the Paris Commune. 'Ministerialism' was subsequently condemned by the Second International and Millerand was expelled from the socialist party.

power." "[2] Here certainly is a struggle between two classes that is as clearly defined as it can be; but it seems to me absurd to assert that it was in this way that Marx understood the struggle which, according to him, was the essence of socialism.

I believe that the authors of the French law of 11 August 1848 had their heads full of these classical references when they decreed punishment against those who, by speeches and newspaper articles, sought 'to trouble the public peace by stirring up contempt and hatred amongst the citizens'. The terrible insurrection of the month of June was just over, and it was firmly believed that the victory of the Parisian workers would have produced, if not an attempt to put communism into practice, at least serious requisitions on the rich in favour of the poor; it was hoped that an end could be put to civil wars by making it more difficult to propagate *doctrines of hatred* capable of rousing the proletariat against the bourgeoisie.

Today, parliamentary socialists no longer believe in insurrection; if they still sometimes speak of it, it is to give themselves an air of importance; they teach that the ballot-box has replaced the gun, but the means of acquiring power might have changed without there being a change of mental attitude. Electoral literature seems inspired by the purist demagogic doctrines: socialism appeals to all the discontented without troubling itself about the place they occupy in the world of production; in a society as complex as ours and as subject to economic upheavals, there are an enormous number of discontented people in all classes; – that is why socialists are often found in places where one would least expect to find them. Parliamentary socialism speaks as many languages as it has types of clients. It addresses itself to workmen, to small employers, to peasants, and, in spite of Engels, it aims at reaching farmers;[3] at times it is patriotic, at others it rants against the army. No contradiction is too great – experience having shown that it is possible, in the course of an electoral campaign, to group together forces which, according to Marxist conceptions, should normally be antagonistic. Besides, cannot a parliamentary deputy be of service to electors in every economic situation?

<hr>

[2] Aristotle, *Politique*, bk VIII, chapter VII, 19. [Aristotle, *The Politics*, (Harmondsworth, Penguin, 1992), bk V, chapter IX.]
[3] F[riedrich] Engels, 'La Question agraire et le socialisme', translated in *Le Mouvement socialiste* [44], 15 October 1900, p. 453. It has often been pointed out that certain socialist candidates had separate posters for the town and the country.

In the end the term 'proletariat' becomes synonymous with the oppressed; and there are the oppressed in all classes:[4] the German socialists have taken a great interest in the princess of Coburg.[5] One of the most distinguished reformers, Henri Turot, for a long time editor of *La Petite République*[6] and municipal councillor in Paris, has written a book on the 'proletarians of love', by which title he designates the lowest class of prostitutes. If one day they give the right to vote to women he will doubtless be called upon to draw up a statement of the aims of this special proletariat.

B. – Contemporary democracy in France finds itself somewhat bewildered by the tactics of class struggle; this explains why parliamentary socialism does not mingle with the main body of the parties of the extreme Left.

In order to understand this situation we must remember the important part played by the revolutionary wars in our history; an enormous number of our political ideas originated in war; war presupposes the union of national forces against the enemy and our French historians have always severely criticized those insurrections which hampered the defence of the homeland. It seems that our democracy is harder on its rebels than monarchies are; the Vendéens[b] are still denounced daily as infamous traitors. All of the articles published by Clemenceau[c] to combat the ideas of

---

[4] Hampered by the monopoly of the licensed stockbrokers, the other brokers of the Stock Exchange are thus *financial proletarians*, and amongst them more than one socialist admirer of Jaurès can be found.

[5] The socialist deputy Sudekum, *the best-dressed man in Berlin*, played a large part in the abduction of the princess of Coburg; let us hope that he had no financial interest in this *affair*. At the time he represented Jaurès' newspaper in Berlin.

[6] H[enri] Turot was for some considerable time one of the editors of the nationalist newspaper *L'Eclair*, and of *La Petite République* at the same time. When [Ernest] Judet [1851–1943] took over management of *L'Eclair* he dismissed his socialist contributor.

[b] The counter-revolutionary rebellion in the Vendée, which began in March 1793, was the most significant of the internal revolts directed against the Revolution. Its repression was characterized by the indiscriminate slaughter of the population of the region.

[c] Georges Clemenceau (1841–1929); Radical-Socialist deputy and journalist; one of the dominant political figures of the Third Republic. Famous for his statement that 'the Revolution is a bloc', it was also Clemenceau who led the journalistic campaign to secure the release of Dreyfus. He was later prime minister during the First World War.

Hervé[d] are inspired by the purest revolutionary tradition, and he clearly says so himself: 'I stand by and shall always stand by the old-fashioned patriotism of our fathers of the Revolution', and he scoffs at the people who would 'suppress international wars in order to hand us over *in peace to the pleasures of civil war*' (*L'Aurore*, 12 May 1905).

For some considerable time the republicans denied that there was a struggle between the classes in France; they had such a horror of revolt that they would not recognize the facts. Judging all things from the abstract point of view of the *Déclaration des droits de l'homme*, they said that the legislation of 1789 had been created in order to abolish all distinction of class in law: it was for this reason that they were opposed to proposals for social legislation which, almost always, reintroduced the idea of class and distinguished certain groups of citizens as being unfitted for the use of liberty. 'The Revolution was supposed to have suppressed classes,' wrote a sad Joseph Reinach in *Le Matin* of 19 April 1895; 'but they spring up again at every step ... It is necessary to point out these aggressive returns of the past, but they must not be allowed to pass unchallenged; they must be resisted.'[7]

Electoral dealings have led many republicans to recognize that the socialists obtain great successes by using the passions of jealousy, of deception or of hate which exist in the world; then they became aware of the class struggle and many have borrowed the jargon of the parliamentary socialists: in this way the party that is called Radical-Socialist was born. Clémenceau even asserts that he knows *moderates* who became socialists overnight: 'In France', he said, 'the socialists that I know[8] are excellent radicals who, thinking that social reforms do not advance quickly enough to please them, argue that it is good tactics to claim the greater in order to get the less. How

---

[7] J[oseph] Reinach, *Démagogues et Socialistes* [Paris, Chailley, 1896], p. 198.
[8] Clemenceau knows all the socialists in parliament very well and from long experience.

[d] Gustave Hervé (1871–1944); leading antimilitarist campaigner in the years prior to 1914. His inflammatory articles led to his trial in 1901 in what became known as 'l'affaire Hervé'. Acquitted, he was nevertheless imprisoned for four years in 1905 for distributing antimilitarist material to army recruits. When released the following year, he established *La Guerre sociale*, further increasing the popularity of 'Hervéisme' in the socialist movement. Nevertheless, in 1914 he rallied to the defence of the Republic and immediately renamed his journal *La Victoire*.

many names and how many secret avowals I could quote to support what I say! But that would be useless, for nothing is less mysterious' (*L'Aurore*, 14 August 1905).

Léon Bourgeois[e] – who was not willing to sacrifice himself completely to the new methods and who, perhaps because of this, left the Chamber of Deputies for the Senate – said, at the congress of his party in July 1905: 'The class struggle is a fact, but it is a cruel fact. I do not believe that it is by prolonging it that the solution of the problem will be attained; I believe that the solution rather lies in its suppression, in making all men consider themselves as partners in the same work.' It would therefore seem to be a question of creating social peace by legislation, in showing to the poor that the government has no greater concern than to improve their lot and by imposing the necessary sacrifices upon people who possess a fortune judged to be too great for the harmony of the classes.

Capitalist society is so rich, and the future appears to it in such optimistic colours, that it endures the most frightful burdens without complaining overmuch: in America politicians waste large amounts of taxation shamelessly; in Europe military preparation consumes sums that increase every year;[9] social peace might very well be bought by a few additional sacrifices.[10] Experience shows that the bourgeoisie allows itself to be plundered quite easily, provided that a little pressure is brought to bear and that they are intimidated by the fear of revolution: the party which can most skilfully manipulate the spectre of revolution will possess the future; this is what the Radical party is beginning to understand; but however clever its clowns may be, it will have some difficulty in finding

---

[9] At the conference in The Hague the German delegate declared that his country bore the expense of the armed peace with ease; Léon Bourgeois held that France bore 'as lightly the personal and financial obligations that national defence imposed upon its citizens'. Ch[arles] Guieysse, who cites this speech, thinks that the tsar has asked for a limitation of military expenditure because Russia was not yet rich enough to maintain herself at the level of the great capitalist countries: *La France et la paix armée* [Paris, Pages Libres, 1905], p. 45.

[10] That is why Briand, on 9 June 1907, told his constituents at Saint-Etienne that the Republic had made a *sacred pledge* to the workers about old-age pensions.

[e] Léon Bourgeois (1851–1925); politician and prime minister between 1895–6; in his *La Solidarité* (1896), he expounded the doctrine known as solidarism, which sought to highlight the social obligations of the rich to the poor, and accordingly advocated a programme of social reform and progressive taxation.

any who can dazzle the big Jewish bankers as well as do Jaurès and his friends.

C. – Syndicalist organization gives a third value to the class struggle. In each branch of industry, employers and workmen form antagonistic groups which have continual discussions, which negotiate and make agreements. Socialism brings along its terminology of social struggle and thus complicates conflicts that might have remained of a purely private order; corporative exclusivism, which so resembles the sense of belonging to a locality or to a race, is thus consolidated, and those who represent it like to think that they are accomplishing a higher duty and are doing excellent work for socialism.

It is well known that the litigants who are strangers in a town are generally very badly treated by the judges of the commercial courts sitting there because they try to give judgements in favour of their fellow townspeople. Railway companies pay fantastic prices for land the value of which is fixed by juries recruited from among the neighbouring landowners. I have seen Italian sailors overwhelmed with fines for alleged infractions of the law by fishing arbitrators with whom they had come to compete on the strength of ancient treaties. – Many workers are in the same way inclined to assert that in all their disputes with the employers the worker has morality and justice on his side; I have heard the secretary of a *syndicat*, so fanatically reformist that he denied the oratorical talent of Guesde,[f] declare that no one had class feeling so strongly developed as he had, – because he argued in the way I have just indicated, – and he concluded that the revolutionaries did not possess a monopoly of the right conception of class struggle.

It is understandable that many people have considered this corporative spirit as no better than parochialism and that they have tried to destroy it by employing methods very analogous to those which have so much weakened the jealousies which formerly existed in France between the provinces. A more general culture and the intermixing with people of another region rapidly destroy

[f] Mathieu Bazile ('Jules') Guesde (1845–1922); Marxist and founder of the Parti Ouvrier Français; as an ardent campaigner for socialism, he was famous for his oratorical skills both in parliament and the country at large, regularly touring France and speaking to vast audiences.

provincialism: by frequently bringing the important men of the *syndicats* into contact with the employers and by providing them with opportunities to take part in discussions of a general nature in joint commissions, would it not be possible to destroy the corporative feeling? – Experience shows that this is possible.

II

The efforts which have been made to remove the causes of hostility which exist in modern society have undoubtedly had some effect, – although the peacemakers may be much deceived about the extent of their work. By showing a few officials of the *syndicats* that the members of the bourgeoisie are not such terrible men as they had believed, by overwhelming them with politeness in commissions set up in ministerial offices or at the Musée Social, and by giving them the impression that there is a *natural and republican equity* above class prejudices and hatreds, it has been possible to change the attitude of a few revolutionaries.[11] A great confusion in the mind of the working classes was caused by the conversion of a few of their old leaders; the former enthusiasm of more than one socialist has given way to discouragement; many workers have wondered whether trade union organization was becoming a kind of politics, a means of personal advancement.

But simultaneously with this development, which filled the heart of the peacemakers with joy, there was a recrudescence of the revolutionary spirit in a large section of the proletariat. Since the governments of the Republic and the philanthropists have taken it into their heads to exterminate socialism by developing social legislation and by moderating the resistance of the employers in strikes, it has been observed, more than once, that the conflicts have become more acute than formerly.[12] This is frequently explained by saying that it

[11] When it comes to social buffoonery there are very few new things under the sun. Aristotle has already laid down the rules of social peace; he said that the demagogues 'should in their harangues appear to be concerned only with the interests of the rich, just as in oligarchies the government should only seem to have in view the interests of the people' [Aristotle, *Politique*: Aristotle, *The Politics*, bk V, chapter IX]. That is a text which should be inscribed on the door of the offices of the Direction du Travail.

[12] Cf. G[eorges] Sorel, *Insegnamenti sociale [dell'economia contemporanea* (Palermo, Sandron, 1907)], p. 343. [See *Social Foundations of Contemporary Economics* (New Brunswick, NJ, Transaction Books, 1984), p. 285].

is only an accident imputable to the bad old ways; people like to delude themselves with the hope that everything will be perfectly fine on the day when manufacturers have a better sense of the practices of social peace.[13] I believe, on the contrary, that we are in the presence of a phenomenon that flows quite naturally from the conditions in which this alleged pacification is carried out.

I observe, first of all, that the theories and actions of the peacemakers are founded on the notion of duty and that duty is something entirely indeterminate – whilst law seeks rigid definition. This difference is due to the fact that the latter finds a real basis in the economics of production, while the former is founded on sentiments of resignation, goodness and sacrifice: and who can judge whether someone who submits to duty has been sufficiently resigned, good and self-sacrificing? The Christian is convinced that he will never succeed in doing all that the Gospel demands of him; when he is free from all economic ties (in a monastery) he invents all sorts of pious obligations, so that he may bring his life nearer to that of Christ, who loved men to the point that He accepted such an ignominious fate that they might be redeemed.

In the economic world, everyone limits his duty according to his unwillingness to give up certain profits; if the employer is always convinced that he has done his duty, the worker will be of the contrary opinion, and no argument could settle the matter: the first will believe that he has been heroic, and the second will treat this supposed heroism as shameful exploitation.

For our great high priests of duty, the contract to work is not a form of sale; nothing is so simple as a sale; nobody troubles himself to find out whether the grocer or the customer is right when they agree on the price of cheese; the customer goes where he can buy at the best price and the grocer is obliged to change his prices when his customers leave him. But when a strike takes place it is quite another thing: all the well-intentioned people, the men of progress and the friends of the Republic, begin to discuss the question of

---

[13] In his speech of 11 May 1907 Jaurès said that nowhere had there been such violence as there was in England during the period when both the employers and the government refused to recognize the trade unions. 'They have given way; there is now vigorous and strong action, which is at the same time legal, firm and wise.'

which of the two parties is in the right: *to be in the right is to have fulfilled one's whole social duty.* Le Play has given much advice on the means of organizing labour with a view to the strict observance of duty; but he could not fix the extent of the mutual observations involved; he put his faith in the discretion of each party, a proper sense of place in the social hierarchy, and the master's intelligent estimation of the real needs of the workman.[14]

The employers generally agree to discuss disputes on these lines; to the demands of the workers they reply that they have already reached the limit of possible concessions – while the philanthropists wonder whether the selling price will not allow a slight increase in wages. Such a discussion presupposes that it is possible to ascertain the exact extent of social duty and what sacrifices an employer must continue to make in order *to maintain his position*: as there is no reasoning capable of resolving such a problem, the *wise men* suggest recourse to arbitration; Rabelais[g] would have suggested recourse to the chance of dice. When the strike is important, parliamentary deputies loudly call for an enquiry, with the object of discovering if the leaders of industry are properly fulfilling their *duties as good masters.*

Results are achieved in this way, which nevertheless seem so absurd, because, on the one hand, the large employers have been brought up with civic, philanthropic and religious ideas,[15] and, on the other, because they cannot show themselves too stubborn when certain things are demanded by people occupying high positions in the country. Conciliators stake their pride on succeeding and they would be extremely offended if industrial leaders prevented them from making social peace. The workers are in a more favourable position because the prestige of the peacemakers is much less amongst them than with the capitalists: the latter therefore give way much more easily than the workers in letting the well intentioned have the glory for ending the conflict. It is noticeable that these methods only rarely succeed when the matter is in the hands of

[14] F[réderic] Le Play, *L'Organisation du travail* [Paris, Dentu, 1870], chap. II, [section] 21, [pp. 143–5].

[15] About the forces which tend to maintain the sentiments of moderation see [Sorel,] *Insegnamenti sociali*, Part 3, chap. V. [See Sorel, *Social Foundations*, pp. 289–99.]

[g] François Rabelais (c. 1494–1553); writer; best known for *Pantagruel et Gargantua.*

former workers who have become rich: literary, moral or sociological considerations have very little effect upon people born outside the ranks of the bourgeoisie.

The people who are called upon to intervene in disputes in this way are misled by what they have seen of certain secretaries of the *syndicats*, whom they find much less intransigent than they expected and who seem to them ready to understand the idea of social peace. In the course of arbitration meetings more than one revolutionary has shown that he aspires to become a member of the lower middle class, and there are many intelligent people who imagine that socialist and revolutionary conceptions are only an accident that might be avoided by establishing better relations between the classes. They believe that the working-class world understands the economy entirely from the standpoint of duty and is persuaded that harmony would be established if a better social education were given to citizens.

Let us see what influences are behind the other movement that tends to make conflict more acute.

The workers quickly perceive that the activity of conciliation and arbitration rests upon no economico-juridical foundation and their tactics have been conducted – instinctively, perhaps – in accordance with this fact. Since the feelings and, above all, the pride of the peacemakers are in question, a strong appeal must be made to their imaginations and they must be given the idea that they have to accomplish a titanic task; demands are therefore piled up, figures fixed in a haphazard way, and no one worries about exaggerating them; often the success of a strike depends on the cleverness with which a member of a *syndicat* (who thoroughly understands the spirit of *social diplomacy*) has been able to introduce demands which are in themselves very minor but which are capable of giving the impression that the employers are not fulfilling their social duty. Upon many occasions writers who concern themselves with these questions have been surprised that several days elapse before the strikers have settled what exactly they have to demand, and that, in the end, demands are put forward that had not been mentioned in the course of the previous discussions. This is easily understood when we consider the bizarre conditions under which the discussion of the interested parties is carried on.

I am amazed that there are no professional observers of strikes who would not undertake to draw up lists of the workers' demands; they would obtain all the more success in conciliation councils as they would not let themselves be dazzled by fine words as easily as the workers' delegates.[16]

When everything is over there is no shortage of workers who do not forget that the employers had at first declared that no concession was possible: they are thus led to believe that the employers are either ignorant or liars; these are not consequences conducive to the development of social peace!

So long as the workers submitted without protest to the authority of the employers, they believed that the will of their masters was completely dominated by economic necessities; after the strike they realize that this necessity is not of a very rigid kind and that, if energetic pressure from below is brought to bear upon the will of the master, a way will then be found to escape the pretended fetters of the economy; thus (within practical limits) capitalism appears to the workers to be *unfettered* and they reason as if this was entirely the case. What in their eyes restrains this liberty is not the necessity that arises from competition but the ignorance of the captains of industry. In this way is introduced the notion of the *inexhaustibility of production*, which is one of the axioms of the theory of class struggle in the socialism of Marx.[17]

Why then speak of social duty? Duty has meaning in a society in which all the parts are intimately connected with one another; but if capitalism is inexhaustible, solidarity is no longer founded upon the economy and the workers think they would be dupes if they did not demand all that they could obtain; they look upon the employer as an adversary with whom one comes to terms after a war. *Social duty no more exists than does international duty.*

These ideas are, I admit, a little confused in many minds; but they exist in a far more substantial way than the supporters of social peace imagine; the latter are content with appearances and never

---

[16] The French law of 27 December 1892 seems to have foreseen this possibility; it stipulates that the delegates on conciliation boards should be chosen among the interested parties; it thus keeps out those professionals whose presence would render precarious the prestige of the authorities and of the philanthropists.

[17] Sorel, *Insegnamenti sociali*, p. 390. [See Sorel, *Social Foundations*, p. 321.]

penetrate to the hidden roots that sustain the present tendencies of socialism.

Before passing to other considerations, we must note that our Latin countries present a great obstacle to the formation of social peace; the classes are more sharply separated by external character-istics than they are in Saxon countries; these differences greatly embarrass the leaders of *syndicats* when they abandon their former manners and take up a position in the official or philanthropic world:[18] this world has welcomed them with great pleasure ever since it has been understood that the tactic of gradually trans-forming union officials into members of the middle class can pro-duce excellent results; but their comrades distrust them. In France this distrust has become much more strong since the entry of a significant number of anarchists into the syndicalist movement, because the anarchist has a horror of everything that recalls the activities of politicians – devoured by the desire to climb into the upper classes of society and already having the capitalist spirit when they were still poor.[19]

Social policy has introduced new elements which must now be taken into account. First of all, we can observe that today the workers *count* in the world in the same way as the different productive groups that demand to be protected: they must be treated with the same care as wine producers or sugar manufacturers.[20] There is nothing settled about protectionism; the custom duties are fixed so

[18] Everyone who has seen trade union leaders close up is struck by the extreme difference which exists between France and England from this point of view; the leaders of the English trade unions rapidly become gentlemen without anyone blaming them for it (P[aul] de Rousiers, *Le Trade-unionisme en Angleterre* [Paris, Colin, 1897], pp. 309 and 322). Whilst correcting these proofs I read an article by Jacques Bardaux, pointing out that a carpenter and a miner had been made knights by Edward VII (*Les Débats*, 16 December 1907).

[19] Some years ago Arsène Dumont invented the term 'social capillarity' to express the slow ascent of classes. If syndicalism followed the guidance of the peacemakers it would be a powerful agent of social capillarity.

[20] It has often been pointed out that the workers' organization in England is a simple union of interests, for the purpose of immediate material advantages. Some writers are very pleased with this situation because, quite rightly, they see it as an obstacle to socialist propaganda. *Annoying the socialists*, even at a cost to economic progress and to the safety of the culture of the future, that is the great aim of certain great *idealists* of the philanthropic bourgeoisie.

as to satisfy the desires of very influential people who wish to increase their incomes; social policy proceeds in the same manner. The protectionist government claims to have knowledge which enables it to measure what should be granted to each group, so as to defend the producers without injuring the consumers; similarly, it is declared that social policy will take into consideration the interests of both the employers and the workers.

Few people, outside the faculties of law, are so naive as to believe that the State can carry out such a programme: in fact, members of parliament resolve partially to satisfy the interests of those who are most influential in elections without provoking too-lively protests from the people who are sacrificed. There is no other rule than the true or presumed interest of the electors: every day the customs commission alters its tariffs and it declares that it will not stop altering them until it succeeds in securing prices which it considers remunerative to the people for whom it has undertaken the part of providence; it keeps a watchful eye on the operations of importers; every lowering of price attracts its attention and provokes enquiries designed to discover if it is not possible to raise values artificially. Social policy operates in exactly the same way: on 27 June 1905 the proposer of a law regulating the hours of work in the mines told the Chamber of Deputies: 'Should the application of the law give rise to disappointment amongst the workers, *we have undertaken* to bring forward a new bill without delay.' This worthy man spoke exactly like the proposer of an import tariff law.

There are plenty of workmen who understand perfectly well that all the rubbish of parliamentary literature only serves to disguise the true motives which guide the government. The protectionists succeed by subsidizing a few important party leaders or by financing newspapers which support the policies of these leaders; the workers have no money but they have at their disposal a far more effective means of action – they can *inspire fear*, and for several years they have not denied themselves this expedient.

At the time of the discussion of the law regulating labour in the mines, the question of threats addressed to the government arose several times: on 5 February 1902, the president of the commission told the Chamber that those in power had lent 'an attentive ear to clamourings from without, [that they had been] inspired by the sentiment of benevolent generosity by allowing themselves to be

moved, *despite the tone in which they were couched*, by the demands
of the workers and the long cry of suffering of the miners'. A little
later he added: 'We have accomplished a work of social justice . . .
a work of benevolence also, in going to those who toil and who
suffer like friends solely desirous of working in peace and under
honourable conditions, and we must not, by a brutal and too egotis-
tic refusal to unbend, allow them to follow impulses which, *while
not actual revolts*, would have as many victims.' All these confused
phrases served to hide the terrible fear that gripped this grotesque
deputy.[21] In the sitting of 6 November 1905, in the Senate the
minister declared that the government was not willing to give way
to threats but that it was necessary to open not only ears and mind
but also the heart to 'respectful demands'(!); a good deal of water
had passed under the bridge since the day when the government
had promised to pass the law under the threat of a general strike.[22]

I could choose other examples to show that the most decisive
factor in social politics is the cowardice of the government. This
was shown in the plainest possible way in the recent discussions on
the closure of employment offices and on the law which sent to the
civil courts appeals against the decisions of the arbitrators in industrial disputes. Nearly all the leaders of the *syndicats* know how to
make excellent use of this situation and they teach the workers that
it is not a question of demanding favours but that they must profit
from *bourgeois cowardice* to impose the will of the proletariat. There
is too much evidence in support of these tactics for them not to
take root in the world of the working class.

One of the things which appears to me to have most astonished the
workers during the last few years has been the timidity of the forces
of law and order in the presence of a riot: the magistrates who have
the right to demand the services of soldiers dare not use their power
to the utmost, whilst officers allow themselves to be abused and

---

[21] This imbecile has become minister of commerce. All his speeches on this question
are full of nonsense; he was a doctor of the insane and perhaps has been influenced
by the logic and the language of his clients.

[22] The minister declared that he was creating 'real democracy' and that it was dema-
gogy 'to give way to external pressure, to haughty summonses which, for the most
part, are only higher bids and baits addressed to the credulity of people whose
life is hard'.

struck with a patience hitherto unknown in them. It has become more and more evident every day that working-class violence in strikes possesses an extraordinary efficacy: prefects, fearing that they may be obliged to use legal force against insurrectionary violence, bring pressure to bear on employers in order to compel them to give way; the safety of factories is now looked upon as a favour which the prefect can dispense as he pleases; consequently, he arranges the use of his police so as to intimidate the two parties and to bring them skilfully to an agreement.

It did not take much time for leaders of the *syndicats* to grasp this situation, and it must be admitted that they have used the weapon that has been put into their hands with great skill. They endeavour to intimidate the prefects by popular demonstrations, which have the potential for serious conflict with the police, and they commend riotous behaviour as the most effective way of obtaining concessions. It is rare that, after a certain time, the administration, itself worried and frightened, does not seek to influence the leaders of industry and to impose an agreement upon them, which becomes an encouragement for the propagandists of violence.

Whether we approve or condemn what is called the *direct and revolutionary method*, it is clear that it is not about to disappear; in a country as warlike as France there are profound reasons that would assure a considerable popularity for this method, even if its enormous efficacy had not been demonstrated by so many examples. This is the great social fact of the present hour and we must seek to understand its significance.

I cannot refrain from noting here a reflection made by Clemenceau with regard to our relations with Germany and that applies equally well to social conflicts when they take on a violent aspect (which seems likely to become more and more general in proportion as a cowardly bourgeoisie continues to pursue the dream of social peace): 'There is no better means', he said, '[than the policy of perpetual concessions] for making the opposite party ask for more and more. Every man or every power, whose action consists solely in surrender, can only finish by self-annihilation. Everything that lives resists; that which does not resist allows itself to be cut up piecemeal' (*L'Aurore*, 15 August 1905).

A social policy based upon bourgeois cowardice, which consists in always surrendering before the threat of violence, cannot fail to engender the idea that the bourgeoisie is condemned to death and that its disappearance is only a matter of time. Every conflict which gives rise to violence thus becomes a vanguard fight, and no one can foresee what will come out of such skirmishes; the great battle never materializes, but each time that they come to blows the strikers hope that it is the beginning of the great *Napoleonic battle* (the one that will crush the vanquished definitively); in this way, the practice of strikes engenders the notion of the catastrophic revolution.

A keen observer of the contemporary working-class movement has expressed the same ideas: 'They, like their ancestors [the French revolutionaries], are for struggle, for conquest; through force they desire to accomplish great works. Only the war of conquest interests them no longer. Instead of thinking of battles, they now think of strikes; instead of setting up their ideal as a battle against the armies of Europe, they now set it up as the general strike in which the capitalist regime will be destroyed.'[23]

The theorists of social peace shut their eyes to these embarrassing facts; they are doubtless ashamed to admit their cowardice, just as the government is ashamed to admit that its social politics are carried out under the threat of disturbances. It is curious that people who boast of having read Le Play have not observed that his conception of the conditions of social peace was very different from that of his stupid successors. He supposed the existence of a bourgeoisie of serious moral habits, imbued with the feelings of its own dignity and having the energy necessary to govern the country without recourse to the old traditional bureaucracy. To these men, who possessed both riches and power, he aspired to teach *social duty towards their subjects*. His system presumed an undisputed authority; it is well known that he deplored the licence of the press under Napoleon III as scandalous and dangerous; his reflections on this subject seem somewhat amusing to those who compare the newspapers of that time to those of today.[24] Nobody in his day would have believed

[23] Guieysse, [*La France*], p. 125.
[24] Speaking of the elections of 1869, he said that there had been 'violences of language which France had not heard before, even in the worst days of the Revolution': *L'Organisation du travail* [Paris, Dentu, 1871], 3rd edn, p. 340. Obviously he had in mind the Revolution of 1848. In 1873, he declared that the emperor could not congratulate himself on having abrogated the system of restraint on the press before having reformed the morals of the country: *La Réforme sociale en France* [Tours, Mame, 1874], 5th edn, III, p. 356.

that a great country would accept peace at any price; his point of view on this matter did not differ greatly from that of Clemenceau. He would never have admitted that one could have the weakness and hypocrisy to disguise the cowardice of a bourgeoisie incapable of defending itself with the name of social duty.

The cowardice of the bourgeoisie strongly resembles that of the English Liberal Party, which constantly proclaims its total confidence in arbitration between nations: arbitration nearly always produces disastrous results for England.[25] But these *wise men* prefer to pay out, or even to compromise the future of their country, rather than face the horrors of war. The English Liberal Party has always the word *justice* on its lips, exactly like our bourgeoisie; we might very well ask ourselves if all the high morality of our great contemporary thinkers is not founded on a degradation of the sentiment of honour.

---

[25] [Sir Henry] Sumner Maine [1822–88] observed a long while ago that it was England's fate to have advocates who aroused little sympathy (*Le Droit international*, French trans., [Paris, Thorin, 1890], p. 279). [See *International Law* (London, J. Murray, 1890).] Many English people believe that by humiliating their country they will rouse more sympathy for themselves: this is not proven.

II The decadence of the bourgeoisie and violence

I. Parliamentarians who have to inspire fear. – Parnell's methods. – Casuistry; fundamental identity of the parliamentary socialist groups.
II. Degeneration of the bourgeoisie brought about by peace. – Marx's conceptions of necessity. – Part played by violence in the restoration of former social relationships.
III. Relation between revolution and economic prosperity. – The French Revolution. – The Christian conquest. – Invasion of the barbarians. – Dangers that threaten the world.

I

It is very difficult to understand proletarian violence as long as we try to think in terms of the ideas disseminated by bourgeois philosophy; according to this philosophy, violence is a relic of barbarism which is bound to disappear under the progress of enlightenment. It is therefore quite natural that Jaurès, who has been brought up on bourgeois ideology, should have a profound contempt for the people who praise proletarian violence; he is astonished to see educated socialists in agreement with the syndicalists; he wonders by what extraordinary act of bad faith men who have proved themselves thinkers can accumulate *sophisms* in order to give the appearance of reason to *the dreams of stupid people who are incapable of thought.*[1] This question greatly worries the friends of Jaurès, who are only too willing to treat the representatives of the *new school* as demagogues and to accuse them of seeking the applause of the impulsive masses.

Parliamentary socialists cannot understand the ends pursued by the *new school*; they imagine that ultimately all socialism can be reduced to the means of getting into power. Is it possible that they think that the followers of the *new school* wish to make a higher bid for the confidence of simple electors and cheat the socialists of the seats provided for them? Again, the apology for violence might have the very unfortunate result of disgusting the workers with electoral politics, and this would tend to reduce the chances of socialist candidates by multiplying the number of abstentions from voting! 'Do you wish to revive civil war?' they ask. To our great statesmen this seems insane.

Civil war has become very difficult since the discovery of new firearms and since the cutting of rectilinear streets in our capital cities.[2] The recent events in Russia seem even to have shown that governments can count much more than was supposed on the energy of their officers; nearly all French politicians had predicted the imminent fall of tsarism at the time of the defeats in Manchuria, but the Russian army, in the presence of rioting, did not display the weakness shown by the French army during our revolutions; nearly everywhere, repression was rapid, effective and even merciless. The discussions which took place at the congress of social democrats at Jena show that the parliamentary socialists no longer count upon an armed struggle to take possession of the State.

Does that mean that they are completely opposed to violence? It would not be in their interest for the people to remain completely calm; a certain amount of agitation suits them, but it must be within well-defined limits and controlled by politicians. When he considers it useful for his purposes, Jaurès makes advances to the

---

[1] This is apparently the way in which the proletarian movement is spoken of in the world of refined socialism.

[2] Cf. the reflections of Engels in the preface to the new edition of articles by Marx which he published in 1895 under the title of *The Class Struggles in France from 1848 to 1850*. This preface is missing from the French translation. In the German edition a passage has been left out, the social democratic leaders considering certain phrases of Engels not sufficiently politic.

Confédération Générale du Travail;[3] sometimes he instructs his peaceable clerks to fill his paper with revolutionary phrases; he is past master in the art of utilizing popular anger. Unrest, cleverly channelled, is extremely useful to parliamentary socialists, who boast to the government and to the rich bourgeoisie of their ability to moderate revolution; they can thus arrange the success of financial affairs in which they are interested, obtain minor favours for many influential electors, and get social laws voted in order to appear important in the eyes of simpletons who imagine that these socialists are great reformers of the law. For this to succeed there must always be a certain amount of agitation and the bourgeois must always be kept in a state of fear.

It is conceivable that a regular system of diplomacy might be established between the socialist party and the State each time an economic conflict arises: *two powers* would settle the specific difference. In Germany, the government enters into negotiations with the Church every time that the clergy stand in the way of the administration. Socialists have even been urged to imitate Parnell,[a] who so often found a means of imposing his will on England. This resemblance with Parnell is all the greater in that his authority did not rest only on the number of votes at his disposal, but mainly upon the terror that every Englishman felt at the merest announcement of agrarian troubles in Ireland. A few acts of violence, controlled by a parliamentary group, were very useful to Parnellian policy, just as they are also useful to the policy of Jaurès. In both cases, a parliamentary group *sells peace of mind to the conservatives*, who do not dare use the force they command.

This kind of democracy is difficult to conduct, and after the death of Parnell the Irish do not seem to have continued it with the same success as in his time. In France, it presents a particular difficulty because in perhaps no other country are the workers as difficult to direct: it is easy enough to arouse popular anger, but it is not easy

---

[3] According to the necessities of the moment, he is either for or against the general strike. According to some, he voted for the general strike at the International Congress in 1900; according to others, he abstained.

[a] Charles Stewart Parnell (1846–91); Irish nationalist leader; after the elections of 1885, which left the Irish nationalists holding the balance of power, he exercised considerable political influence.

to stifle it. As long as there are no very rich and strongly centralized *syndicats*, whose leaders are in continuous contact with politicians,[4] it will be impossible to know exactly to what lengths violence will go. Jaurès would very much like to see the existence of such associations of workers, for the day when the general public perceives that he is not in a position to moderate revolution his prestige will vanish in an instant.

Everything becomes a matter of valuation, estimation and opportunism; much skill, tact and calm audacity are necessary to carry out such diplomacy: to make the workers believe that you are carrying the flag of revolution, the bourgeoisie that you are holding back the danger which threatens them, and the country that you represent an irresistible current of opinion. The great mass of electors understands nothing of what happens in politics and has no grasp of economic history; they are on the side of those who seem to possess power and you can obtain everything you wish from them when you can prove that you are strong enough to make the government capitulate. But you must not go too far, because the bourgeoisie might wake up and the country might give itself over to a resolutely conservative statesman. A proletarian violence that escapes all valuation, estimation and opportunism may jeopardise everything and ruin socialist diplomacy.

This diplomacy is played at all levels: with the government, with the leaders of parliamentary groups, and with influential electors. The politicians seek to draw the greatest possible advantage from the discordant forces operating in the field of politics.

Parliamentary socialism feels a certain embarrassment from the fact that, at its origin, socialism took its stand on absolute principles and appealed for a long time to the same sentiments of revolt as the most advanced republican party. These two circumstances prevent the following of a policy such as that frequently recommended by Charles Bonnier:[b] this writer, who was for a long time the principal

---

[4] Gambetta complained that the French clergy was 'acephalus'; he would have liked a select body to be formed from within it with which the government could discuss matters ([François Clément] Garilhe, *Le Clergé séculier français au XIXe siècle* [Paris, Savaète, 1899], pp. 88–9). Syndicalism has no head with which it would be possible to carry on diplomatic relations usefully.

[b] Charles Bonnier (1863–?); Guesdist publicist; author of numerous articles in such socialist journals as *Le Socialiste*, *Le Devenir social*, etc.

theorist of the Guesdist party, would like the socialists to follow closely the example of Parnell, who used to negotiate with the English parties without being controlled by any of them; in the same way, it might be possible to come to an agreement with the conservatives, if the latter pledged themselves to grant better conditions to the proletariat than the radicals (*Le Socialiste*, 27 August 1905). This policy seemed scandalous to many people. Bonnier was thus obliged to dilute his thesis: he then contented himself with asking that the party should act in the best interests of the proletariat (17 September 1905); but how is it possible to know where these interests lie when the principle of class struggle is no longer taken as your single and absolute rule?

Parliamentary socialists believe that they possess the special faculties which enable them to take into account not only the material and immediate interests reaped by the working class but also the moral reasons which compel socialism to form part of the great republican family. Their congresses spend their energies in putting together formulas designed to regulate socialist diplomacy, in defining what alliances are allowed and what are forbidden, in reconciling the abstract principle of class struggle (which they are anxious to retain verbally) with the reality of agreements with politicians. Such an undertaking is madness; and therefore leads to equivocations when it does not force deputies into attitudes of deplorable hypocrisy. Each year problems have to be rediscussed, because all diplomacy requires a flexibility incompatible with the existence of perfectly clear statutes.

The casuistry that Pascal scoffed at so much was not more subtle and more absurd than that which is to be found in the polemics between what are called the *socialist schools*. Escobar[c] would have some difficulty finding his bearings amid the distinctions of Jaurès; the moral theology of *responsible socialists* is not among the least buffooneries of our time.

All moral theology can be divided into two tendencies; there are casuists who say that we must be content with opinions having a

---

[c] Antonio Escobar (1558–1669); Spanish Jesuit; known especially for the doctrine that the sole determinant of the moral value of an action is the moral intent of the agent, the actions themselves being of no moral significance. He produced an anthology of Jesuit opinions which, as an example of casuistry, was pilloried relentlessly by Pascal in his attack upon the Jesuits in his *Lettres provinciales*.

slight probability; others wish that we should always adopt the strictest and most certain position. This distinction was bound to be encountered amongst our parliamentary socialists. Jaurès prefers the soft and conciliatory method, provided that means are found to make it agree, somehow or other, with first principles and that it has behind it a few respectable authorities: he is a *probabilist* in the strongest sense of the term – or even a *laxist*. Vaillant[d] recommends the strong and belligerent method which, in his opinion, alone is in accordance with the class struggle and which has in its favour the unanimous support of all the old authorities; he is a *tutoirist* and a kind of Jansenist.

Jaurès no doubt believes that he is acting for the greatest good of socialism, just as the most easy-going casuists believed themselves to be the best and most useful defenders of the Church; they did indeed prevent weak Christians from falling into irreligion and led them to practise the sacraments – exactly as Jaurès prevents the rich Intellectuals who have come to socialism by way of the Dreyfusard movement from drawing back in horror before the class struggle and induces them to finance the party's newspapers. In Jaurès' eyes Vaillant is a dreamer who does not see the reality of the world, who intoxicates himself with the fantasy of an insurrection that has now become impossible and who does not understand the great advantages which may be got from universal suffrage by a skilful politician.

Between the two methods there is only a difference of degree and not one of kind, as is believed by those parliamentary socialists that call themselves revolutionaries. On this point Jaurès has a great intellectual superiority over his adversaries, because he has never cast doubt upon the fundamental identity of the two methods.

Both of these methods suppose an entirely dislocated bourgeois society, rich classes who have lost all sentiment of their class interest, men ready to follow blindly the lead of people who have taken up the business of directing public opinion. The Dreyfus affair showed that the enlightened bourgeoisie was in a strange mental state: people who had long and loudly served the conservative cause campaigned together with anarchists, took part in violent attacks on the army, or even enrolled in the socialist party; on the other hand,

[d] Marie-Edouard Vaillant (1840–1915); founder of the Parti Socialiste Révolutionnaire, and an enthusiastic advocate of the autonomy of the syndicalist movement.

newspapers, which make it their business to defend traditional institutions, dragged the magistrates of the court of appeal into the mire.
This strange episode in our contemporary history has brought to
light the state of dislocation of the classes.

Jaurès, who was very much mixed up in all the events of the
Dreyfusard movement, had very quickly judged the mentality of
the upper bourgeoisie, into which he had not yet penetrated. He
saw that this upper bourgeoisie was terribly ignorant, self-
satisfyingly foolish, and politically absolutely impotent; he recognized that with people who understand nothing of the principles of
capitalist economics it is easy to contrive a policy of compromise on
the basis of an extremely broad socialism; he calculated – in order
to become the leader of people devoid of ideas – the extent to which
it was necessary to mix together: the flattery of the superior intelligence of the imbeciles the seduction of whom was aimed at, appeals
to the disinterested sentiments of speculators who pride themselves
in having invented the ideal, and threats of revolution. Experience
has shown that he had a very remarkable intuition of the forces
which existed at that precise moment in the bourgeois world. Vaillant, on the contrary, is very little acquainted with this world; he
believes that the only weapon that can be employed to move the
bourgeoisie is fear; doubtless, fear is an excellent weapon, but it
might provoke an obstinate resistance beyond a certain limit. Vaillant does not possess those remarkable qualities of suppleness of
mind, and perhaps even of peasant duplicity, which shine in Jaurès
and which have often caused people to say that he would have made
a wonderful cattle-dealer.

The more closely the history of these last years is examined, the
more the discussions concerning the two methods will be recognized
as puerile: the supporters of the two methods are equally opposed
to proletarian violence, because it escapes from the control of the
people engaged in parliamentary politics. Revolutionary syndicalism
cannot be controlled by the so-called revolutionary socialists of
parliament.

II

The two methods favoured by official socialism presuppose the
same historical datum. The ideology of a timorous, humanitarian
bourgeoisie professing to have freed its thought from the conditions

of its existence is grafted on to the degeneration of the capitalist economy; the race of bold captains who made the greatness of modern industry disappears to make way for an ultra-civilized aristocracy that demands to be left in peace. This degeneration fills our parliamentary socialists with joy. Their role would vanish if they were confronted with a bourgeoisie which was energetically engaged on the paths of economic progress, which regarded timidity with shame and which was proud in looking after its class interests. In the presence of a bourgeoisie which has become almost as stupid as the nobility of the eighteenth century, their power is enormous. If the degradation of the upper middle classes continues to progress at the pace it has taken in the last few years, our official socialists may reasonably hope to reach their goal of their dreams and sleep in sumptuous mansions.

Two accidents alone, it seems, would be able to stop this movement: a great foreign war, which might reinvigorate lost energies and which, in any case, would doubtless bring into government men with the will to govern;[5] or a great extension of proletarian violence, which would make the revolutionary reality evident to the bourgeoisie and would lead to their disgust with the humanitarian platitudes with which Jaurès lulls them to sleep. It is with these two great dangers in mind that the latter deploys all his skills as a popular orator: European peace must be maintained at any price; a limit must be put on proletarian violence.

Jaurès is convinced that France will be perfectly happy on the day when the editors of his journal and its shareholders can draw freely upon the resources of the public Treasury; it is an illustration of the celebrated proverb: 'When Augustus had drunk, Poland was inebriated.'[e] A socialist government of this kind would without doubt ruin the country, which would be run with the same care for financial order as *L'Humanité* has been administered; but what does the future of the country matter, provided that the new regime

---

[5] Cf. G[eorges] Sorel, *Insegnamenti sociali [dell'economia contemporanea* (Palermo, Sandron, 1907)], p. 388. [See Georges Sorel, *Social Foundations of Contemporary Economics* (New Brunswick, NJ, Transaction Books, 1984), p. 317.] The hypothesis of a great European war seems very far-fetched at the moment.

[e] The origin of this peculiar proverb appears to be found in Voltaire's *Epître à l'Impératrice de Russie, Catherine II.*

gives a good time to a few professors, who imagine that they have invented socialism, and to a few Dreyfusard financiers?

Before the working class could also accept this *dictatorship of incapacity*, it must itself become as stupid as the bourgeoisie and must lose all revolutionary energy, whilst at the same time its masters would have lost all capitalist energy. Such a future is not impossible; and a great deal of hard work is being done to stupefy the workers for this purpose. The Direction du Travail and the Musée Social are doing their best to carry out this marvellous task of idealistic education, which is decorated with the most pompous names and which is presented as a means of civilizing the proletariat. The syndicalists very much disturb our professional idealists, and experience shows that a strike is sometimes sufficient to ruin all the *work of education* which these manufacturers of social peace have patiently built over several years.

In order properly to understand the consequences of the very singular regime in the midst of which we are living, we must refer back to Marx's conception of the passage from capitalism to socialism. These conceptions are well known; yet we must continually return to them, because they are often forgotten or at least undervalued by the official writers of socialism; it is necessary to insist on them strongly each time that we have to argue about the anti-Marxist transformation which contemporary socialism is undergoing.

According to Marx, capitalism, by reason of the inner laws of its nature, is carried along a path which leads the world of today to the doors of a future world with the exactness of the evolution of organic life. This movement comprises a long period of capitalist construction and it ends with a rapid destruction which is the work of the proletariat. Capitalism creates: the heritage that socialism will receive, the men who will suppress the present regime, and the means of bringing about this destruction; – at the same time, this destruction preserves the results obtained in production.[6] Capitalism begets new ways of working; it throws the working class into organizations of protest through the pressure it exerts on wages;

---

[6] This notion of *revolutionary conservation* is very important; I have signalled something analogous in the passage between Judaism and Christianity (*Le Système historique de Renan* [Paris, Jacques, 1906], pp. 72–3, 171–2, 467).

it restricts its own political base by competition, which constantly eliminates industrial leaders. Thus, after having solved the great problem of industrial labour – about which utopians formulated so many naive or stupid hypotheses – capitalism provokes the birth of the cause which will overthrow it; and thus renders useless everything that the utopians have written to induce enlightened people to carry out reforms; and it gradually ruins the traditional order, against which the criticisms of the ideologues have shown themselves to be so deplorably incompetent. It might therefore be said that capitalism plays a role analogous to that attributed by Hartmann to the Unconscious in nature, since it prepares the coming of social forms that it does not intend to produce. Without any coordinated plan, without any directing idea, without an ideal of the future world, it determines an inevitable evolution; it draws from the present all that it can give for historical development; in an almost mechanical manner, it does all that is necessary in order that a new era might appear and that every link will be broken with the ideology of the present times, despite preserving the acquisitions of the capitalist economy.[7]

Socialists should therefore abandon the search (initiated by the utopians) for a means of inducing the enlightened bourgeoisie to prepare the *transition to a better system of legislation*; their sole function consists in explaining to the proletariat the greatness of the revolutionary role which it is called upon to play. By ceaseless criticism the proletariat must be brought to perfect its organizations; it must be shown how to develop the embryonic forms of its organizations of resistance, so that it may build institutions that have no parallel in the history of the bourgeoisie and form ideas that depend solely upon the position of producer in large-scale industry, borrowing nothing from bourgeois thought. The aim must be to acquire *habits* of liberty with which the bourgeoisie are no longer acquainted.

This doctrine will obviously be inapplicable if the bourgeoisie and the proletariat do not oppose each other with all the severity they possess and all the forces at their disposal; the more the bourgeoisie is ardently capitalist, the more the proletariat will be full of

---

[7] Cf. what I have said on the transformation Marx wrought on socialism in *Insegnamenti sociali*, pp. 179–86. [See Sorel, *Social Foundations*, pp. 167–71.]

warlike spirit and confident of its revolutionary strength, the more the success of the movement will be certain.

The bourgeoisie with which Marx was familiar in England was still, in the great majority, animated by the conquering, insatiable and pitiless spirit which, at the beginning of the modern epoch, had characterized the creators of new industries and the discoverers of unknown lands. When we are studying the modern economy, we should always bear in mind this similarity between the capitalist type and the warrior type; it is with very good reason that the men who directed gigantic enterprises were named *captains of industry*. This type is still found today in all its purity in the United States: there are encountered the indomitable energy, the audacity based upon an accurate appreciation of its strength, the cold calculation of interests, which are the qualities of great generals and great capitalists.[8] According to Paul de Rousiers,[f] every American feels himself capable of 'trying his luck' on the battlefield of business,[9] so that the general spirit of the country is in complete harmony with that of the millionaires; our men of letters are very surprised to see these latter condemning themselves to lead to the end of their lives a galley-slave existence without ever thinking of leading a nobleman's life, as the Rothschilds do.

In a society so enfevered by the passion for the success which can be obtained through competition, all the actors walk straight before them like veritable automata, without concerning themselves with the great ideas of the sociologists; they are subject to very simple forces and not one of them dreams of escaping from the circumstances of his condition. It is only then that the development of capitalism is carried out with the inevitability which struck Marx

---

[8] I will come back to this resemblance in chapter VII, [section] III.

[9] P[aul] de Rousiers, *La Vie américaine: l'éducation et la société* [Paris, Firmin-Didot, 1899], p. 19. 'Fathers give very little advice to their children and let them learn for themselves, as they say over there' (p. 14). 'Not only does [the American] wish to be independent, but he wishes to be powerful': *La Vie américaine: ranches, fermes et usines* [Paris, Firmin-Didot, 1899], p. 6.

[f] Paul de Rousiers (1857–1934); sociologist and leading member of the Le Play school. Sorel was an attentive reader of the writings of de Rousiers and in this text, as in so many others, Sorel makes frequent reference to his empirical investigations of America and Britain. It was upon the basis of de Rousiers' *Le Trade-unionisme en Angleterre* (1897) that Sorel first drew attention to the importance of trade unions in *L'Avenir socialiste des syndicats* (1898).

so strongly and which seemed to him comparable to that of a natural law. If, on the contrary, the bourgeoisie, led astray by the *nonsense* of the preachers of ethics and sociology, returns to the *ideal of conservative mediocrity*, seeks to correct the *abuses* of the economy and wishes to break with the barbarism of their predecessors, then one part of the forces which were to further the development of capitalism is employed in hindering it, chance is introduced and the future of the world becomes completely indeterminate.

This indetermination grows still greater if the proletariat converts to the idea of social peace at the same time as its masters, or even simply if they consider everything from a corporative point of view; while socialism gives to every economic conflict a general and revolutionary colour.

The conservatives are not mistaken when they see in the compromises which lead to collective contracts and in corporative particularism the best means of avoiding the Marxist revolution;[10] but they escape one danger only to fall into another and risk being devoured by parliamentary socialism.[11] Jaurès is as enthusiastic as the priests about measures which distance the working classes from the Marxist revolution; I believe that he understands better than they do what the result of social peace will be; he builds his own hopes upon the simultaneous ruin of both the capitalist spirit and the revolutionary spirit.

It is urged in objection to the people who defend the Marxist conception that it is impossible for them to stop the double movement of degeneration which is dragging the bourgeoisie and the proletariat away from the paths that the theory of Marx assigned to them. They can probably influence the working classes and it is hardly to be denied that the violence of strikes does keep the revolutionary spirit alive; but how can they hope to give back to the bourgeoisie an ardour which is extinguished?

[10] There is constant talk today of organizing labour, i.e. of utilizing the corporative spirit by subjecting it to the direction of *well-intentioned people* and freeing the workers from the yoke of *sophists*. The responsible people are [Albert] de Mun, Charles Benoist (the amusing specialist in constitutional law), Arthur Fontaine and the band of democratic priests . . . and finally Gabriel Hanotaux!

[11] Vilfredo Pareto laughs at the simple bourgeois who are happy no longer to be threatened by intractable Marxists and who fall into the snare of the conciliatory Marxists (*Systèmes socialistes* [Paris, Giard et Brière, 1902–3], II, p. 453).

It is here that the role of violence in history appears as of utmost importance; because in an indirect manner it can operate on the bourgeoisie so as to reawaken them to a sense of their own class interests. On many occasions attention has been drawn to the danger of certain acts of violence which compromised *admirable social works*, disgusted employers who were disposed to arrange the happiness of their employees, and developed egoism where formerly the most noble sentiments reigned.

To repay with *black ingratitude* the *benevolence* of those who wish to protect the workers,[12] to meet with insults the homilies of the defenders of human fraternity and to respond by blows to the advances of the propagators of social peace: all that is assuredly not in conformity with the rules of the fashionable socialism of M. and Mme Georges Renard,[13] but it is a very practical way of indicating to the bourgeoisie that they must occupy themselves with their own affairs and that only.

I also believe that it would be very useful to thrash the orators of democracy and the representatives of the government in order that none of them should be under any illusion about the character of acts of violence. These acts can only have historical value if they are *the brutal and clear expression of class struggle*: the bourgeoisie must not be allowed to imagine that, aided by cleverness, social science or noble sentiments, they might find a better welcome at the hands of the proletariat.

The day when the bosses perceive that they have nothing to gain by works which promote social justice or by democracy, they will understand that they have been badly advised by the people who

---

[12] Cf. Sorel, *Insegnamenti sociali*, p. 53. [See Sorel, *Social Foundations*, p. 73.]

[13] Mme G. Renard has published in the 26 July 1900 edition of *La Suisse* an article full of lofty sociological considerations about the workers' fête given by Millerand (Léon de Seilhac, *Le Monde socialiste* [Paris, Lecoffre, 1904], pp. 307–9). Her husband has solved the grave problem of who will drink Clos-Vougeot in the society of the future (G[eorges] Renard, *Le Régime socialiste* [Paris, Alcan, 1898], p. 175). [Georges Renard (1847–1930), socialist and academic, was for a time editor of *La Revue socialiste*. Sorel here makes reference to Renard's chapter in *Le Régime socialiste* discussing the question of value, where Renard's example is that of the fine Burgundian wines of the Clos Vougeot. Under socialism those prepared to pay the high price will benefit society as a whole! The reference to the article by his wife alludes to her account of how workers attending the event were greeted 'graciously' by Millerand and his wife, clothed in her 'long white dress' and playing the perfect 'hostess'.]

persuaded them to abandon their trade of creators of productive forces for the noble profession of educators of the proletariat. Then there is some chance that they will rediscover a part of their energy and that a moderate or conservative economy may appear as absurd to them as it did to Marx. In any case, the separation of the classes being more clearly attenuated, the movement of the economy will have some chance of developing with greater regularity than today.

The two antagonistic classes therefore influence each other in a partly indirect but decisive manner. Capitalism drives the proletariat into revolt, because in daily life the bosses use their force in a direction opposed to the desires of their workers; but this revolt does not entirely determine the future of the proletariat; the latter organize themselves under the influence of other causes, and socialism, inculcating the revolutionary idea, prepares it to suppress the enemy class. Capitalist force is at the base of this entire process and it operates in an imperious manner.[14] Marx supposed that the bourgeoisie had no need to be incited to employ force; but we are faced with a new and very unforeseen fact: a bourgeoisie which seeks to weaken its own strength. Must we believe that the Marxist conception is dead? By no means, because proletarian violence comes upon the scene at the very moment when the conception of social peace claims to moderate disputes; proletarian violence confines employers to their role as producers and tends to restore the class structure just when they seemed on the point of intermingling in the democratic morass.

Not only can proletarian violence ensure the future revolution but it also seems the only means by which the European nations, stupefied by humanitarianism, can recover their former energy. This violence compels capitalism to restrict its attentions solely to its material role and tends to restore to it the warlike qualities it formerly possessed. A growing and solidly organized working class

[14] In an article written in September 1851 (the first of a series published under the title *Révolution et Contre-Révolution* [Paris, Giard et Brière, 1900]), Marx established the following parallelism between the development of the bourgeoisie and the proletariat: to a numerous, rich, concentrated and powerful bourgeoisie corresponds a numerous, strong, concentrated and intelligent proletariat. Thus he seems to have thought that the intelligence of the proletariat depends on the historical conditions which secured the power of the bourgeoisie in society. He says again that the true characteristics of class struggle only exist in countries where the bourgeoisie has recast government in conformity with its needs.

can force the capitalist class to remain ardent in the industrial struggle; if a united and revolutionary proletariat confronts a rich bourgeoisie eager for conquest, capitalist society will reach its historical perfection.

Thus proletarian violence has become an essential factor in Marxism. Let us add once more that, if properly conducted, it will have the result of suppressing parliamentary socialism, which will no longer be able to pose as the leader of the working classes and as the guardian of order.

III

The Marxist theory of revolution assumes that capitalism will be struck to the heart while it is still full of vitality, when it achieves its historical mission of complete industrial efficiency and whilst the economy is still advancing. Marx does not seem to have asked himself what would happen if the economic system was declining; he never dreamt of the possibility of a revolution which would take a return to the past, or even social conservation, as its ideal.

Today we can see that this might easily come to pass: the friends of Jaurès, the priests and the democrats all take the Middle Ages as their ideal for the future; they would like competition to be tempered, wealth limited and production subordinated to needs. These are dreams that Marx regarded as reactionary[15] and consequently as negligible, because it seemed to him that capitalism was embarked on a path of irresistible progress; but today we see considerable forces grouped together in the endeavour of reforming the capitalist economy, with the aid of laws, in a medieval direction. Parliamentary socialism would like to combine with the moralists, the Church and democracy with the aim of arresting the movement of

---

[15] 'Those who, like Sismondi, would return to the just distribution of production, while preserving the existing bases of society, are *reactionaries*, since, to be consistent, they should also desire to re-establish all the other conditions of past times ... In existing society, in the industry based upon individual exchanges, the anarchy of production, which is the *source of so much poverty*, is at the same time the *source of all progress*': Marx, *Misère de la philosophie* [Paris, Giard et Brière], 1896, pp. 90–1.

capitalism; and, given the extent of bourgeois cowardice, this would not perhaps be impossible.

Marx likened the movement from one historical era to another to a civil inheritance: the new age inherits prior acquisitions. If the revolution took place during a period of economic decadence, would not the inheritance be very much compromised and could there be any hope of seeing the speedy reappearance of economic progress? The ideologists hardly concern themselves with this question: they are sure that the decadence will stop on the day that the public Treasury is at their disposal; they are dazzled by the immense reserve of riches which would be delivered up to their pillage; what banquets there would be, what loose women and what opportunities for self-display! We, on the other hand, who have no such prospect before our eyes, have to ask whether history can furnish us with any guidance on this subject that will enable us to conjecture what would be the result of a revolution accomplished in times of decadence.

The researches of de Tocqueville[g] enable us to study the French Revolution from this point of view. He greatly shocked his contemporaries when, a half-century ago, he showed them that the Revolution had been far more conservative than had been supposed until then. He pointed out that the most characteristic institutions of modern France dated from the *ancien régime* (centralization, excessive regulation, administrative tutelage of the communes, exemption of civil servants from the jurisdiction of the courts); he found only a single important innovation: the coexistence, which was established in year VIII, of isolated civil servants and deliberative councils. The principles of the *ancien régime* reappeared in 1800 and the old customs were received back in favour.[16] Turgot[h] seemed to him

---

[16] [Alexis de] Tocqueville, *L'Ancien Régime et la Révolution (Oeuvres complètes)* [Paris, Calmann-Lévy, 1866], Part 2, chaps. 1, 3, 4, pp. 89, 91, 94, 288. [See *The Ancien Regime and the French Revolution* (London, Fontana, 1969), pp. 52–60, 70–83.]

[g] Alexis de Tocqueville (1805–59); historian and politician; author of two of the great texts of French liberal thought in the nineteenth century: *De la Démocratie en Amérique* (1835 and 1840, 2 vols.) and *L'Ancien Régime et la Révolution* (1856).

[h] Anne-Robert-Jacques Turgot (1727–81); economist and administrator; appointed controller-general of finance, where he introduced radical reforms of the fiscal system and measures to facilitate free trade. He was a friend of the *philosophes*.

to be an excellent example of the Napoleonic administrator who embodied 'the ideal of a civil servant in a democratic society subject to an absolute government'.[17] He was of the opinion that the partition of land, which it is customary to place to the credit of the Revolution, had begun long before and had not advanced at an exceptionally rapid pace under its influence.[18]

It is certain that Napoleon did not have to make an extraordinary effort to put the country once more upon a monarchical footing. He found France quite ready and had only a few corrections of detail to make in order to profit by the experience acquired since 1789. The administrative and fiscal laws had been drawn up during the Revolution by people who had applied the methods of the *ancien régime*; they still remain in force today, almost intact. The men he employed served their apprenticeship under the *ancien régime* and under the Revolution; they all resemble each other; in their governmental practices they are all men of the preceding period; they all work with an ardour for the greatness of His Majesty.[19] The real merit of Napoleon lay in his not trusting too much to his own genius, in not giving himself up to the dreams which had so often deluded the men of the eighteenth century and had led them to desire to regenerate everything from top to bottom – in short, in his full recognition of the principle of historical heredity. It follows from this that the Napoleonic regime may be looked upon as an experiment showing clearly the enormous part played by conservation throughout the greatest revolutions.

Indeed, I think that the principle of conservation may even be extended to include things military and to show that the armies of the Revolution and the Empire were an extension of former institutions. In any case, it is very curious that Napoleon should have made no essential innovations in military equipment and that it should have been the fire-arms of the *ancien régime* which so greatly contributed to securing the victories of the revolutionary troops. It was only under the Restoration that the artillery was improved.

---

[17] Tocqueville, *Mélanges. Fragments historiques et notes sur l'Ancien Régime, la Révolution et l'Empire* [Paris, Calmann-Lévy, 1864], pp. 155–6.
[18] Tocqueville, *L'Ancien Régime et la Révolution*, pp. 35–7. [See *The Ancien Regime and the French Revolution*, pp. 53–5.]
[19] L[ouis] Madelin also comes to this conclusion in an article in the *Débats* of 6 July 1907, on the prefects of Napoleon I.

The ease with which the Revolution and the Empire succeeded in their work of radically transforming the country while still retaining such a large number of the acquisitions of the past is bound up to a fact to which our historians have not always called attention and that Taine does not seem to have noticed: the industrial economy was making great progress and this progress was such that by 1780 everybody believed in the dogma of the infinite progress of mankind.[20] This dogma, which was to exercise so great an influence upon modern thought, would be a bizarre and inexplicable paradox if it were not considered as bound up with economic progress and with the feeling of absolute confidence that this economic progress engendered. The wars of the Revolution and of the Empire only stimulated this feeling further, not only because they were glorious but also because they caused a great deal of money to enter the country and thus contributed towards the development of production.[21]

The triumph of the Revolution astonished nearly all its contemporaries and it seems that the most intelligent, the most thoughtful and the best informed as regards political matters were the most surprised; this was because reasons drawn from ideology could not explain this paradoxical success. It seems to me that even today the question is hardly less obscure to historians than it was to our ancestors. The primary cause of this triumph must be sought in the economy; it is because the *ancien régime* was struck by rapid blows while production was making great strides that the contemporary world was born with comparatively little labour and could so rapidly be assured of a vigorous life.

We, on the other hand, possess a dreadful historical experience of a great transformation taking place at a time of economic decadence; I mean the victory of Christianity and the fall of the Roman Empire which closely followed it.

---

[20] Tocqueville, *L'Ancien Régime et la Révolution*, pp. 254–62 [see *The Ancien Regime and the French Revolution*, pp. 189–99] and *Mélanges*, p. 62. Cf. chapter IV, part IV, of my study on *Les Illusions du progrès* [Paris, Rivière, 1908]. [In English see *The Illusions of Progress* (Berkeley, University of California Press, 1969), pp. 111–16.]

[21] Kautsky has insisted strongly on the role played by the treasures of which the French armies took possession (*La Lutte des classes en France en 1789*, French trans. [Paris, Jacques, 1901], pp. 104–6).

All the old Christian authors agree in informing us that the new religion brought no serious improvement in the situation of the world; political corruption, oppression and disasters continued to crush the people as in the past. This was a great disillusion for the fathers of the Church; at the time of the persecutions the Christians had believed that God would overwhelm Rome with favours on the day that the Empire ceased to persecute the faithful; now the Empire was Christian and the bishops had becomes personages of the first rank, yet everything continued to go as badly as in the past. Even more disheartening, the immorality, so often denounced as the result of idolatry, had spread to the adorers of Christ. Far from imposing a far-reaching reform upon the profane world, the Church itself had become corrupted by imitating the profane world: it began to resemble an imperial administration, and the factions which tore it apart were much more moved by the appetite for power than by religious motives.

It has often been asked whether Christianity was not the cause, or at least one of the principal causes, of the fall of Rome. Gaston Boissier[i] contests this opinion by endeavouring to show that the decadent movement observed after Constantine is a continuation of a movement which had existed for some time and that it is not possible to see whether Christianity accelerated or retarded the death of the ancient world.[22] This amounts to saying that the extent of the conservation was very significant; we can, by analogy, imagine what would follow from a revolution which brought our official socialists to power: institutions remaining almost as they are today, all bourgeois ideology would be preserved; the bourgeois State would dominate with its ancient abuses; if economic decadence had begun, it would be accentuated.

Shortly after the Christian conquest, the barbarian invasions began: more than one Christian wondered whether an order in conformity with the principles of the new religion was not at

---

[22] G[aston] Boissier, *La Fin du paganisme* [Paris, Hachette, 1891], IV, chapter III. [For Sorel's long commentary on this text see *La Ruine du monde antique* (Paris, Jacques, 1902); a shorter version originally appeared as 'La Fin du paganisme' in *L'Ere nouvelle* during 1894.]

[i] Gaston Boissier (1823–1908); professor at the Collège de France; historian and publisher of numerous books on ancient history.

last going to appear; this hope was all the more reasonable as the barbarians had been converted on coming into the Empire and because they were not tainted by the corruptions of Roman life. From the economic point of view, a regeneration seemed possible, since the world was perishing under the weight of urban exploitation; the new masters, who had coarse rural manners, would not live as great lords but as heads of large landed estates; perhaps, therefore, the land would be better cultivated. The illusions of Christian authors contemporary with the invasions can be compared to those of the numerous utopians who hoped to see the modern world regenerated by the virtues which they attributed to the man of average condition: the replacing of very rich classes by new social strata should bring about morality, happiness and universal prosperity.

The barbarians did not establish any progressive state of society; there were few in number and almost everywhere they simply took the place of the old lords, led the same life as the lords had done, and were devoured by urban civilization. In France, the Meroving-ian dynasty has been made the subject of particularly thorough investigation; Fustel de Coulanges[j] has used all his erudition in throwing light on the conservative character it assumed; its con-servatism appeared to him to be so strong that he was even able to say that there had been no real revolution, and he represented the whole of the history of the late Middle Ages as a movement which carried on that of the Roman Empire, with only a little acceler-ation.[23] 'The Merovingian government', he said, 'is more than three parts the continuation of that which the Roman Empire gave to Gaul.'[24]

Economic decadence was accentuated under these barbarian kings; no renascence could take place until very long afterwards, after the world had gone through a long series of trials. At least

---

[23] N[uma]-D[enis] Fustel de Coulanges, *Les Origines du régime féodal* [Paris, Hach-ette, 1890], pp. 566–7. I do not deny that there is a good deal of exaggeration in the thesis of Fustel de Coulanges, but the element of conservatism was undeniable.

[24] N[uma]-D[enis] Fustel de Coulanges, *La Monarchie absolue* [Paris, Hachette, 1888], p. 650.

---

[j] Numa-Denis Fustel de Coulanges (1830–89); professor at the University of Stras-bourg and at the Sorbonne; historian of the classical world as well as of the history of France.

four centuries of barbarism had to be gone through before a progressive movement showed itself; society was compelled to descend to a state not far removed from its origins, and Vico was to find in this phenomenon an illustration of his doctrine of *ricorsi.* Thus a revolution that took place in a time of economic decadence had forced the world to pass again through a period of almost primitive civilization and stopped all progress for several centuries.

These dreadful events have been many times invoked by the adversaries of socialism; I do not deny the validity of the argument but two details must be added which may perhaps appear of small importance to professional sociologists: such events presuppose 1) an economic decadence; 2) an organization which assures a very perfect conservation of the current ideology. On many occasions the *civilized* socialism of our professors has been presented as a safeguard of socialism: I believe that it would produce the same effect as was produced by the classical education given by the Church to the barbarian kings: the proletariat would be corrupted and stupefied as the Merovingians were, and economic decadence would only be more certain under the action of these would-be civilizing agents.

The danger which threatens the future of the world may be avoided if the proletariat hold on with obstinacy to revolutionary ideas, so as to realize as much as possible Marx's conception. Everything may be saved if the proletariat, by their use of violence, manage to re-establish the division into classes and so restore to the bourgeoisie something of its energy: that is the great aim towards which the whole thought of men who are not hypnotized by the events of the day but who think of the conditions of tomorrow must be directed. Proletarian violence, carried on as a pure and simple manifestation of the sentiment of class struggle, appears thus as a very fine and heroic thing; it is at the service of the immemorial interests of civilization; it is not perhaps the most appropriate method of obtaining immediate material advantages, but it may save the world from barbarism.

To those who accuse the syndicalists of being obtuse and ignorant people, we have the right to ask them to consider the economic decadence for which they are working. Let us salute the revolutionaries as the Greeks saluted the Spartan heroes who defended Thermopylae and helped preserve civilization in the ancient world.

III Prejudices against violence

I. Old ideas relative to the Revolution. – Change resulting from the war of 1870 and from the parliamentary regime.
II. Drumont's observations on the ferocity of the bourgeoisie. – The judicial Third Estate and the history of the law courts. – Capitalism against the cult of the State.
III. Attitude of the Dreyfusards. – Jaurès' judgements on the Revolution: his adoration of success and his hatred for the vanquished.
IV. Antimilitarism as proof of an abandonment of bourgeois traditions.

I

The ideas current among the general public on the subject of proletarian violence are not based on the observation of contemporary facts nor on a rational interpretation of the present syndicalist movement; they derive from an infinitely simpler mental process, a comparison of the present with the past; they are shaped by the memories that the word *revolution* evokes almost automatically. It is presumed that the syndicalists, merely because they call themselves revolutionaries, wish to reproduce the history of the revolutionaries of [17]93. The Blanquists,[a] who look upon themselves as the legitimate owners of the terrorist tradition, consider that for this very

---

[a] The supporters of the ideas of Louis-Auguste Blanqui (1805–81), who was a lifelong believer in the conspiratorial and insurrectional route to socialism.

reason they are called upon to direct the proletarian movement;[1] they display much more condescension to the syndicalists than do the other parliamentary socialists; they are inclined to assert that the workers' organizations will come to understand in the end that they cannot do better than to put themselves under their tuition. It seems to me that Jaurès himself, when writing the *Histoire socialiste* of [17]93, thought more than once of the teachings which this long dead past might yield to him for the conduct of the present.

Proper attention has not always been given to the great changes which have taken place since 1870 in the way the Revolution is judged; yet these changes must be considered if we wish to understand contemporary ideas relative to violence.

For a very long time the Revolution appeared to be essentially a succession of glorious wars which a people, famished for liberty and carried away by the noblest passions, had maintained against a coalition of all the powers of oppression and error. The riots and the *coups d'état*, the struggles between parties often devoid of any scruple and the banishing of the vanquished, the parliamentary debates and the adventures of illustrious men, in a word, all the events of its political history were, in the eyes of our fathers, only very secondary accessories to the wars of Liberty.

For about twenty-five years, changing the form of government in France had been at issue; after campaigns before which the memories of Caesar and Alexander paled, the *Charte* of 1814[b] had definitively incorporated the parliamentary system, Napoleonic legislation and the Church established by the Concordat[c] into the national tradition; war had given an irrevocable judgement whose preambles,

[1] The reader may usefully refer to a very interesting chapter of Bernstein's book, *Socialisme théorique et social-démocratie pratique* [Paris, Stock, 1900], pp. 47–63. Bernstein, who knows nothing of the preoccupations of our present-day syndicalism, has not, in my opinion, drawn from Marxism all that it contains. Moreover, his book was written at a time when it was still impossible to understand the revolutionary movement, in view of which these reflections are written.

[b] The constitutional charter of 4 June 1814 restored the monarchy, in the shape of Louis XVIII, to power, but at the same time it formally recognized many of the social and administrative changes resulting from the revolutionary and Napoleonic periods.

[c] The Concordat of 1801, an agreement between Pope Pius VII and Napoleon Bonaparte, defined the relationship between Church and State in France, recognizing the pre-eminence of the Catholic religion.

as Proudhon said, had been dated from Valmy, from Jemmapes, and from fifty other battlefields, and whose conclusions had been accepted at Saint-Ouen by Louis XVIII.[2] Protected by the prestige of the wars of Liberty, the new institutions had become inviolable and the ideology that was built up to explain them became a faith which seemed for a long time to have for the French the value which the revelation of Jesus has for the Catholics.

From time to time eloquent writers have thought that they could set up a current of reaction against these doctrines, and the Church had hopes that it might get the better of what it called the *error of liberalism*. A long period of admiration for medieval art and of contempt for the period of Voltaire seemed to threaten the new ideology with ruin; but all these attempts to return to the past left no trace except in literary history. There were times when those in power governed in the least liberal manner, but the principles of the modern regime were never seriously threatened. This fact could not be explained by the power of reason or by some law of progress; its cause lies simply in the epic of the wars which had filled the French soul with an enthusiasm analogous to that provoked by religions.

This military epic gave an epic colour to all the events of internal politics; the competition between parties was thus raised to the level of an *Iliad*; politicians became giants and the Revolution, which Joseph de Maistre denounced as satanical, was made divine. The bloody scenes of the Terror were episodes without great importance by the side of the enormous slaughter of war, and the means were found to envelop them in a dramatic mythology; riots were elevated to the same rank as illustrious battles; and it was in vain that calmer historians endeavoured to bring the Revolution and the Empire down to the plane of common history. The prodigious triumphs of the revolutionary and imperial armies rendered all criticism impossible.

The war of 1870 changed all that. At the moment of the fall of the Second Empire,[d] the immense majority in France still believed very

---

[2] [Pierre-Joseph] Proudhon, *La Guerre et la paix* [Paris, Lacroix, 1869], V, chap. III.

[d] The Second Empire (1852–70), with Napoleon III as its emperor, came crashing to an end on the battlefield of Sedan, when the emperor himself was taken prisoner and was forced to accept an unconditional surrender.

strongly the legends which had been spread about the armies of
volunteers, the miraculous role of the representatives of the people,
and improvised generals; experience produced a cruel disillusion.
Tocqueville had written: 'The Convention created the policy of the
impossible, the theory of furious madness, the cult of blind audacity.'[3] The disasters of 1870 brought the country back to practical,
prudent and ordinary conditions; the first result of these disasters
was the development of the conception most opposed to that spoken
of by Tocqueville; the idea of opportunism, which has now been
introduced even into socialism.

Another consequence was the change which took place in all revolutionary values, and notably the modification in the opinions
which were held on the subject of violence.

After 1871 everyone in France thought only of the search for the
most appropriate means of setting the country on its feet again.
Taine endeavoured to apply the methods of the most scientific psychology to this question and he looked upon the history of the
Revolution as a social experiment. He hoped to be able to make
quite clear the danger presented in his opinion by the Jacobin spirit
and thereby to induce his contemporaries to change the course of
French politics by abandoning ideas which had been incorporated
into the national tradition and which were all the more solidly
rooted in people's minds because nobody had ever discussed their
origin. Taine failed in his enterprise, as Le Play and Renan failed,
as all those will fail who wish to found an intellectual and moral
reform on investigations, on scientific syntheses and on
demonstrations.

It cannot be said, however, that Taine's immense labour was
accomplished to no purpose; the history of the Revolution was thoroughly overhauled; the military epic no longer dominates judgements about political events. The life of men, the inner workings
of factions, the material needs that determine the tendencies of the
great masses have now come to the foreground. In the speech which
he made on 24 September 1905, at the inauguration of the
monument to Taine at Vouziers, the deputy Hubert, while giving
full homage to the great and many-sided talent of his illustrious

---

[3] A[lexis] de Tocqueville, *Mélanges:* [*Fragments historiques et notes sur l'Ancien
Régime. La Révolution et l'Empire* (Paris, Calmann-Lévy, 1865)], p. 189.

compatriot, expressed a regret that the epic side of the Revolution had been disregarded by him in a systematic manner. These are superfluous regrets: the epic vision can no longer govern this political history: an idea of the grotesque effects to which this preoccupation to return to old methods leads can be obtained by reading Jaurès' *Histoire socialiste*: in vain does Jaurès revive all the most melodramatic images of the old rhetoric; the only effect he manages to produce is one of absurdity.

The prestige of the revolutionary days has been directly hit by the comparison with contemporary civil struggles: there was nothing during the Revolution which could bear comparison with the battles that covered Paris in blood in 1848[e] and in 1871;[f] 14 July [1789] and 10 August [1792] seem to us now mere scuffles which would not have made a serious government tremble.

There is another reason, still hardly recognized by professional writers on revolutionary history, which has contributed a great deal to taking all the romance out of these events. There can be no national epic about things which the people cannot picture to themselves as reproducible in the near future; popular poetry implies the future much more than the past; it is for this reason that the adventures of the Gauls, of Charlemagne, of the Crusades, of Joan of Arc, cannot form the object of a narrative capable of moving anyone but literary people.[4] Since we have begun to believe that contemporary governments cannot be brought down by riots like those of 14 July and 10 August, we have ceased to regard these days as having an epic character. Parliamentary socialists, who would like to utilize the memory of the Revolution in order to excite the ardour of the people and who, at the same time, ask them to put all their

---

[4] It is very remarkable that in the seventeenth century [Nicholas] Boileau [1636–1711] had already pronounced against the supernatural Christian epic. This was because his contemporaries, however religious they might have been, did not expect that angels would come to help Vauban to capture fortresses; they did not doubt what was recounted in the Bible, but they did not see matter in it for epics, because these marvels were not destined to be reproduced.

[e] Between 23–6 June 1848 rioting, followed by bitter street fighting, occurred on the streets of Paris. The so-called 'journées de juin' led to severe reprisals from the government of the Second Republic, with 1,500 protesters shot without trial.

[f] The Paris Commune was brought to an end when the French army stormed the city walls. The so-called 'semaine sanglante' (21–8 May) saw widespread fighting across Paris, with approximately 25,000 defenders killed.

confidence in parliamentarism, are very inconsistent, because they are themselves working to ruin the epic whose prestige they wish to maintain in their speeches.

But then what remains of the Revolution when we have taken away the wars against the coalition and that of the victorious days of the people? What remains is not very savoury: police operations, proscriptions and the sittings of servile courts of law. The employment of the force of the State against the vanquished shocks us all the more because so many of the leaders of the Revolution were soon to distinguish themselves amongst the servants of Napoleon and to employ the same policing zeal on behalf of the emperor as they did on behalf of the Terror. In a country which has been convulsed by so many changes of regime and which, as a consequence, has known so many recantations, there is something particularly odious about political justice because the criminal of today might become the judge of tomorrow: General Malet could say before the council of war that condemned him in 1812 that, had he succeeded, he would have had for his accomplices the whole of France and his judges themselves.[5]

It serves no purpose to carry these reflections further; the slightest observation suffices to show that proletarian violence recalls a mass of painful memories of those past times: instinctively people start to think of the committees of revolutionary inspection, of the brutalities of suspicious agents, coarsened and frightened by fear, of the tragedies of the guillotine. One understands, therefore, why the parliamentary socialists make such great efforts to persuade the public that they have the souls of sensible shepherds, that their hearts are overflowing with good feelings and that they have only one passion: *a hatred of violence*. They would readily give themselves out to be the protectors of the bourgeoisie against proletarian violence; and in order to heighten their prestige as humanitarians they never fail to shun all contact with anarchists; sometimes they even shun this contact with an abruptness which is not without a certain element of cowardice and hypocrisy.

---

[5] Ernest Hamel, *Histoire de la conspiration du général Malet* [Paris, Librairie de la Société des Gens de Lettres, 1873], p. 241. According to some newspapers, Jaurès, in his evidence before the court of assizes of the Seine on 5 June 1907, in the Bousquet-Lévy trial, said that the police officers would show more consideration for the accused, Bousquet, when he had become a legislator.

When Millerand was the unquestioned chief of the socialist party in parliament, he advised his party to *be afraid to frighten*; and, as a matter of fact, socialist deputies would find few votes if they did not manage to convince the general public that they are very reasonable people, great enemies of the old practices of the men of blood, and solely preoccupied in meditating on the philosophy of future law. In a long speech given on 8 October 1905 at Limoges, Jaurès strove to reassure the bourgeoisie much more than had been done hitherto: he informed them that a victorious socialism would be generous and that he was studying different ways in which former property holders would be indemnified. A few years ago Millerand promised indemnities to the poor (*La Petite République*, 25 March 1898); now everybody will be put on the same footing, and Jaurès assures us that Vandervelde[g] has written things on this subject full of profundity. I am quite willing to take his word for it!

The social revolution is conceived by Jaurès as a kind of bankruptcy; substantial annuities will be given to the bourgeoisie of today; then, from generation to generation, these annuities will decrease. These plans must seem very appealing to financiers accustomed to drawing great advantages from bankruptcies; I have no doubt that the shareholders of *L'Humanité* think these ideas marvellous; they will be made liquidators of the bankruptcy and will pocket large fees, which will compensate them for the losses which the newspaper has caused them.

In the eyes of the contemporary bourgeoisie everything is admirable which dispels the idea of violence. Our bourgeoisie desire to die in peace – after them the deluge.

II

Let us now examine the violence of [17]93 a little more closely and endeavour to see whether it can be identified with that of contemporary syndicalism.

---

[g] Emile Vandervelde (1866–1938); Belgian socialist and one of the prominent figures of the Second International.

Fifteen years ago, Drumont,[h] speaking of socialism and of its future, wrote these sentences, which then appeared exceedingly paradoxical to many people: ' "Salute the worker leaders of the Commune", the historian, who is always something of a prophet, might say to conservatives, "You will never see their like again! . . . those who are about to come are malicious, wicked and vindictive in a different way from the men of 1871. Henceforward, a new feeling takes possession of the French proletariat: hatred." '[6] These were not the airy words of a man of letters: Drumont had learned what he knew of the Commune and of the socialist world through Malon,[i] of whom he gave a very appreciative portrait.

This sinister prediction was founded upon the idea that the worker was getting farther and farther away from the national tradition and nearer to the bourgeoisie, which is much more prone than he is to bad feeling. 'It was the bourgeois element', said Drumont, 'which was the most ferocious during the Commune, the vicious and bohemian bourgeoisie of the Latin quarter; amid this dreadful crisis, the popular element remained *human, that is French* . . . Among the internationalists who formed part of the Commune, four only . . . pronounced themselves in favour of violent measures.'[7] Clearly, Drumont has got no farther than that naive philosophy of the eighteenth century and of the utopians prior to 1848, according to which men will follow the injunctions of the moral law all the better for not having been spoilt by civilization; in descending from the superior classes to the poorer classes a greater number of good qualities are found; good is only natural to individuals who have remained close to a state of nature.

This theory about the nature of classes led Drumont to a rather curious historical speculation: none of our revolutions was so bloody

---

[6] [Edouard] Drumont, *La Fin d'un monde* [Paris, Savine, 1889], pp. 137–8.
[7] *Ibid.*, p. 128.

[h] Edouard Drumont (1844–1917); nationalist writer; author of the anti-Semitic best-seller *La France juive* (1886) and editor of *La Libre parole*, which he established in 1892. In 1889 he published *La Fin d'un monde*, mixing his anti-Semitism with socialist themes of anticapitalism, whilst also rehabilitating the workers of the Paris Commune. He there acknowledged his debt to socialist Benoît Malon.
[i] Benoît Malon (1841–93); journalist and writer; one of the founders of the First International and a leading member of the Paris Commune. He subsequently established *La Revue socialiste* in 1880 and came to adopt an increasingly reformist position.

as the first, because it was conducted by the bourgeoisie: – 'in proportion as the people become more intimately mixed with revolutions they become less ferocious' – 'when, for the first time, the
proletariat had acquired an effective share of authority it was less
bloodthirsty than the bourgeoisie.'[8] We cannot remain content with
the easy explanations which satisfied Drumont, but it is certain that
something has changed since [17]93. We have to ask ourselves
whether the ferocity of the old revolutionaries was not due to
reasons depending on the past history of the bourgeoisie, so that in
confusing the abuses of the revolutionary bourgeois force of [17]93
with the violence of our revolutionary syndicalists a grave error
would be committed: the word *revolutionary* would, in this case,
have two perfectly distinct meanings.

The Third Estate, which filled the assemblies in the revolutionary
epoch and may be called the official Third Estate, was not a body
of agriculturalists and leaders of industry: power was never in the
hands of manufacturers but in the hands of legal people. Taine was
very much struck by the fact that out of 577 deputies of the Third
Estate in the Constituent Assembly, there were 373 'unknown barristers and lawyers of a minor order, notaries, King's attorneys,
court-roll commissioners, judges and recorders of the presidial
bench, bailiffs and lieutenants of a district, simple practitioners shut
up since their youth within the narrow circle of a mediocre jurisdiction or the routine of continual scribbling, without any other escape
than philosophical wanderings through imaginary spaces under the
guidance of Rousseau and Raynal'.[9] We have some difficulty nowadays in understanding the importance that lawyers possessed in
pre-revolutionary France: but a multitude of jurisdictions existed;
property owners were extremely punctilious in going to law about
questions which today appear to us as of minor importance but
which seemed of enormous importance to them on account of the

---

[8] *Ibid.*, p. 136.
[9] [Hippolyte] Taine, *La Révolution*, I [*L'Anarchie* (Paris, Hachette, 1878)], p. 155.
[Guillaume Raynal (1713–96); historian and editor of the *Mercure de France*; his
best-known work was *Histoire philosophique et politique des établissements et du commerce des Européens dans les deux Indes* (1770). This ran to over fifty editions before
the end of the century and strongly criticized the colonial activities of the European powers.]

dovetailing of feudal law with the law of property; functionaries of the judicial order were found everywhere and they enjoyed the greatest prestige with the people.

This class brought to the Revolution a great deal of administrative capacity; it was owing to them that the country was able to pass easily through the crisis which shook it for ten years and that Napoleon was able to reconstruct regular administrative services so rapidly; but this class also brought a mass of prejudices which caused those of its representatives who occupied high positions to commit grave errors. It is impossible, for example, to understand the behaviour of Robespierre if we compare him to the politicians of today; we must always see in him the serious lawyer, taken up with his duties, anxious not to tarnish the professional honour of an orator of the bar; moreover, he had literary leanings and was a disciple of Rousseau. He had scruples about legality which astonish the historians of today; when he was obliged to take important decisions and to defend himself before the Convention, he showed a simplicity that bordered on stupidity. The famous law of the 22nd Prairial,[j] with which he has so often been reproached and which gave so rapid a pace to the revolutionary courts, is the masterpiece of his type of mind: the whole of the *ancien régime* is found in it, expressed in clear-cut formulas.

One of the fundamental ideas of the *ancien régime* had been the employment of the penal procedure to ruin any power which was an obstacle to the monarchy. It seems that in all primitive societies the penal law, at its inception, was a protection granted to the chief and to a few privileged persons whom he honoured with special favour; it is only much later that the legal power serves to safeguard indiscriminately the persons and the goods of all the inhabitants of a country. The Middle Ages being a return to the customs of very ancient times, it was natural that they should reproduce exceedingly archaic ideas about justice and that the courts of justice should come to be considered primarily as instruments of royal greatness. An historical accident happened to favour the extraordinary

---

[j] This law authorized the arrest of anyone who 'either by their conduct, their contacts, their words or their writings, showed themselves to be supporters of tyranny, of federalism or to be enemies of liberty'. This sweeping law prepared the way for widespread repression.

development of this theory of criminal administration. The Inquisition furnished a model for courts which, set in motion on very slight pretexts, prosecuted people who embarrassed authority, with great persistence, and made it impossible for them to harm the latter. The royal State borrowed from the Inquisition many of its procedures and nearly always followed the same principles.

The Crown constantly demanded of its courts of law that they should work for the enlargement of its territory; it seems strange to us today that Louis XIV should have had annexations proclaimed by commissions of magistrates; but he was following established practice; many of his predecessors had used the Parlement to confiscate feudal manors for very arbitrary motives. Justice, which seems to us today to be created to secure the prosperity of production and to permit its free and constantly widening development, seemed previously to have the task of securing the greatness of the monarchy: *its essential aim was not the administration of justice but the welfare of the State.*

It was very difficult to establish strict discipline in the services set up by the monarchy for war and administration; enquiries had continually to be carried out in order to punish unfaithful and disobedient employees; for this purpose, kings employed men taken from their courts of law; thus they came to confuse acts of disciplinary surveillance with the repression of crimes. Lawyers must transform everything according to their habits of mind; in this way, negligence, ill will or carelessness became revolt against authority, crime or treason.

The Revolution piously inherited this tradition, and gave an importance to imaginary crimes which was all the greater because its political courts of law functioned in the midst of a population maddened by the seriousness of the peril; it seemed quite natural to explain the defeats of generals by criminal intentions and to guillotine people who had not been able to realize hopes fostered by a public opinion that had often returned to the superstitions of childhood. Our penal code still contains not a few paradoxical articles dating from this time: today it is not easy to understand how a citizen can be seriously accused of plotting or of keeping up a correspondence with foreign powers or their agents in order to induce them to begin hostilities or to enter into war with France or to provide them with the means to do so. Such a crime supposes that the State can be imperilled by the act of one person; this appears scarcely credible to us.[10]

Trials against enemies of the king were always carried out in an exceptional manner; the procedures were simplified as much as possible; flimsy proofs which would not have sufficed for ordinary crimes were accepted; the intention was to make a terrible and profoundly intimidating example. All of this is to be found again in Robespierre's legislation. The law of the 22nd Prairial contents itself with rather vague definitions of political crime, so as not to let any enemy of the Revolution escape; and the kinds of proof required are worthy of the purest tradition of the *ancien régime* and of the Inquisition: 'The proof necessary to condemn the *enemies of the people* is any kind of document, material, moral, verbal or written, which can naturally obtain the assent of any just and reasonable mind. Juries in giving their verdict should be guided by what love of their country indicates to their conscience; their aim is the *triumph of the Republic and the ruin of its enemies*.' In this celebrated terrorist law we have the strongest expression of the doctrine of the State.[11]

The philosophy of the eighteenth century rendered these methods still more formidable. It professed, in fact, to formulate a return to natural law; humanity had been, till then, corrupted by the fault of a small number of people whose interest it had been to deceive it; but the means of returning to the principles of primitive goodness, of truth and of justice had at last been discovered; all opposition to so excellent a reform, one so easy to apply and so certain of success, was the most criminal act imaginable; the innovators were resolved to show themselves inexorable in destroying the evil influence which bad citizens might exercise for the purpose of hindering the regeneration of humanity. Indulgence was a culpable weakness, for it amounted to nothing less than the sacrifice of the happiness of the many to the caprices of incorrigible people who gave proof of an incomprehensible obstinacy, who refused to recognize evidence and who only lived on lies.

---

[10] Yet this was the article that was applied to Dreyfus without anybody, moreover, having attempted to prove that France had been in danger.

[11] Even the details of this law can only be explained by comparing them with the rules of the old penal law.

From the Inquisition to the political justice of the monarchy, and from this to the revolutionary tribunals, there was a constant progress towards greater arbitrariness in laws, the extension of the use of force and the amplification of authority. For some considerable time the Church had felt doubts about the value of the exceptional methods practised by its inquisitors.[12] The monarchy, especially when it had achieved its full maturity, was troubled with very few scruples about the matter; but the Revolution displayed the scandal of its superstitious cult of the State in the full light of day.

A reason of an economic kind gave to the State at that time a strength that the Church had never possessed. At the beginning of the modern age, governments, by their maritime expeditions and the encouragement they gave to industry, had played a very great part in production; but in the eighteenth century this part had become exceptionally important in the minds of theorists. At the time people had their heads full of great projects; they conceived kingdoms as vast companies undertaking to cultivate new lands and they made efforts to ensure the good working of these companies. Thus the State was the God of the reformers. 'They desired', wrote Tocqueville, 'to borrow the authority of the central power and to use it to break up and to remake everything according to a new plan which they have conceived themselves: the central power alone appeared to them capable of accomplishing such a task. The power of the State must be limitless, as are its rights; all that is necessary is to persuade the State to make suitable use of its power.'[13] The physiocrats[k] seemed ready to sacrifice individuals to the general good; they had no great love of liberty and thought the idea of a balance of powers absurd; they hoped to convert the State; their system is defined by Tocqueville as 'a democratic despotism'; the government would have been, in theory, the representative of

---

[12] Modern authors, by taking literally certain instructions of the Papacy, have been able to maintain that the Inquisition had been relatively indulgent, having regard to the customs of the time.

[13] [Alexis de] Tocqueville, *L'Ancien Régime et la Révolution* [Paris, Calmann-Lévy, 1866], p. 100. [See *The Ancien Regime and the French Revolution* (London, Fontana, 1969), p. 95.]

[k] The physiocrats were eighteenth-century advocates of the new science of political economy. They believed that land was the source of all wealth.

everybody, controlled by an enlightened public opinion; in practice, it was an absolute master.[14] One of the things which most astonished Tocqueville in the course of his studies of the *ancien régime* was the admiration felt by the physiocrats for China, which appeared to them as the model of good government because it was run exclusively by valets and clerks who were carefully catalogued and chosen by competition.[15]

Since the Revolution there has been such a dramatic upheaval of ideas that we have difficulty in understanding correctly the conceptions of our fathers.[16] The capitalist economic system has thrown full light on the extraordinary power of the individual; the confidence which the men of the eighteenth century had in the industrial capacities of the State appear puerile to everybody who has studied production elsewhere than in the insipid books of the sociologists, who still preserve very carefully the cult of the stupidities of the past; the law of nature has become an inexhaustible subject of amusement for people who have the slightest knowledge of history; the employment of the courts of law as a means of coercing a political adversary arouses universal indignation, whilst people with ordinary common sense hold that it ruins all judicial conceptions.

Sumner Maine points out that the relationships between governments and citizens have been completely overturned since the end of the eighteenth century; formerly the State was always supposed to be good and wise; consequently, any attempt to hinder its working was looked upon as a grave offence; the liberal system, on the contrary, supposes that the citizen, left free, chooses the best outcome and that he exercises the first of his rights in criticizing the government, which has passed from the position of master to that of servant.[17] Maine does not say what is the reason for this transformation; the reason seems to me to be, above all, an economic one. In the new state of things, political crime is an act of simple

---

[14] *Ibid.*, pp. 235–40. [See *The Ancien Regime and the French Revolution*, pp. 178–83.]

[15] *Ibid.*, p. 241. [See *The Ancien Regime and the French Revolution*, pp. 183–4.]

[16] In the history of judicial ideas in France, full consideration must be given to the dividing up of landed property, which, by multiplying the independent heads of productive units, contributed more to the spread of judicial ideas among the masses than was ever done among the literate classes by the finest treatises on philosophy.

[17] [Sir Henry] Sumner Maine, *Essais sur le gouvernement populaire*, French trans. [Paris, Thorin, 1887], p. 20. [See *Popular Government* (London, J. Murray, 1884).]

revolt which cannot carry with it disgrace of any kind and which is combated for reasons of prudence, but which no longer merits the name of crime for its author in no way resembles a criminal.

We are not perhaps better, more human, more sensitive to the misfortunes of others than the men of [17]93; I should even be rather disposed to assert that the country is probably less moral than it was at that time; but we are no longer dominated to the same extent that our fathers were by this superstition of the God-State, to which they sacrificed so many victims. The ferocity of the members of the National Convention is easily explained by the influence of the conceptions which the Third Estate derived from the detestable practices of the *ancien régime*.

III

It would be strange if the old ideas were completely dead; the Dreyfus affair showed us that the immense majority of the officers and the priests still conceived justice in the manner of the *ancien régime* and looked upon condemnations for reasons of State as quite natural.[18] This should not surprise us, for these two types of people, never having any direct relationship with production, can understand nothing about law. The revolt of the enlightened public against the practices of the ministry of war was so great that for a moment it might have been believed that reasons of State would soon no longer be accepted (outside the two categories mentioned above) except by the readers of *Le Petit Journal*, whose mentality would thus be characterized and shown to be much the same as that which existed a century ago.[1] By cruel experience, we know now, alas!, that the State still had its high priests and its fervent advocates amongst the Dreyfusards.

The Dreyfus affair was hardly over when the government of republican defence began another political prosecution in the name

---

[18] The extraordinary and illegal severity which was brought to bear in the application of the penalty is explained by the fact that the aim of the trial was to terrify certain spies who, by their situation, were out of reach; whether Dreyfus was guilty or not troubled his accusers little; the essential thing was to protect the State from treachery and to reassure the French people, who were maddened by the fear of war.

[1] *Le Petit Journal* was a popular newspaper founded in 1863.

of reasons of State and accumulated almost as many lies as the army general staff had accumulated in the trial of Dreyfus. No serious person today can doubt that the great plot for which Déroulède, Buffet and Lur-Saluces were condemned was an invention of the police:[m] the siege of what has been called the Fort Chabrol was arranged in order to make Parisians believe that they had been on the eve of a civil war. The victims of this judicial crime were granted an amnesty but the amnesty should not have sufficed: if the Dreyfusards had been sincere they should have demanded that the Senate recognize the scandalous error which the lies of the police had caused it to commit: I believe that, on the contrary, they seem to have found it in line with the principles of eternal justice to maintain for as long as possible a conviction founded on the most evident fraud.

Jaurès and many other eminent Dreyfusards commended General André and Combes for having organized a regular system of secret accusations. Kautsky strongly reproached him for his conduct; the German writer demanded that socialism should not continue to represent 'the wretched practices of the bourgeois Republic' as great democratic actions, and that it should remain 'faithful to the principle which declares that the informer is the worst kind of rascal'(*Les Débats*, 13 November 1904). The saddest thing about this affair is that Jaurès asserted that Colonel Hartmann (who protested against the system of secret reports) had himself employed similar methods.[19] The latter wrote to him: 'I pity you that you have come to defend today and by such means the guilty acts which, with us, you condemned a few years ago; I pity you that you should

[19] In *L'Humanité*, 17 November 1904, there is a letter from Paul Guieysse and from Vazeilles declaring that nothing of this kind can be imputed to Colonel Hartmann. Jaurès follows this letter with a strange commentary: he considers that the informers acted in perfect good faith and he regrets that the colonel should have provided 'imprudently, further matter for the systematic campaign of the reactionary newspapers'. Jaurès has no suspicion that this commentary made his own case much worse, and that it was not unworthy of a disciple of Escobar. [See 'L'Incident Hartmann', *L'Humanité*, 17 November 1904.]

[m] Paul Déroulède (1846–1914) was leader of the Ligue des Patriotes; in 1899 he led a farcical attempted coup to overthrow the Third Republic. The comte Eugène de Lur-Saluces (1852–1922) and André Buffet were leading representatives of the royalist cause and were put on trial with Déroulède. All three were sent into exile for ten years.

believe yourself obliged to make the republican regime responsible for the vile proceedings of the police spies who dishonour it' (*Les Débats*, 5 November 1904).

Experience has always shown us hitherto that our revolutionaries plead reasons of State as soon as they get into power, that they then employ police methods and look upon justice as a weapon which they may use unfairly against their enemies. Parliamentary socialists do not escape this universal rule; they preserve the old cult of the State; they are therefore prepared to commit all the misdeeds of the *ancien régime* and of the Revolution.

A fine collection of unpleasant political maxims might be composed by going through Jaurès' *Histoire socialiste*: I have never had the patience to read the 1,824 pages devoted to the story of the Revolution between 10 August 1792 and the fall of Robespierre; I have simply turned over the pages of this tedious book and have seen that it contained a mixture of philosophy at times worthy of M[onsieur] Pantalon[n] and a policy fitting a purveyor to the guillotine. For a long time I had concluded that Jaurès would be capable of every ferocity against the vanquished; I saw that I was not mistaken; but I would not have thought that he was capable of so much platitude: in his eyes the vanquished are always in the wrong and victory fascinates our great defender of eternal justice so much that he is ready to consent to every proscription demanded of him. 'Revolutions', he says, 'claim from a man the most frightful sacrifices, not only of his rest, not only of his life but of human tenderness and pity.'[20] Why write so much, then, about the inhumanity of the executioners of Dreyfus? They also sacrificed 'human tenderness' to what appeared to them to be the safety of the country.

A few years ago, the republicans were extremely indignant with the comte de Vogüé[o] who, when receiving Hanotaux[p] into the Académie Française, called the *coup d'état* of 1851 'a somewhat harsh

[20] J[ean] Jaurès, *La Convention* [Paris, Jules Rouff, 1901, II], p. 1732.

[n] Monsieur Pantalon is a name derived from the seventeenth-century school of Italian comedy: it is meant to indicate the combination of the farcical and the burlesque.
[o] Eugène-Melchior, vicomte de Vogüé (1848–1910); novelist and writer, known especially for his studies of Russian literature.
[p] Gabriel Hanotaux (1853–1941); diplomat and historian.

police operation'.[21] Jaurès, taught by revolutionary history, now reasons in exactly the same way as the jovial vicomte;[22] he praises, for example, 'the policy of vigour and of wisdom' that consisted of forcing the Convention to expel the Girondins 'with a certain appearance of legality'.[23]

The massacres of September 1792[q] are a little embarrassing for him; legality is not very evident here, but he has big words and bad reasons for every wretched cause; the behaviour of Danton[r] was not very worthy of admiration at the time of these sad events, but Jaurès has to excuse him because Danton was triumphant during this period. 'He did not think that it was his duty as a revolutionary and patriotic minister to enter upon a struggle with these *misguided popular forces*. How can we purify the metal of the bells when they are sounding the alarm of imperilled liberty?'[24] It seems to me that Cavaignac might have explained his conduct in the Dreyfus affair in the same way: to the people who accused him of being hand in hand with the anti-Semites he might have answered that his duty as a patriotic minister did not compel him to enter upon a struggle with the misguided populace and that when the safety of national defence is at stake we cannot purify the metal of the bells which are sounding the alarm of the country in danger.

When he comes to the period when Camille Desmoulins[s] sought to stir up a movement of opinion capable of stopping the Terror,

[21] This was on 24 March 1898, at a particularly critical moment of the Dreyfus affair, when the nationalists were demanding that agitators and enemies of the army should be swept away. J[oseph] Reinach says that De Vogüé openly invited the army to begin again the work of 1851 (*Histoire de l'affaire Dreyfus* [Paris, Editions de la Revue Blanche, 1901–11], III, p. 545).

[22] De Vogüé has the habit in his polemics of thanking his adversaries for having given him much amusement: that is why I take the liberty of calling him jovial, although his writings are rather soporific.

[23] Jaurès, [*La Convention*, I], p. 1434.

[24] *Ibid.*, [I], p. 1434.

[q] At the end of August 1792 approximately 3,000 suspected opponents of the Revolution were arrested. In the first week of September between 1,100 and 1,400 of them were massacred in acts of popular justice.

[r] Georges-Jacques Danton (1759–94); revolutionary politician and leader of the government formed after the fall of the monarchy in 1792. A moderate, he was executed in 1794.

[s] Camille Desmoulins (1760–94); associate of Danton; it was in his journal, *Le Vieux Cordelier*, that he protested against the violent excesses of the Terror: for this he was himself executed.

Jaurès speaks energetically against this attempt. He does acknowledge a few pages later on, however, that the system of the guillotine
could not last forever; but Desmoulins, having succumbed, is wrong
in the eyes of our *humble* worshipper of success. Jaurès accuses
the author of *Le Vieux Cordelier* of forgetting the conspiracies, the
treasons, the corruptions and all the dreams with which the terrorists fed their infatuated imaginations; he even had the irony to speak
of 'free France' and pronounced this sentence worthy of a Jacobin
pupil of Joseph Prudhomme:[1] 'The knife of Desmoulins was chis-
elled with an incomparable art; but he planted it at the heart of the
Revolution'.[25] When Robespierre no longer commands the majority
in the Convention he is, as a matter of course, put to death by the
other terrorists by virtue of the legitimate workings of the parliamentary institutions of the day; but to appeal to *mere public opinion*
against the leaders of the government, that was Desmoulins' 'crime'.
His crime was also that committed by Jaurès at the time he
defended Dreyfus against the great leaders of the army and the
government; how many times has not Jaurès been accused of com-
promising the national defence? But that time is a long way back;
and our orator had then not yet tasted the advantages of power and
did not possess a theory of the State as ferocious as that which he
possesses today.

I think that I have said sufficient to enable me to conclude that if,
by chance, our parliamentary socialists come to power they will
prove themselves worthy successors of the Inquisition, of the *ancien
régime* and of Robespierre; political courts will be at work on a large
scale and we may even suppose that the *unfortunate* law of 1848
which abolished the death penalty for political matters will be repealed. Thanks to this *reform* we might again see the State triumphing
by the hand of the executioner.

Proletarian acts of violence have no resemblance to these proscriptions; they are purely and simply acts of war; they have the
value of military manoeuvres and serve to mark the separation of

---

[25] *Ibid.*, [II], p. 1731.

[1] A character created by the caricaturist Henri Monnier, meant to signify the prosperous self-contented bourgeois of the July Monarchy (1830–48) and known, above
all, for his platitudes on all subjects.

classes. Everything in war is carried out without hatred and without the spirit of revenge; in war the vanquished are not killed; non-combatants are not made to bear the consequences of the disappointments which the armies may have experienced on the field of battle;[26] force is then displayed according to its own nature, without ever professing to borrow anything from the judicial proceedings which society sets up against criminals.

The more syndicalism develops by abandoning the old superstitions which come to it, via the men of letters, professors of philosophy and historians of the Revolution, from the *ancien régime* and from the Church, the more will social conflicts assume the character of simple struggle similar to those of armies on campaign. We cannot censure too severely those who teach the people that they ought to carry out we know not what highly idealistic decrees of a progressive justice. They work to maintain those ideas about the State which provoked the bloody acts of [17]93, whilst the idea of class struggle, on the contrary, tends to refine the conception of violence.

IV

Syndicalism in France is engaged in an antimilitarist campaign that shows clearly the immense distance which separates it from parliamentary socialism in its conception of the State. Many newspapers believe that this is merely an exaggerated humanitarian movement, provoked by the articles of Hervé; this is a great error. We would be mistaken in believing that it was merely a protest against the harshness of discipline, the length of military service or the presence, in the higher ranks, of officers hostile to existing political institutions;[27] these are the reasons which led many members of the bourgeoisie to applaud declamations against the army at the time of

---

[26] I bring to notice here a fact which is perhaps not very well known: the Spanish war at the time of Napoleon was the occasion of innumerable atrocities, but Colonel Laffaille says that in Catalonia the murders and the cruelties were never committed by Spanish soldiers who had been enlisted for some time and who had become familiar with correct behaviour in war. (*Mémoires sur les campagnes de Catalogne de 1808 à 1814* [Paris, Anselin et Pochard, 1826], pp. 164–5).

[27] According to Joseph Reinach, an error was made after the war in giving too much power to the former students of the military schools; the old nobility and the Catholic party were thus able to monopolize the high command.

the Dreyfus affair, but they are not the reasons of the syndicalists.

The army is the clearest and the most tangible of all the possible manifestations of the State and the one which is most firmly connected to its origins. The syndicalists do not propose to reform the State, as the men of the eighteenth century did; they want to destroy it,[28] because they wish to realize this idea of Marx's: the socialist revolution ought not to culminate in the replacement of one governing minority by another.[29] The syndicalists outline their doctrine still more clearly when they give it a more ideological aspect and declare themselves antipatriotic – following the example of the *Communist Manifesto*.

On this issue, it is impossible that there should be the slightest understanding between the syndicalists and the official socialists; the latter speak of breaking up everything, but they attack the men in power rather than power itself; they hope to possess the force of the State and they are aware that, on the day that they control the government, they will need to have an army; they will carry on foreign politics and, consequently, they in their turn will have to praise the feeling of devotion for the homeland.

The parliamentary socialists fully understand that antipatriotism is strongly held in the hearts of the socialist workers and they make great efforts to reconcile the irreconcilable; they are anxious not to oppose too strongly ideas to which the proletariat has become attached, but at the same time they cannot abandon their cherished State, which promises them so much enjoyment. They have stooped to the most comical oratorical acrobatics in order to get over the difficulty. For instance, after the sentence of the Court of Assizes of the Seine, condemning Hervé and the antimilitarists, the National Council of the socialist party passed a resolution condemning this 'verdict of hate and fear', declaring that a class justice could not respect 'liberty of opinion', protesting against the employment of troops in strikes and affirming 'resolutely the necessity for action and for an international understanding among the workers for the

[28] 'The society which will organize production on the basis of a free and equal association of producers will transport the whole machinery of the State to where its place will be henceforward – in the museum of antiquities, by the side of the spinning wheel and the bronze age': ([Friedrich] Engels, *Les Origines de la société*, French trans. [Paris, Jacques, n.d.], p. 281.

[29] *Le Manifeste communiste*, trans. [Charles] Andler [Paris, G. Bellais, 1901], I, p. 39.

suppression of war' (*Le Socialiste*, 20 January 1906). All this is very clever but the fundamental question is avoided.

Thus it cannot any longer be contested that there is an absolute opposition between revolutionary syndicalism and the State; in France this opposition takes the particularly harsh form of antipatriotism, because the politicians have devoted all their skill to spreading confusion in the people's minds about the essence of socialism. On the issue of patriotism there can be no compromises and halfway positions; it is therefore here that the syndicalists have been forced to take a stand when the bourgeois of every description have employed all their powers of seduction to corrupt socialism and to distance the workers from the revolutionary idea. They have been led to deny the idea of patriotism by one of the necessities that are always encountered in the course of history,[30] and which philosophers sometimes have great difficulty in explaining – because the choice is imposed by external conditions and not freely made for reasons drawn from the nature of things. This character of historical necessity gives to the existing antipatriotic movement a strength which it would be useless to attempt to dissimulate by means of sophistries.[31]

We have the right to conclude from this that syndicalist violence, perpetrated in the course of strikes by proletarians who desire the overthrow of the State, must not be confused with the acts of savagery which the superstition of the State suggested to the revolutionaries of [17]93 when they had power in their hands and were able to oppress the conquered – following the principles which they had received from the Church and from the monarchy. We have the right to hope that a socialist revolution carried out by pure syndicalists would not be defiled by the abominations which sullied the bourgeois revolutions.

---

[30] After the trial of Hervé, Léon Daudet wrote: 'Those who followed these debates were thrilled by the theatrical testimonies of the secretaries of the *syndicats*': *La Libre Parole*, 31 December 1905.

[31] Yet Jaurès had the audacity to declare in the Chamber on 11 May 1907 that there was only 'on the surface of the workers' movement a few paradoxical and outrageous formulas which originated, not from the negation of the homeland, but from condemnation of the abuse to which the word and the idea were so often put'. Language like this could only have been used before an assembly that is completely ignorant of the workers' movement.

IV The proletarian strike

I. The confusion of parliamentary socialism and the clarity of the general strike. – Myths in history. – Experimental proof of the value of the general strike.
II. Research carried out to perfect Marxism. – Means of throwing light upon it, starting from the general strike: class struggle; – preparation for the revolution and absence of utopias; – irrevocable character of the revolution.
III. Scientific prejudices against the general strike; doubts about science. – The clear and obscure parts in thought. – Economic incompetence of parliaments.

I

Every time that we attempt to obtain an exact conception of the ideas behind proletarian violence we are forced to go back to the notion of the general strike; but this same notion may provide many other services and throw an unexpected light on all the other obscure parts of socialism. In the last pages of the first chapter I compared the general strike to the Napoleonic battle which definitively crushes an adversary; this comparison will help us to understand the ideological role of the general strike.

When today's military writers discuss the new methods of war necessitated by the employment of troops infinitely more numerous than those of Napoleon and equipped with weapons much more deadly than those of the time, they nevertheless imagine that wars will be decided in Napoleonic battles. The new tactics proposed must fit into the drama Napoleon had conceived; no doubt the detailed development of the combat will be quite different from what it used to be; but the end must always be the catastrophic defeat of the enemy. The methods of military instruction are intended to prepare the soldier for this great and terrible action in which everybody must be prepared to take part at the first signal. From the highest to the lowest, the members of a really solid army always have in mind this catastrophic outcome of international conflicts.

The revolutionary *syndicats* argue about socialist action in exactly the same way as the military writers argue about war; they enclose the whole of socialism in the general strike; they look upon every combination as one that should culminate in this fact; they see in each strike a model, a test, a preparation for the great final upheaval.

The *new school*, which calls itself Marxist, syndicalist and revolutionary, declared in favour of the idea of the general strike as soon as it became clearly conscious of the true sense of its own doctrine, of the consequences of its activity and of its own originality. It was thus led to break with the old official, utopian and political coteries that held the general strike in horror and, in stark contrast, to launch itself into the true movement of the revolutionary proletariat – which, for a long time, had made adherence to the general strike the *test* by means of which the socialism of the workers was distinguished from that of the amateur revolutionaries.

Parliamentary socialists can only have a great influence if, through the use of a very confused language, they can impose themselves on very diverse groups: they must have working-class constituents simple enough to allow themselves to be duped by high-sounding phrases about the future collectivism; they are compelled to represent themselves as profound philosophers to stupid members of the bourgeoisie who wish to appear well informed about social questions; it is very necessary for them to be able to exploit rich people who think that they are earning the gratitude of humanity by taking shares in the enterprises of political socialism. This influence is founded upon gibberish and our great men endeavour, sometimes only too successfully, to spread confusion among the ideas of their readers; they detest the general strike because all the propaganda surrounding it is too socialistic to please philanthropists.

In the mouths of these would-be representatives of the proletariat all socialist formulas lose their real sense. The class struggle still remains the great principle, but it must be subordinated to national solidarity.[1] Internationalism is an article of faith about which the most moderate declare themselves ready to take the most solemn oaths; but patriotism also imposes sacred duties.[2] The emancipation of the workers must be the work of the workers themselves, as their newspapers tell us every day, but real emancipation consists in voting for a professional politician, in securing for him the means of obtaining a comfortable situation, in subjecting oneself to a leader. In the end the State must disappear and they are very careful not to dispute what Engels has written on the subject; but this disappearance will take place only in a future so far distant that one must prepare oneself for it by using the State, meanwhile, as a means of allowing politicians to gorge themselves; and the best means of bringing about the disappearance of the State consists in strengthening temporarily the governmental machine. Gribouille, who threw himself into the water in order to escape getting wet in the rain, would not have reasoned otherwise. And so on and so on.

Whole pages could be filled with the outlines of the contradictory, comical and quack arguments which form the substance of the harangues of our great men; nothing embarrasses them and they know how to combine, in pompous, impetuous and nebulous speeches, the most absolute intransigence with the most supple opportunism. A learned exponent of socialism has maintained that the art of reconciling opposites by means of nonsense is the most obvious result of his study of the works of Marx.[3] I confess my extreme

[1] *Le Petit Parisien*, which makes a speciality of addressing socialist and working-class questions, warned strikers on 31 March 1907, that they 'must never imagine that they are above the duties of social solidarity'.

[2] At the time when the antimilitarists were beginning to occupy public attention, *Le Petit Parisien* was distinguished by its patriotism: on 8 October 1905, it published articles on 'The sacred duty' and 'The worship of the Tricolour Flag which has carried our glories and our liberties all over the world'; on 1 January 1906, it congratulated the jury of the Seine, arguing: 'The flag has been avenged for the insults flung by its detractors on this noble emblem. When it is carried through the streets it is saluted. The jury has done more than bow to it; they have gathered round it with respect.' This is certainly a very cautious socialism.

[3] Two motions had been discussed at length by the National Council, one proposing that departmental federations should be invited to enter the electoral struggle wherever it was possible, the other that candidates should be put forward

incompetence in these difficult matters; moreover, I make no claim whatever to be counted among the people upon whom politicians confer the title of learned; yet I cannot easily bring myself to admit that this is the sum and substance of Marxist philosophy.

The controversy between Jaurès and Clemenceau demonstrates quite incontestably that our parliamentary socialists can succeed in imposing themselves upon the public only through their gibberish and that, as a result of continually deceiving their readers, they have finally lost all sense of honest discussion. In *L'Aurore* of 4 September 1905, Clemenceau accuses Jaurès of muddling the minds of his supporters 'with metaphysical subtleties into which they are incapable of following him'; there is nothing to object to in this accusation, save the use of the word 'metaphysical'; Jaurès is no more a metaphysician than he is a lawyer or an astronomer. In the issue of 26 October, Clemenceau proves that his opponent possesses 'the art of falsifying his texts' and he ends by saying: 'It seemed to me instructive to expose certain polemical practices which we wrongly supposed to be the monopoly of the Jesuits.'[a]

Against this noisy, garrulous and lying socialism, which is exploited by ambitious people of every description, which amuses a few buffoons and is admired by decadents, stands revolutionary syndicalism, which endeavours, on the contrary, to leave nothing in a state of indecision; its ideas are honestly expressed, without trickery and without insinuation; no attempt is made to dilute doctrines by a stream of confused commentaries. Syndicalism strives to employ methods of expression which throw a full light on things, which put them exactly in the place assigned to them by their nature, and which bring out the whole value of the forces in play. Opposition, instead of being glossed over, must be thrown into sharp relief if we are to follow syndicalist thinking; the groups that are struggling against each other must be shown to be as separate as possible; finally, the movements of the revolting masses are presented so as to make a deep and lasting impression on the souls of the rebels.

everywhere. One member got up and said: 'I should be glad of your earnest attention, for the argument which I am about to state may at first sight appear strange and paradoxical. [These two motions] are not irreconcilable, if we try to solve the contradiction according to the *natural Marxist method of resolving all contradiction*': *Le Socialiste*, 7 October 1905. It seems that nobody understood. And, in fact, it was unintelligible.

[a] For Jaurès' reply see *Réplique à Clemenceau* (Paris, Editions de l'Humanité, 1906).

Ordinary language could not produce these results in any very certain manner; appeal must be made to collections of images which, *taken together and through intuition alone*, before any considered analyses are made, are capable of evoking the mass of sentiments which correspond to the different manifestations of the war undertaken by socialism against modern society. The syndicalists solve this problem perfectly by concentrating the whole of socialism in the drama of the general strike; there is thus no longer any place for the reconciliation of opposites through the nonsense of *official thinkers*; everything is clearly mapped out, so that only one interpretation of socialism is possible. This method has all the advantages that integral knowledge has over analysis, according to the doctrine of Bergson; and perhaps it might be possible to cite many other examples which would demonstrate equally well the worth of the famous professor's doctrines.[4]

The possibility of the actual realization of the general strike has been much discussed; it has been stated that the socialist war could not be decided in one single battle; to the practical and scientific *wise men* it seems that the difficulty of setting the great mass of the proletariat in motion at the same time would be prodigious; the difficulties of detail which such an enormous struggle would present have been analysed. It is the opinion of the socialist-sociologists, as also of the politicians, that the general strike is a popular dream characteristic of the beginnings of the working-class movement; cited is the authority of Sidney Webb, who has decreed that the general strike is an illusion of youth,[5] of which the English workers – whom the practitioners of serious science have so often presented to us as the depositories of the true conception of the working-class movement – soon rid themselves.

That the general strike is not popular in contemporary England is a poor argument to bring against the historical significance of the idea, for the English are distinguished by an extraordinary lack of understanding of the class struggle; their ideas have remained very

---

[4] The nature of these articles will not allow of any long discussion of this subject; but I believe that it would be possible to develop still further the application of Bergson's ideas to the theory of the general strike. Movement, in Bergsonian philosophy, is looked upon as an undivided whole; which leads us precisely to the catastrophic conception of socialism.

[5] [Jean] Bourdeau, *L'Evolution du socialisme* (Paris, Alcan, 1901), p. 232. [Sidney Webb (1859–1947); Fabian socialist; author of numerous books and pamphlets, including *The History of Trade Unionism* (1897) and *Industrial Democracy* (1902).]

much dominated by medieval influences; the guild, privileged or at least protected by the law, still seems to them the ideal of working-class organization; it is for England that the term *working-class aristocracy*, as a name for the trade unionists, was invented and, as a matter of fact, trade unionism pursues the acquisition of legal privileges.[6] We might therefore say that the aversion felt by England for the general strike should be looked upon as strong presumptive evidence in favour of the latter by all those who look upon the class struggle as the essence of socialism.

Moreover, Sidney Webb enjoys a reputation for competence that is much exaggerated; he has had the merit of wading through uninteresting documents and has had the patience to produce one of the most extremely indigestible compilations on the history of trade unionism that exists; but he has a mind of the narrowest description which could only impress people unaccustomed to reflection.[7] Those people who introduced his fame into France knew nothing at all about socialism; and if he is really in the first rank of contemporary authors of economic history, as his translator affirms,[8] it is because the intellectual level of these historians is rather low; moreover, many examples show us that it is possible to be a most illustrious professional historian and yet possess a mind something less than mediocre.

Neither do I attach any importance to the objections made to the general strike based on considerations of a practical order; to want to construct hypotheses about the nature of the struggles of the future and the means of suppressing capitalism, on the model furnished by historical accounts, is a return to the old methods of the utopians. There is no process by which the future can be predicted

---

[6] This is seen, for example, in the efforts made by the trade unions to obtain laws absolving them from the civil responsibilities of their actions. [Sorel uses the English 'trade union' in this passage and footnote.]

[7] [Gabriel] Tarde could never understand the reputation enjoyed by Sidney Webb, who seemed to him to be a worthless scribbler.

[8] [Albert] Métin, *Le Socialisme en Angleterre* [Paris, Alcan, 1901], p. 210. This writer received from the government a *certificate of socialism*; on 26 July 1904, the French commissioner-general at the Saint-Louis exhibition said: 'M. Métin is animated by the best democratic spirit; he is an excellent republican; *he is even a socialist* whom working-class organizations should welcome as a friend' (*Association ouvrière*, 30 July 1904). An amusing study could be made of the persons who possess certificates of this kind given to them either by the government, the Musée Social, or the *well-informed press*.

scientifically, nor even one which enables us to discuss whether one hypothesis about it is better than another; innumerable memorable examples have shown that the greatest men have committed prodigious errors in thus desiring to make predictions about even the least distant futures.[9]

And yet we are unable to act without leaving the present, without considering the future, which seems forever condemned to escape our reason. Experience shows that the *framing of the future in some indeterminate time* may, when it is done in a certain way, be very effective and have few inconveniences; this happens when it is a question of myths, in which are found all the strongest inclinations of a people, of a party or of a class, inclinations which recur to the mind with the insistence of instincts in all the circumstances of life, and which give an aspect of complete reality to the hopes of immediate action upon which the reform of the will is founded. We know that these social myths in no way prevent a man from knowing how to profit from the observations he makes in the course of his life and form no obstacle to the pursuit of his normal occupations.[10]

The truth of this can be shown by numerous examples.

The first Christians expected the return of Christ and the total ruin of the pagan world, with the inauguration of the kingdom of the saints, at the end of the first generation. The catastrophe did not come to pass, but Christian thought profited so greatly from the apocalyptic myth that certain contemporary scholars maintain that the whole preaching of Christ referred solely to this one point.[11] – The hopes that Luther and Calvin had formed of the religious exaltation of Europe were by no means realized; very quickly these fathers of the Reformation seemed men of a past era; for present-day Protestants they belong rather to the Middle Ages than to modern times, and the problems which troubled them most occupy very little place in contemporary Protestantism. Must we for that reason deny the immense result that came from their dreams of Christian renovation? – We can readily admit that the real

[9] The errors committed by Marx are numerous and sometimes enormous (cf. G[eorges] Sorel, *Saggi di critica del marxismo* [Palermo, Sandron, 1903], pp. 51–7).

[10] It has often been remarked that English and American sectarians, whose religious exaltation was fed by apocalyptic myths, were often none the less very practical men.

[11] At the present time this doctrine occupies an important place in German exegesis; it was introduced into France by the Abbé Loisy.

developments of the Revolution did not in any way resemble the enchanting pictures which created the enthusiasm of its first adherents; but without those pictures would the Revolution have been victorious? The myth was heavily mixed up with utopias,[12] because it had been formed by a society passionately fond of imaginative literature, full of confidence in the *little science* and very little acquainted with the economic history of the past. These utopias came to nothing; but it may be asked if the Revolution was not a much more profound transformation than those dreamed of by the people who in the eighteenth century had invented social utopias. – In our own time Mazzini pursued what the wise men of his day called a mad chimera; but it can no longer be denied that, without Mazzini, Italy would never have become a great power and that he did more for Italian unity than Cavour[b] and all the politicians of his school.

A knowledge of what the myths contain in the way of details which will actually form part of the history of the future is then of small importance; they are not astrological almanacs; it is even possible that nothing which they contain will come to pass – as was the case with the catastrophe expected by the first Christians.[13] In our own daily life, are we not familiar with the fact that what actually happens is very different from our preconceived notion of it? And that does not prevent us from continuing to make resolutions. Psychologists say that there is heterogeneity between the ends in view and the ends actually realized: the slightest experience of life reveals this law to us, which Spencer transferred into nature in order to arrive at his theory of the multiplication of effects.[14]

Myths must be judged as a means of acting on the present; all discussion of the method of applying them as future history is

---

[12] Cf. the Letter to Daniel Halévy, [section] IV.

[13] I have tried to show how this social myth, which has disappeared, was succeeded by a piety which has remained extremely important in Catholic life; this evolution from the social to the individual seems to me quite natural in a religion (*Le Système historique de Renan*, [Paris, Jacques, 1906], pp. 374–82).

[14] I believe, moreover, that the whole of Spencer's evolutionism is to be explained as an application of the most commonplace psychology to physics. [Herbert Spencer (1820–1903); English philosopher; he coined the phrase 'the survival of the fittest' and did so as part of a broader theory of evolution; evolution was seen as a universal movement from the simple to the complex, the criterion of complexity being the differentiation of their parts and their integration.]

[b] Camillo Benso Cavour (1810–61); the leading politician behind the drive for the unification of Italy, secured in 1861.

devoid of sense. *It is the myth in its entirety which is alone important*: its parts are only of interest in so far as they bring out the main idea. No useful purpose is served, therefore, in arguing about the incidents which may occur in the course of the social war and about the decisive conflicts which may give victory to the proletariat; even supposing the revolutionaries to have been wholly and entirely deluded in setting up this imaginary picture of the general strike, this picture may yet have been, in the course of the preparation of the revolution, a great element of strength if it had embraced all the aspirations of socialism and if it had given to the whole body of revolutionary thought a precision and a rigidity which no other method of thought could have given.

To estimate, then, the significance of the idea of the general strike, all the methods of discussion which are current among politicians, sociologists or people with pretensions to practical science, must be abandoned. Everything which its opponents endeavour to establish may be conceded to them without reducing in any way the value of the thesis which they think they have refuted; it matters little whether the general strike is a partial reality or simply a product of the popular imagination. All that it is necessary to know is whether the general strike contains everything that socialist doctrine expects of the revolutionary proletariat.

To solve this question we are no longer compelled to argue learnedly about the future; we are not obliged to indulge in lofty reflections about philosophy, history or economics; we are not in the domain of ideologies, but we can remain on the level of observable facts. We have to question men who take a very active part in the real revolutionary movement among the proletariat, who do not aspire to climb into the bourgeoisie and whose mind is not dominated by corporative prejudices. These men may be deceived about an infinite number of political, economic or moral questions; but their testimony is decisive, sovereign and irrefutable when it is a question of knowing what are the ideas which most powerfully move them and their comrades, which most appeal to them as being identical with their socialist conceptions, and thanks to which their reason, their hopes and their way of looking at particular facts seem to make but one indivisible unity.[15]

---

[15] This is another application of Bergson's theories.

Thanks to these men, we know that the general strike is indeed what I have said: the *myth* in which socialism is wholly comprised, i.e. a body of images capable of evoking instinctively all the sentiments which correspond to the different manifestations of the war undertaken by socialism against modern society. Strikes have engendered in the proletariat the noblest, the deepest and the most moving sentiments that they possess; the general strike groups them all in a coordinated picture and, by bringing them together, gives to each one of them its maximum intensity; appealing to their painful memories of particular conflicts, it colours with an intense life all the details of the composition presented to consciousness. We thus obtain that intuition of socialism which language cannot give us with perfect clearness – and we obtain it as a whole, perceived instantaneously.[16]

We may urge yet another piece of evidence to prove the power of the idea of the general strike. If this idea was a pure chimera, as is so frequently said, parliamentary socialists would not attack it with such heat; I do not remember that they ever attacked the senseless hopes which the utopians have always held up before the dazzled eyes of the people.[17] In the course of a polemic about realizable social reforms, Clemenceau brought out the Machiavellianism in the attitude of Jaurès when he is confronted with popular illusions: he shelters his conscience beneath 'some cleverly balanced sentence', but one so cleverly balanced that it 'will be received without thinking by those who have the greatest need to probe into its substance, while they will drink in with delight the delusive rhetoric of terrestrial joys to come' (*L'Aurore*, 28 December 1905). But when it is a question of the general strike it is quite another thing; our politicians are no longer content with complicated reservations; they speak violently and endeavour to induce their listeners to abandon this conception.

It is easy to understand the reason for this attitude: politicians have nothing to fear from the utopias which present a deceptive

[16] This is the global knowledge of Bergson's philosophy.

[17] I do not remember that the official socialists have ever shown up all the ridiculousness of the novels of [Edward] Bellamy [1850–1918], which have had so great a success. These novels needed criticism all the more because they presented to the people an entirely middle-class ideal of life. They were a natural product of

image of the future to the people and turn 'men towards immediate realizations of terrestrial felicity which anyone who looks at these matters scientifically knows can only be very partially realized after long efforts'. (This is what socialist politicians do, according to Clemenceau.) The more readily the electors believe in the *magical forces of the State*, the more they will be disposed to vote for the candidate who promises marvels; in the electoral struggle each candidate tries to outbid the other: in order that the socialist candidates may put the Radicals to rout, the electors must be credulous enough to believe every promise for the future;[18] our socialist politicians, therefore, take very good care not to combat these comfortable utopias in any very effective way.

If they struggle against the general strike, it is because they recognise, in the course of their propaganda tours, that the idea of the general strike is so well adapted to the working-class soul that there is the possibility of its dominating the latter in the most absolute manner and of leaving no place for the desires which the parliamentarians are able to satisfy. They perceive that this idea is so effective as a motive force that once it has entered into the minds of the people they can no longer be controlled by leaders and thus that the power of the deputies would be reduced to nothing. In short, they feel in a vague way that the whole socialist movement might easily be absorbed by the general strike, which would render useless all the compromises between political groups in view of which the parliamentary regime has been built up.

The opposition of the official socialists therefore furnishes a confirmation of our first enquiry into the significance of the general strike.

II

We must now proceed further and enquire whether the picture furnished by the general strike is really complete; that is to say, whether it comprises all those features of the struggle which are recognized by modern socialism. But, first of all, we must state the problem more precisely; this will be easy if we start from the

America, a country that is ignorant of the class struggle; but in Europe would not the theorists of the class struggle have understood them?

[18] In the article which I have already quoted, Clemenceau recalls that Jaurès made use of these outbidding tactics in a long speech which he made at Béziers.

explanations given above on the nature of this conception. We have
seen that the general strike must be considered as an undivided
whole; consequently, no details about ways and means will be of
the slightest help to the understanding of socialism; it must even be
added that there is always a danger of losing something of this
understanding if an attempt is made to split up this whole into
parts. We will now endeavour to show that there is a fundamental
identity between the chief tenets of Marxism and the coordinated
aspects furnished by the picture of the general strike.

This affirmation is certain to appear paradoxical to many who have
read the publications of the most authoritative Marxists. In fact, for
a very long time there existed a marked hostility to the general
strike in Marxist circles. This tradition has done a great deal of
harm to the progress of Marx's doctrine; and it is a very good
illustration of the way in which, as a rule, disciples tend to restrict
the application of their master's ideas. The *new school* had considerable difficulty in liberating itself from these influences; it was
formed by people who had received the Marxist imprint in a very
marked degree; and it was a long time before it recognized that the
objections brought against the general strike arose from the incapacity of the official representatives of Marxism rather than the
principles of the doctrine itself.[19]

The *new school* began its emancipation on the day when it
perceived clearly that the formulas of socialism were often very
far from the spirit of Marx and when it recommended a return
to this spirit. It was not without a certain element of stupefaction
that it realised that it had credited the master with would-be
inventions that came from his predecessors or which were commonplaces at the time when the *Communist Manifesto* was drawn
up. According to one author who – in the opinion of the government and of the Musée Social – is considered to be well

[19] In an article, *Introduction à la métaphysique*, published in 1903, Bergson points out
that disciples are always inclined to exaggerate the points of difference between
masters and that 'the master in so far as he formulates, develops, translates into
abstract ideas what he brings is already in a way his own disciple' (*Cahiers de la
Quinzaine*, 12th of the IV series [17 February 1903], pp. 22–3). [See 'Introduction
to metaphysics', in H[enri] Bergson, *The Creative Mind* (New York, Greenwood
Press, 1968), p. 235.]

informed: 'the accumulation [of capital in the hands of a few individuals] is one of the great discoveries of Marx, one of the discoveries of which he was most proud'.[20] With all due deference to the historical science of this notable university expert, this theory was one which was widely known long before Marx had ever written a word and it had become an established truth in the socialist world by the end of the reign of Louis-Philippe.[c] There are many Marxist theses of the same kind.

A decisive step towards reform was made when those Marxists who aspired to think for themselves began to study the syndicalist movement; they discovered that 'the genuine members of the *syndicats* have more to teach us than they have to learn from us'.[21] This was the beginning of wisdom; it was a step towards the realist method which had led Marx to his true discoveries; in this way a return might be made to those methods which alone merit the name philosophical, 'because true and fruitful ideas are so many close contacts with currents of reality' and they 'owe most of their clearness to the light which the facts, and the applications to which they led, have by reflection shed on them – the clarity of a concept being scarcely anything more at bottom than the certainty, at last obtained, of manipulating the concept profitably'.[22] And yet another profound thought of Bergson may be usefully quoted: 'We do not obtain an intuition of reality, that is, *an intellectual sympathy with the most intimate part of it*, unless we have won its confidence by a long fellowship with its superficial manifestations. And it is not merely a question of assimilating the most conspicuous facts; so immense a mass of facts must be *accumulated and fused* together, that in this fusion all the preconceived and premature ideas which observers may unwittingly have put into their observations will be certain to neutralize each other. Only in this way can the bare

---

[20] Métin, [*La Socialisme*], p. 191.
[21] G[eorges] Sorel, *L'Avenir socialiste des syndicats* [Paris, Jacques, 1898], p. 12. [See 'The Socialist Future of the Syndicates', in John L. Stanley (ed.), *From Georges Sorel: Essays in Socialism and Philosophy* (New York, Oxford University Press, 1976), p. 75.]
[22] Bergson [*Introduction à la métaphysique*], p. 21. [See 'Introduction to metaphysics', pp. 233–4.]

[c] Louis-Philippe (1773–1850) was deposed in the revolution of 1848, bringing the July Monarchy (1830–48) to an end.

materiality of the known facts be exposed to view.' Finally, what Bergson calls an *integral experience* is obtained.[23]

Thanks to the new principle, people very soon came to recognize that the propositions with which people had tried to encircle and enclose socialism were deplorably inadequate and were often more dangerous than useful. It is the superstitious respect paid by social democracy to the mere text of its doctrines that nullified every attempt in Germany to perfect Marxism.

When the *new school* had acquired a full understanding of the general strike and had thus obtained a profound intuition of the working-class movement, it saw that all the socialist theories, interpreted in the light of this powerful construction, took on a clarity which till then they had lacked; it perceived that the clumsy and rickety apparatus which had been manufactured in Germany to explain Marx's doctrines had to be rejected if the contemporary transformation of the proletarian idea was to be followed exactly; it discovered that the idea of the general strike enabled them to explore profitably the whole vast domain of Marxism which until then had remained practically unknown to the pundits who professed to be guiding socialism. Thus the fundamental principles of Marxism are perfectly intelligible only with the aid of the picture of the general strike and, on the other hand, the full significance of this picture, it may be supposed, is only apparent to those deeply versed in Marxist doctrine.

A. – First of all, I will speak of the class struggle, which is the point of departure for all socialist thought and which stands in such great need of elucidation as sophists have endeavoured to give a false idea of it.

1) Marx speaks of society as if it were divided into two fundamentally antagonistic groups; observation, it has often been urged, does not justify this thesis of dichotomy and it is true that a certain effort of the will is necessary before we can find it verified in the phenomena of everyday life.

The organization of a capitalist workshop furnishes a first approximation and piece-work plays an essential part in the formation of the class idea; in fact, it throws into relief the very clear

[23] *Ibid.*, pp. 24–5. [See 'Introduction to metaphysics', p. 237.]

opposition of interests about the price of commodities:[24] the workers feel themselves under the thumb of the employers in the same way that peasants feel themselves in the power of the merchants and the money-lenders of the towns; history shows that no economic opposition has been more clearly felt than this latter power; since civilization has existed, country and town have formed two hostile camps.[25] Piece-work also shows that in the wage-earning world there is a group of men somewhat analogous to the retail shop-keepers, possessing the confidence of the employer and not belonging to the world of the proletariat.

The strike throws a new light on all this; it separates the interests and the different ways of thinking of the two groups of wage-earners much better than do the daily circumstances of life. It then becomes clear that the administrative group has a natural tendency to become a little aristocracy; for these people, State socialism would be advantageous because they would go up one in the social hierarchy.

But all these oppositions become extraordinarily clear when conflicts are seen as being enlarged to the size of the general strike; then all the parts of the economico-judicial structure, in so far as the latter is looked upon from the point of view of the class struggle, reach the summit of their perfection; society is plainly divided into two camps, and only into two, on the field of battle. No philosophical explanation of the facts observed in practical affairs could furnish such vivid light as the extremely simple picture that the evocation of the general strike puts before our eyes.

2) It would be impossible to conceive of the disappearance of capitalist dominance if we did not suppose an ardent sentiment of revolt, always present in the soul of the worker; but experience shows that, very often, the revolts of a day are very far from possessing a really specifically socialist character; more than once the most violent outbursts have depended on passions which could be satisfied inside the bourgeois world; many revolutionaries have been seen to abandon their old intransigence when they found themselves

---

[24] I do not know whether the *experts* have always quite understood the function of piece-work. It is evident that the well-known formula – 'the producer should be able to buy back his product' – arose from reflections on the subject of piece-work.

[25] 'It may be said that the economic history of society turns on this antithesis' of town and country. (*Le Capital* [Paris, Librariè du progrès, 1875], I, p. 153, col. 1). [See *Capital*, (New York, Charles H. Kerr, 1906), p. 387.]

on the road to fortune.[26] – It is not only considerations of a material kind which produce these frequent and scandalous conversions; vanity, much more than money, is the great motive force in the passage of the revolutionary into the bourgeoisie. – All that would be of negligible importance if it were only a question of a few exceptional people; but it has often been maintained that the psychology of the working masses is so easily adapted to the capitalist order that social peace would be rapidly obtained if the employers on their part would make a few sacrifices.

G[ustave] Le Bon says that it is a mistake to believe in the revolutionary instincts of the crowd, that their tendencies are conservative, that the whole power of socialism lies in the rather muddled state of mind of the bourgeoisie; he is convinced that the masses will always go to a Caesar.[27] There is a good deal of truth in these judgements, which are founded on a very wide knowledge of history, but the theories of G. Le Bon must be corrected in one respect; they are only valid for societies that lack the conception of class struggle.

Observation shows that this conception is maintained with an indestructible vitality in every environment which has been touched by the idea of the general strike: the day when the slightest incidents of daily life become symptoms of the state of struggle between the classes, when every conflict is an incident in the social war, when every strike engenders the perspective of a total catastrophe, on that day there is no longer any possibility of social peace, of resignation to routine, or of enthusiasm for philanthropic or successful employers. The idea of the general strike has such motive power behind it that it drags into the revolutionary track everything it touches. In virtue of this idea, socialism remains ever young; all attempts to bring about social peace seem childish; desertions of

---

[26] It may be remembered that in the eruption on Martinique a governor perished who, in 1879, had been one of the protagonists of the socialist congress at Marseilles. The Commune itself was not fatal to all its partisans; several have had fairly successful careers; the ambassador of France in Rome was amongst those who, in 1871, demanded the death of the hostages.

[27] G[ustave] Le Bon, *Psychologie du socialisme* [Paris, Alcan, 1902], 3rd edn, p. 111 and pp. 457–9. The author, who a few years ago was treated as an imbecile by the little bullies of university socialism, is one of the most original physicists of our time. [Here Sorel makes reference to the polemic between Le Bon and Jean Perrin, future winner of the Nobel prize for physics, that took place in the pages of *La Revue du mois* at the end of 1907.]

comrades into the ranks of the bourgeoisie, far from discouraging the masses, only excite them still more to rebellion; in a word, the line of cleavage is never in danger of disappearing.

3) The successes obtained by politicians in their attempts to make what they call the proletarian influence felt in bourgeois institutions constitute a very great obstacle to the maintenance of the notion of class struggle. The world has always been carried on by compromises between opposing parties and order has always been provisional; no change, however inconsiderable, can be looked upon as impossible in a time like ours, which has seen so many novelties introduced in an unexpected manner. Modern progress has been brought about by successive compromises; why not pursue the aims of socialism by methods which have succeeded so well? Many means of satisfying the more pressing desires of the unfortunate classes can be thought of. For a long time these proposals for improvement were inspired by a conservative, feudal or Catholic spirit; we wished, said the inventors, to rescue the masses from the influence of the Radicals. The latter, seeing their political influence threatened, not so much by their old enemies as by socialist politicians, today invent all kinds of projects of a progressive, democratic, free-thinking colour. We are beginning at last to be threatened with socialist compromises!

Enough attention has not always been paid to the fact that many kinds of political, administrative and financial organization can adjust themselves to the domination of a bourgeoisie. We must not always attach too much importance to violent attacks on the bourgeoisie; they may be motivated by the desire to reform and to perfect capitalism.[28] There are, it seems, quite a number of people today who, though not in the least desiring the disappearance of the capitalist regime, would willingly abolish inheritance, such as the followers of Saint-Simon.[29]

---

[28] I know, for instance, a very enlightened Catholic who gives vent with singular acrimony to his contempt for the French middle class; but his ideal is Americanism, i.e. a very young and very active capitalism.

[29] P[aul] de Rousiers was very much struck by the way rich fathers in the United States forced their sons to earn their own living; he often met 'Frenchmen who were profoundly shocked by what they called the egoism of American fathers. It seemed revolting to them that a rich man should leave his son to earn his own living, that he did nothing *to set him up in life*': *La Vie américaine: l'éducation et la société* [Paris, Firmin-Didot, 1899], p. 9. [Claude-Henri de Rouvray, comte de

The general strike destroys all the theoretical consequences of every possible social policy; its supporters look upon even the most popular reforms as having a bourgeois character; so far as they are concerned, nothing can weaken the fundamental opposition of the class struggle. The more the policy of social reforms becomes preponderant, the more will socialism feel the need of placing against the picture of progress which it is the aim of this policy to bring about, the picture of the complete catastrophe furnished so perfectly by the general strike.

B. – Let us now examine, with the aid of the conception of the general strike, certain very essential aspects of the Marxist revolution.

1) Marx says that, on the day of the revolution, the proletariat will be disciplined, united and organized by the very mechanism of production. This exceedingly concentrated formula would not be very intelligible if we did not read it in connection with its context; according to Marx, the working class is bowed beneath a system in which 'abject poverty, oppression, slavery, degradation and exploitation increase' and against which it is organizing an ever-increasing resistance until the day when the whole social structure breaks up.[30] The accuracy of this famous description has been many times disputed; it seems to be more suited to the period of the *Manifesto* (1847) than to the time of *Capital* (1867); but this objection must not stop us and it may be thrust to one side by means of the theory of myths. The different terms which Marx uses to describe the preparation for the decisive combat are not to be taken literally as statements of fact about a determined future; it is the description in its entirety which should engage our attention, and taken in this way it is perfectly clear: Marx wishes us to understand that the whole preparation of the proletariat depends solely upon the organization of a stubborn, increasing and passionate resistance to the present order of things.

Saint-Simon (1760–1825); one of the utopian socialists much vilified by Karl Marx. Largely ignored during his lifetime, his followers (most notably Armand Bazard (1791–1832) and Barthélemy-Prosper Enfantin (1796–1832)) developed his ideas in such texts as *L'Exposition de la doctrine saint-simonienne* (1828–30), where, amongst other radical proposals, they recommended the abolition of property rights.]

[30] Marx, *Le Capital*, I, p. 342, col. 1. [See *Capital*, p. 836.]

This thesis is of supreme importance if we are to have a sound understanding of Marxism; but it is often contested, if not in theory, at least in practice; the proletariat, it is held, should prepare for the part it is to play in the future by other ways than those of revolutionary syndicalism. Thus the exponents of cooperation hold that a prominent place in the work of emancipation must be given to their own particular remedy; the democrats say that it is essential to abolish all the prejudices arising from the old Catholic influence, etc. Many revolutionaries believe that, however useful syndicalism may be, it is not in itself sufficient to organize a society which needs a new philosophy, a new code of laws, etc.; as the division of labour is a fundamental law of the world, socialists should not be ashamed to apply to specialists in philosophy and law, of whom there is never any lack. Jaurès never stops repeating this kind of rubbish. This *expansion* of socialism is contrary to Marxist theory as also to the conception of the general strike; but it is evident that the general strike makes a much more forcible appeal to the mind than any formula.

2) I have called attention to the danger for the future of civiliz-ation presented by revolutions that take place in an era of economic decline not all the Marxists seem to have formed a clear idea of Marx's thought on this subject. The latter believed that the great catastrophe would be preceded by an enormous economic crisis, but the crises Marx had in mind must not be confused with economic decline; crises appeared to him as the result of a too-risky venture on the part of production, which creates productive forces out of proportion to the means of regulation which the capitalist system automatically brings into play. Such a venture supposes that the future was looked upon as favourable to very large enterprises and that the conception of economic progress prevailed absolutely at the time. In order that the lower middle classes, who are still able to find tolerable conditions of existence under the capitalist regime, may join hands with the proletariat, it is essential that they can picture the future of production as being as bright with hope as the conquest of America formerly appeared to the English peasants who left old Europe to throw themselves into a life of adventure.

The general strike leads to the same conclusions. The workers are accustomed to seeing their revolts against the restrictions imposed by capitalism succeed during periods of prosperity; so that it may be said that if you once identify revolution and general strike it then becomes impossible to conceive that an essential transformation of the world can take place in a time of economic decline. The workers are equally aware that the peasants and the artisans will not join hands with them unless the future appears so rosy-coloured that industry will be able to ameliorate the lot not only of the producers but that of everybody.[31]

It is very important always to lay stress on the high degree of prosperity which industry must possess in order that the realization of socialism may be possible; for experience shows us that it is by seeking to stop the progress of capitalism and to preserve the forms of existence of classes who are on the decline that the prophets of social peace endeavour to capture popular favour. The connections which link revolution to the constant and rapid progress of industry must be demonstrated in a striking manner.[32]

3) Too much stress cannot be laid on the fact that Marxism condemns every hypothesis about the future constructed by the utopians. Professor Brentano of Munich relates that in 1869 Marx wrote to his friend Beesly (who had published an article on the future of the working class) to say that up till then he had looked upon him as the sole revolutionary Englishman and that henceforth he looked upon him as a reactionary – for, he said, 'whoever draws up a programme for the future is a reactionary'.[33] He considered that the proletariat had no need to take lessons from the learned inventors of solutions to social problems but simply to take up

---

[31] It is not difficult to see that the propagandists are obliged to refer frequently to this aspect of the social revolution: this will take place while the intermediary classes are still in existence, but when they become sickened by the farce of social peace and when a period of such great economic progress has been reached that the future will appear in colours favourable to everybody.

[32] Kautsky has often dwelt on this idea, of which Engels was particularly fond.

[33] Bernstein said about this story that Brentano might have exaggerated a little, but that 'the phrase quoted by him was not inconsistent with Marx's general line of thought' ([Eduard] Bernstein, 'Des Forces de la démocratie industrielle', *Le Mouvement socialiste* [2], 1 September 1899, p. 270). Of what can utopias be composed? Of the past and often of a very far-off past; it is probably for this reason that Marx called Beesly a *reactionary* while everybody else was astonished at his revolutionary boldness. The Catholics are not the only people to be hypnotized by the Middle Ages, and Yves Guyot pokes fun at the '*collectivist troubadourism*' of Lafargue ([Paul] Lafargue and Y[ves] Guyot, *La Propriété* [*Origine et évolution: thèse communiste par P. Lafargue; réfutation par Y. Guyot*], [Paris, Delagrave, 1895], pp. 121–2).

where capitalism left off. There was no need for programmes of the future; the programmes were already worked out in the workshops. The idea of a technological continuity dominates the whole of the Marxist position.

Experience gained in strikes leads us to a conception identical with that of Marx. The workers who put down their tools do not go to their employers with schemes for the better organization of labour and do not offer them assistance in the management of their business; in short, utopias have no place in economic conflicts. Jaurès and his friends are well aware that this is a very strong argument against their own ideas of the way in which socialism is to be realized: they would like even now to have fragments of the industrial programmes manufactured by learned sociologists and accepted by the workers introduced into strike negotiations; they would like to see the creation of what they call *industrial parliamentarism* which, exactly as in the case of political parliamentarism, would imply masses who are led and demagogues that show them the way. This would be the apprentice stage of their sham socialism and might begin at once.

With the general strike all these fine things disappear; the revolution appears as a revolt, pure and simple, and no place is reserved for sociologists, for fashionable people who are in favour of social reforms, and for Intellectuals who have embraced *the profession of thinking for the proletariat.*

C. – Socialism has always inspired fear because of the enormous element of the unknown which it contains; people feel that a transformation of this kind would permit of no turning back. The utopians used all their literary art in the endeavour to lull anxiety by pictures of the future so enchanting that all fear might be banished; but the more they accumulated fine promises, the more did thoughtful people suspect traps – and in this they were not completely mistaken, for the utopians would have led the world to disasters, tyranny and stupidity if they had been listened to.

Marx was firmly convinced that the social revolution of which he spoke would constitute an *irrevocable transformation* and that it would mark an absolute separation between two historical eras; he often returned to this idea whilst Engels endeavoured to show, by means of images that were sometimes a little grandiose, how

economic emancipation would be the point of departure of an era
having no relationship with the past. Rejecting all utopias, these
two founders renounced all the resources by which their predecessors had rendered the prospect of a great revolution less intimidating; but however strong the impressions which they employed
might have been, the effects which they produced are still very
inferior to those produced by the evocation of the general strike.
This conception makes it impossible not to see that a kind of irresistible wave will pass over the old civilization.

There is something really frightening in this; but I believe that
it is absolutely essential that this feature of socialism should be
insisted upon if it is to have its full educational value. Socialists
must be convinced that the work to which they are devoting themselves is a *serious, formidable and sublime work*; it is only on this
condition that they will be able to bear the innumerable sacrifices
imposed on them by a propaganda which can produce neither honours, profits nor even immediate intellectual satisfaction. Even if
the only result of the idea of the general strike was to make the
socialist conception more heroic, it should on that account alone be
looked upon as having an incalculable value.

The resemblances which I have just established between Marxism
and the general strike might be carried still further and deepened;
if they have been overlooked hitherto, it is because we are much
more struck by the form of things than by their content; a large
number of people find great difficulty in believing that there can be
any parallelism between a philosophy based on Hegelianism and the
constructions made by men entirely devoid of higher culture. Marx
had acquired in Germany a taste for very condensed formulas and
these formulas were so admirably suited to the conditions in the
midst of which he worked that he naturally made great use of them.
When he was writing, there had been none of the great and numerous events which would have enabled him to speak with a detailed
knowledge of the means by which the proletariat may prepare itself
for the revolution. This absence of knowledge gained from experience very much hampered Marx's thought; he avoided the use of
too-precise formulas which would have had the inconvenience of
giving a kind of sanction to existing institutions that seemed value-
less to him; he was happy therefore to be able to find in German

academic writing a habit of abstract language which allowed him to avoid all discussion of detail.[34]

No better proof perhaps can be given of Marx's genius than the remarkable agreement which is found to exist between his views and the doctrine that revolutionary syndicalism is today building slowly and laboriously, keeping always strictly to strike tactics.

III

For some time yet, the conception of the general strike will have considerable difficulty in being accepted in circles which are not specially dominated by strike tactics. I think that it might be useful at this point to enquire into the motives which explain the repugnance felt by many intelligent and sincere people who are disturbed by the novelty of the syndicalist point of view. All the members of the *new school* know that they had to make great efforts in order to overcome the prejudices of their education, to set aside the associations of ideas which sprang up spontaneously in their mind, and to reason along lines which in no way corresponded to those which they had been taught.

During the nineteenth century there existed an incredible scientific ingenuousness which was the direct outcome of the illusions that had aroused so much excitement towards the end of the eighteenth century.[35] Because astronomers had managed to calculate the tables of the moon, it was believed that the aim of science was to forecast the future with accuracy; because Le Verrier had been able to indicate the probable position of the planet Neptune – which had never been seen and which accounted for the disturbances of the

---

[34] I have elsewhere put forward the hypothesis that Marx, in the penultimate chapter of the first volume of *Capital*, perhaps wished to demonstrate the difference between the evolution of the proletariat and that of bourgeois force. He said that the working class is disciplined, united and organized by the very mechanism of capitalist production. There is perhaps an indication of a movement towards liberty, opposed to the movement towards automatism which will be discussed later when we come to consider bourgeois force ([Sorel], *Saggi di critica*, pp. 46–7).

[35] The history of scientific superstitions is of the deepest interest to philosophers who wish to understand socialism. These superstitions have remained dear to our democracy, as they had been dear to the great minds of the *ancien régime*; I have touched on a few of the aspects of this history in *Les Illusions du progrès*. Engels was often under the influence of these errors, from which Marx himself was not always free.

planets – it was believed that science could remedy the defects of society and indicate what measures should be taken to bring about the disappearance of the unpleasant things in the world. It may be said that this was the *bourgeois conception of science*: it certainly corresponds very closely to the mental attitude of those capitalists who, ignorant of the perfected techniques of the workshop, yet direct industry and always find ingenious inventors to get them out of their difficulties. For the bourgeoisie, science is a mill which produces solutions to all the problems we are faced with:[36] science is no longer considered as a perfected means to knowledge, but only as a recipe for procuring certain advantages.[37]

I have said that Marx rejected all attempts to determine the conditions of a future society: too much stress cannot be laid upon this point, for it shows that Marx took his stand outside bourgeois science. The doctrine of the general strike also repudiates this science and many professors consequently accuse the *new school* of having negative ideas only; their own aim, on the other hand, is the noble one of constructing universal happiness. The leaders of social democracy, it seems to me, have not been very Marxist on this point; a few years ago Kautsky wrote a preface to a somewhat comic utopia.[38]

I believe that among the motives which led Bernstein to part from his old friends must be counted the horror which he felt for their utopias. If Bernstein had lived in France and had known our revolutionary syndicalism, he would soon have perceived that the latter was on the true Marxist track: but neither in England nor in Germany did he find a working-class movement which could guide him; wishing to remain attached to realities, as Marx had been, he thought that it was better to carry on a policy of social reform, pursuing practical ends, than to lull himself asleep to the sound of fine phrases about the happiness of future humanity.

[36] Marx cites this curious phrase by Ure, written about 1830: 'This invention supports the doctrine already developed by us: if *capital enlists the aid of science*, the rebel hand of labour always learns how to be tractable': *Le Capital*, I, p. 188, col. 2. [See *Capital*, p. 477.]

[37] To use the language of the *new school*, science was considered from the point of view of the consumer and not from the point of view of the producer.

[38] Atlanticus, [Carl Ballod], *Ein Blick in den Zukunfisstaat* [Stuttgart, Dietz, 1898]. E[rnest] Seillière reviewed this book in the *Débats* of 16 August 1899.

The worshippers of this useless pseudo-science did not allow themselves to be stopped by the objection, legitimate in this case, that their methods of calculation were entirely inadequate in their means of determination. Their conception of science, being derived from astronomy, supposes that everything can be expressed by some mathematical law. Evidently there are no laws of this kind in sociology; but man is always susceptible to analogies connected with the forms of expression: it was thought that a high degree of perfection had been attained and that something had already been accomplished for science when – starting from a few principles not offensive to common sense and which seemed confirmed by a few common experiences – it had been found possible to present a doctrine in a simple, clear and deductive manner. This so-called science is simply chatter.[39]

The utopians excelled in the art of exposition in accordance with these prejudices; the more their exposition satisfied the requirements of a school book, the more convincing they thought their inventions were. I believe that the contrary of this belief is the truth and that we should distrust proposals for social reform all the more when every difficulty seems solved in a apparently satisfactory manner.

I should like to examine here, very briefly, a few of the illusions which have arisen out of what may be called the *little science*, which believes that when it has attained clarity of exposition that it has

---

[39] 'It has not been enough noticed how feeble is the reach of deduction in the psychological and moral sciences ... Very soon appeal has to be made to common sense, that is to say, to the continuous experience of the real, in order to infect the consequences deduced and bend them along the sinuosities of life. *Deduction succeeds in things moral only metaphorically*, so to speak': [Henri] Bergson, *L'Evolution créatrice* [Paris, Alcan, 1907], pp. 231–2. [See *Creative Evolution* (London, Macmillan, 1911), p. 224.] Newman had already written something similar to this but in more precise terms: 'Thus it is that the logician for his own purposes, and most usefully as far as these purposes are concerned, turns rivers, full, winding and beautiful, into navigable canals ... His business is not to ascertain facts in the concrete but to find and dress up middle terms; and provided that they and the extremes which they go between are not equivocal, either in themselves or in their use. Supposing he can enable his pupils to show well in a *viva voce* disputation ... he has achieved the main purpose of his profession': *Grammaire de l'assentiment* [French trans. (Paris, Bloud, 1907)], pp. 261–2. [See *An Essay in Aid of a Grammar of Assent*, (London, Burnes, Oates & Co., 1870)]. There is no weakness in this denunciation of small talk.

attained truth. This *little science* has contributed a great deal towards creating the crisis of Marxism and every day we hear the *new school* accused of delighting in the obscurities of which Marx has so often been accused, while French socialists and Belgian sociologists, on the contrary . . . !

Perhaps the best way of giving an accurate idea of the error committed by these sham scientists against whom the *new school* wages war will be to examine the general characteristics of some social phenomena and to run through some of the achievements of the mind, beginning with the highest.

A. – 1) The positivists, who represent, in an eminent degree, mediocrity, pride and pedantry, had decreed that philosophy was to give way before *their science*; but philosophy is not dead and it has acquired a new and vigorous lease of life thanks to Bergson, who, far from wishing to reduce everything to science, has claimed for the philosopher the right to proceed in a manner quite opposed to that employed by the scientist. It might be said that metaphysics has reclaimed the lost ground by demonstrating to man the illusion of so-called scientific solutions and by bringing the mind back to the mysterious region which the *little science* abhors. Positivism is still admired by a few Belgians, the employees of the Office du Travail, and General André;[40] but these are people who count for very little in the world of thought.

2) Religions do not seem to be on the point of disappearing. Liberal Protestantism is dying because it attempted, at all costs, to give a perfectly rationalistic exposition of Christian theology. A. Comte[d] manufactured a caricature of Catholicism, in which he had

---

[40] A few years ago, this illustrious warrior (?) was instrumental in blocking the candidature for the Collège de France of Paul Tannery [1843–1903], whose erudition was universally recognized in Europe, in favour of a positivist. The positivists constitute a lay congregation which is ready for any dirty work. [General Louis-Joseph-Nicolas André (1838–1913) was minister of war between 1900–4. He was forced to resign as a result of the so-called 'affaire des fiches', when it was revealed that he had introduced a system of promotion in the army which depended upon political affiliation to the Republic (and, by implication, to positivism).]

[d] Auguste Comte (1798–1857); sociologist and philosopher; author of the *Cours de philosophie positive* (1830–42); towards the end of his life he attempted to turn his positivist philosophy into a Religion of Humanity which copied many of the organizational and devotional practices of the Catholic Church.

retained only the administrative, hierarchical and disciplinary machinery of that Church; his attempt obtained success only with those people who like to laugh at the simplicity of those they were duping. In the course of the nineteenth century, Catholicism recovered strength to an extraordinary degree because it would abandon nothing; it even strengthened its mysteries and, what is very curious, it gains ground in cultivated circles where the rationalism which was formerly in fashion at the University is scoffed at.[41]

3) Nowadays we look upon the old claim made by our fathers that they had created a science of art or even that they could describe a work of art in so adequate a manner that the reader could obtain from a book an exact aesthetic appreciation of a picture or of a statue as a perfect example of pedantry. Taine's efforts in the direction first mentioned are very interesting but only as regards the history of the various schools. His methods give us no useful information about the works themselves. As for the descriptions, they are only of value if the works themselves are of small aesthetic quality and if they belong to what is sometimes called *literary painting*. The poorest photograph of the Parthenon conveys a hundred times as much information as a volume devoted to the praise of the marvels of this monument; it seems to me that the famous *Prière sur l'Acropole*, so often praised as one of the finest passages in Renan, is a rather remarkable example of rhetoric and that it is much more likely to render Greek art unintelligible to us than to make us admire the Parthenon. Despite all his enthusiasm for Diderot (which is sometimes comical and expressed nonsensically), Joseph Reinach[e] is obliged to acknowledge that his hero was lacking in artistic feeling in his famous *Salons*, because Diderot appreciated most of all those pictures which offered possibilities of literary dissertation.[42] Brunetière could say that Diderot's *Salons* were the

---

[41] Pascal protested eloquently against those who considered obscurity an objection against Catholicism and it is with reason that Brunetière looked upon him as being one of the most anticartesian of the men of his time (*Etudes critiques [sur l'histoire de la littérature française]*, 4th series, [Paris, Hachette, 1891], pp. 144–9).

[42] J[oseph] Reinach, *Diderot* [Paris, Hachette, 1894], pp. 116–17, 125–7, 131–2.

[e] Joseph Reinach (1856–1921); a supporter of Gambetta and later a member of parliament; he was from the outset one of the principal advocates of the Dreyfusard cause; author of the *Histoire de l'affaire Dreyfus* (1901–11).

corruption of criticism, because he discussed works of art in them as if they were books.[43]

The impotence of speech is due to the fact that art flourishes best on mystery, half shades and indeterminate outlines; the more speech is methodical and perfect, the more likely is it to eliminate everything that distinguishes a masterpiece; it reduces the masterpiece to the proportions of an academic product.

As a result of this preliminary examination of the three highest achievements of the mind, we are led to believe that it is possible to distinguish in every complex body of knowledge a clear and an obscure region, and to say that the latter is perhaps the most important. The mistake made by the mediocre consists in the statement that this second part must disappear with the progress of enlightenment and that eventually everything will be explained in terms of the *little science*. This error is particularly abhorrent as regards art and, above all perhaps, as regards modern painting, which seeks more and more to render combinations of shades to which no attention was formerly paid on account of their lack of stability and of the difficulty of rendering them by speech.[44]

B. – 1) In ethics, the part that can be expressed easily in clearly reasoned expositions is that which has reference to the equitable relations between men; it contains maxims which are to be found in many different civilizations; consequently it was for a long time believed that a summary of these precepts might form the basis of a natural morality applicable to the whole of humanity. The obscure part of morality is that which has reference to sexual relationships; this is not easily expressed in formulas; to understand it thoroughly you must have lived in a country for a great number of years. It is, moreover, the fundamental part; when it is known, the whole psychology of a people is understood; the supposed uniformity of the first system in reality then conceals many differences; almost identical maxims may correspond to very different applications; their clearness was only a delusion.

[43] [Ferdinand] Brunetière, *Evolution des genres* [*dans l'histoire de la littérature*], [Paris, Hachette, 1898], p. 122. Elsewhere he calls Diderot a *philistine*, p. 153.

[44] It is to the great credit of the *impressionists* that they showed that these fine shades can be rendered by painting; but some few among them soon began to paint according to the formulas of a school and then there appeared a scandalous contrast between their works and their avowed aims.

2) In legislation, everybody sees immediately that the law regulating contracts and debts constitutes the clearest part, that which is called scientific; here again there is a great uniformity in the rules adopted by different peoples, and it was believed that it was eminently desirable to draw up a common code founded on a rational revision of those that existed; but in practice it is again found that, in different countries, the courts generally attach different meanings to these supposed common principles; that is because there is something individual and particular in each maxim. The mysterious region is the family, whose organization influences all social relationships. Le Play was very struck by an opinion of Tocqueville on this subject: 'I am astonished', said this great thinker, 'that ancient and modern publicists have not attributed a greater influence on the progress of human affairs to the laws of inheritance. These laws, it is true, refer to civil affairs but they should be placed at the head of all political institutions, for they have an incredible influence on the social condition of peoples, of which political laws are only an expression.'[45] This remark governed all the researches of Le Play.

This division of legislation into a clear and an obscure region has one curious consequence: it is very rare for people who are not members of the legal professions to undertake any discussion of the principles of justice; they know that it is necessary to have an intimate knowledge of certain rules of law in order to be able to argue about these questions: an outsider would run the risk of making himself ridiculous if he were to venture on an opinion; but on the question of divorce, of paternal authority, of inheritance, every man of letters believes himself as learned as the cleverest lawyer, because in this obscure region there are no well-defined principles nor regular deductions.

3) In economics, the same distinction is, perhaps, still more evident; questions relative to exchange can be easily expounded; the methods of exchange are very much alike in the different countries, and it is hardly likely that any very violent paradoxes will be ventured about monetary circulation; on the other hand, everything

---

[45] [Alexis de] Tocqueville, *De la démocratie en Amérique* [Paris, Calmann-Lévy, 1864], I, chap. 3. [See *Democracy in America* (New York, Alfred A. Knopf, 1976), I, p. 47.] [Frédéric] Le Play, *La Réforme sociale en France, déduite de l'observation comparée des peuples européens* [Tours, Mame, 1874], chap. 17, [section] IV.

relative to production presents a complexity which is sometimes inextricable; it is in production that local traditions are most strongly maintained; ridiculous utopias regarding production may be invented indefinitely without shocking the common sense of readers. Nobody denies that production is the fundamental part of any economic system; this is a truth which plays a great part in Marxism and which has been acknowledged even by authors who have been unable to understand its importance.[46]

C. – Let us now examine how parliamentary assemblies work. For a long time it was believed that their principal function was that of arguing out the most important questions of social organization and, above all, those relating to the constitution; in such matters it is possible to proceed from first principles by way of deduction to clear and concise conclusions. Our forefathers excelled in this scholastic type of argument, which forms the luminous part of political discussions. Now that the question of the constitution is scarcely ever discussed, certain great laws still give rise to fine oratorical contests; thus on the question of the separation of Church and State, the professional expounders of first principles were heard and even applauded; it was the opinion of all that the debates had rarely reached so high a level, and this was because the question was one that lent itself to academic discussion. But when, as more frequently happens, commercial laws and social measures are discussed, then we see the stupidity of our representatives displayed in all its splendour; ministers, presidents and chairs of committees, experts, vie with each other in displays of stupidity. The reason for this is that we are now dealing with economic questions and the mind is no longer guided by simple rules; in order to be able to give an opinion worthy of consideration on these questions one must have had a practical acquaintance with them, and this is not the case with our honourable members. Among them may be found many representatives of the *little science*; on 5 July 1905 a well-known specialist in

---

[46] In my *Introduction a l'économie moderne* [Paris, Jacques, 1903]. I have shown how this distinction may be used to throw light on many questions which had till then remained exceedingly obscure, and notably to show the exact value of certain important arguments used by Proudhon.

venereal diseases[47] declared that he had not studied political economy, having 'a certain distrust for that conjectural science'. We must doubtless understand from this that it is more difficult to argue about production than it is to diagnose syphilis.

The *little science* has engendered a fabulous number of sophistries which we continually come across and which go down very well with people who possess the stupid and mediocre culture distributed by the University. These sophistries consist in putting very different things on the same plane from a love of logical simplicity; thus sexual morality is reduced to the equitable relations between contracting parties, the family code to that of regulating debts and agreements, and production to exchange.

Because, in nearly every country and in every age, the State has undertaken to regulate circulation, both of money and of banknotes, or has laid down a legal system of measures it does not by any means follow that there would be the same advantage in entrusting to the State, for mere love of uniformity, the management of great enterprises: yet this argument is one of those which appeal most strongly to many medical students and nurselings of the law schools. I am convinced that Jaurès is even now unable to understand why industry has been abandoned by lazy legislators to the anarchical tendencies of egotists; if production is really the base of everything, as Marx says, it is criminal not to place it in the front rank, not to subject it to a great legislative action conceived on the same lines as those parts of legislation which owe their clearness to their abstract character, i.e. not to order and arrange it so that it rests on great principles analogous to those which are brought forward when constitutional laws are discussed.

Socialism is necessarily very obscure, since it deals with production, i.e. with the most mysterious part of human activity, and since it proposes to bring about a radical transformation of that region which it is impossible to describe with the clearness that is to be found in more superficial regions. No effort of thought, no

---

[47] Dr [Victor] Augagneur [1855–1931] was for a long time one of the glories of that class of Intellectuals who looked upon socialism as a variety of Dreyfusism; his great protests in favour of Justice have brought him to the governorship of Madagascar, which proves that virtue is sometimes rewarded.

progress of knowledge, no rational induction will ever dispel the mystery which envelops socialism; and it is because Marxism fully recognized this mystery as being a feature of socialism that it acquired the right to serve as the starting point of socialist enquiry.

But we must hasten to add that this obscurity lies only in the language by which we endeavour to describe the *methods* of realizing socialism; this obscurity may be said to be *scholastic* only; it does not in the least prevent us picturing the proletarian movement in a way that is exact, complete and striking, and this may be achieved by the aid of that powerful construction which the proletarian mind has conceived in the course of social conflicts and which is called the general strike. It must never be forgotten that the perfection of this method of representation would vanish in a moment if any attempt were made to resolve the general strike into a sum of historical details: it must *be taken as an undivided whole and the passage from capitalism to socialism conceived as a catastrophe whose development defies description.*

The professors of the *little science* are really difficult to satisfy. They assert very loudly that they will only admit into thought ideas that are clear and distinct; – as a matter of fact, this is a rule which is insufficient for purposes of action, for we do nothing great without the help of warmly coloured and sharply defined images which absorb the whole of our attention; – now, is it possible to find anything more satisfying from their point of view than the general strike? – But, they say, we ought only to rely on those realities which are given by experience: is then the picture of the general strike made up of tendencies which were not obtained directly from observation of the revolutionary movement? Is it a work of pure reason, manufactured by armchair experts attempting to solve the social problem according to the rules of logic? Is it something arbitrary? Is it not, on the contrary, a spontaneous product analogous to those others which students of history come across in periods of action? They insist and invoke the rights of the critical spirit; nobody dreams of disputing them; of course, this picture of the general strike must be tested, and that is what I have tried to do above; but the critical spirit does not consist in replacing *historical data* by the *charlatanism of a sham science.*

If it is desired to criticize the basis of the idea of the general strike, the attack must be directed against the revolutionary tendencies which it groups together and displays in action; by no other method worthy of attention can one hope to prove to the revolutionaries that they are wrong in giving all their energies to the cause of socialism and that their real interests would be better served if they were politicians; they have known this for a long time and their choice is made; as they do not take up a utilitarian standpoint, any advice they may be given will be in vain.

We are perfectly aware that the historians of the future are bound to discover that we laboured under many illusions, because they will see behind them a finished world. We, on the other hand, must act and nobody can tell us today what these historians will know; nobody can furnish us with the means of modifying our motor images in such a way as to avoid their criticisms.

Our situation resembles somewhat that of physicists who work at huge calculations based on theories which are not destined to endure for ever. We have nowadays abandoned all hope of discovering a complete science of nature; the spectacle of modern scientific revolutions is not encouraging for scientists and has no doubt led many people, naturally enough, to proclaim the bankruptcy of science – and yet we should be mad if we handed the management of industry over to sorcerers, mediums and miracleworkers. The philosopher who *does not seek to make a practical application of his theories* may take up the point of view of the future historian of science, and then dispute the absolute character of present-day scientific theories; but he is as ignorant as the present-day physicist when he is asked how to correct the explanations given by the latter; must he therefore take refuge in scepticism?

Today, no philosophers worthy of consideration accept the sceptical position; their great aim, on the contrary, is to prove the legitimacy of a science which, however, makes no claim to know the real nature of things and which confines itself to relations which can be utilized for practical ends. It is because sociology is in the hands of people who are incapable of any philosophical reasoning that it is possible for us to be attacked (in the name of the *little science*) for being content with methods founded on the laws of action which are revealed to us in all great historical movements.

To proceed scientifically means, first of all, to know what forces exist in the world and then to take measures whereby we may utilize them, by reasoning from experience. This is why I say that, by accepting the idea of the general strike, although we know that it is a myth, we are proceeding exactly as a modern physicist does who has complete confidence in his science, although he knows that the future will look upon it as antiquated. It is we who really possess the scientific spirit, while our critics have lost touch both with modern science and philosophy; – and having proved this, we are quite easy in our minds.

V The political general strike

I. Use made of the *syndicats* by politicians. – Pressure on parliaments. – The general strikes in Belgium and Russia.

II. Differences in the two currents of ideas corresponding to the two conceptions of the general strike: class struggle; the State; the aristocracy of thought.

III. Jealousy fostered by politicians. – War as a source of heroism and of pillage. – Dictatorship of the proletariat and its historical antecedents.

IV. Force and violence. – Marx's ideas about force. – Necessity of a new theory in the case of proletarian violence.

I

Politicians are people whose wits are singularly sharpened by their voracious appetites and in whom the hunt for fat jobs develops the cunning of *apaches*.[a] They hold purely proletarian organizations in horror and discredit them as much as they can; frequently they even deny their efficacy, in the hope of alienating the workers from groups which, they say, have no future. But when they perceive that their hatred is powerless, that their abuse does not hinder the working of these detested organizations and that they have become

---

[a] This is one of several references made to '*apaches*' in the text. While the origin of the name is obvious, the *apaches* were an early twentieth-century version of thugs or petty criminals, for the most part living in the infamous 'zones' that ringed the city of Paris.

strong, then they seek to turn to their own profit the forces which the proletariat has created.

The cooperative societies were for a long time denounced as useless to the workers; since they have prospered, more than one politician has cast languishing eyes on their cash box and would like to see the party supported from income from the bakery and the grocery, as the Israelite administrative councils in many countries live off the dues from the Jewish butchers.[1]

The *syndicats* may be very useful in electoral propaganda; a certain amount of skill is needed to utilize them profitably, but politicians do not lack lightness of touch. Guérard, the secretary of the railway worker's *syndicat*, was once one of the most ardent revolutionaries in France; in the end, however, he understood that it was easier to play with politics than to prepare the general strike;[2] he is today one of those men in whom the Direction du Travail has most confidence, and in 1902 he went to a great deal of trouble in order to secure the election of Millerand. In the constituency where the *socialist minister* was a candidate there is a very large railway station and, without the support of Guérard, Millerand would probably have been defeated. In *Le Socialiste* of 14 September 1902, a Guesdist denounced this conduct, which seemed to him doubly scandalous: because the congress of the railway workers had decided that the *syndicat* should not enter into politics and because a former Guesdist deputy was standing against Millerand. The author of the

[1] In Algeria the scandals in the administration of these administrative councils, which had become sinks of electoral corruption, compelled the government to reform them; but the recent law concerning the separation of the Churches and the State will probably bring about a return to the old practices.

[2] An attempt to organize a railway strike was made in 1898, about which Joseph Reinach says: 'A very shady individual, Guérard, who had founded an association of railway workers and employees which had a membership of 20,000, intervened [in the conflict of the navvies of Paris] with the announcement of a general strike of his union . . . Brisson authorized search warrants, had the stations occupied by the military, and placed lines of sentries along the tracks: nobody came out': *Histoire de l'affaire Dreyfus* [Paris, Editions de la Revue Blanche, 1901–11], IV, pp. 310–11. – Today the Guérard union is in such good favour that the government has granted it permission to start a big lottery. On 14 May 1907, Clemenceau spoke of it in the Chamber as a body of 'sensible and reasonable people' opposed to the machinations of the Confédération du Travail. [The strike of 1898 was an abject failure and convinced Eugène Guérard (1859–1931) that the tactics of the revolutionary strike would lead to defeat: after this, as Sorel indicates, he became an indefatigable opponent of the 'revolutionaries' within the CGT, and one of the leaders of its reformist faction.]

article feared that 'the corporative groups were on the wrong track and that, although they started out to *utilize* politics, they might finally find themselves the *tools* of a party'. He was quite right; in any deals between the representatives of the *syndicats* and the politicians, it will always be the latter who will reap the greater advantage.

Politicians have more than once intervened in strikes, desiring to destroy the prestige of their adversaries and to capture the confidence of the workers. The Longwy basin strikes[b] in 1905 arose out of the efforts of a *republican federation*, which attempted to organize the *syndicats* that might serve its ends as against those of the employers;[3] the business did not quite take the turn desired by the promoters of the movement, who were not familiar enough with this kind of operation. Some socialist politicians, on the other hand, possess consummate skill in combining instincts of revolt into electoral forces. It was inevitable, therefore, that a few people should be struck by the idea that the great movements of the masses might be used for political ends.

The history of England affords more than one example of a government giving way when numerous demonstrations against its proposals took place, even though it was strong enough to repel by force any attack on existing institutions. It seems to be an admitted principle of parliamentary government that the majority cannot persist in pursuing schemes which give rise to popular demonstrations of too serious a kind. It is one of the applications of the system of compromise on which this system is founded; no law is valid when it is looked upon by a minority as being so oppressive that it arouses them to violent opposition. Large riotous demonstrations are an indication that the moment is not far off when an armed revolt might break out; governments that are respectful of the old traditions give way before such demonstrations.[4]

[3] [Alphonse Merrheim, 'Le Mouvement ouvrier dans le bassin de Longwy'] *Le Mouvement socialiste* [168–9] (1–15 December 1905), [pp. 425–82].
[4] The clerical party thought that it would be able to make use of these tactics to block the application of the law regarding religious organizations; it hoped that some show of violence would cause the government to give way, but the latter

[b] The Longwy basin in Lorraine was the centre of France's iron and mineral industries. Starting in the spring of 1905 and continuing into the autumn of that year there took place a series of large and, at times, violent strikes, in which strikers were killed by troops.

Between the first simple threat of trouble and a riot a political general strike might take place, which could assume any one of a large number of forms: it might be peaceful and of short duration, its aim being to show the government that it is on the wrong track and that there are forces which could resist it; it might also be the first act of a series of bloody riots.

During the last few years parliamentary socialists have not been so sure that they would soon come to power and they have recognized that their authority in the two Chambers is not destined to increase indefinitely. When there are no exceptional circumstances to force the government to buy their support with large concessions, their parliamentary power is much reduced. It would therefore be a great advantage to them if they could bring outside pressure to bear on recalcitrant majorities, thus appearing to threaten the conservatives with a formidable insurrection.

If there were in existence rich working-class federations, highly centralized and in a position to impose a strict discipline on their members, socialist deputies would not have very much trouble in inflicting their leadership occasionally upon their colleagues. All that they would have to do would be to take advantage of an opportunity that was favourable to a movement of revolt, in order to stop some branch of industry for a few days. It has more than once been proposed that the government should be brought to a standstill in this fashion by a stoppage in the working of the mines or of the railways.[5] For such tactics to produce the full effect desired, the strike must break out unexpectedly at the word of command of the party and must stop at the moment when the latter has signed an agreement with the government. It is for these reasons that politicians are so very much in favour of the centralization of the *syndicats* and that they talk so much about discipline.[6] It is well

stuck to its guns, and it may be said that one of the mainsprings of the parliamentary system was thus broken, since there are fewer obstacles than formerly to the dictatorship of parliament.

[5] In 1890 the national congress of the Guesdist party at Lille passed a resolution by which it declared that the general strike of the miners was actually possible and that a general strike of the miners by itself would bring about the results that are expected in vain from a stoppage of every trade.

[6] 'There may be room in the party for individual initiative but the arbitrary fancies of the individual must be put down. The safety of the party lies in its rules; we must steadfastly abide by them. It is the constitution freely chosen by ourselves, which binds us together, and which will enable us to conquer together or to die.'

understood that this discipline is one which must subject the proletariat to their command. Associations which are very decentralized
and grouped into *bourses du travail* would offer them far fewer
guarantees of success; so that all those who are not in favour of a
solid concentration of the proletariat round the party leaders are
regarded by the latter as anarchists.

The political general strike has this immense advantage, that it
does not greatly imperil the precious lives of the politicians; it is an
improvement upon the *moral insurrection* of which the *Mountain*[c]
made use in the month of May 1793 in order to force the Convention to expel the Girondins from its midst; Jaurès, who is afraid of
alarming his clients, the financiers (just as the members of the
Mountain were afraid of alarming the Departments), greatly admires
any movement which is free from the violent acts that *distress
humanity*;[7] he is not, therefore, an irreconcilable opponent of the
political general strike.

Recent events have given a very great impetus to the idea of the
political general strike. The Belgians obtained the reform of the
constitution by a display which has been decorated, perhaps rather
ambitiously, with the name of the general strike.[d] It now appears
that these events did not have the tragic aspect with which they
have sometimes been credited; the ministry was very pleased to be
put in a position to compel the Chamber to accept an electoral bill
which the majority disapproved of; many liberal employers were
very much opposed to this ultra-clerical majority; what happened,
therefore, was something quite contrary to the proletarian general
strike, since the workers served the ends of the State and of the
capitalists. Since those already distant times there has been another
attempt to bring pressure to bear on the central authority, with the

Thus spoke a learned exponent of socialism [Louis Révelin (1865–1918)] at the
National Council (*Le Socialiste*, 7 October 1905). If a Jesuit expressed himself
thus, there would be an outcry about monkish fanaticism.

[7] Jean Jaurès, *La Convention* [(Paris, Jules Rouoff, 1901), II], p. 1384.

[c] As France dissolved into civil war the deputies of the Girondin faction were
purged from the Convention, after the insurrectionary *journées* of 31 May and 2
June. The *Mountain*, or *Montagnards*, were so named because they sat on the
highest benches of the Convention.

[d] In 1893 a successful mass strike was called in Belgium demanding universal
suffrage.

aim of establishing a more democratic system of suffrage; this attempt failed completely; the ministry, this time, was no longer secretly on the side of the promoters in wishing to adopt a new electoral law. Many Belgians were very much astonished at their failure and could not understand why the king did not dismiss his ministers to please the socialists; he had previously insisted on the resignation of his clerical ministers in the face of liberal opposition; in fact, this king understood nothing of his duties and, as was said at the time, he was only a *cardboard cut-out king*.

This Belgian experience is not without interest, because it brings home to us the fact that the proletarian general strike and the political general strike are diametrically opposed to one another. Belgium is one of those countries where the trade union movement is the weakest;[e] the whole socialist organization is founded on the bakers', grocers' and drapers' shops that are run by committees of the party; the worker, accustomed from of old to a clerical discipline, remains an *inferior* who believes himself obliged to follow the leadership of people who sell him the commodities he needs at a slight reduction and who assail him with Catholic or socialist speeches. Not only do we find grocery set up as a priestcraft, but it is also from Belgium that we get the well-known theory of public services against which Guesde wrote such a violent pamphlet in 1883[f] and which Deville called in the same year a Belgian imitation of collectivism.[8] The whole of Belgian socialism tends towards the development of State industrialism and the constitution of a class of worker-civil servants who would be firmly disciplined under the iron hand of leaders accepted by democracy.[9] It is quite natural, therefore, that in such a country the general strike should be conceived in a political form; in such conditions, the only aim of the popular insurrection must

[8] [Gabriel] Deville, *Le Capital* [*de Karl Marx, résumé et accompagné d'un aperçu sur le socialisme scientifique* (Paris, Flammarion, 1883)], p. 10.

[9] Paul Leroy-Beaulieu recently proposed calling the whole body of government employees 'the Fourth Estate' and those in private employment 'the Fifth Estate'; he said that the first tended to form hereditary castes (*Les Débats*, 28 November 1905). As time goes on, the distinction between the two groups will grow more pronounced; the first group is a great source of support to socialist politicians who wish to discipline it perfectly and to subordinate the industrial producers to it.

[e] See Sorel's earlier article 'Le Socialisme en Belgique', *L'Ouvrier des deux mondes* 2 (1898), pp. 244–7.

[f] J[ules] Guesde, *Services publics et socialisme* (Paris, Oriol, 1883).

be to pass power from one group of politicians to another – the people still remaining the passive beast that bears the yoke.[10] The very recent troubles in Russia have helped to popularize the idea of the general strike among professional politicians.[g] Many people were surprised at the results produced by the great concerted stoppages of work; but what really happened and what followed from these disturbances is not very well known. People who are acquainted with the country believe that Witte was in contact with many of the revolutionaries and that he was delighted at being able to obtain, by terrifying the tsar, the dismissal of his enemies and the grant of institutions which, in his opinion, would put obstacles in the way of any return to the old regime. It is very remarkable that for a long time the government seemed paralysed and the administration reduced to anarchy, while, from the moment Witte thought it necessary in his personal interests to act vigorously, repression was rapid; that day arrived (as several people had foreseen) when the financiers needed to revive Russian credit. It seems hardly probable that the previous insurrections ever had the irresistible power attributed to them; *Le Petit Parisien*, which was one of the French newspapers that did most to secure the fame of Witte, said that the great strike of October 1905 came to an end on account of the hunger of the workers; according to this newspaper, the strike had even been *prolonged for a day* in the hope that the Poles would take part in the movement and would obtain concessions as the Finns had done; then it congratulated the Poles for having been *wise enough not to budge* and for not having given a pretext for German intervention (*Le Petit Parisien*, 7 November 1905).

We must not allow ourselves, therefore, to be too much dazzled by certain descriptions, and Ch[arles] Bonnier was right when, in

---

[10] This does not prevent Vandervelde from comparing the future world to the Abbey of Thelma, celebrated by Rabelais, where everybody did as he pleased, and from saying that he aspires to an 'anarchist community' ([Jules] Destrée and [Emile] Vandervelde, *Le Socialisme en Belgique* [Paris, Giard et Brière, 1898], p. 289). Oh, the magic of big words!

[g] In 1905 a wave of strikes and protests led to the establishment of the St Petersburg soviet, led by Trotsky. It was in these conditions that Witte extracted a constitutional manifesto from the tsar that introduced an element of constitutional and representative government.

Le Socialiste of 18 November 1905, he cast doubt on the account that had been given of events in Russia; he had always been an irreconcilable opponent of the general strike and he pointed out that there was no resemblance at all between what had happened in Russia and what the 'genuine syndicalists in France' look forward to. In his opinion, the strike in Russia had merely been the consummation of a very complex process, one method out of the many employed, which had succeeded owing to the exceptionally favourable circumstances in which it had occurred.

We have here, then, a criterion which will serve to distinguish two kinds of movement generally designated by the same name. We have studied a proletarian general strike which is an undivided whole; now we have to consider the general political strike which combines the incidents of economic revolt with many other elements depending on systems foreign to the economy. In the first case, no detail ought to be considered by itself; in the second, everything depends upon the art with which heterogeneous details are combined. In this case the parts must be considered separately, their importance estimated, and an attempt made to harmonize them. One would think that such a task ought to be looked upon as purely utopian (or even quite absurd) by the people who are in the habit of bringing forward so many *practical* objections to the proletarian general strike; but if the proletariat, left to itself, can do nothing, politicians are equal to anything. Is it not one of the dogmas of democracy that the genius of demagogues can overcome all obstacles?

I will not stop here to discuss what chances of success these tactics have and I leave it to the speculators who read *L'Humanité* to discover how the political general strike may be prevented from degenerating into anarchy. My only concern in the following pages will be to throw full light on the great difference between the two conceptions of the general strike.

II

We have seen that the idea of the syndicalist general strike contains within itself the whole of proletarian socialism; not only are all its real elements found therein, but they are, moreover, grouped in the same way as in social struggles and their movements are exactly those proper to their own nature. It would, in contrast, be impossible to find any image which would represent as perfectly the socialism of politicians; yet, by making the political general strike the pivotal point in the tactics of those socialists who are at the same time revolutionary and parliamentary, it becomes possible to obtain an exact notion of what it is that separates the latter from the syndicalists.

A. – We perceive immediately that the political general strike does not presuppose a class struggle concentrated on the field of battle in which the proletariat attacks the bourgeoisie – the division of society into two antagonistic armies disappears – for this kind of revolt is possible with any kind of social structure. In the past many revolutions were the result of coalitions between discontented groups; socialist writers have often pointed out that the poorer classes have more than once allowed themselves to be massacred to no purpose, save to place power in the hands of new rulers who, with great astuteness, had managed to utilize for their own advantage a passing discontent of the people against the former authorities.

It seems, indeed, that the Russian liberals had hoped to see something of the kind happen in 1905; they were delighted at the number of peasant and working-class insurrections; it has even been asserted that they heard with great satisfaction of the reverses of the army in Manchuria;[11] they believed that a frightened government would have recourse to their enlightenment; as there is a large number of sociologists among them, the *little science* would thus have obtained a huge success; but it is probable that the people would have been left to twiddle their thumbs.

It is, I suppose, for much the same kind of reason that the capitalistic shareholders of *L'Humanité* are such admirers of certain strikes; they look upon the proletariat as a very convenient instrument with which to clear the ground and they feel certain from their study of

---

[11] The correspondent of *Les Débats*, in the issue of 25 November 1906, related how the members of the Douma had congratulated a Japanese journalist on the victories of his compatriots (cf. *Les Débats*, 25 December 1907).

history that it will always be possible for a socialist government to bring rebels to reason. Moreover, are not the laws against anarchists, made in an hour of madness, still carefully preserved? They are stigmatised as *wicked laws*;[h] but they may yet serve to protect capitalist–socialists.[12]

B. – 1) Further, it would no longer be true to say that the whole organization of the proletariat was contained within revolutionary syndicalism. Since the syndicalist general strike would no longer be the entire revolution, other organizations would have been created side by side with the *syndicats*; as the strike could only be one detail cleverly dovetailed into many other incidents that must be set going at the propitious moment, the *syndicats* would have to await the word of command of the political committees, or at least work in perfect agreement with the committees which represent the superior intelligence of the socialist movement. In Italy, Ferri[i] has represented this agreement in a rather comical manner, by saying that socialism has need of two legs; this figure of speech was borrowed from Lessing,[j] who little thought that it might become one of the principles of sociology. In the second scene of *Minna von Barnhelm*, the innkeeper says to Just that a man cannot stand on one glass of brandy any more than he can walk on one leg; he also adds that all good things are three in number and that a rope of four strands is all the stronger. I am not aware that sociology has made any use of these other aphorisms, which are worth just as much as the one Ferri misused.

[12] We may also ask how much the old enemies of military justice desire the abolition of the courts martial. For a long time, the nationalists were able to maintain with some show of reason that they were retained in order that Dreyfus, if the court of appeal ordered a third trial, should not be brought up before a court of assizes; a court martial can be more easily chosen than a jury.

[h] Following the assassination of President Carnot by the anarchist Caserio, the government passed a series of laws in 1894 authorizing drastic repression of the anarchist movement and of anarchist propaganda. The subject of stormy debate, these laws became known as the 'lois scélérates'. It was after this that the anarchists began to enter the *syndicats*.

[i] Enrico Ferri (1856–1929); criminologist and professor at the University of Rome; he was also one of the leading figures on the left wing of the Italian socialist party. Associated with a socialism inspired by positivism, his writings were widely translated into French, German and English.

[j] Gottfried Ephraim Lessing (1729–81); German dramatist and critic; *Minna von Barnhelm*, written in 1767, was a comedy.

2) If the syndicalist general strike is connected with the idea of an era of great economic progress, the political general strike calls up, instead, that of a period of decline. Experience shows that classes on the downward slope are more easily captured by the fallacious harangues of politicians than classes on the rise, so that there seems to be a close relation between the political perspicacity of men and the conditions under which they live. Prosperous classes may often act very imprudently, because they have too much confidence in their own strength, face the future with too much boldness and are overcome for the moment by a frenzied desire for glory. Enfeebled classes habitually put their trust in people who promise them the protection of the State, without ever trying to understand how this protection could possibly harmonize their discordant interests; they readily enter into every coalition formed for the purpose of forcing concessions from the government; they greatly admire charlatans who speak with self-assurance. Socialism must be exceedingly careful if it is not to fall to the level of what Engels called bombastic anti-Semitism,[13] and the advice of Engels on this point has not always been followed.

The political general strike presupposes that very diverse social groups shall possess the same faith in the magical force of the State; this faith is never lacking amongst groups on the decline and its existence enables windbags to represent themselves as able to do everything. The political general strike would be greatly helped by the stupidity of philanthropists; and this stupidity is always a result of the degeneration of the rich classes. Its chances of success would be enhanced by the fact that it would have to deal with cowardly and discouraged capitalists.

3) Under such conditions it would no longer be possible to ignore plans for the future state of society; these plans, on which Marxism pours ridicule and which the syndicalist general strike ignores, would become an essential element of the new system. A political general strike could not be proclaimed until it was known with absolute certainty that the complete framework of the future organization was ready. This is what Jaurès intended to convey in his articles of 1901 when he said that modern society 'will recoil from

---

[13] [Friedrich] Engels, 'La question agraire et le socialisme', in *Le Mouvement socialiste* [44] (October 15, 1900), p. 462. Cf. pp. 458–9 and p. 463.

an enterprise as indeterminate and as empty as the [syndicalist strike] as one draws back from the precipice'.[14]

There are plenty of young barristers without a future career who have filled enormous notebooks with their detailed projects for social organization. If we have not yet been favoured with the breviary of the revolution which Lucien Herr announced in 1900,[k] we know at least that regulations have been framed for the establishment of the book-keeping branch of the collectivist society, and [Ernest] Tarbouriech has even gone into the question of the printed forms to be recommended for the use of the future bureaucracy.[15] Jaurès is continually bewailing the fact that so many lights are condemned to remain under the capitalist bushel; and he feels convinced that the revolution depends very much less on the conditions Marx had in mind than on the efforts of unknown geniuses.

C. – I have already called attention to the terrifying nature of the revolution as conceived by Marx and the syndicalists and I have said that it is very important that its character of absolute and irrevocable transformation should be preserved, because it contributes powerfully to giving socialism its high educational value. The profoundly serious work which is being carried on by the proletariat could not be viewed with any approval by the comfort-loving followers of our politicians; the latter desire to reassure the bourgeoisie and promise not to allow the people to give themselves up entirely to their anarchical instincts. They explain to the bourgeoisie that they do not by any means dream of suppressing the great State machine, but rather as wise socialists desire two things: to take possession of this machine so that they may improve its operation and make it run to further their friends' interests as much as possible – and to assure the stability of government, which will be very advantageous

[14] [Jean] Jaurès, *Etudes socialistes* [Paris, Ollendorf, 1902], p. 107.
[15] Many idiotically serious things like this may be found in Tabouriech's *La Cité future* [*: Essai d'une utopie scientifique* (Paris, Stock, 1902)] – people who call themselves well informed say that Arthur Fontaine [1860–1931], directeur du travail, has some astonishing solutions to the social question in his portfolios and that he will reveal them on the day that he retires. Our successors will bless him for having saved up for them pleasures we shall not know.

[k] In 1900 Herr, Charles Andler and others launched the Bibliothèque Socialiste. Among the texts announced, but never published, was Herr's own *La Révolution sociale*. Herr was a notorious non-publisher.

for all business men. Tocqueville had observed that, since the beginning of the nineteenth century, the administrative institutions of France having changed very little, revolutions had no longer produced any very great upheavals.[16] Socialist financiers have not read Tocqueville but they understand instinctively that the preservation of a highly centralized, very authoritarian and very democratic State puts immense resources at their disposal and protects them from proletarian revolution. The transformations which their friends, the parliamentary socialists, may carry out will always be of a very limited scope and it will always be possible, thanks to the State, to correct any imprudence they may commit.

The general strike of the syndicalists drives away from socialism all financiers who are in search of adventures; the political strike rather pleases them, because it would be carried out in circumstances favourable to the power of politicians – and consequently to the operations of their financial allies.[17]

Marx supposes, exactly as the syndicalists do, that the revolution will be absolute and irrevocable, because it will place the forces of production in the hands of *free men*, i.e. of men who are capable of running the workshop created by capitalism without any need of masters. This conception would not at all suit the financiers and the politicians whom they support, for both are only fit to exercise the noble profession of masters. Therefore, the authors of all enquiries into *moderate socialism* are forced to acknowledge that the latter implies the division of society into two groups: the first forms an elite organized as a political party, which has adopted the mission of thinking for the thoughtless masses and which imagines that,

---

[16] [Alexis de] Tocqueville, *L'Ancien Régime et la Révolution*. [Paris, Calmann-Lévy, 1864], p. 297. [See *The Ancien Regime and the French Revolution* (London, Fontana, 1969), pp. 219–20.]

[17] In *L'Avant-Garde* of 29 October 1905 may be read the report of Lucien Rolland to the National Council of the Unified Socialist Party on the election at Florac of Louis Dreyfus, a speculator in grain and a shareholder of *L'Humanité*. 'I was greatly pained', says Rolland, 'to hear one of the *kings of the time* speak in the name of our Internationale, of our red flag, of our principles, and cry "Long live the social republic!".' Those whose only knowledge of this election has been gained from the official report published in *Le Socialiste* of 28 October 1905, will have gained a singularly false idea of it. Official socialist documents should be mistrusted. I do not believe that, during the Dreyfus affair, the friends of the general staff ever distorted the truth so much as the official socialists did on this occasion.

because it allows the latter to enjoy the results of its superior enlightenment, it has done something admirable;[18] – the second is the whole body of the producers. The political elite has no other profession than that of using its intellect and they find that it is strictly in accordance with the principles of immanent justice (of which they are the sole owners) that the proletariat should work to feed them and to furnish them with the means for an existence that only distantly resembles an ascetic's.

This division is so evident that generally no attempt is made to hide it: the officials of socialism constantly speak of the party as an organism having a life of its own. At the International Socialist Congress of 1900, the party was warned against the danger it ran in following a policy which might separate it too much from the proletariat; it must inspire the masses with confidence if it desires to have their support on the day of the great battle.[19] The great reproach which Marx levelled at his adversaries in the Alliance was this separation of the leaders and the led, which had the effect of reinstating the State[20] and which is today so marked in Germany . . . and elsewhere.

III

A. – We will now carry our analysis of the ideas grouped around the political strike a little farther and enquire first of all what becomes of the notion of class.

1) It will no longer be possible to distinguish the classes by the place occupied by their members in capitalist production; we go

---

[18] The Intellectuals are not, as is so often said, men who think: they are people *who have adopted the profession of thinking* and who take an *aristocratic salary* on account of the nobility of this profession.

[19] For example, Vaillant says: 'Since we have to fight this great battle, do you think that we can win it if we have not the proletariat behind us? We must have the proletariat; and we shall not have it if we have discouraged it, if we have shown it that the Party no longer represents its interests, no longer *represents* the war of the working class against the capitalist class': ['Compte rendu sténographique non officiel de la version française du cinquième Congrès socialiste international, tenu à Paris du 23 au 27 septembre 1900'], *Cahiers de la Quinzaine*, 16th cahier of the IIᵉ series, pp. 159–60. This number contains the shorthand notes of the proceedings of the Congress.

[20] [Friedrich Engels, Paul Lafargue and Karl Marx,] *L'Alliance de la démocratie socialiste et l'Association internationale des travailleurs* [Hamburg–London, A. Darson, 1873], p. 14.

back to the old distinction between rich groups and poor groups; such was the division between the classes as it appeared to those earlier socialists who sought to reform the iniquities of the actual distribution of riches. The social Catholics also take up this position and endeavour to improve the lot of the poor, not only by charity but also by a large number of institutions which aim at the mitigation of the wretchedness caused by the capitalist economy. It seems that even today things are considered from this point of view in circles that admire Jaurès as a prophet; I have been told that the latter sought to convert Buisson[1] to socialism by making an appeal to the goodness of his heart and that these two oracles had a very ludicrous discussion as to the best way to *remedy the defects* of society.

The masses believe that they are suffering from the iniquitous consequences of a past which was full of violence, ignorance and wickedness; they are confident that the *genius of their leaders* will render them less unhappy; they believe that democracy, if it were only free, would replace a malevolent hierarchy by a benevolent hierarchy.

The leaders, who foster this sweet illusion in their men, see the situation from quite another point of view; the present social organization revolts them just in so far as it creates obstacles to their ambition; they are less shocked by the existence of classes than by their own inability to attain the positions already acquired by elder men; on the day when they have penetrated far enough into the sanctuaries of the State, into drawing-rooms and places of amusement, they cease, as a rule, to be revolutionary and speak learnedly of evolution.

2) The sentiment of revolt which is met with in the poorer classes will henceforth be coloured by a violent jealousy. Our democratic newspapers foster this passion with considerable skill, imagining that this is the best means of dulling the minds of their readers and of keeping up the circulation of the paper; they exploit the scandals that arise from time to time amongst the rich; they lead their readers

---

[1] Ferdinand Buisson (1871–1932); Protestant academic and politician; committed above all to the idea of a 'secular faith' as the basis necessary to secure the stability and longevity of the Republic. An ardent Dreyfusard, after his election as a parliamentary deputy in 1902 he supported Combes in his policy of separating Church and State.

to feel a savage pleasure when they see shame entering the household of one of the great ones of the earth. With a really astonishing impudence, they pretend that they are thus serving the cause of refined morality, which they hold as much to heart, they say, as the well-being and the liberty of the poorer classes! But it is probable that their own interests are the sole motives for their actions.[21]

Jealousy is a sentiment which seems to belong, above all, to passive beings; leaders have active sentiments, and with them jealousy is transformed into a thirst to obtain, at whatever cost, the most coveted positions by employing any means which enables them to set aside people who stand in the way of their onward march. In politics, people are no more held back by scruples than they are in sport, and we hear every day of cases where competitors of all kinds of contests seek to improve their chances by some trickery or other.

3) The *masses who are led* have a very vague and extremely simple idea of the means by which their lot can be improved; the demagogues easily get them to believe that the best way is to utilize the State to *pester* the rich; we thus pass from jealousy to vengeance, and it is well known that vengeance is a sentiment of power, especially with the weak. The history of the Greek cities and of the Italian republics of the Middle Ages is full of instances of fiscal laws which were very oppressive on the rich and which contributed not a little towards the ruin of governments. In the fifteenth century, Aeneas Sylvius (later Pope Pius II) noted with astonishment the extraordinary prosperity of the commercial towns of Germany and the great liberty enjoyed there by the bourgeoisie who, in Italy, were persecuted.[22] If our contemporary social policy were examined closely, it would be seen that it, too, was steeped in ideas of jealousy and vengeance; many regulations have been framed more with the idea of annoying employers than of improving the situation of the workers; when the clericals are in a minority they never fail to

---

[21] I note here, in passing, that *Le Petit Parisien*, the importance of which as an organ of the policy of social reform is so great, took up strongly the case of the princess of Saxony and the charming private tutor Giron. This newspaper, which is very fond of giving sermons to the people, cannot understand why the outraged husband obstinately refuses to take back his wife. On 14 September 1906, it said that 'she had broken with the ordinary moral code'; it may be concluded from this that the moral code of *Le Petit Parisien* is something quite out of the ordinary.

[22] [Johannes] Janssen, *L'Allemagne et la Réforme*, French trans. [Paris, Plon, 1887], I, p. 361.

recommend severe regulations in order to be revenged on Freemason employers.[23]

The leaders obtain all sorts of advantages from these methods; they alarm the rich and exploit them for their own personal profit; they cry louder than anybody against the privileges of wealth and know how to obtain for themselves all the enjoyments which the latter procures; by making use of the evil instincts and the stupidity of their followers, they realize the curious paradox that they get the people to applaud the inequality of conditions in the name of democratic equality. It would be impossible to understand the success of demagogues, from the time of Athens to contemporary New York, if due account was not taken of the extraordinary power of the idea of vengeance in extinguishing reasonable reflection.

I believe that the only means by which the pernicious influence of the demagogues may be wiped out are those employed by socialism in propagating the notion of the proletarian general strike; it awakens in the depth of the soul a sentiment of the sublime proportionate to the conditions of a gigantic struggle; it forces the desire to satisfy jealousy by malice into the background; it brings to the fore the pride of free men and thus protects the worker from the charlatanism of ambitious leaders eager for pleasures.

B. – The great differences that exist between the two general strikes (or the two socialisms) become still more obvious when social struggles are compared to war; in fact, war may also give rise to two opposite systems of ideas, so that quite contradictory things can be said about it, all based on incontestable facts.

War may be considered from its noble side, i.e. as it has been considered by poets celebrating armies which have been particularly illustrious; proceeding thus we find in war:

1) The idea that the profession of arms cannot compare to any other profession, – that it puts the man who adopts this profession in a class which is superior to the ordinary conditions of life, – that history is based entirely on the adventures of warriors, so that the economic life only existed to maintain them.

[23] The application of social laws gives rise, in France at least, to very singular inequalities of treatment; judicial proceedings depend on political or financial conditions. The case of the rich fashion designer may be remembered who was decorated by Millerand and against whom proceedings had so often been taken for infringements of the laws for the protection of work-girls.

2) The sentiment of glory which Renan so justly looked upon as one of the most singular and the most powerful creations of human genius, and which has been of such incomparable value in history.[24]

3) The ardent desire to try one's strength in great battles, to submit to the test which gives the military calling its claim to superiority, and to conquer glory at the peril of one's life.

There is no need for me to insist on these features of war at any great length for readers to understand the part played in ancient Greece by this conception of war. The whole of classical history is dominated by the idea of war conceived heroically; in their origin, the institutions of the Greek republics had as their basis the organization of armies of citizens; Greek art reached its apex in the citadels; philosophers conceived of no other possible form of education than that which fostered in youth the heroic tradition, and if they endeavoured to keep the study and practice of music within bounds it was because they wished to prevent the development of sentiments foreign to discipline; social utopias were created with a view to maintaining a nucleus of homeric warriors in the cities, etc. In our own times, the wars of Liberty have been scarcely less fruitful in ideas than those of the ancient Greeks.

There is another aspect of war which does not possess this character of nobility and on which the pacifists always dwell.[25] The object of war is no longer war itself; its object is to allow politicians to satisfy their ambitions: the foreigner must be conquered in order that they themselves may obtain great and immediate material advantages; the victory must also give the party which led the country during the time of success so great a preponderance that it can distribute favours to its followers; finally, it is hoped that the citizens will be so intoxicated by the spell of victory they will overlook the sacrifices which they are called upon to make and will allow themselves to be carried away by enthusiastic conceptions of the future. Under the influence of this state of mind, the people permit the government to develop its authority in an improper manner, without any protest, so that every conquest abroad may be

---

[24] [Ernest] Renan, *Histoire du peuple d'Israël* [Paris, Calmann-Lévy, 1887–93], IV, pp. 199–200.
[25] The distinction between the two aspects of war is the basis of Proudhon's book on *La Guerre et la paix* [Paris, Lacroix, 1869].

considered as having for its inevitable corollary a conquest at home made by the party that holds power.

The syndicalist general strike presents a very great number of analogies with the first conception of war: the proletariat organizes itself for battle, separating itself distinctly from the other parts of the nation, and regarding itself as the great motive power of history, all other social considerations being subordinated to that of combat; it is very clearly conscious of the glory which will be attached to its historical role and of the heroism of its militant attitude; it longs for the final contest in which it will give proof of the whole measure of its valour. Pursuing no conquest, it has no need to make plans for utilizing its victories: it counts on expelling the capitalists from the productive domain and on taking their place in the workshop created by capitalism.

This conception of the general strike manifests in the clearest manner its indifference to the material profits of conquest by affirming that it proposes to suppress the State; the State has always been, in fact, the organizer of the war of conquest, the dispenser of its fruits, and the reason for the existence of the dominating groups which profit by its enterprises – the cost of which is borne by the general body of society.

Politicians adopt the other point of view; they argue about social conflicts in exactly the same manner as diplomats argue about international affairs; all the actual fighting apparatus of conflict interests them very little; they see in the combatants nothing but instruments. The proletariat is their army, which they love in the same way that a colonial administrator loves the troops which enable him to bring large numbers of negroes under his authority; they apply themselves to the task of training the proletariat, because they are in a hurry to win quickly the great battles which will deliver the State into their hands; they keep up the ardour of their men, as the ardour of troops of mercenaries has always been kept up, by promises of pillage, by appeals to hatred, and also by the small favours which their occupancy of a few political places already enables them to distribute. But the proletariat for them is *cannon fodder* and nothing else, as Marx said in 1873.[26]

[26] [Engels, Lafargue and Marx,] *L'Alliance de la démocratie socialiste*, p. 15. Marx accused his opponents of modelling their policy on Napoleonic lines.

The strengthening of the State is at the basis of all their conceptions; in the organizations which they at present control, the politicians are already preparing the framework of a strong, centralized
and disciplined authority, which will not be hampered by the criticism of an opposition, which will be able to enforce silence and
which will give currency to its lies.

C. – In socialist literature the question of a future *dictatorship of
the proletariat* is constantly raised, but nobody likes to explain it;
sometimes this formula is improved and the epithet *impersonal* is
added to the substantive *dictatorship*, though this addition does not
throw much light on the question. Bernstein pointed out that this
dictatorship would probably be that 'of club orators and of literary
men'[27] and he was of the opinion that the socialists of 1848, when
speaking of this dictatorship, had in view an imitation of 1793, 'a
central, dictatorial and revolutionary authority, upheld by the terrorist dictatorship of the revolutionary clubs'; he was alarmed by
this prospect and he asserted that all the workers with whom he
had had the opportunity of conversing were very mistrustful of the
future.[28] Hence he concluded that it would be better to base socialist
policy and propaganda upon a more evolutionary conception of
modern society. His analysis seems to me to be inadequate.

In the dictatorship of the proletariat we may first of all notice a
harking back to the *ancien régime*; socialists have for a long time
been dominated by the idea that capitalist society must be likened
to the feudal system. I scarcely know any idea more false and more
dangerous; they imagine that the new feudalism would disappear
beneath the influence of forces analogous to those which ruined the
old feudal system. The latter succumbed beneath the attacks of a

---

[27] Bernstein evidently had in mind here a well-known article by Proudhon, from
which, moreover, he quotes a fragment on p. 47 of his book. This article closes
with imprecations against the Intellectuals: 'Then you will know what a revolution
is, that has been set going by lawyers, accomplished by artists, and conducted by
novelists and poets. Nero was an artist, a lyric and a dramatic artist, a passionate
lover of the ideal, a worshipper of the antique, a collector of medals, a tourist, a
poet, an orator, a swordsman, a sophist, a Don Juan, a Lovelace, a nobleman full
of wit, fancy, and fellow-feeling, overflowing with love of life and love of pleasure.
That is why he was Nero': *Le Représentant du peuple*, 29 April 1848.

[28] [Eduard] Bernstein, *Socialisme théorique et social-démocratie pratique* [Paris, Stock,
1900], pp. 298 and 226.

strong and centralized power, imbued with the conviction that it had received a mandate from God to employ exceptional measures against evil; the kings of the new model,[29] who established the modern monarchical system, were terrible despots wholly destitute of scruples; but great historians have absolved them from all blame for the acts of violence they committed, because they wrote in times when feudal anarchy, the barbarous manners of the old nobles and their lack of culture, when joined to a want of respect for the ideas of the past,[30] seemed crimes against which it was the duty of the royal power to act energetically. It is, therefore, probably with a view to treating the leaders of capitalism with a wholly royal energy that there is much talk today of the dictatorship of the proletariat.

Later on, royalty relaxed its despotism and constitutional government took its place; it is also said that the dictatorship of the proletariat will weaken over time and disappear in order, finally, to give way to an *anarchical society*, but how this will come about is not explained. Royal despotism did not fall by itself or by the goodness of sovereigns; one must be very simple indeed to suppose that the people who would profit by demagogic dictatorship would willingly abandon its advantages.

What Bernstein saw quite plainly was that the dictatorship of the proletariat corresponds to a division of society into masters and servants, but it is curious that he did not perceive that the idea of the political strike (which he now, to a certain extent, accepts) is connected in the closest manner with this dictatorship of the politicians which he fears. The men who had managed to organize the proletariat in the form of an army, ever ready to obey orders, would be generals who would set up a state of siege in the vanquished society; we should therefore have, on the day following the revolution, a dictatorship exercised by those politicians who in the society of today already form a compact group.

I have already recalled what Marx said about the people who reinstated the State by creating in contemporary society an embryo

---

[29] Cf. [Georg Gottfried] Gervinus, *Introduction à l'histoire du XIXe siècle*, French trans. [Paris, Lacroix, 1876], p. 27.

[30] The history of the Papacy very much embarrasses modern writers; some of them are fundamentally hostile to it on account of their hatred of Christianity, but many are led to condone the greatest faults of papal policy in the Middle Ages on account of the natural sympathy that inclines them to admire all the efforts made by theorists to tyrannize the world.

of the future society of masters. The history of the French Revolution shows us how these things occur. The revolutionaries made arrangements whereby their administrative staff was ready to take possession of authority immediately, the moment that the old administration decamped, so that there was no break in the system of domination. There are no bounds to Jaurès' admiration for these operations, which he describes in the course of his *Histoire socialiste*, and whose significance he does not exactly understand, even if he guesses the analogy they bear to his own conceptions of social revolution. The inertia of the men of that time was so great that sometimes the substitution of the old by the new officials was accomplished under conditions bordering on farce; we always find a supernumerary State (an *artificial State*, to use an expression of that time) which is organized in advance by the side of the legal State, which considers itself a *legitimate* power before it becomes a *legal* power, and which profits by some slight incident to take up the reins of government as they slip from the feeble hands of the constituted authorities.[31]

The adoption of the red flag is one of the most singular and most characteristic episodes of this period. This symbol was used in times of disaffection to give warning that martial law was about to be set up; on 10 August 1792, it became the revolutionary symbol, in order to proclaim 'the martial law of the people against rebels to the executive power'. Jaurès comments on this incident in these terms: 'It is we, the people, who are now the law ... We are not rebels. The rebels are in the Tuileries, and it is against the factions of the court and the party of the constitutional monarchy that we raise, in the name of the country and of liberty, the flag of legal

---

[31] One of the ludicrous comedies of the Revolution is that related by Jaurès in *La Convention* [II], pp. 1386–8. In the month of May 1793 an insurrectionary committee was set up at the bishop's palace, which formed an *artificial State*, and which on May 31 repaired to the town hall and declared that the people of Paris withdrew all powers from every constituted authority; the general council of the Commune, having no means of defence, 'was forced to give in', but not without assuming an air of high tragedy: pompous speeches, embracings all round, 'to prove that there was neither wounded vanity on the one part, nor pride of domination on the other'; finally, this buffoonery was terminated by an order which reinstated the council which had just been dismissed. Jaurès is delightful here: the revolutionary committee 'freed [the legal authority] from all the fetters of legality'. This happy thought is a reproduction of the well-known phrase of the Bonapartists: 'Abandon legality in order to return to the law.'

repressions.'[32] Thus the insurgents began by proclaiming that they had legitimate authority; they were fighting against a State which has only the appearance of legitimacy and they take the red flag to symbolize the re-establishment by force of the real order; as victors, they would treat the conquered as conspirators and would demand that their plots be punished. The real conclusion of all these fine ideas was to be the massacre of the prisoners in September.

All this is perfectly simple and the political general strike would develop in the same way with similar outcomes. In order that this strike should succeed, the greater part of the proletariat must be members of the *syndicats* which are under the control of political committees; there must thus be a complete organization made up of the men who will take over the government, and it should be necessary only to make a simple transmutation in the personnel of the State. The organization of the *artificial State* would have to be more complete than it was at the time of the Revolution, because the conquest of the State by force does not seem so easy to accomplish as formerly; but the principle would be the same. It is even possible that, since the transmission of authority operates nowadays in a more perfect fashion, thanks to the new resources at the disposal of the parliamentary system, and since the proletariat would be thoroughly well organized under the official *syndicats*, we should see the social revolution culminate in a wonderful system of slavery.

IV

The study of the political strike leads us to a better understanding of a distinction we must always have in mind when we reflect on contemporary social questions. Sometimes the terms 'force' and 'violence' are used in speaking of acts of authority, sometimes in speaking of acts of revolt. It is obvious that the two cases give rise to very different consequences. I think that it would be better to adopt a terminology which would give rise to no ambiguity, and that the term 'violence' should be employed only for the second sense; we should say, therefore, that the object of force is to impose a certain social order in which the minority governs, while violence

---

[32] [Jean] Jaurès, *La Législative*, [Paris, J. Rouff, 1901, I], p. 1288.

tends to the destruction of that order. The bourgeoisie have used force since the beginning of modern times, while the proletariat now reacts against the middle class and against the State by violence.

For a long time I was convinced that it is very important to deepen our understanding of the theory of social forces, which, in large measure, may be compared to the dynamic forces acting on matter; but I was not able to perceive the capital distinction in question here until I had come to consider the general strike. Moreover, I do not think that Marx had ever examined any other form of social constraint except force. In my *Saggi di critica del marxismo* I endeavoured, a few years ago, to sum up the arguments of Marx with respect to the adaptation of man to the conditions of capitalism and I presented these arguments in the following manner, on pages 38–40.

'1) There is a social system which is to a certain extent mechanical, in which man seems subject to true *natural laws*; classical economists place at the beginning of things that automatism which is in reality the last product of the capitalist regime. "But the advance of capitalist production", says Marx,[33] "develops a working class who, by education, tradition and habit, look upon the conditions of that mode of production as self-evident laws of nature." The intervention of an intelligent will in this mechanism would appear as an exception.

2) There is a regime of emulation and of fierce competition which impels men to set aside traditional obstacles, to seek constantly for what is new, and to imagine conditions of existence which seem to them to be better. According to Marx, it is in this revolutionary task that the bourgeoisie excelled.

3) There is a regime of violence which plays an important part in history and which assumes several distinct forms:

a) On the lowest level we find a scattered kind of violence which resembles the struggle for life, which acts through economic conditions and which carries out a slow but sure expropriation;

[33] *Le Capital* [Paris, Librairie du Progrès, 1875,] I, p. 327, col. 1. [See *Capital* (New York, Charles H. Kerr, 1906), p. 809.]

violence of this character works especially with the aid of fiscal arrangements;[34]

b) Next comes the concentrated and organized force of the State, which acts directly on labour, "to *regulate wages*, i.e. to force them within the limits suitable to surplus value making, to lengthen the working day, and to maintain the labourer himself in the normal degree of dependence; this is an essential element of primitive accumulation";[35]

c) We have finally violence properly so-called, which occupies so great a place in the history of primitive accumulation and which constitutes the principal subject of history.'

A few supplementary observations may be useful here.

We must first of all observe that these different phases are placed in a logical sequence, starting from states which most resemble an organism and in which no independent will appears, and ending in states in which individual wills bring forward their considered plans; but the historical order is quite the contrary of this order.

At the origin of capitalist accumulation we find some very distinct historical facts, which each appear in its proper time, with its own characteristics, and under conditions so clearly marked that they are described in the records. We find, for instance, the expropriation of the peasants and the suppression of the old legislation which had constituted 'serfdom and the industrial hierarchy'. Marx adds: 'The history of this expropriation is not a matter of conjecture; it is inscribed in the annals of humanity in indelible letters of blood and fire.'[36]

Farther on, Marx shows how the dawn of the modern age was marked by the conquest of America, the enslavement of negroes and the colonial wars: 'The different methods of primitive accumulation which the capitalist era brought about are divided in a more or less

---

[34] Marx points out that in Holland taxation was used to raise the price of necessities artificially; this was the application of a principle of government: this system had a deleterious effect on the working class and ruined the peasant, the artisan and the other members of lower middle classes; but it secured the absolute submission of the workers to their masters, the manufacturers. (*Le Capital*, I, p. 338, col. 2). [See *Capital*, p. 829.]

[35] *Ibid.*, p. 327, col. 1. [See *Capital*, p. 809.]

[36] *Ibid.*, p. 315. [See *Capital*, p. 786.]

chronological order first of all [between] Portugal, Spain, France and England, until the latter combined the lot, during the last thirty years of the seventeenth century, into a systematic whole, embracing simultaneously the colonial system, public credit, modern finance and the protectionist system. Some of these methods are backed by the employment of brute force; but all, without exception, exploit the power of the State, the concentrated and organized force of society, in order to precipitate violently the passage from the feudal economic order to the capitalist economic order, and to shorten the phases of the transition.' It is on this occasion that he compared force to a midwife, and says that it multiplies the social movement.[37]

Thus we see that economic forces are closely bound up with political power and that finally capitalism perfects itself to the point of being able to dispense with any direct appeal to the forces of repression, except in very exceptional circumstances. 'In the ordinary run of things, the worker can be left to the action of the *natural laws* of society, i.e. to his dependence on capital, engendered, guaranteed and perpetuated by the very mechanism of production.'[38]

When we reach the last historical stage, the action of independent wills disappears and the whole of society resembles an organized body, working automatically; observers can then establish an economic science which appears to them as exact as the sciences of physical nature. The error of many economists consisted in their ignorance of the fact that this system, which seemed natural and primitive to them,[39] is the result of a series of transformations that might not have taken place, and which always remains a very

---

[37] *Ibid.*, p. 336, col. 1. [See *Capital*, pp. 823–4.] The German text says that force is an 'oekonomische Potenz' (*Das Kapital*, 4th edn, p. 716); the French text says that force is an 'agent économique'. [Charles] Fourier calls geometric progressions *puissancielles* (*Le Nouveau Monde industriel et sociétaire* [Paris, Bossange, 1829], p. 376). Marx evidently used the word 'Potenz' in the sense of a multiplier; cf. in *Le Capital*, p. 176, col. 1 the term 'travail puissancié' for labour of a multiplied productivity. [The original English edition has 'labour of a higher degree and efficacy'.]

[38] [*Le Capital*, I], p. 327, col. 1. [See *Capital*, p. 809.]

[39] 'Natural', in the Marxist sense, is that which resembles a physical movement as opposed to the idea of creation by an intelligent will; for the deists of the eighteenth century, 'natural' was that which had been created by God and which was both primitive and excellent; this is still, it seems, the view of G[ustave] de Molinari.

unstable structure, for it could be destroyed by force, as it had been created by the intervention of force; – moreover, contemporary economic literature is full of complaints relating to the interventions of the State which upset *natural laws*.

Today economists are little disposed to believe that these *natural laws* are in reality laws of nature: they are well aware that the capitalist regime was reached slowly, but they consider that it was reached by a progress which should enchant the minds of all enlightened men. This progress, in fact, is demonstrated by three remarkable facts: it has become possible to set up a science of economics; law can be stated in the simplest, surest and most elegant formulas, since the law of contract dominates the whole of advanced capitalism; the caprices of the rulers of the State are no longer so apparent, and thus the path towards liberty is open. Any return to the past seems to them a crime against science, law and human dignity.

Socialism looks upon this evolution as being a history of bourgeois force and it sees only differences of degree where the economists imagine that they are discovering difference of kind: whether force manifests itself under the aspect of historical acts of coercion, or of fiscal oppression, or of conquest, or labour legislation, or whether it is wholly bound up with the economic system, it is always bourgeois force labouring, with more or less skill, to bring about the capitalist order.

Marx endeavoured to describe the details of this evolution very carefully: but he gave very little detail about the organization of the proletariat. This gap in his work has often been explained; he found in England an enormous mass of materials concerning the history of capitalism, materials that were fairly well arranged and which had already been discussed by economists; he was therefore able to investigate thoroughly the different peculiarities of the evolution of the bourgeoisie; but he was not very well furnished with matter on which he could argue about the organization of the proletariat. He was obliged, therefore, to remain content with an explanation, in very abstract formulas, of his ideas on the subject of the path which the proletariat had to take in order to arrive at the final revolutionary struggle. The consequence of this inadequacy of Marx's work was that Marxism deviated from its real nature.

The people who pride themselves on being orthodox Marxists have not wished to add anything essential to what their master has written and they have always imagined that, in order to argue about the proletariat, they must make use of what they had learned from the history of the bourgeoisie. They have never suspected, therefore, that a distinction should be drawn between the *force* that aims at authority, endeavouring to bring about an automatic obedience, and the *violence* that would smash that authority. According to them, the proletariat must acquire force just as the bourgeoisie acquired it, use it as the latter used it, and end finally by establishing a socialist State which will replace the bourgeois State.

As the State formerly played a most important part in the revolutions that abolished the old economic systems, so it must again be the State that should abolish capitalism. The workers should therefore sacrifice everything to one end alone: that of putting into power men who solemnly promise them to ruin capitalism for the benefit of the people; that is how a parliamentary socialist party is formed. Former socialist activists provided with modest jobs, the educated bourgeoisie, frivolous and eager to be in the public eye, and Stock Exchange speculators, all imagine that a golden age might spring up for them as the result of a cautious – a very cautious – revolution which would not seriously disturb the traditional State. Quite naturally, these future masters of the world dream of reproducing the history of bourgeois force and they are organizing themselves so that they may be able to draw the greatest possible profit from this revolution. Quite a good number of such clients might find a place in the new hierarchy, and what Paul Leroy-Beaulieu[m] calls the 'Fourth Estate' would become really a *lower middle class*.[40]

---

[40] In an article in *Le Radical* (2 January 1906), Ferdinand Buisson shows that those classes of workers who are more favoured at the present time will continue to rise above the others; the miners, the railway workers, employees in the State factories or municipal services who are well organized, form a 'working-class aristocracy' which succeeds all the more easily because it has continually to discuss all kinds of affairs with corporate bodies who 'stand for the recognition of the rights of man, the sovereignty of the national, and the authority of universal suffrage'. Beneath this nonsense is to be found merely the recognition of the relationship existing between politicians and obsequious followers.

[m] Paul Leroy-Beaulieu (1843–1916); economist; author of *L'Etat moderne et ses fonctions* (1898) and professor of political economy at the Collège de France. He was one of the Third Republic's leading exponents of economic liberalism and consistently opposed State intervention, in part because it would produce privileged groups dependent upon the State.

The whole future of democracy might easily depend upon this *lower middle class*, which hopes to make use, for its own great personal advantage, of the strength of genuinely proletarian organizations.[41] The politicians believe that this class will always have peaceful tendencies, that it may be organized and disciplined, and that since leaders of such prudent *syndicats* understand the action of the State in the same way, this class will form an excellent body of followers. They would like to make use of them to govern the proletariat; it is for this reason that Ferdinand Buisson and Jaurès are in favour of *syndicats* for the minor grades of civil servants, who, upon entering the *bourses du travail*, would inspire the proletariat with the idea of imitating their own feeble and peaceful attitude.

The political general strike concentrates the whole of this conception into one easily understood picture: it shows how the State would lose nothing of its strength, how the transmission of power from one privileged class to another would take place, and how the mass of producers would merely change masters. These masters would very probably be less able than those of today; they would make more flowery speeches than the capitalists; but there is every evidence that they would be much harder and much more insolent than their predecessors.

The *new school* approaches the question from quite another point of view: it cannot accept the idea that the historic mission of the proletariat is to imitate the bourgeoisie; it cannot conceive that a revolution as vast as that which would abolish capitalism could be attempted for a negligible and doubtful result, for a change of masters, for the satisfaction of theorists, politicians and speculators, all worshippers and exploiters of the State. It does not wish to restrict itself to the formulas of Marx; although he gave no other theory than that of bourgeois force, that, in the eyes of the *new school*, is no reason for restricting oneself to the scrupulous imitation of bourgeois force.

In the course of his revolutionary career, Marx was not always happily inspired and too often he followed inspirations which

---

[41] 'A portion of the nation *attaches itself to the proletariat* to demand its rights', says Maxime Leroy in a book devoted to the defence of civil servants' *syndicats* (*Les Transformations de la puissance publique* [Paris, Giard et Brière, 1907], p. 216).

belong to the past; he even allowed a quantity of outdated ideas that he found in the utopians to creep into his writings. The *new school* does not in the least feel itself bound to admire the illusions, the faults and the errors of the man who did so much to work out revolutionary ideas; it endeavours to separate what disfigures the work of Marx from what will immortalize his name; its attitude is thus the reverse of that of the official socialists, who wish to admire in Marx that which is not Marxist. We shall therefore attach no importance whatsoever to the numerous extracts which may be quoted against us to prove that Marx often understood history as the politicians do.

We now know the reason for his attitude: he did not know the distinction, which appears to us today so obvious, between bourgeois force and proletarian violence, because he did not move in circles which had acquired a satisfactory notion of the general strike.[42] We now possess sufficient material to enable us to understand the syndicalist strike as thoroughly as we do the political strike; we know what differentiates the proletarian movement from the older bourgeois movement; we find in the attitude of the revolutionaries towards the State a means of elucidating ideas which were still very confused in Marx's mind.

The method which has served us to mark the difference that exists between bourgeois force and proletarian violence may also serve to solve many questions which arise in the course of researches about the organization of the proletariat. In comparing attempts to organize the syndicalist strike with attempts to organize the political strike, we may often judge what is good and what is bad, i.e. what is specifically socialist and what has bourgeois tendencies.

Popular education, for example, seems to be wholly carried on in a bourgeois spirit; the whole historic effort of capitalism has been to bring about the submission of the masses to the conditions of the capitalist economic system, so that society might become an organism; the whole revolutionary effort tends to create *free men*; but democratic rulers adopt as their mission the accomplishment of the

---

[42] The inadequacies and the errors contained in Marx's work in respect of everything concerning the revolutionary organization of the proletariat may be cited as memorable examples of that law which prevents us from *thinking* anything but that which has actual basis in life. Let us not confuse *thought* and *imagination*.

moral unity of France. This moral unity is the automatic discipline of the producers who would be happy to work for the glory of their intellectual leaders.

It may be said, too, that the greatest danger which threatens syndicalism would be an attempt to imitate democracy; it would be better for it to remain content for a time with weak and chaotic organizations rather than that it should fall beneath the sway of *syndicats* that would copy the political forms of the bourgeoisie.

The revolutionary syndicalists have never yet made this mistake, because those who seek to lead them into an imitation of bourgeois methods happen to be adversaries of the syndicalist general strike and thus have stood self-confessed as enemies.

VI The ethics of violence

I. Observations of P[aul] Bureau and of P[aul] de Rousiers. – The era of martyrs. – Possibility of maintaining the cleavage with very little violence, thanks to a catastrophic myth.
II. Old habits of brutality in schools and workshops. – The dangerous classes. – Indulgence for crimes of cunning. – Informers.
III. Law of 1884 passed to intimidate conservatives. – Part played by Millerand in the Waldeck-Rousseau ministry. – Motives behind present ideas on arbitration.
IV. Search for the sublime in morality. – Proudhon. – No moral development in trade unionism. – The sublime in Germany and the catastrophic conception.

I

There are so many legal precautions against violence and our education is directed towards so weakening our tendencies towards violence that we are instinctively inclined to think that any act of violence is a manifestation of a return to barbarism. If industrial societies have so often been contrasted favourably with military ones, it is because peace has always been considered the greatest of blessings and the essential condition of all material progress: this last point of view explains why, since the eighteenth century and almost without interruption, economists have been in favour of strong central authorities and have troubled little about political liberties. Condorcet[a] levels this reproach at the followers of Quesnay,[b] whilst Napoleon III had probably no greater admirer than Michel Chevalier.[1]

It may be asked whether there is not a little stupidity in the admiration of our contemporaries for gentle methods; I see, in fact, that several authors, remarkable for their perspicacity and their interest in the ethical side of every question, do not seem to have the same fear of violence as our official professors.

P[aul] Bureau[c] was extremely surprised to find in Norway a rural population which had remained profoundly Christian: the peasants, nevertheless, carried a dagger at their belt; when a quarrel ended with a stabbing the police enquiry generally came to nothing for lack of witnesses ready to come forward and give evidence.

The author concludes thus: 'In men, a soft and effeminate character is more to be feared than their feeling of independence, however exaggerated and brutal, and a stab given by a man who is virtuous in his morals, but violent, is a social evil less serious and more easily curable than the excessive profligacy of young men reputed to be more civilized'.[2]

I borrow a second example from P[aul] de Rousiers who, like P[aul] Bureau, is a fervent Catholic and especially interested in questions of morality. He narrates how, towards 1860, the country of Denver, the great mining centre of the Rocky Mountains, was cleared of the bandits who infested it; the American magistracy being impotent,

---

[1] One day Michel Chevalier came beaming into the editorial room of *Le Journal des débats*: 'His first words were: I have achieved liberty! Everybody was agog; he was asked to explain. He meant the liberty of the slaughter-houses': [Ernest] Renan, *Feuilles détachées* [Paris, Calmann-Lévy, 1892], p. 149. [Michel Chevalier 1806–79; economist and disciple of Saint-Simon; he played a key role in bringing about the free-trade treaty of 1860 signed by Napoleon III with Britain.]

[2] P[aul] Bureau, *Le Paysan des fjords de Norwège* [Paris, Bureaux de la Science sociale, 1906], pp. 114 and 115.

[a] Antoine-Nicolas de Condorcet (1743–94); mathematician and philosopher; author of the *Tableau historique des progrès de l'esprit humain* (1795). Condorcet was a friend and admirer of Turgot who, as controller-general of finance, sought to introduce reforms removing barriers to free trade.

[b] François Quesnay (1694–1774); a leading member of the physiocrats.

[c] Paul Bureau (1865–1923); professor of law at the Institut Catholique; a leading member of the Le Play school. He was one of the few Catholics who rallied to the Dreyfusard cause, becoming a member of the Comité Catholique pour la Défense du Droit.

courageous citizens undertook the work: 'lynch law was frequently put into operation; a man accused of murder or of theft might be arrested, condemned and hanged in less than a quarter of an hour, if an energetic vigilance committee could get hold of him . . . The honest American has the excellent practice of not allowing himself to be crushed on the pretext that he is virtuous; a law-abiding man is not necessarily timid, as is often the case with us; on the contrary, he is convinced that his interests ought to be considered before those of the habitual criminal or of the gambler. Moreover, he possesses the necessary energy to resist and the kind of life he leads makes him capable of resisting effectively, even of taking the initiative and the responsibility of a serious step when circumstances demand it . . . Such a man, placed in a new country, full of natural resources, wishing to take advantage of the riches it contains and to acquire a superior situation in life by his labour, will not hesitate to suppress, in the name of the higher interests he represents, the bandits who compromise the future of this country. That is why, twenty-five years ago at Denver, so many corpses were dangling above the little wooden bridge thrown across Cherry Creek.'[3]

This is the considered opinion of P[aul] de Rousiers, for he returns elsewhere to this question: 'I know', he says, 'that lynch law is generally considered in France as a symptom of barbarism . . . ; but if honest virtuous people in Europe think thus, virtuous people in America think quite otherwise.'[4] He highly approved of the vigilance committee of New Orleans which, in 1890, 'to the great satisfaction of all virtuous people', hanged *mafiosi* acquitted by the jury.[5]

In Corsica, at the time when the *vendetta* was the regular means of remedying the deficiencies or correcting the action of a too-halting justice, the people do not appear to have been less moral than today. Before the French conquest, Kabylie had no other means of punishment but private vengeance, yet the Kabyles were not a bad people.

It may be conceded to those in favour of mild methods that violence may hamper economic progress and even, when it goes beyond

---

[3] [Paul] de Rousiers, *La Vie américaine: ranches, fermes et usines* [Paris, Fermin-Didot, 1899], pp. 224–5.

[4] [Paul] de Rousiers, *La Vie américaine: l'éducation et la société* [Paris, Fermin-Didot, 1899], p. 218.

[5] *Ibid.*, p. 221.

a certain limit, that it may be a danger to morality. This concession cannot be used as an argument against the doctrine set forth here, because I consider violence only from the point of view of its ideological consequences. It is, in fact, certain that a great development of brutality accompanied by much blood-letting is quite unnecessary in order to induce the workers to look upon economic conflicts as the reduced facsimiles of the great battle which will decide the future. If a capitalist class is energetic, it is constantly affirming its determination to defend itself; its frank and consistently reactionary attitude contributes at least as greatly as proletarian violence towards keeping distinct that cleavage between the classes which is the basis of all socialism.

We may make use here of the great historical example provided by the persecutions which Christians were obliged to suffer during the first centuries. Modern authors have been so struck by the language of the fathers of the Church and by the details given in the Acts of the Martyrs[d] that they have generally imagined the Christians as outlaws whose blood was constantly being spilt. The cleavage between the pagan world and the Christian world was extraordinarily well marked; without this cleavage the latter would never have acquired all its characteristic features; but this cleavage was maintained by a combination of circumstances very different from that formerly imagined.

Nobody believes any longer that the Christians took refuge in subterranean quarries in order to escape the searches of the police; the catacombs were dug out at great expense by communities with large resources at their disposal, under land generally belonging to powerful families that protected the new cult. Nobody has any doubt now that before the end of the first century Christianity had its followers among the Roman aristocracy; 'in the very ancient catacomb of Priscilla . . . has been found the family vault in which was buried from the first to the fourth centuries the Christian line of the Acilii'.[6] It seems also that the old belief that the number of martyrdoms was very great must be abandoned.

[6] P[aul] Allard, *Dix leçons sur le martyre* [Paris, Lecoffre, 1905], p. 171.

[d] The 'Acts of the Martyrs' is a multiauthored text used in the early liturgy. It details the trials, etc., of the martyrs, and was held to be a reasonable source.

Renan still asserted that the literature of martyrdom should be taken seriously: 'The details of the Acts of the Martyrs', he said, 'may be false for the most part; the dreadful picture which they unroll before us was nevertheless a reality. The true nature of this terrible struggle has often been misconceived . . . but its seriousness has not been exaggerated.'[7] The researches of Harnack[e] lead to quite another conclusion; the language of the Christian authors was entirely disproportionate to the actual importance of the persecutions; there were very few martyrs before the middle of the third century. Tertullian is the writer who has most strongly indicated the horror that the new religion felt for its persecutors, and yet here is what Harnack says: 'If, with the help of the works of Tertullian, we consider Carthage and Northern Africa we shall find that before the year 180 there were in those regions no cases of martyrdom, and that from that year to the death of Tertullian (after 220), and adding Numidia and the Mauritanias, scarcely more than two dozen could be counted.'[8] It must be remembered that at that time there was in Africa a rather large number of Montanists,[f] who extolled the glory of martyrdom and denied that anyone had the right to fly from persecution.

P[aul] Allard contests Harnack's proposition with arguments which seem to me to be somewhat weak;[9] he is unable to understand the enormous distance which can exist between the conceptions of the persecuted and reality. 'The Christians', says the German

[7] [Ernest] Renan, *L'Eglise chrétienne* [Paris, Calmann-Lévy, 1879], p. 137.
[8] Allard, [*Dix leçons*], p. 137.
[9] [P. Allard, 'M. Harnack et le nombre de martyrs'], *Revue des questions historiques* [34] (July 1905), [pp. 235–46].

[e] Adolf von Harnack (1850–1931); professor of church history at the University of Berlin and an outspoken liberal Protestant scholar. Harnack's two great works, *History of Dogma* (1886–9) and *What is Christianity?* (1901) pursue the related theme of the perversion of Christianity as an ethical doctrine by the rise of dogma associated with the institution of the Church. The process was accentuated through contact with the hellenic world, producing the 'formulation of Christian faith as Greek culture understood it and justified it to itself'. This, and the subsequent development of the Catholic Church, led to the essence of Christianity being hidden from view. Harnack's self-declared task was to rediscover that essence by removing the theological accretions of the centuries and returning to the Jesus of history and His Gospel.
[f] The Montanists were a heretical Christian movement founded in the second century which sought strict obedience to the principles of primitive Christianity.

professor, 'were able to complain of being persecuted flocks and yet such persecutions were exceptional; they were able to look upon themselves as models of heroism and yet they were rarely put to the proof'; and I call attention to the end of this sentence: 'they were able to place themselves above the majesty of the world and yet at the same time to make themselves more and more at home in it'.[10]

There is something paradoxical at first sight in the situation of the Church which had its followers in the upper classes, who were obliged to make many concessions to custom in order to live, and who could yet hold beliefs based on the idea of an absolute cleavage. The inscriptions on the catacomb of Priscilla show us 'the continuance of the faith through a series of generations of the Acilii, among whom were to be found not only consuls and magistrates of the highest order, but also priests, priestesses, even children, members of the illustrious idolatrous colleges, reserved by privilege for patricians and their sons'.[11] If the Christian system of ideas had been rigorously determined by material facts, such a paradox would have been impossible.

The statistics of persecutions therefore play no great part in this question; what was of much greater importance than the frequency of the punishments were the remarkable occurrences which took place during the scenes of martyrdom. It was through these rather rare but very heroic events that the ideology was constructed: there was no necessity for the martyrdoms to be numerous in order to prove, by the test of experience, the absolute truth of the new religion and the absolute error of the old, to establish thus that there were two incompatible ways and to make it clear that the reign of evil would come to an end. 'In spite of the small number of martyrs', says Harnack, 'we may estimate at its true value the courage needed to become a Christian and to live as one; above all, we ought to praise the conviction of the martyr whom a word or a gesture could save and who preferred death to such freedom.'[12] Contemporaries, who saw in martyrdom a *judicial proof* testifying to the honour of Christ,[13] drew from these facts quite other conclusions than those

[10] Allard, *Dix leçons*, p. 142. Cf. what I have said in *Le Système historique de Renan* [Paris, Jacques, 1906], pp. 312–15.
[11] Allard, *Dix leçons*, p. 206.
[12] *Ibid.*, p. 142.
[13] Sorel, *Le Système historique de Renan*, pp. 335–6.

which a modern historian with modern preoccupations might draw from them; no ideology was ever more remote from the facts than that of the early Christians.

The Roman administration dealt very severely with anyone who showed a tendency to disturb the public peace and especially with any accused person who defied its majesty. In striking down from time to time a few Christians who had been denounced to it (for reasons which have generally remained hidden from us) it did not think that it was accomplishing an act which would ever interest posterity; it seems that the general public itself hardly ever took any great notice of these punishments; and this explains why the persecutions left scarcely any trace on pagan literature. The pagans had no reason to attach to martyrdom the extraordinary importance which the faithful and those who already sympathized with them attached to it.

This ideology would certainly not have been formed in so paradoxical a manner had it not been for the firm belief that people had in the catastrophes described by the numerous apocalypses which were composed at the end of the first century and at the beginning of the second; it was everyone's conviction that the world was to be delivered up completely to the reign of evil and that Christ would then come and give the final victory to the elect. Any case of persecution borrowed from the mythology of the Antichrist something of its fearful dramatic character; instead of being valued on its actual importance as a misfortune that had befallen a few individuals, a lesson for the community or a temporary check on propaganda, it became an incident of the war carried on by *Satan, prince of this world*, who was soon to reveal his Antichrist. Thus the cleavage sprang at the same time from the persecutions and from the feverish expectation of a decisive battle. When Christianity had developed sufficiently, the apocalyptic literature ceased to be cultivated to any great extent, although the root idea continued to exercise its influence; the Acts of the Martyrs were drawn up in such a way that they might excite the same feelings that the apocalypse excited; it may be said that they replaced them;[14] we sometimes find in the

---

[14] It is probable that the first Christian generation had no clear idea of the possibility of replacing the apocalypses imitated from Jewish literature by the Acts of the Martyrs; this would explain why we possess no accounts prior to the year 155 (letter of Smyrniotes telling of the death of Saint Polycarpe) and why all memory of a certain number of very ancient Roman martyrs has been lost.

literature of the persecutions, set down as clearly as in the apocalypses, the horror which the faithful felt for the ministers of Satan
who persecuted them.[15]

It is possible, therefore, to conceive socialism as being perfectly
revolutionary, although there may only be conflicts that are short
and few in number, provided that these have strength enough to
evoke the idea of the general strike: all the events of the conflict
will then appear under a magnified form and, the idea of catastrophe
being maintained, the cleavage will be perfect. Thus the objection
often urged against the revolutionaries may be set aside: there is
no danger of civilization succumbing under the consequences of a
development of brutality, since the idea of the general strike may
foster the notion of class struggle by means of incidents which
would appear to bourgeois historians as being of small importance.

When the governing classes, no longer daring to govern, are
ashamed of their privileged position, are eager to make advances to
their enemies and proclaim their horror of all division in society, it
becomes much more difficult to maintain in the minds of the proletariat this idea of cleavage without which socialism cannot fulfil its
historical role. So much the better, declare the *wise men*; we may
then hope that the future of the world will not be left in the hands
of brutes who do not even respect the State, who laugh at the high
ideals of the bourgeoisie, and who have no more respect for the
professional expounders of lofty thought than for priests. Let us
therefore do more and more every day for the disinherited, say these
gentlemen; let us show ourselves more Christian, more philanthropic, or more democratic (according to the temperament of
each); let us unite for the accomplishment of our *social duty*. We
shall thus get the better of these dreadful socialists who think it
possible to destroy the prestige of the Intellectuals now that the
Intellectuals have destroyed that of the Church. As a matter of fact,
these clever moral schemes have failed; it is not difficult to see why.

The specious reasoning of these gentlemen, the high priests of
social duty, supposes that violence cannot increase and may even
diminish in proportion as the Intellectuals make polite comments,

[15] [Ernest] Renan, *Marc-Aurèle* [*et la fin du monde antique* (Paris, Calmann-Lévy, 1882)], p. 500.

utter platitudes and put on airs in honour of the union of the classes. Unfortunately for these great thinkers, things do not happen in this way; violence does not diminish in the proportion that it should diminish according to the principles of advanced sociology. There are, in fact, socialist scoundrels who, profiting from bourgeois cowardice, entice the masses into a movement which every day becomes less like that which ought to result from the sacrifices consented to by the bourgeoisie in order to obtain peace. If they dared, the sociologists would declare that the socialists cheat and use unfair methods, so little do the facts come up to their expectations.

However, it was only to be expected that the socialists would not allow themselves to be beaten without having used all the resources which the situation offered them. People who have devoted their lives to a cause which they identify with the regeneration of the world, could not hesitate to make use of any weapon that might serve to develop to a greater degree the spirit of the class struggle, seeing that greater efforts were being made to suppress it. Existing social conditions favour the production of an infinite number of acts of violence and there has been no hesitation in urging the workers not to refrain from brutality when this might do them service. Philanthropic leaders of the bourgeoisie having given a kindly welcome to members of the *syndicats* who were willing to come and discuss matters with them, in the hope that these workers, proud of their aristocratic acquaintances, would give peaceful advice to their comrades, saw suspicions of treason soon appear against the supporters of social reform. Finally, and this is the most remarkable fact in the whole business, antipatriotism becomes an essential element of the syndicalist programme.[16]

The introduction of antipatriotism into the working-class movement is all the more remarkable because it came just when the government was about to put the theories about the solidarity of the classes into action. It was in vain that Léon Bourgeois approached the proletariat with his most amiable airs and graces; without success, he assured the workers that capitalist society was

[16] As we consider everything from an historical point of view, it is of small importance to know what reasons were actually in the mind of the first apostles of antipatriotism; reasons of this kind are almost never the right ones; the essential thing is that for the revolutionary workers antipatriotism appears an inseparable part of socialism.

one great family and that the poor had a right to share in the general riches; he maintained that the whole of contemporary legislation was directed towards the application of the principles of solidarity. The proletariat replied to him by denying, in the most brutal fashion, the social compact, by denying the duty of patriotism. At the moment when it seemed that a means of suppressing the class struggle had been found, it springs up again in a particularly displeasing form.[17]

Thus all the efforts of the *wise men* only brought about results in flat contradiction to their aims; it is enough to make one despair of sociology! If they had any common sense and if they really desired to protect society against an increase of brutality, they would not drive the socialists into the necessity of adopting the tactics that are forced on them today; they would remain quiet instead of devoting themselves to social duty; they would bless the propagandists of the general strike who, as a matter of fact, endeavour to *render the maintenance of socialism compatible with the minimum of brutality*. But these *wise men* are not blessed with common sense; and they have yet to suffer many blows, many humiliations and many losses of money, before they decide to allow socialism to follow its own course.

II

We must now carry our investigation farther and enquire what are the motives behind the great aversion felt by moralists for acts of violence; a very brief summary of a few very curious changes which have taken place in the customs of the working classes is, first of all, indispensable.

A. – I observe firstly that nothing is more remarkable than the change which has taken place in the methods of bringing up children; formerly, it was believed that the cane was the most necessary instrument of the schoolmaster; today corporal punishments have disappeared from our public schooling. I believe that the competition which the latter had to maintain against the Church schools

---

[17] This propaganda produced results which went far beyond the expectations of its promoters, and which would be inexplicable without the revolutionary idea.

played a very great part in this progress; the Christian Brothers
applied the old principles of clerical pedagogy with extreme severity; and these, as is well known, involve an excessive amount of
corporal punishment inflicted for the purpose of taming the demon
who prompted so many of the child's bad habits.[18] The government
was intelligent enough to set up in opposition to this barbarous
system a milder form of education, which brought it a great deal of
sympathy; it is not at all improbable that the severity of clerical
punishments is largely responsible for the present wave of hatred
against which the Church is struggling with such difficulty. In 1901
I wrote: 'If [the Church] were well advised, it would suppress
entirely that part of its activities devoted to children; it would do
away with its schools and workrooms; it would thus do away with
the principal sources of anticlericalism; – far from showing any
desire to adopt this course, it seems to be its intention to develop
these establishments still further, and thus it is ensuring a bright
future for popular hatred against the clergy.'[19] What has happened
since 1901 surpasses my predictions.

Formerly, customs of great brutality existed in factories and
especially in those where it was necessary to employ men of superior
strength, to whom was given the name of 'big breeches'; in the end
these men managed to get entrusted with the task of engaging other
men, because 'any individual taken on by others was subjected to
an infinite number of humiliations and insults'; the man who wished
to enter *their* workshop had to buy them a drink and on the following day to treat all his fellow-workers. 'The notorious *When's it to
be?* would be started; everybody gets tipsy ... *When's it to be?* is the
devourer of savings; in a workshop where *When's it to be?* is the
custom, you must stand your turn or beware.' Denis Poulot, from
whom I borrow these details, observes that machinery did away
with the prestige of the 'big breeches', who were scarcely more than
a memory when he wrote in 1870.[20]

[18] Cf. [Ernest] Renan, *Histoire du peuple d'Israël* [Paris, Calmann-Lévy, 1887–93],
IV, pp. 289 and 296; Y[ves] Guyot, *La Morale* [Paris, Doin, 1883] pp. 212–15;
Alphonse Daudet, *Numa Roumestan*, [*Moeurs parisiennes* (Paris, Charpentier,
1881)], chap. IV.
[19] G[eorges] Sorel, *Essai sur l'Eglise et l'Etat* [Paris, Jacques, 1901], p. 63.
[20] Denis Poulot, [*Question sociale:*] *Le Sublime* [*ou le travailleur comme il est en 1870
ou comme il peut être* (Paris, Flammarion, 1887)], pp. 150–3. I quote from the
edition of 1887. This author says that the 'big breeches' very much hampered
progress in the ironworks. [The French is given as 'grosses culottes': in Poulot's

The customs of the *compagnonnages*[g] were for a long time remarkable for their brutality; before 1840, there were constant brawls, often ending in bloodshed, between groups with different rites. Martin Saint-Léon, in his book on the *compagnonnages*, gives extracts from really barbarous songs;[21] initiation into the lodge was accompanied by the severest tests; young men were treated as if they were pariahs in the *Devoirs de Jacques et de Subise*: ' "*Compagnons* [carpenters] have been known', says Perdiguier, 'to call themselves the Scourge of the Foxes [candidates for admission], the Terror of the Foxes ... In the provinces a fox works rarely in the towns; he is hunted back, as they say, into the brushwood." '[22] There were many secessions when the tyranny of the companions came into opposition with the more liberal habits which prevailed in society. When the workers were no longer in need of protection, especially for the purpose of finding work, they were no longer so willing to submit to the demands which had formerly seemed to be of little consequence in comparison with the advantages of the *compagnonnage*. The struggle for work more than once brought candidates for admission into opposition with companions who wished to reserve certain privileges.[23] We might find still other reasons to explain the decline of an institution which, while rendering many important services, had contributed very much to maintaining the idea of brutality.

Everybody agrees that the disappearance of these old brutalities is an excellent thing; from this opinion it was so easy to pass to the

account, these men are described as exercising a virtual dictatorship in the workshop.]

[21] Martin Saint-Léon, *Le Compagnonnage* [Paris, Colin, 1901], pp. 115, 125, 270–3, 277–8. [Etienne Martin Saint-Léon (1860–1934) was librarian of the Musée Social.]

[22] *Ibid.*, p. 97. Cf. pp. 91–2, 107.

[23] In 1823 the companion joiners claimed La Rochelle as theirs, a town which they had for a long time neglected as being of too little importance; they had previously only broken their journey at Nantes and Bordeaux (*ibid.*, p. 103). L'Union des Travailleurs du Tour de France was formed between 1830–2 as a rival organization to the *compagnonnage*, following the refusals with which the latter had met a few rather modest demands for reforms presented by the candidates for admission (pp. 108–16, 126, 131).

[g] The *compagnonnages* were workmen's associations, membership of which was often necessary to secure employment. At their height around 1820, the *compagnonnages* had a tradition of violent rivalry and ritualistic initiation ceremonies.

idea that all violence is an evil, that this step was bound to have been taken; and, in fact, the great mass of the people, who are not accustomed to thinking, have come to this conclusion, which is now accepted as a dogma by the *bleating herd* of moralists. They have not asked themselves what there is in brutality which is reprehensible.

When we no longer remain content with current stupidity we discover that our ideas about the disappearance of violence depend much more on a very important transformation which has taken place in the criminal world than on ethical principles. I shall now endeavour to prove this.

B. – The scholars of the bourgeoisie do not like to concern themselves with anything relating to the dangerous classes;[24] that is one of the reasons why their observations relating to the history of customs always remain superficial; it is not very difficult to see that it is a knowledge of these classes which alone enables us to penetrate the mysteries of the moral thought of peoples.

The dangerous classes of past times practised the simplest forms of offence, that which was nearest to hand, that which is nowadays left to groups of young louts without experience and without judgement. Offences of brutality seem to us today as something so abnormal that when the brutality has been great we often ask ourselves whether the culprit is in possession of all his senses. This transformation has evidently not come about because criminals have become moral, but because they have changed their method of procedure to suit the new economic conditions, as we shall see later on. This change has had the greatest influence on popular thought.

We all know that, by using brutality, associations of criminals manage to maintain excellent discipline among themselves; when we see a child ill-treated we instinctively suppose that its parents have criminal habits; the methods used by the old schoolmasters, which the ecclesiastical houses persist in preserving, are those of vagabonds who steal children to make clever acrobats or interesting beggars of them. Everything that reminds us of the morals of the dangerous classes of the past is odious to us.

There is a tendency for the old ferocity to be replaced by cunning, and many sociologists believe that this is a real progress; some

---

[24] On 30 March 1906, Monis said to the Senate: 'We cannot write in a legal text that prostitution *exists* in France for both sexes.'

philosophers, who are not in the habit of following the herd, do not see exactly how this constitutes progress from the point of view of morality: 'If we are revolted by the cruelty, by the brutality of past times', says Hartmann, 'it must not be forgotten that uprightness, sincerity, a lively sentiment of justice, pious respect before holiness of morals, characterized the ancient peoples; whilst today we see predominant lies, duplicity, treachery, the spirit of deception, the contempt for property, disdain for instinctive probity and legitimate customs, the value of which are no longer understood.[25] Robbery, deceit and fraud increase in spite of legal repression more rapidly than brutal and violent crimes (such as pillage, murder and rape) decrease. Egoism of the basest kind shamelessly breaks the sacred bonds of the family and friendship in every case in which these oppose its desires.'[26]

At the present time money losses are generally looked upon as accidents to which we are constantly exposed and that are easily made good again, while bodily accidents are not so easily reparable; fraud is therefore regarded as infinitely less serious than brutality. Criminals benefit from this change which has come about in legal sentencing.

Our penal code was drawn up at a time when the citizen was pictured as a rural proprietor occupied solely with the adminis-tration of his property as a good family man, saving to secure an honourable position for his children; large fortunes made in busi-ness, in politics or by speculation were rare and were looked upon as monstrosities; the defence of the savings of the middle classes was one of the first concerns of the legislator. The previous judicial system had been still more severe in the punishment of fraud, for the royal declaration of 5 August 1725 punished a fraudulent bank-rupt with death; it would be difficult to imagine anything further removed from our present customs. We are now inclined to

---

[25] Hartmann here bases his statements on the authority of the English naturalist [Alfred Russell] Wallace [1823–1913], who has greatly praised the simplicity of life among Malays; there must surely be a considerable element of exaggeration in this praise, although other travellers have made similar observations about some of the tribes of Sumatra. Hartmann wishes to show that there is no progress towards happiness, and this preoccupation leads him to exaggerate the happiness of the ancients.

[26] [Eduard von] Hartmann, *Philosophie de l'inconscient* [French trans. (Paris, Baillière, 1877)], II, pp. 464–5.

consider that offences of this sort can, as a rule, only be committed as a result of the imprudence of the victims and that it is only exceptionally that they deserve severe penalties; and we, on the contrary, content ourselves with light punishment.

In a rich society where business is on a very large scale, and in which everybody is wide awake in defence of his own interests, as in America, crimes of fraud never have the same consequences as in a society that is forced to practise a rigid economy; as a matter of fact, these crimes seldom cause a serious or lasting disturbance in the economic system; it is for this reason that Americans put up with the excesses of their politicians and financiers with so little complaint. P[aul] de Rousiers compares the American to the captain of a ship who, during a dangerous voyage, has no time to look after his thieving cook. 'When you point out to Americans that they are being robbed by their politicians, they usually reply: Of course we are quite aware of that! But as long as business is good and politicians do not get in the way, it will not be very difficult for them to escape the punishment they deserve.'[27]

In Europe also, since it has become easy to make money, ideas analogous to those current in America have spread among us. Big-businessmen have been able to escape punishment because in their hour of success they were clever enough to make friends in all circles; we have finally come to believe that it would be extremely unjust to condemn bankrupt merchants and lawyers who retire ruined after moderate catastrophes, while the princes of financial swindling continue to lead happy lives. Gradually the new industrial system has created a new and extraordinary indulgence for all crimes of fraud in the great capitalist countries.[28]

In those countries where the old parsimonious and non-speculative economy still prevails, the relative estimation of acts of brutality and acts of fraud has not followed the same evolution as in America, England and France; this is why Germany has preserved so many of the customs of former times[29] and does not feel

[27] De Rousiers, *La Vie américaine: l'éducation et la société*, p. 217.
[28] Several small countries have adopted these ideas, thinking by such imitation to reach the greatness of the large countries.
[29] It must be noticed that in Germany there are so many Jews in the world of speculation that American ideas do not spread very easily. The speculator appears to the majority as a *foreigner who is robbing the nation*.

the same horror that we do for brutal punishments; these never seem to them, as they do to us, only suitable to the most dangerous classes.

There has been no lack of philosophers to protest at this softening of sentences; after what we have related earlier about Hartmann, we shall expect to meet him among those who protest: 'We are already', he says, 'approaching the time when theft and lying condemned by the law will be despised as vulgar errors, as gross clumsiness, by the clever cheats who know how to preserve the letter of the law while infringing the rights of other people. For my part, I would much rather live amongst the ancient Germans, at the risk of being killed on occasion, than be obliged, as I am in modern cities, to look on every man as a swindler or a rogue unless I have evident proofs of his honesty.'[30] Hartmann takes no account of economic conditions; he argues from an entirely personal point of view and never looks at what goes on around him; nobody today wants to run the risk of being killed by ancient Germans; a fraud or a theft are very easily reparable.

C. – Finally, in order to get to the heart of contemporary thought, it is necessary to examine the way in which the public judges the relations existing between the State and criminal associations; such relations have always existed; these associations, after having practised violence, have ended by employing cunning, or at least their acts of violence have become somewhat exceptional.

Today we should think it very strange if magistrates were to put themselves at the head of armed bands, as they did in Rome during the last years of the Republic. In the course of the Zola trial,[h] the anti-Semites recruited bands of paid demonstrators, who were instructed to display patriotic indignation; the government of Méline[i] protected these antics, which for some months had great success and helped considerably in hindering a fair revision of the sentence on Dreyfus.

[30] Hartmann, [*Philosophie de l'inconscient*], p. 465.

[h] Emile Zola (1840–1902); novelist and author of the famous open letter 'J'accuse', denouncing the miscarriage of justice perpetrated upon Captain Dreyfus. This and other activities relating to the Dreyfus case earned him both a trial and criminal sentence in 1898, to avoid which he fled to England.

[i] Jules Félix Méline (1838–1925); prime minister from April 1896 to June 1898.

I believe that I am not mistaken in saying that these tactics of the supporters of the Church have been the principal cause of all measures directed against Catholicism since 1901; the liberal bourgeoisie would never have accepted these measures if they had not still been under the influence of the fear they had felt during the Dreyfus affair; the chief argument that Clemenceau used to stir up his followers to fight against the Church was that of fear: he never ceased to denounce the danger which the Republic ran in the continued existence of the *Roman faction*: the laws about the congregations, about education and the administration of the churches were made with the object of preventing the Catholic party again taking up its former warlike attitude and that Anatole France[j] so often compared to La Ligue:[k] they were *laws inspired by fear*. Many conservatives felt this so strongly that they regarded with displeasure the recent resistance opposed to the inventories of the churches; they considered that the employment of bands of *pious apaches* would make the middle classes still more hostile to their cause;[31] it was not a little surprising to see Brunetière, who had been one of the admirers of the anti-Dreyfusard *apaches*, advise submission; this was because experience had enlightened him as to the consequences of violence.

Associations that work by cunning provoke no such reaction from the public; at the time of the clerical Republic,[l] the society of Saint Vincent-de-Paul was an excellent centre of surveillance over officials of every order and grade; it is not surprising therefore that Freemasonry has been able to render services to the government headed by the Radical Party of exactly the same kind as those which

---

[31] At a meeting of the Municipal Council of Paris on 26 March 1906, the prefect of police said that the resistance was organized by a committee sitting at 86, rue de Richelieu, which hired *pious apaches* at between three and four francs a day. He asserted that fifty-two priests had promised him either to facilitate the inventories or to be content with a merely passive resistance. He accused the Catholic politicians of having forced the hands of the clergy.

[j] Anatole France (1844–1924); novelist, Dreyfusard and enthusiastic supporter of the anticlerical measures of Combes.
[k] La Ligue, founded in 1576 to defend Catholics against Huguenots (French Protestants) and led by Henri, 3rd duke of Guise. It continued its seditious activities until the conversion of Henri IV to the Catholic faith.
[l] A reference to the early years of the Third Republic (between 1871–7), when conservative forces led by President Macmahon sought to secure a government of 'moral order' with close links to the Catholic Church.

Catholic philanthropy was able to render to former governments.[m] The history of recent spying scandals has shown very plainly what the point of view of the country actually was.

When the nationalists obtained possession of the documents containing information about officers of the army, which had been compiled by the dignitaries of the Masonic Lodges, they believed that their opponents were lost; the panic which prevailed in the Radical camp for some time seemed to justify their hopes; but before long democracy showed only derision for what they called the 'petty virtue' of those who publicly denounced the methods of General André and his accomplices. In those difficult days Henry Bérenger[n] showed that he understood admirably the ethical standards of his contemporaries; he did not hesitate to approve of what he called the 'legitimate supervision of the governing classes exercised by the organizations of the vanguard'; he denounced the cowardice of the government which had 'allowed [those] who had undertaken the difficult task of opposing the military caste and the Roman Church, of examining and denouncing them, to be branded as informers' (*L'Action*, 31 October 1904); he loaded with insults the few Dreyfusards who dared to show their indignation; the attitude of Joseph Reinach appeared particularly scandalous to him; in his opinion the latter should have felt himself extremely honoured by being tolerated in the Ligue des Droits de l'Homme,[o] which had decided at last to lead 'the good fight for the defence of the rights of the citizen, sacrificed too long to those of *one* man' (*L'Action*, 12 December 1904). Finally, a law of amnesty was voted declaring that no one wanted to hear anything more of these trifles.

There was some opposition in the provinces,[32] but was it very serious? I am inclined to think not, when I read the documents

---

[32] The people in the provinces are not, as a matter of fact, so accustomed as the Parisians are to indulgence towards non-violent trickery and brigandage.

[m] Another reference to the 'affaire des fiches'. The government, led by Radical Party politician Emile Combes from 1902–5, was eager to 'republicanize' both the army and the administration and thus used the Freemasons to provide information about its army officers and civil servants.

[n] Henry Bérenger (1867–1952); anticleric; editor of the anti-Catholic *L'Action*, a daily founded in 1903.

[o] Founded in response to the Dreyfus affair, the Ligue des Droits de l'Homme quickly became one of the principal organizations defending not just the rights of individual citizens but the broader principles of republican government.

published by Péguy in the ninth number of the sixth series of the *Cahiers de la Quinzaine*. Some people, used to speaking a verbose, sonorous and nonsensical language, doubtless found themselves a little uncomfortable under the smiles of the leading grocers and eminent chemists who constituted the elite of the learned and musical societies before which they had been accustomed to hold forth on Justice, Truth and Light. They found it necessary to adopt a stoical attitude.

Could anything be finer than this passage from a letter of Professor Bouglé,[p] an eminent doctor of social science, which I find on page 13: 'I am very happy to learn that at last the *Ligue* is going to speak. *Its silence astonishes and frightens us.*' He must be a man who is easily astonished and frightened. Francis de Pressensé[q] also suffered some anxiety of mind; he is a specialist in this sort of thing; but his feelings were of a very distinguished kind, as is only proper for an aristocratic socialist. He was afraid that democracy was threatened with a new 'persecution', resembling that which had done so much harm to virtuous democrats during the Panama scandal.[33] When he saw the public quietly accept the complicity of the government with a philanthropic association which had turned into a criminal association, he turned his avenging thunders against the protesters. Amongst the most comical of these protesters I pick out a political pastor from Saint-Etienne called L[ouis] Comte. He wrote, in the extraordinary language employed by the members of the Ligue des Droits de l'Homme: 'I had hoped that the Affair would have definitively cured us of the moral malaria from which we suffer and that it would have cleansed the republican conscience

---

[33] ['La délation aux Droits de l'homme'], *Cahiers de la Quinzaine*, 9th of the VI series [1905], p. 9. F[rancis] de Pressensé was, at the time of the Panama affair, Hébrard's principal clerk; we know that the latter was one of the principal beneficiaries from the Panama booty, but that has not injured his position in the eyes of the austere Huguenots; *Le Temps* continues to be the organ of moderate democracy and of the ministers of the Gospel. [The Panama scandal erupted in 1889 when the failure of the French company launched to build the Panama Canal revealed widespread bribery and corruption in the government.]

[p] Celestin Bouglé (1870–1940); Durkheimian sociologist, Dreyfusard and member of the Ligue des Droits de l'Homme.

[q] Francis Dehaut de Pressensé (1853–1914); diplomat; journalist; elected president of the Ligue des Droits de l'Homme in 1903; born into a distinguished Protestant family he became a socialist and close friend of Jaurès.

of the clerical virus with which it is impregnated. It has done nothing. We are more clerical than ever.'[34] Accordingly, this austere man remained in the Ligue! Protestant and bourgeois logic! It is always possible that the Ligue might be able to render some small service to the deserving ministers of the Holy Gospel.

I have dwelt rather lengthily on these grotesque incidents because they seem to me to characterize very aptly the moral ideas of the people who claim to lead us. Henceforth it must be accepted that politico-criminal associations which work by cunning have a recognized place in any democracy that has attained its maturity. P[aul] de Rousiers believes that America will one day cure itself of the evils which result from the guilty machinations of its politicians. Ostrogorski,[r] after making a long and detailed enquiry into *Democracy and the Organization of Political Parties*, believes that he has found remedies which will enable modern States to free themselves from exploitation by political parties. These are Platonic vows; no historical experience justifies the hope that a democracy can be made to work in a capitalist country, without the criminal abuses experienced everywhere today. When Rousseau demanded that democracy should not tolerate the existence in its midst of any private association, he reasoned from his knowledge of the republics of the Middle Ages; he knew this history better than his contemporaries did and was struck with the enormous part played at that time by politico-criminal associations; he asserted the impossibility of reconciling *reason* in a democracy with the existence of such forces; but we ought to learn from experience that there is no way of bringing about their disappearance.[35]

---

[34] *Ibid.*, p. 13. [What Péguy took the importance of this affair to be is clear in his remark that: 'of all the events which show the decomposition of the Dreyfusard movement in France, the decomposition of socialism in France, the decomposition of the political system and, unhappily perhaps, also the decomposition of the Republic, it was obvious from the beginning that one of the most serious was this spying affair': *ibid.*, p. XVII.]

[35] Rousseau, stating the question in an abstract way, appeared to condemn every kind of association and our governments for a long time used his authority to subject every association to arbitrary power.

[r] Moisei Yakovlevich Ostrogorski (1854–1919); Russian-born political scientist; best known for his study of British and American political parties, *Democracy and the Organization of Political Parties* (1902). Ostrogorski, like Roberto Michels, concluded that political parties, irrespective of ideology, were necessarily hierarchical in organization. To enhance democracy, he recommended the formation of *leagues*.

III

The preceding explanations enable us to understand the ideas about the proper function of the workers' *syndicats* formed by enlightened democrats and the *wise men.*

Waldeck-Rousseau has often been congratulated on having carried the law on the *syndicats* in 1884.[s] In order to give an account of what was expected from this law we must recall the situation of France at that time: severe financial embarrassments had compelled the government to sign agreements with the railway companies that the Radicals denounced as acts of brigandage; colonial policy gave opportunities for extremely hostile opposition and was thoroughly unpopular;[36] the discontent that, a few years later, took the form of Boulangism[t] was already very marked and the elections of 1885 very nearly gave a majority to the conservatives.

Waldeck-Rousseau, without being a very profound seer, was yet sharp enough to understand the danger that might threaten the Opportunist Republic[u] and cynical enough to look for means of defence in a politico-criminal organization capable of checkmating the conservatives.

At the time of the Empire, the government had tried to manipulate the mutual benefit societies in such a way as to control the white-collar workers and a section of the artisans; later on, it believed it might be possible to find, in working men's associations, a weapon with which it might be capable of ruining the authority which the liberal party had over the people and of terrifying the rich classes who had obstinately opposed the government since 1863.

---

[36] In his [*La*] *Morale*, published in 1883, Y[ves] Guyot violently attacks this policy. 'In spite of the disastrous experiences [of two centuries], we are taking Tunisia, we are on the point of going to Egypt, we are setting out for Tonkin, we dream of the conquest of Central Africa' (p. 339).

[s] This law, sponsored by Waldeck-Rousseau, repealed the Le Chapelier law of 1791 and gave workers the legal right of association. In intention, it was very much an attempt to foster pragmatic, responsible trade unions on the British model.
[t] The Boulangist movement, inspired by the person of General Georges Boulanger (1837–91), was a short-lived but very popular nationalist protest movement against the Third Republic.
[u] A reference to the political dominance of the Opportunists between 1879–85. Led by figures such as Gambetta and Jules Ferry, the term 'opportunism' denoted a policy of pursuing those reforms which were deemed to be practically possible.

Waldeck-Rousseau was inspired by these examples and hoped to organize among the workers a hierarchy under the direction of the police.[37]

In a circular of 25 August 1884, Waldeck-Rousseau explained to the prefects that they ought not to confine themselves to their too-limited function of enforcing respect for the law; they must stimulate the spirit of association and 'smooth away the difficulties which were bound to arise from inexperience and lack of practice in this new liberty'. Their task would be so much the more useful and important if they succeeded in inspiring greater confidence in the workers; in diplomatic terms, to take moral leadership of the union movement:[38] 'Although the government is not obliged by the law of March 21 [1884] to take any part in the search for solutions to [the great economic and social problems], it cannot be indifferent to them and I am convinced that it is *its duty to participate* and to put its services and zeal at the disposal of all the parties concerned.' It will be necessary to act with a great deal of prudence so as 'not to excite mistrust', to show the workmen's associations how very much the government interests itself in their development, and advise them 'when they make applications'. The prefects must prepare themselves for 'this role of counsellor and *energetic collaborator* by a thorough study of legislation and of similar organizations which exist in France and abroad'.

In 1884 the government did not in the least foresee that the *syndicats* might participate in a great revolutionary agitation and the circular spoke with a certain irony of 'the hypothetical peril of an antisocial federation of all the workers'. Today one is very tempted to smile at the ingenuousness of the man who has often been represented to us as the *king of cunning*; but to account for his illusions it is necessary to go back to the writings of the democrats of that period. In 1887, in the preface to the third

---

[37] I have pointed this out in ['L'ancienne et la nouvelle métaphysique'] *L'Ere nouvelle* (March 1894), p. 339.

[38] According to the socialist deputy, Marius Devèze, the prefect of the Gard undertook this leadership of the union movement under the minister Combes (*Etudes socialistes*, p. 323) – I find in the *France du Sud-Ouest* (25 January 1904), a notice announcing that the prefect of La Manche, delegated by the government, the sub-prefect, the mayor and the municipality, officially inaugurated the *bourse du travail* at Cherbourg.

edition of *Le Sublime*, Denis Poulot,[v] an experienced manufac-
turer, former mayor of the eleventh *arrondissement* and a follower
of Gambetta, said that the *syndicats* would kill strikes; he believed
that the revolutionaries had no serious influence on the organized
workmen and saw in the primary schools a sure means of bringing about the disappearance of socialism; like nearly all the
Opportunists of his day he was much more preoccupied with the
'blacks' than the 'reds'.[w] Yves Guyot himself does not seem to
have much more insight than Waldeck-Rousseau, because in his
La Morale (1883) he considered collectivism to be merely a word;
he denounced the existing legislation which 'aims at hindering
the workers from organizing themselves for the sale of their
labour at the highest possible price and for the discussion of
their interests', and he expected that what the *syndicats* would
lead to would be the 'organization of the sale of labour on a
wholesale basis'. The priests are violently attacked by him, and
the Chagot family is denounced because it forces the miners of
Montceau to go to Mass.[39] Everybody then counted on the workers' organizations to destroy the authority of the clerical party.

If Waldeck-Rousseau had had the slightest foresight, he would
have perceived the advantage that the conservatives have tried to
draw from the law on the *syndicats* with a view to attempting the
restoration of *social peace* in the country districts under their own
leadership. Some years ago the peril which the Republic ran in the
formation of an agrarian party was denounced;[40] the result has not
lived up to the hopes of agricultural *syndicats*, but it might have
been serious; Waldeck-Rousseau never suspected it for an instant;

[39] Guyot, [*La*] *Morale* pp. 293, 183–4, 122, 148 and 320. [The coal company at
Montceau-les-Mines, like many others, maintained a strict paternalistic employment policy, with jobs and promotion determined by Church attendance. In the
strikes of 1901, the miners of Montceau-les-Mines placed religious freedom
amongst their demands.]

[40] [Robert] de Rocquigny, *Les Syndicats agricoles et leur oeuvre* [Paris, Colin, 1900],
pp. 42, 391–4.

[v] Denis Poulot, *Question sociale. Le sublime ou le travailleur comme il est en 1870 ou
ce qu'il peut être* (Paris, Flammarion, 1887). An ex-foreman turned businessman,
Poulot divided workers into seven categories, with at one extreme the respectable
and loyal 'true worker' and, the other, the reprobate 'sublime'. An opponent of
socialism, Poulot hoped that capital–worker cooperation would facilitate gradual
and peaceful reform.

[w] The 'blacks' were the supporters of clerical reaction; the 'reds' were the socialists.

in his circular he does not seem even to have suspected the material services that the new associations would render to agriculture.[41] If he had had any idea of what might come to pass, he would have taken precautions in the drawing up of the law; it is certain that neither the minister who drew up the law nor the parliamentary committee that discussed the law understood the importance of the word 'agricultural', which was introduced by means of an amendment proposed by Oudet, the senator for the Doubs.[42]

Workmen's associations directed by democrats, using cunning, threats and sometimes even a certain amount of violence, could have been of the greatest service to the government in the struggle against the conservatives, then so threatening. Those people who have recently transformed Waldeck-Rousseau into the father of his country will probably protest against such a disrespectful interpretation of his policy; but this interpretation will not seem altogether improbable to the people who remember the cynicism with which he, who is now represented as a *great liberal*, then governed: one had the impression that France was about to enter on a regime which would recall the follies, the luxuries and the brutality of the Caesars. Moreover, when unforeseen circumstances brought Waldeck-Rousseau back to power, he immediately resumed his former policy and tried to use the *syndicats* against his adversaries.

In 1899 it was no longer possible to attempt to put the workers' associations under the direction of the prefects in the way indicated by the circular of 1884; but there were other methods which might be tried and, by including Millerand in his government, Waldeck-Rousseau thought he had carried out a masterstroke. As Millerand had been able to make himself leader of the socialists, until then divided into irreconcilable groups, might he not become the *broker* who would discreetly manipulate the *syndicats* by influencing their leaders? Every means of seduction was employed in order to bring the workers to reason and to inspire them with confidence in the higher officials of the government of republican defence.

[41] This is all the more remarkable since the *syndicats* are represented in the circular as *capable of aiding French industry* in its struggle against foreign competition.
[42] It was thought to be merely a question of permitting agricultural labourers to form themselves into unions; Tolain declared, in the name of the committee, that he had never thought of excluding them from the benefits of the new law (de Rocquigny, [*Les Syndicats*], p. 10). As a rule, the agricultural unions have served as commercial agencies for landowners, etc.

One cannot help being reminded of the policy that Napoleon, in signing the Concordat, intended to follow; he had recognized that it would not be possible for him, as for Henry VIII, directly to influence the Church. 'Failing that method', said Taine, 'he adopts another, which leads to the same end but ... [h]e does not want to change the beliefs of his peoples; he respects spiritual things and wishes to *control them without interfering with them* and without becoming entangled himself in them; he wants to make them square with his policy, but by the influence of temporal things.'[43] In the same way Millerand was commissioned to assure the workmen that their socialist convictions would not be interfered with; the government only wanted to direct the action of the *syndicats* and to make them fit in with its own policy.

Napoleon had said: 'You will see how I shall be able to utilize the priests.'[44] Millerand was instructed to gratify in every way the vanity of the leaders of the *syndicats*,[45] while the mission of the prefects was to induce the employers to grant material concessions to the workers; it was thought that such a Napoleonic policy would give results as considerable as those obtained from the policy pursued in regard to the Church. Dumay,[x] the minister of public worship, had succeeded in creating a docile episcopacy formed of men whom the ardent Catholics contemptuously called *violet prefects;*[y] by putting a shrewd head of service in the office of the minister, might it not be possible to create *red prefects?*[46] All this was

[43] [Hippolyte] Taine, *Le Régime moderne* [Paris, Hachette, 1894], II, p. 10.
[44] *Ibid.*, p. 11.
[45] This is what Mme Georges Renard very sensibly points out in her report of a workmen's fête given by Millerand (L[éon] de Seilhac, *Le Monde socialiste* [Paris, Lecoffre, 1904], p. 308).
[46] Millerand did not keep on the former head of the Office du Travail, who was doubtless not pliant enough for the new policy. It seems to me clearly established that at that time considerable attention was being given in this government department to a kind of enquiry as to the state of feeling among the activists of the *syndicats*, evidently in order to ascertain in what way they might be advised. This was revealed by Ch[arles] Guieysse [in 'M. Combes et ses caciques'] in the *Pages libres* of 10 December 1904, [pp. 485–9]; the protestations of the department and those of Millerand do not appear to have been very serious (*La Voix du peuple*, 18, 25 December 1904; 1 January, 25 June, 27 August 1905).

[x] Charles Dumay (1843–1906); director of the Administration des Cultes from 1887 to 1906.
[y] A reference to the Catholic bishops who were thought to be too friendly towards the republican government.

fairly well thought out and corresponded perfectly with the kind of talent possessed by Waldeck-Rousseau, who was all his life a great admirer of the Concordat and was fond of negotiating with Rome; it was not unpleasing for him to negotiate with the *reds*; the very originality of the enterprise would have been enough to charm a mind like his that delighted in subtlety.

In a speech of 1 December 1905, Marcel Sembat,[z] who had been in a particularly good position to know what had happened at the time of Millerand, related several anecdotes which very much astonished the Chamber. He told them how the government, in order to make itself disagreeable to the nationalist municipal councillors of Paris and to reduce their influence on the *bourses du travail*, had asked 'the *syndicats* to make applications to it that would justify' the reorganization of that establishment. A certain amount of scandal was caused by the march-past of the red flags before the official platform at the inauguration of the monument by Dalou in the Place de la Nation;[aa] we now know that this happened as a result of negotiations; the prefect of police had hesitated, but Waldeck-Rousseau authorized these revolutionary ensigns. The fact that the government denied having any relations with the *syndicats* is of no importance; a lie more or less would not trouble a politician of Waldeck-Rousseau's calibre.

The exposure of these manoeuvres shows that the ministry depended on the *syndicats* to frighten the conservatives; ever since then it has become easy to understand the attitude they have adopted in the course of several strikes: on the one hand, Waldeck-Rousseau proclaimed with great fervour the necessity of giving the protection of public force to every single worker who wished to work in spite of the strikers; whilst, on the other, he has more than once shut his eyes to acts of violence; the reason for this is that he found it necessary to annoy and frighten the Progressists[47] and

[47] It may be questioned whether Waldeck-Rousseau did not go too far and thus started the government on a very different road from that which he wanted it to take; I do not think that the new law about associations would have been voted except under the influence of fear, but it is certain that its final wording was much more anticlerical than its promoter would have wished. [The Progressists were

[z] Marcel Sembat (1862–1922); socialist politician and journalist.
[aa] On 19 November 1899 a big procession was organized to mark the inauguration of a statue by Dalou, the 'Triumph of the Republic'. Representatives of the labour movement and many other organizations of the Left participated.

because he meant to reserve to himself the right of forcible intervention for the moment when his political interests required the
disappearance of all political disorder. In the precarious state of his
authority in the country he believed it possible to govern only by
fear and by imposing himself as the supreme arbitrator in industrial
disputes.[48]

To transform the *syndicats* into politico-criminal associations
which could serve as auxiliaries of democratic government: such
was the plan of Waldeck-Rousseau from 1884 onwards. The *syndicats* were to play a part analogous to that played by the Masonic
Lodges, the latter being useful in spying on government employees,
the former designed to threaten the interests of those employers
who were not on the side of the administration; the Freemasons
being rewarded by decorations and favours given to their friends,
the workers being authorized to extract extra wages from their
employers. This policy was simple and cheap.

In order that this system may work properly, a certain moderation in the conduct of the workers is necessary; not only must
violence be used with discretion but the demands must not exceed
certain limits. The same principles must be applied in this case as
in the bribery of politicians; everybody approves as long as the politicians are reasonable in their demands. People who are in business
know that there is quite an art to bribery; certain intermediaries
have acquired a special skill in estimating the amount of the presents
that should be offered to high officials or to deputies who can get
bills passed.[49] If financiers are almost always obliged to have
recourse to the services of specialists, there is all the more reason
why the workers, who are quite unaccustomed to the practices of
this world, must need intermediaries to fix the sum which they can
exact from their employers without exceeding reasonable limits.

We are thus led to consider arbitration in an entirely new light
and to understand it in a really scientific manner, since, instead of

descended from the Opportunists; moderate republicans, they moved steadily
rightwards and increasingly antisocialist. In the elections of 1899 they secured 254
deputies and voted against the government of Waldeck-Rousseau.]
[48] In a speech on 21 June 1907, Charles Benoist complains that the Dreyfus affair
had thrown discredit on *reasons of State* and had led the government to appeal to
the elements of disorder in the nation in order to create order.
[49] I suppose that no one is ignorant of the fact that no important undertaking is
carried through without bribery.

allowing ourselves to be duped by abstractions, we shall explain it by means of the dominant ideas of bourgeois society, which invented it and which wants to impose it on the workers. It would be evidently absurd to go to a pork butcher's shop, order him to sell us a ham at less than the marked price, and then ask him to submit the question to arbitration; but it is not absurd to promise to a group of employers the advantages to be derived from the fixity of wages for several years and to ask the *specialists* what present remuneration this guarantee is worth; this remuneration may be considerable if business is expected to be good during that time. Instead of bribing some influential person, the employers raise their workers' wages; from their point of view there is no difference. As for the government, it becomes the benefactor of the people and hopes that it will do well in elections; that is its special benefit. To the politician, the electoral advantages that result from a successful conciliation are worth more than a very large bribe.

It is easy to understand now why all politicians have so great an admiration for arbitration; it is because an enterprise conducted without bribery is inconceivable to them. Many of our politicians are lawyers, and clients who confide their cases to them attach great weight to their parliamentary influence; it is for this reason that a former minister of justice is always sure of getting remunerative lawsuits even when he is not that talented, because he has means of influencing the magistrates, with whose failings he is very familiar and whom he could ruin if he wished. The great political barristers are sought out by financiers who have serious difficulties to overcome in the law courts, who are accustomed to bribing on a large scale and in consequence pay royally. The world of employers thus appears to our rulers as a world of adventurers, gamblers and parasites of the Stock Exchange; they consider that this rich and criminal class must expect to submit from time to time to the demands of other social groups; their conception of the ideal capitalist society would be a *compromise between conflicting appetites under the auspices of political lawyers.*[50]

---

[50] I borrow from a celebrated novel by Léon Daudet a description of the character of the barrister Méderbe: 'The latter was a curious character, tall, thin, of a well-set-up figure, surmounted by a head like a dead fish, green impenetrable eyes, oiled and flattened hair, his whole appearance being frozen and rigid . . . He had chosen the profession of a barrister as being one which would supply his own and

The Catholics would not be sorry, now they are in opposition, to find support in the working classes; it is not only flattery that they address to the workers in order to convince them that it would be greatly to their advantage to abandon the socialists. They would also very much like to organize politico-criminal *syndicats*, just as Waldeck-Rousseau hoped to do twenty years ago; but the results they have obtained up till now have been very moderate. Their aim is to save the Church and they think that well-disposed capitalists might sacrifice a part of their profits to give the Christian *syndicats* the concessions necessary to assure the success of this religious policy. Recently, a well-informed Catholic, who interests himself in social questions, told me that in a few years the workers would be obliged to recognize that their prejudices against the Church had no foundation. I think that he deludes himself as much as Waldeck-Rousseau did when in 1884 he regarded the idea of a revolutionary federation of *syndicats* as ridiculous; but the material interest of the Church so blinds Catholics that they are capable of every kind of stupidity.

The social Catholics[bb] have a way of looking at economic questions that makes them resemble our vilest politicians very closely. In fact, it is difficult for the clerical world to conceive that things can happen otherwise than by grace, favouritism and bribery.

I have often heard a lawyer say that a priest can never be made to understand that certain actions that the law does not punish are nevertheless villainies; and I have been told by a bishop's notary that, while a clientele composed of convents is an excellent one, it is at the same time very dangerous, because convents frequently

his wife's need of money . . . He took part chiefly in financial cases, on account of the large profit to be made out of them, and of the secrets he learned from them; he was employed in such cases on account of his semi-political, semi-judicial relations, which always secured him victory in any case he pleaded. He charged fabulous fees. *What he was paid for was certain acquittal.* This man had enormous power . . . He gave one the impression of a bandit armed for social life and sure of impunity': *Les Morticoles* [Paris, Charpentier, 1894], pp. 287–8. It is clear that many of these traits are copied from those of the man the socialists so often called the Eiffel barrister, before they made him the demi-god of republican defence. [In the Panama affair, Waldeck-Rousseau defended Gustave Eiffel.]

[bb] Following Leo XIII's encyclical *Rerum novarum* of 1891, there developed a variety of social Catholic movements prepared to 'rally' to the Republic. For the most part they advocated moderate social reform along corporatist lines.

want fraudulent deeds drawn up. Many people, seeing during the last fifteen years so many ostentatious monuments erected by the religious congregations, have wondered if a wave of madness was not passing over the Church; they are unaware that these building operations enable a crowd of pious rascals to live at the expense of the Church treasury. The imprudence of those congregations which persist in carrying on long and costly lawsuits against the public treasury has often been pointed out; this tactic enables the Radicals to work up a lively agitation against the monks by denouncing the avarice of people who claim to have taken vows of poverty; but these cases make plenty of business for the army of pious hagglers. I do not think that I am exaggerating when I say that more than a third of the fortune of the Church has been wasted for the benefit of these vampires.

A widespread dishonesty therefore prevails in the Catholic world, which leads the devout to believe that economic conditions depend chiefly on the caprices of the people who hold the purse. Everybody who has profited from an unexpected gain – and for them all profit from capital is an unexpected gain[51] – ought to share the profit with those people who have a right to his affection or to his esteem: first of all the priests,[52] and then his parishioners. If he does not respect this obligation, he is a rogue, a Freemason or a Jew; no violence is too great to be used against such a tool of Satan. When, therefore, priests are heard using revolutionary language, we need not take them literally and believe that these vehement orators have socialist sentiments; it simply indicates that the capitalists have not been sufficiently generous.

Here again there is a case for arbitration; recourse must be had to men with great experience of life in order to ascertain exactly what sacrifices the rich must submit to on behalf of the poor dependents of the Church.

IV

The study we have just made has not led us to think that the theorists of social peace are on the way to an ethic worthy of

[51] I do not think that there exists a class less capable of understanding the economics of production than the priests.

[52] In Turkey when a high palace dignitary receives a bribe, the sultan takes the money and then gives a certain proportion back to his employee; what proportion

acknowledgement; we now pass to a counterproof and enquire whether proletarian violence might not be capable of producing the effect in vain expected from the tactics of moderation.

First of all, it must be noticed that modern philosophers seem to agree in demanding a kind of sublimity from the ethics of the future, which will distinguish it from the petty and insipid morality of the Catholics. The chief thing with which the theologians are reproached is that they make too great use of the concept of probabilism; nothing seems more absurd (not to say more scandalous) to contemporary philosophers than to count the opinions which have been emitted for or against a maxim, in order to find out whether we ought to shape our conduct by it or not.

Professor Durkheim[cc] said recently, at the Société Française de Philosophie (11 February 1906), that it would be impossible to suppress the *sacred* in *ethics* and that what characterized the sacred was its incommensurability with other human values; he recognized that his sociological researches led him to conclusions very near to those of Kant; he asserted that utilitarian morality had misunderstood the problem of duty and obligation. I do not want to discuss these arguments here; I simply cite them to show to what point the character of the sublime impresses itself on authors who, by the nature of their work, would seem to be the least inclined to accept it.

No writer has defined more forcibly than Proudhon the principles of that morality which modern times have in vain sought to realize: 'To feel and to assert the dignity of man', he says, 'first in everything in connection with ourselves, then in the person of our neighbour, and that without a shadow of egoism, without any consideration either of divine or communal sanction: therein lies *right*. To be ready to defend that dignity in every circumstance with energy, and if necessary against oneself: therein lies *justice*.'[53] Clemenceau, who doubtless can hardly be said to make personal use of this morality, expressed the same thought when he writes: 'Without the dignity of the human

---

is given back depends on the sultan's disposition at the moment. The sultan's ethical code in these matters is also that of the social Catholics.

[53] [Pierre-Joseph] Proudhon, *De la Justice dans la Révolution et dans l'Eglise* [Paris, Lacroix, 1868–70], I, p. 216.

[cc] Emile Durkheim (1858–1917); sociologist. The text referred to is Durkheim's 'La Détermination du fait moral', published in the *Bulletin de la société française de philosophie* 6 (1906), pp. 169–212.

person, without independence, liberty and justice, life is but a bestial state not worth the trouble of preserving' (*L'Aurore*, 12 May 1905).

One well-founded reproach has been brought against Proudhon, as well as against many others of the great moralists; it has been said that his maxims were admirable, but that they were doomed to remain ineffective. And, in fact, experience does prove, unfortunately, that those precepts which the historians of ideas call the most noble precepts are, as a rule, entirely ineffective. This was evident in the case of the Stoics; it was no less remarkable in Kantianism; and it does not seem as if the practical influence of Proudhon has been very noticeable. In order that a man may suppress the tendencies against which morality struggles, he must have in himself a powerful motive, a *conviction* which must dominate his whole consciousness, and act before the calculations of reflection have time to enter his mind.

It may even be said that all the fine arguments by which authors hope to induce men to act morally are more likely to lead them down the slope of probabilism; as soon as we consider an act to be accomplished, we are led to ask ourselves if there is not some means of escaping the strict obligations of duty. A[uguste] Comte supposed that human nature would change in the future and that the cerebral organs which produce altruism (?) would destroy those which produce egoism; in saying this he very likely bore in mind the fact that moral decision is instantaneous and comes instinctively from the depths of man's nature.

At times Proudhon is reduced, like Kant, to appeal to a kind of scholasticism for an explanation of the paradox of moral law: 'To feel himself in others, to the point of sacrificing every other interest to this sentiment, to demand for others the same respect as for himself and to be angry with the unworthy creature who suffers others to be lacking in respect for him, as if the care of his dignity did not concern himself alone, such a faculty at first sight seems a strange one ... There is a tendency in every man to develop and force the acceptance of that which is essentially himself, his own dignity. It results from this that, the essential in man being identical and one for all humanity, each of us is aware of himself at the same time as individual and as species; and that an insult is felt by a third party and by the offender himself as well as by the injured person, that in consequence the protest is common. This is precisely what is meant by Justice.'[54]

Religious ethics claim to possess this source of action that is wanting in lay ethics;[55] but here it is necessary to make a distinction if an error, into which so many authors have fallen, is to be avoided. The great mass of Christians do not carry out the real Christian ethic, that which the philosopher considers as really peculiar to their religion; the society people who profess Catholicism are chiefly pre-occupied with probabilism, mechanical rites and proceedings more or less related to magic, which are calculated to assure their present and future happiness in spite of their sins.[56]

Theoretical Christianity has never been a religion suited to society people; the doctors of the spiritual life have always reasoned about those people who were able to escape from the conditions of ordi-nary life. 'When the Council of Gangres, in 325', said Renan, 'declared that the maxims of the Gospel about poverty, the renunci-ation of the family, and virginity, were not intended for the ordinary Christian, the perfectionists made places apart where the evangelical life, too lofty for the common run of men, could be practised in all its rigour.' He remarks, moreover, very justly that the 'monastery took the place of martyrdom so that the precepts of Jesus might be carried out somewhere';[57] but he does not carry this comparison far enough: the lives of the great hermits were a material struggle against the infernal powers which pursue them even to the desert,[58] and this struggle was to continue that which the martyrs had waged against their adversaries.

These facts show us the way to a right understanding of the nature of lofty moral convictions; these never depend on reasoning or on

[54] *Ibid.*, pp. 216–17.
[55] Proudhon thinks that this was also lacking in pagan antiquity: 'During several centuries, polytheistic societies had customs, but no ethics. In the absence of a morality solidly based on principles, the customs gradually disappeared': *ibid.*, p. 173.
[56] Heinrich Heine claims that the Catholicism of a wife is a very good thing for a husband, because the wife is never oppressed by the burden of her sins; after confession she begins again 'to chatter and to laugh'. Moreover, there is no danger of her relating her sin (*L'Allemagne*, 2nd edn [Paris, Michel-Lévy, 1860], II, p. 322).
[57] Renan, *Marc-Aurèle*, p. 558.
[58] Catholic saints do not struggle against abstractions but often against apparitions which present themselves with all the signs of reality. Luther also had to fight the devil, at whom he threw his inkpot.

any education of the individual will; they depend upon a state of war in which men voluntarily participate and which finds expression in well-defined myths. In Catholic countries the monks carry on the struggle against the prince of evil who triumphs in this world and would subdue them to his will; in Protestant countries small fanatical sects take the place of the monasteries.[59] These are the battlefields that enable Christian morality to hold its own, with that character of sublimity which today still fascinates many minds and which gives it sufficient lustre to occasion in society a few pale imitations.

When one considers a less accentuated state of the Christian ethic, one is struck by seeing to what extent it depends on struggle. Le Play, who was an excellent Catholic, often contrasted (to the great scandal of his co-religionists) the solidity of the religious convictions he encountered in countries of mixed religions with the spirit of inactivity that prevails in the countries exclusively submitted to the influence of Rome. Among the Protestant peoples, the more vigorously the Established Church is assailed by dissident sects the greater the moral fervour developed. We thus see that conviction is founded on the competition of communions, each of which regards itself as the army of truth fighting the armies of evil. In such conditions it is possible to find sublimity; but when religious warfare is much weakened, probabilism, mechanical rites and proceedings having a certain resemblance to magic take first place.

We can point out quite similar phenomena in the history of modern liberal ideas. For a long time our fathers regarded from an almost religious point of view the *Déclaration des droits de l'homme*, which seems to us today only a colourless collection of abstract and confused formulas, without any great practical bearing. This was due to the fact that formidable struggles had been undertaken on account of the institutions which were associated with this document: the clerical party asserted that it would demonstrate the fundamental error of liberalism; everywhere it organized campaigning organizations intended to enforce its authority on the people and on the government; it boasted that it would be able to destroy the defenders of the [1789] Revolution before long. At the time when

[59] [Renan, *Marc-Aurèle*], p. 627.

Proudhon wrote his book on Justice, the conflict was far from being
ended; thus the whole book is written in a warlike tone astonishing
to the reader of today; the author speaks as if he were a veteran of
the wars of Liberty; he would be revenged on the temporary conquerors who threaten the acquisitions of the Revolution; he
announces the dawn of the great revolt.

Proudhon hopes that the duel will be soon, that the forces will
meet with their whole strength, and that there will be a Napoleonic
battle, finally destroying the opponent. He often speaks in a language which would be appropriate to the epic. He did not perceive
that his abstract arguments would seem weak when, later on, his
belligerent ideas had disappeared. There is a ferment all through
his soul which colours it and gives a hidden meaning to his thought,
very far removed from the scholastic sense.

The savage fury with which the Church proceeded against
Proudhon's book shows that the clerical camp had exactly the same
conception of the nature and consequences of the conflict as he had.

As long as the sublime imposed itself in this way on the modern
spirit, it seemed possible to create a lay and democratic ethic; but
in our time such an enterprise would seem almost comic; everything
is changed now that the clericals no longer seem formidable; there
are no longer any liberal convictions, since the liberals have ceased
to be animated by their former warlike passions. Today everything
is in such confusion that the priests claim to be the best of democrats; they have adopted the *Marseillaise* as their party hymn; and
if a little persuasion is exerted they will have illuminations on the
anniversary of 10 August 1792. Sublimity has vanished from the
ethics of both parties, giving place to a morality of extraordinary
meanness.

Kautsky[dd] is evidently right when he asserts that in our time the
advancement of the workers has depended on their revolutionary
spirit: 'It is hopeless', he says, at the end of a study on social reform
and revolution, 'to try, by means of moral homilies, to inspire the
English workman with a more exalted conception of life, a feeling
of nobler effort. The ethics of the proletariat spring from its revolutionary aspirations; these are what give it the greatest force and

---

[dd] Karl Kautsky (1854–1938); one of the leaders of the German socialist party and
for many years the supreme representative of Marxist orthodoxy.

elevation. It is the idea of revolution which has raised the proletariat from its degradation.'[60] It is clear that, for Kautsky, morality is always subordinate to the sublime.

The socialist point of view is quite different from that of the former democratic literature; our fathers believed that the nearer man approached to nature the better he was and that a man of the people was a sort of savage; that consequently the lower we descend down the social scale the more virtue we find. In support of this idea, the democrats have many times called attention to the fact that during revolutions the poorest people have often given the finest examples of heroism; they explain it by assuming that these obscure heroes were true children of nature. I explain it by saying that, these men being engaged in a war which was bound to end in either their triumph or enslavement, the sentiment of sublimity was bound to be engendered by the conditions of the struggle. During a revolution the higher classes as a rule show themselves in a particularly unfavourable light; this for the reason that, belonging to a defeated army, they experience the feelings of the defeated, of supplicants and of those about to surrender.

When working-class circles are *reasonable*, as the professional sociologists wish them to be, when conflicts are confined to disputes about material interests, there is no more opportunity for the sublime than when agricultural unions discuss the subject of the price of guano with manure merchants.

It has never been thought that discussions about prices could possibly exercise any ethical influence upon men; the experience of sales of livestock would lead to the supposition that in such cases those interested are led to admire cunning rather than good faith; the *ethical values* recognized by horse-dealers have never passed for very elevated. Amongst the important things accomplished by the agricultural unions, De Rocquigny reports that in 1896 'the munici-pality of Marmande, having wanted to impose on beasts brought to the fair a tax which the cattle-breeders *considered unfair* ... the

[60] Karl Kautsky, *La Révolution sociale*, French trans. [Paris, Rivière, 1901], pp. 123–4. I have pointed out elsewhere that the decay of the revolutionary idea in the minds of former activists who have become *moderates* seems to be accompanied by a moral decadence that I have compared to that which as a rule one finds in the case of a priest who lost his faith (*Insegnamenti sociali* [*dell'economia contemporanea* (Palermo, Sandron, 1907)], pp. 344–5). [See *Social Foundations of Contemporary Economics* (New Brunswick, NJ, Transaction Books, 1984), p. 286.]

breeders went on strike and stopped supplying in the market of Marmande, with such effect that the municipality found itself forced to give in'.[61] This was a very peaceful procedure which produced profitable results to the peasants; but it is quite clear that nothing ethical was involved in such a dispute.

When politicians intervene there is, almost necessarily, a noticeable lowering of ethical standards, because they do nothing for nothing and only act on condition that the favoured association is one of their customers. We are very far here from the path of the sublime, we are on that which leads to the practices of politico-criminal societies.

In the opinion of many well-informed people, the transition from violence to cunning which shows itself in contemporary strikes in England cannot be too much admired. The great object of the trade unions is to obtain a recognition of the right to employ threats disguised in diplomatic formulas: their desire is that their delegates, when doing the round of the workshops, should not be interfered with, and therefore that they can fulfil their mission of bringing those that wish to work to understand that it would be in their interests to follow the *directions* of the trade unions; they *consent* to express their *desires* in a form which will be perfectly clear to the listener, but which could be presented in a court of law as a solidarist sermon. I protest that I cannot see what is so admirable in this tactic, which is worthy of Escobar. In the past the Catholics have often employed similar methods of intimidation against the liberals; I understand thus perfectly well why so many *wise men* admire the trade unions, but I find the morality of the *wise men* to be not very admirable.

It is true that in England violence has, for a long time, been void of all revolutionary character. Whether corporate advantages are pursued by means of blows or by craft, there is not much difference between the two methods; yet the pacific tactics of the trade unions indicate an hypocrisy which would be better left to the *wise men*. In the countries where the conception of the general strike exists, the blows exchanged between workmen and the representatives of the

---

[61] De Rocquigny, [*Les Syndicats*], pp. 379–80. I am curious to know how exactly a tax can be iniquitous: mystery and the Musée Social. These *wise men* speak a special language.

bourgeoisie have an entirely different significance; their consequences are far-reaching and they may beget the sublime.

I am convinced that in order to understand, at least in part, the
dislike that Bernstein's doctrines rouse in German social democracy
we must bear in mind these considerations about the nature of the
sublime. The German has been brought up on sublimity to an
extraordinary extent: first by the literature connected with the wars
of Independence,[62] then by the revival of the taste for the old
national songs which followed these years, finally by a philosophy
which pursues aims very far removed from vulgar preoccupations.
It must also be remembered that the victory of 1871 has considerably contributed towards giving Germans of every class a feeling of
confidence in their strength that is not to be found to the same
degree in this country at the present: compare, for instance, the
German Catholic party with the chicken-hearted creatures who
form the clientele of the Church in France! Our clergy only think of
humiliating themselves before their adversaries and are quite happy,
provided that there are plenty of evening parties during winter; they
have no recollection of services which are rendered to them.[63]

The German socialist party drew its strength particularly from
the catastrophic idea that its propagandists spread everywhere and
which was taken very seriously as long as the Bismarkian persecutions maintained a warlike spirit amongst its members. This
spirit was so strong that the masses have not yet succeeded in
understanding thoroughly that their leaders are anything but
revolutionaries.

---

[62] Renan even wrote: 'The war of 1813 to 1815 is the only one of the century that
had anything epic and elevated about it ... [it] corresponded to a movement of
ideas and had a real intellectual significance. A man who had taken part in this
great struggle told me that, awakened by the cannonade on the first night that he
passed with the volunteer troops collected in Silesia, he felt that he was witnessing
an immense divine service': *Essais de morale et de critique* [Paris, Michel-Lévy,
1859], p. 116. Compare Manzoni's ode entitled '*Mars 1821*' and dedicated to 'the
illustrious memory of Théodor Koerner, poet and soldier of German independence, killed on the field of battle at Leipzig, a name dear to all those peoples
who are struggling to defend and to reconquer their fatherland'. Our own wars
of Liberty were also epic, but they did not produce a literature as good as the war
of 1813.

[63] Drumont has often denounced this state of mind of the fashionable religious
world.

When Bernstein, who was too intelligent not to know what was the real spirit of his friends on the directing committee, announced that the grandiose hopes which had been raised must be given up, there was a moment of stupefaction; very few people understood that Bernstein's declarations were courageous and honest actions, intended to make the language of socialism accord more with reality. If henceforth it was necessary to be content with the policy of social reform, it was also necessary to negotiate with the parliamentary parties and the government and to behave exactly as the bourgeoisie did; this appeared monstrous to men who had been brought up on theories of catastrophe. Many times the tricks of the bourgeois politicians had been denounced, their astuteness contrasted with the candour and the disinterestedness of the socialists, and the large element of expediency in their attitude of opposition pointed out. It could never be imagined that the disciples of Marx might follow in the footsteps of the liberals. With the new policy, no more heroic characters, no more sublimity, no more convictions! The Germans thought that the world was turned upside down.

It is plain that Bernstein was absolutely right in not wanting to keep up a revolutionary semblance which was in contradiction with the real state of mind of the [socialist] party; he did not find in his own country the elements which existed in France and Italy; he saw no other way therefore of keeping socialism on a basis of reality than that of suppressing all that was deceptive in a revolutionary programme which the leaders no longer believed in. Kautsky, on the contrary, wanted to preserve the veil that hid from the workers the real activity of the socialist party; in this way he achieved much success among the politicians, but more than anyone else he has helped to intensify the crisis of socialism in Germany. It is not by diluting the phrases of Marx in verbose commentaries that the revolutionary idea can be kept intact; but by continually adapting the thought of Marx to facts which are capable of assuming a revolutionary aspect. The general strike alone can produce this result today.

One serious question must now be asked: 'Why is it that in certain countries acts of violence can group themselves around the general strike and produce a socialist ideology capable of inspiring sublimity; and why in others do they seem not to have that power?' Here, national traditions play a great part; the examination of this problem would perhaps throw a strong light on the genesis of ideas; but we will not deal with it here.

VII The ethics of the producers

I. Morality and religion. – Contempt of democracies for morality. –
Ethical preoccupations of the *new school*.
II. Renan's uneasiness about the future of the world. – His conjec-
tures. – The need of the sublime.
III. Nietzsche's ethics. – The role of the family in the genesis of
morality; Proudhon's theory of morality. – The ethics of Aristotle.
IV. Kautsky's hypotheses. – Analogies between the spirit of the
general strike and that of the wars of Liberty. – Fear inspired in
the parliamentarians by this spirit.
V. The worker employed in the factory of advanced production, the
artist and the soldier in the wars of Liberty: desire to surpass previous models; care for exactitude; abandonment of the idea of exact
recompense.

I

Fifty years ago Proudhon pointed out the necessity of giving the
people a morality that would fit new needs. The first chapter of the
preliminary discourses placed at the beginning of *De la Justice dans
la Révolution et dans l'Eglise* is entitled: 'The state of morals in the
nineteenth century. Invasion of moral scepticism; society in danger.
What is the remedy?' There one reads these striking sentences:
'France has lost its morals. Not that, as a matter of fact, the men
of our generation are worse than their fathers ... When I say that
France has lost its morals I mean something very different, that it
has ceased to believe in her own principles. She no longer has either

moral intelligence or conscience, she has almost lost the idea of morals itself. As a result of continual criticism we have come to this sad conclusion: that right and wrong, between which we formerly thought we were able to distinguish, are now vague and indeterminate conventional terms; that all these words, Right, Duty, Morality, Virtue, etc., of which the pulpit and the school talk so much, serve to cover nothing but pure hypotheses, vain utopias and unprovable prejudices; thus that social life, governed by some sort of human respect or by convention, is in reality arbitrary.'[1]

However, he did not think that contemporary society was mortally wounded; he believed that since the Revolution, humanity had acquired an idea of Justice which was sufficiently clear to enable it to triumph over temporary lapses; by this conception of the future he separated himself completely from what was to become the most fundamental idea of contemporary official socialism, which sneers at morality. 'This juridical faith ... this science of right and of duty, which we seek everywhere in vain, that the Church has never possessed, and without which it is impossible for us to live today, I say that the Revolution has created all its principles; that these principles, unknown to us, rule and uphold us, but that, while at the bottom of our hearts affirming them, we shrink from them through prejudice, and it is this infidelity to ourselves that makes our moral poverty and servitude.'[2] He maintains the possibility of bringing light to our minds, of presenting what he calls 'the exegesis of the Revolution'; in order to do this, he examines history, showing how humanity has never ceased to strive towards Justice, how religion has been the cause of corruption and how 'the French Revolution, by bringing about the predominance of the juridical principle [over

---

[1] [Pierre-Joseph] Proudhon, *De la Justice dans la Révolution et dans l'Eglise* [Paris, Lacroix, 1868–70], I, p. 70.

[2] *Ibid.*, p. 74. By *juridical* faith Proudhon here means a triple faith which dominates the family, contracts and political relations. The first is 'the conception of mutual dignity [of husband and wife] which, raising them above the level of the senses, renders them more sacred to the other than dear, and makes their fertile community a religion for them, sweeter than love itself'; – the second 'raising the mind above egotistical appetites, makes them more happy through respect for the right of another than their own fortune'; without the third, 'citizens, giving themselves up to the attractions of individualism, could not, whatever they did, be anything other than a mere aggregate of incoherent and repulsive existences that the first wind will disperse like dust': *ibid.*, pp. 72–3. In the strict sense of the word, juridical faith would be the second of these three.

the religious principle], opens a new epoch, an entirely contrary order of things, the different elements of which it is now our task to determine'.[3] – 'Whatever may happen in the future to our worn-out race', he says at the end of his discourse, 'posterity will recognize that the third age of humanity has its start in the French Revolution; that an understanding of this new law has been given to some of us in all its fullness; that we have not been found completely wanting in the practice of it; and that to perish in this sublime beginning was, after all, not without grandeur. At that hour the Revolution defined itself: then it lived. The rest of the nation does not think at all. Will that *part which lives and thinks* be suppressed by the corpse?'[4]

I said in the preceding chapter that the whole doctrine of Proudhon was subordinated to revolutionary enthusiasm and that this enthusiasm has been extinct since the Church has ceased to be formidable; thus there is nothing astonishing in the fact that the undertaking that Proudhon considered so easy (the creation of a morality absolutely free from all religious belief) seems very uncertain to many of our contemporaries. I find proof of this way of thinking in a speech by Combes delivered during a discussion of the budget of public worship on 26 January 1903: 'At the present moment we look upon the moral ideas taught by the Church as necessary ideas. For my part I find it difficult to accept the idea of a society composed of philosophers such as M[onsieur] Allard,[5] whose primary education would have sufficiently guaranteed them against the perils and trials of life.' Combes is not the kind of man to have ideas of his own; he reproduced an opinion current in his circle.

---

[3] *Ibid.*, p. 93.
[4] The first two epochs are those of paganism and of Christianity. *Ibid.*, p. 104.
[5] This deputy had made a very anticlerical speech from which I quote this curious idea that 'the Jewish religion was the most clerical of all religions, possessing the most sectarian and narrowest type of clericalism'. A little before this he said: 'I myself *am not an anti-Semite* and only make one reproach to the Jews, that of having poisoned Aryan thought, so elevated and broad, with Hebraic monotheism.' He demanded the introduction of the history of religions into the curriculum of the primary schools in order to ruin the authority of the Church. According to him the socialist party saw in 'the intellectual emancipation of the masses the necessary preface to the progress and social evolution of societies'. Is it not rather the contrary which is true? Does not this speech prove that there is an anti-Semitism in free-thinking circles quite as narrow and badly informed as that of the clericals?

This declaration created a great commotion in the Chamber; all the deputies who prided themselves on their knowledge of philosophy took part in the debate; as Combes had referred to the superficial and narrow instruction of our primary schools, F[erdinand] Buisson felt that, as the leading pedagogue of the Third Republic, he ought to protest: 'The education that we give to the child of the people', he said, 'is not a half education; it is the very flower and fruit of civilization gathered during the centuries, from among many peoples, the religions and legal systems of all ages and from the whole of humanity.' An abstract morality of this kind must be entirely devoid of efficacy; I remember having read, in a manual by Paul Bert,[a] that the fundamental principles of morality are based on the teachings of Zoroaster and the Constitution of the year III; these do not seem to me the kind of principles which would be powerful enough to influence a man's conduct.

It might be imagined that the University had arranged its present programme in the hope of imposing moral conduct on its pupils by means of the repetition of precepts; courses on morality are multiplied to such an extent that one might ask oneself if (with a slight difference) the well-known verse of Boileau[b] might not be applied:

Do you like *musk*? It has been put everywhere.

I do not think that there are many people who share the naive confidence of F[erdinand] Buisson and the members of the University in this ethic. G[ustave] de Molinari,[c] exactly like Combes, believes that it is necessary to have recourse to religion, which promises men a reward in the other world and which is thus 'the insurer of justice ... It is religion which, in the infancy of humanity, raised the edifice of morality; it is religion which supports it and which alone can support it. Such are the functions which religion filled and which it continues to fill and which, unpleasant as it may be to the apostles of independent morality,

---

[a] Paul Bert (1833–86); professor of sociology at the Sorbonne and Gambetta's minister of education; author of *L'Instruction civique à l'école* (1882).

[b] Nicolas Boileau (1636–1711); poet and literary critic.

[c] Gustave de Molinari (1819–1912); Belgian Catholic social economist and editor of *Le Journal des economistes*. He was also one of the first to suggest the establishment of labour exchanges or '*bourses du travail*'. Sorel wrote a lengthy review of this Molinari text in *Le Devenir social* 1 (1895), pp. 677–84.

constitute its usefulness.'[6] – 'We must look for help to a more powerful and more active instrument than the interests of society in order to effect those reforms demonstrated by political economy to be necessary, and this instrument can only be found in the religious sentiment associated with the sentiment of justice.'[7]

G[ustave] de Molinari expresses himself in intentionally vague terms; he seems to regard religion as do many modern Catholics (of the Brunetière type); it is a social means of government, which must be suited to the needs of the different classes. People of the higher classes have always considered that they had less need of moral discipline than their subordinates, and it is by making this fine discovery the basis of their theology that the Jesuits have had so much success in the contemporary bourgeoisie. Our author distinguishes four motive forces capable of assuring the accomplishment of duty: 'the power of society invested in the governmental organism, the power of public opinion, the power of the individual conscience and the power of religion'; and he considers that this spiritual mechanism perceptibly lags behind the material mechanism.[8] The first two motive forces may have some influence on capitalists, but none in the workshop; for the worker, the last two motive forces are alone effective and they will become every day more important on account of 'the growth of responsibility in those who are charged with the direction and surveillance of the working of machinery';[9] but, according to G[ustave] de Molinari, we could not conceive the power of individual conscience without that of religion.[10]

I believe then that G[ustave] de Molinari would be inclined to approve of the employers who protect religious institutions; he would ask only, no doubt, that it be done with a little more circumspection than Chagot used at Montceau-les-Mines.[11]

For a long time the socialists have been greatly prejudiced against morality, on account of these Catholic institutions that the large

[6] G[ustave] de Molinari, *Science et religion* [Paris, Guillaumin, 1894], p. 94.
[7] *Ibid.*, p. 198.
[8] *Ibid.*, p. 61.
[9] *Ibid.*, p. 54.
[10] *Ibid.*, pp. 87 and 93.
[11] I have already mentioned that in 1883 Y[ves] Guyot violently denounced the conduct of Chagot, who placed his workmen under the direction of the priests and forced them to go to Mass ([*La*] *Morale* [Paris, Doin, 1883], p. 183).

employers established in their towns; it seemed to them that, in our capitalist society, morality was only a means of assuring the docility of the workers, who are kept in the fear created by superstition. The literature which the bourgeoisie have admired for so long describes conduct so outrageous, so scandalous even, that it is difficult to credit the rich classes with sincerity when they speak of inculcating morality in the people.

The Marxists had a particular reason for showing themselves suspicious in all that concerned ethics; the propagators of social reforms, the utopians and the democrats had so abused the idea of Justice that it was only reasonable to consider all discussions on such a subject as an exercise in rhetoric or as sophistry intended to mislead those who were interested in the working-class movement. This is why, several years ago, Rosa Luxemburg[d] called the idea of Justice 'this old post horse, on which for centuries all the regenerators of the world, deprived of surer means of historic locomotion, have ridden; this ungainly Rosinante, mounted on which so many Quixotes of history have gone in search of the great reform of the world, bringing back from these journeys nothing but black eyes'.[12] From these sarcasms about a fantastic Justice springing from the imagination of utopians, one passed, often too easily, to a coarse facetiousness about the most ordinary morality; a rather sordid selection could easily be made of paradoxes supported by the official Marxists on this subject. Lafargue[e] distinguishes himself particularly from this point of view.[13]

The principal reason that prevented the socialists from studying ethical problems as they deserved was the democratic superstition which has dominated them for so long and which has led them to

---

[12] ['Démocratie industrielle et Démocratie politique',] *Le Mouvement socialiste* [11] (15 June 1899), p. 649.
[13] For example, we read in *Le Socialiste* of 30 June 1901: 'As, in a communist society, the *morality which clogs the brains of the civilized* will have vanished like *a frightful nightmare*, perhaps another ethic will incite women to *flutter about like butterflies*, to use Ch. Fourier's expression, instead of submitting to being the property of a male ... In savage and barbarous communist tribes, women are much more honoured when they distribute their favours to a great number of lovers.'

[d] Rosa Luxemburg (1870–1919); German socialist and theoretician.
[e] Paul Lafargue (1842–1911); idiosyncratic Marxist and author of *Le Droit à la Paresse* (1880). Sorel worked with Lafargue in the early 1890s on the review *Le Devenir social*, but became increasingly critical of his ideas.

believe that, above everything else, the aim of their actions must be the conquest of seats in political assemblies.

From the moment one has anything to do with elections, it is necessary to submit to certain general conditions which impose themselves unavoidably on all parties in every country and at all times. If one is convinced that the future of the world depends on an electoral programme, on compromises between influential people and on the sale of favours, it is not possible to pay much attention to the moral constraints which prevent a man going in the direction of his most obvious interests. Experience shows that in all the countries where democracy can develop its nature freely, the most scandalous corruption is displayed without anyone thinking it necessary to conceal his rascality: Tammany Hall of New York has always been cited as the most perfect example of democratic life and in the majority of our large towns politicians are found who ask for nothing better than to follow the paths of their colleagues in America. So long as a man is faithful to his party he only commits trifling offences; but if he is unwise enough to abandon it, he is immediately discovered to have the most shameful vices: it would not be difficult to show, by means of well-known examples, that our parliamentary socialists practise this singular morality with a certain amount of cynicism.

Electoral democracy greatly resembles the world of the Stock Exchange; in both cases, it is necessary to work upon the simplicity of the masses, to buy the cooperation of the most important papers, and *to assist chance* by an infinity of trickery; there is not a great deal of difference between a financier who puts grand-sounding concerns on the market, which come to grief in a few years, and the politician who promises his fellow citizens an infinite number of reforms, which he does not know how to bring about[14] and which resolve themselves simply into an accumulation of parliamentary papers. Neither one nor the other knows anything about production and yet they manage to obtain control over it, to misdirect it and

[14] On 21 June 1907 Clemenceau, replying to Millerand, told him that in introducing the bill to establish old age pensions without concerning himself where the money was to come from, he had not acted as 'a statesman nor even as a responsible person'. Millerand's reply is entirely characteristic of the pride of the political parvenu: 'Do not talk about things that you know nothing about.' Of what then does he himself speak?

to exploit it shamelessly: they are dazzled by the marvels of modern industry and they each imagine that the world is so rich that they can rob it on a large scale without causing any great outcry amongst the producers; to bleed the taxpayer without bringing him to the point of revolt, that is the whole art of the statesman and the great financier. Democrats and businessmen have a very special science for the purpose of making deliberative assemblies approve of their swindling; parliamentary regimes are as fixed as shareholders' meetings. It is probably because of the profound psychological affinities resulting from these methods of operation that they both understand each other so perfectly: democracy is the paradise of which unscrupulous financiers dream.

The disheartening spectacle presented to the world by these financial and political parasites[15] explains the success that anarchist writers have had for so long: the latter founded their hopes of the regeneration of the world on the intellectual progress of individuals; they never ceased urging the workmen to educate themselves, to be more aware of their dignity as men and to show their devotion to their comrades. This attitude was imposed upon them by their guiding principle: how was the formation of a society of free men conceivable if it was not assumed that individuals had not already acquired the capacity of guiding themselves? Politicians assert that this is a very naive idea and that the world will enjoy all the happiness it can desire on the day when messengers of the new Gospel are able to profit from all the advantages that power procures; nothing will be impossible for a State which turns the editors of *L'Humanité* into princes. If at that time it is considered useful to have free men, they will be manufactured by a few good laws; but it is doubtful if the friends and business associates of Jaurès will find that necessary; it will be sufficient for them if they have servants and taxpayers.

---

[15] I am pleased here to be able to support myself in the incontestable authority of Gérault-Richard who, in *La Petite République* on 19 March 1903, denounced 'the intriguers, the careerists, the half-starved, and the ladies' men [who] are only after the ministerial spoils' and who at that time were trying to bring about the fall of the Combes ministry. We see from the following issue that he is speaking of Waldeck-Rousseau's friends who, like him, were opposed to the destruction of the congregations.

The *new school* is rapidly differentiating itself from official socialism in recognizing the necessity of the improvement of morals;[16] it
is thus fashionable amongst the dignitaries of parliamentary socialism to accuse it of having anarchist tendencies; for my part, I have
no difficulty in acknowledging myself as anarchist in this respect –
since parliamentary socialism professes a contempt for morality
equalled only by that which the vilest representatives of the stock-
broking bourgeoisie have for it.

The *new school* is also sometimes reproached with returning to
the dreams of the utopians; this criticism shows how much our
adversaries misunderstand the works of the old socialists as well as
the present situation. Formerly the aim was to construct a morality
capable of influencing the feelings of society people in such a way
as to make them sympathize with those who in pity were called the
disinherited classes and of inducing them to make some sacrifice in
favour of their unfortunate brethren. The writers of that time pictured the workshop in a very different light from that which it
might have in a society of proletarians dedicated to progressive
work; they imagined that it would resemble drawing-rooms in
which ladies meet to do embroidery; they thus gave a bourgeois
character to the mechanism of production. Finally, they credited
the proletariat with feelings closely resembling those which the
explorers of the eighteenth and nineteenth centuries attributed to
savages – goodness, simplicity and the desire to imitate men of a
superior race. With such hypotheses it was an easy matter to conceive of an organization of peace and happiness; it was only a matter
of making the rich better and the poorer class more enlightened.
These two operations seemed easily realizable, and then the fusion
of the drawing-room and the factory, which had turned the heads
of so many utopians, would be brought about.[17] It is not upon an

[16] This is what Benedetto Croce pointed out [in 'Cristianesimo, socialismo e
methodo storico'] in *La Critica* of July 1907, pp. 317–19. – This writer is well
known in Italy as a remarkably acute critic and philosopher. [This article was
written by Croce after the publication of Sorel's *Le Système historique de Renan*
and was later used as a preface to the Italian translation of *Réflexions sur la violence*.
Sorel corresponded with Croce for over twenty years, the greater part of this
correspondence being published in *La Critica* between 1927–30.]

[17] In the New Harmony colony, founded by R[obert] Owen, the work done was
sparse and of poor quality, but amusements were abundant; in 1826 the duke of

idyllic, Christian or bourgeois model that the *new school* conceives things; it knows that the progress of production requires entirely different qualities from those met in society people; it is on account of the moral qualities which are necessary to improve production that it is so concerned with ethical matters.

It resembles, then, the economists much more than the utopians; like G[ustave] de Molinari, it considers that the moral progress of the proletariat is as necessary as the material improvement of machinery if modern industry is to be lifted to the increasingly high levels that technical science allows it to attain; but it descends farther than this author does into the depths of the problem and does not content itself with vague recommendations about religious duty;[18] in its insatiable desire for reality, it seeks to arrive at the real roots of this process of moral perfection and desires to know how to *create today the ethic of the producers of the future.*

II

At the beginning of any enquiry on modern ethics this question must be asked: under what conditions is regeneration possible? The Marxists are absolutely right in laughing at the utopians and in maintaining that morality is never created by mild preaching, by the ingenious constructions of theorists, or by fine gestures. Proudhon, having neglected this problem, suffered from many illusions about the persistence of forces that gave life to his ethics; experience was soon to prove that his enterprise was to remain fruitless. And if the contemporary world does not contain the roots of a new ethic, what will happen to it? The sighs of a whimpering bourgeoisie will not save it if it has for ever lost its morality.

Very shortly before his death, Renan was much preoccupied with the ethical future of the world: 'Moral values decline, that is a certainty; sacrifice has almost disappeared; one can see the day coming when everything will be incorporated into groups,[19] when organized

Saxe-Weimar was dazzled by the music and the balls (E[douard] Dolléans, *Robert Owen*, [*1771–1858, Individualisme, philosophie, socialisme* (Paris, Alcan, 1907)], pp. 247–68).

[18] G[ustave] de Molinari appears to believe that a natural religion like that of J[ean-Jacques] Rousseau or Robespierre would suffice. We know today that such means have no moral efficacy.

[19] It is clear that Renan had none of the veneration for the corporatist spirit that so many contemporary idealists display.

selfishness will take the place of love and devotion . . . there will be strange upheavals. The two things that alone until now have resisted the decay of reverence, the army[20] and the Church, will soon be swept away in the general torrent.'[21] Renan showed a remarkable insight in writing this at the very moment when so many futile intellects were announcing the renaissance of idealism and foreseeing progressive tendencies in a Church that was at last reconciled to the modern world. But through all his life Renan had been too favoured by fortune not to be optimistic; he believed, therefore, that the evil of the future would consist simply in the necessity of passing through a bad period, and he added: 'No matter, the resources of humanity are infinite. The eternal designs will be fulfilled, the *springs of life* ever forcing their way to the surface will never be dried up.'

Several months before, he had finished the fifth volume of his *Histoire du peuple d'Israël* and this volume, having been printed from the unaltered manuscript, contains a more imperfect expression of his ideas on this subject; it is known that he corrected his proofs very carefully. We find here the most gloomy forebodings; the author even questions whether humanity will ever attain its real end: 'If this globe should happen not to fulfil its purpose, there will be others to carry on to its final end the programme of all life: light, reason, truth.'[22] The times to come frightened him: 'The immediate future is dark. The triumph of light is not assured.' He dreaded socialism and there is no doubt that by socialism he meant the humanitarian idiocy which he saw emerging in the world of the stupid bourgeoisie; it was in this way that he came to think that Catholicism might perhaps be the accomplice of socialism.[23]

On the same page he speaks of the divisions which can exist in a society, and this is of considerable importance: 'Judea and the Graeco-Roman world were like two universes revolving one beside the other under opposing influences . . . The history of humanity

---

[20] He did not see that his son-in-law would agitate violently against the army in the Dreyfus affair.

[21] [Ernest] Renan, *Feuilles détachées* [Paris, Calmann-Lévy, 1892], p. 14.

[22] [Ernest] Renan, *Histoire du peuple d'Israël* [Paris, Calmann-Lévy, 1889–93], V, p. 421.

[23] *Ibid.*, p. 420.

by no means synchronizes in its various parts. Tremble! At this moment, perhaps, the religion of the future is being created . . . and we have no part in it. I envy wise Kimri who saw beneath the earth! It is there that everything is being prepared, it is there that we must look.' – There is in these words nothing of which the theorists of the class struggle could not approve; in them I find the commentary to what Renan said a little later on the subject of the 'springs of life ever forcing their way to the surface'; regeneration is brought about by a class which works subterraneously and which separates itself from the modern world as Judaism separated itself from the ancient world.

Whatever the official sociologists might think, the lower classes are by no means condemned to live on the crumbs which the upper classes let fall; it is good to see Renan protest against this imbecile doctrine. Syndicalism claims to create a truly proletarian ideology; and, whatever the professors of the bourgeoisie say of it, historical experience, as confirmed by Renan, tells us that this is quite possible and that out of it may come the salvation of the world. It is truly underground that the syndicalist movement is being developed; the men who devote themselves to it do not make much noise in society; what a difference between them and the former leaders of democracy working solely for the conquest of power!

These men were intoxicated by the hope that the chances of history might some day make them *republican princes*.[24] While waiting for the wheel of fortune to turn to their advantage in this way, they obtained the moral and material advantages that celebrity procures for all virtuosi in a society which is accustomed to paying well those who amuse it. Many amongst them had their immeasurable pride as their chief motive force, and they fancied that, as their name was bound to shine with singular brilliancy in the annals of history, they might buy that future glory by a few sacrifices.

None of these motives for action exist for the syndicalists of today: the proletariat has none of the servile instincts of society; it does not aspire to walk on all fours behind a former comrade who has become

---

[24] The essence of democracy is concentrated in the phrase of Mme Flocon: 'It is we who are the princesses.' Democracy is happy when it sees a ridiculous creature such as Félix Faure, whom Joseph Reinach compared to the *bourgeois gentilhomme*, treated with princely honours (*Histoire de l'affaire Dreyfus* [Paris, Editions de la Revue Blanche, 1901–11], IV, p. 552).

the chief magistrate or to swoon for joy before the fine clothes of ministers' wives.[25] The men who devote themselves to the revolutionary cause know that they must always live in conditions of great modesty. They pursue their work of organization without attracting attention, and the most insignificant hack who scribbles for *L'Humanité* is much better known than the activists of the Confédération du Travail; for the great mass of the French public Griffuelhes[f] will never have the notoriety of Rouanet;[g] in the absence of material advantages, which they can hardly expect, they have not even the satisfaction that celebrity can give. Putting their whole trust in the movements of the masses, they have no expectation of a Napoleonic glory and they leave the superstition of great men to the bourgeoisie.

It is good that it is so, because the proletariat will be able to develop itself much more surely if it organizes itself in obscurity; socialist politicians do not like occupations which do not provide celebrity (and which consequently are not profitable); they are not therefore disposed to trouble themselves with the work of groups who wish to remain proletarian; they parade about on the parliamentary stage, but that as a rule does not have serious consequences. The men who truly participate in the working-class

---

[25] Parliamentary socialism is very keen on good manners, as we can assure ourselves by consulting Gérault-Richard's numerous articles. I quote at random several examples. On 1 June 1903, he declared in *La Petite République* that Queen Nathalie of Serbia merited 'a call to order' for having listened to the preaching of the Reverend Pastor Coubé at Aubervilliers and Gérault-Richard demanded that she be admonished by the police commissary of her district. On 26 September, he is roused to indignation by the coarseness and the ignorance of good manners exhibited by Admiral Maréchal. Socialist protocol has its mysteries; the wives of socialist citizens are sometimes called 'ladies' and sometimes 'citizenesses'; in the society of the future there will evidently be disputes about the order of preference as there were at Versailles. – On 30 July 1903, Cassagnac makes great fun in *L'Autorité* of his having been taken to task by Gérault-Richard, who had given him lessons in good manners.

[f] Victor Griffuelhes (1874–1922); general secretary of the Confédération Générale du Travail between 1902–9. Apprenticed as a cobbler, Griffuelhes rose to lead the leather workers' union and then the CGT. His two pamphlets – *L'Action syndicaliste* (1908) and *Le Syndicalisme révolutionnaire* (1909) – give a good account of the principles of revolutionary syndicalism during its 'heroic' period.

[g] Gustave Rouanet (1855–1927); journalist and socialist politician; a close associate of Benoît Malon, Rouanet collaborated on *La Revue socialiste*, before later writing for *La Cri du peuple*, *La Petite République* and *L'Humanité*. He had been a favourite object of Sorel's scorn since the 1890s, when the latter objected to Rouanet's contention that Marxism was opposed to the 'French genius'.

movement of today are an example of what have always been regarded as the highest virtues; they cannot, indeed, acquire any of those things which the bourgeois world sees as especially desirable. If then, as Renan asserts,[26] history rewards the resigned abnegation of men who strive uncomplainingly and who accomplish, without profit, a great work of history, we have a new reason for believing in the advent of socialism, since it represents the highest moral ideal ever conceived by man. It is not a new religion which is shaping itself underground, without the aid of bourgeois thinkers; it is *the birth of a virtue*, a virtue that the Intellectuals of the bourgeoisie are incapable of understanding, a virtue which has the power to save civilization – as Renan hoped it would be saved – but only by the total elimination of the class to which Renan belonged.

Let us now examine closely the reasons which made Renan dread a decadence of the bourgeoisie;[27] he was struck by the decay of religious ideas: 'An immense moral, and *perhaps intellectual*, degeneracy will follow on the day of the disappearance of religion from the world. We can dispense with religion, because others have it for us. Those who do not believe are carried along by the more or less believing majority; but when the majority lose this impulse, the men of spirit will go feebly to the attack.' It is the absence of the sentiment of the sublime which Renan dreaded; like all old people in their days of sadness, he thought of his childhood and adds: 'Man is of value in proportion to the religious sentiment which he preserves from his first education and which colours his whole life.' He himself had lived all his life under the influence of the sentiment of sublimity inculcated in him by his mother; we know, in fact, that Madame Renan was a woman of lofty character. But the source of sublimity is drying up: 'Religious people live in a shadow. We live in the shadow of a shadow. *On what will those who come after us live?*'[28]

As was his custom, Renan tried to mitigate the gloom of the outlook which his perspicacity presented to him; he is like so many

---

[26] Renan, [*Histoire du peuple d'Israël*], IV, p. 267.

[27] Renan pointed out one symptom of decadence, on which he did not insist enough and which does not seem to have particularly struck his readers; he was irritated by the restlessness, the claims to originality, and the naive one-upmanship of the young metaphysicians: 'But, my dear fellows, it is useless to give oneself so much headache, merely to change from one error to another': *Feuilles détachées*, p. X. A restlessness of this kind (which puts on today a sociological, socialist or humanitarian air) is a sure sign of anaemia.

[28] Renan, *Feuilles détachées*, pp. XVII–XVIII.

French writers who, wishing to please a frivolous public, never dare to go to the bottom of the problems that life raises;[29] he does not wish to frighten his amiable lady admirers; he adds therefore that it is not necessary to have a religion burdened with dogmas, a religion analogous to Christianity; the religious sentiment should suffice. After Renan, there has been no lack of blabbermouths to entertain us about this vague religious sentiment which should suffice to replace the positive religions which are coming to grief. F[erdinand] Buisson informs us that 'no religious doctrines will survive, but a religious emotion which, far from contradicting either science, art or morality, will steep them in a feeling of profound harmony with the life of the Universe'.[30] This, unless I delude myself, is complete gibberish.

'On what will those who come after us live?' This is the great problem posed by Renan and which the bourgeoisie will never be able to solve. If any doubt is possible on this point, the stupidities uttered by the official moralists would show that the decadence is henceforth fatal; it is not speculations on the harmony of the Universe (even when the Universe is personified) that will give to men that courage which Renan compared with that of a soldier at the moment of attack. The sublime is dead in the bourgeoisie and it is doomed to possess no ethic in the future.[31] The winding-up of the Dreyfus affair, which, to the great indignation of Colonel Picquart,[32]

---

[29] It is Brunetière who addressed this reproach to French literature: 'If you wish to know why Racine and Molière, for example, never attained the depth we find in a Shakespeare or a Goethe ... look towards a woman, and you will find that the defect is due to the influence of the salons and of women' ([Ferdinand Brunetière] *Evolution des genres* [*dans l'historie de la littérature*], 3rd edn [Paris, Hachette, 1898], p. 128).

[30] *Questions de morale* (lectures given by several professors) in the *Bibliothèque des sciences sociales* [Paris, Alcan, 1900], p. 328. [Sorel was one of the contributors to this volume: see 'La Science et la morale', pp. 1–25; 'Les Facteurs moraux de l'évolution', pp. 74–100.]

[31] I must call attention to the extraordinary prudence shown by [Théodule] Ribot [1839–1916] in his *Psychologie des sentiments* [Paris, Alcan, 1896] in dealing with the evolution of morality; it might have been expected that, on the analogy of the other sentiments, he would have come to the conclusion that there was an evolution towards a purely intellectual state and to the disappearance of its efficacy; but he has not dared to draw this conclusion for morality as he did for religion.

[32] I refer to an article published in *La Gazette de Lausanne*, 2 April 1906, from which *La Libre Parole* gave a fairly long extract (cf. Joseph Reinach, [*Histoire*], VI, p. 36). Several months after I had written these lines Picquart was himself the object of exceptionally favourable treatment; he had been conquered by the fatalities of Parisian life, which have ruined stronger men than he. [Georges Picquart (1854–

the Dreyfusards knew how to put to great advantage, has shown that bourgeois sublimity is a Stock Exchange asset. All the intellectual and moral defects of a class tainted with folly showed themselves in that affair.

III

Before examining what qualities the modern industrial system requires of free producers, we must analyse the component parts of morality. Philosophers always have a certain amount of difficulty in seeing clearly into these ethical problems, because they feel the impossibility of harmonizing the ideas which are current at a given time in a class, and yet they imagine it to be their duty to reduce everything to a unity. In order to conceal from themselves the fundamental heterogeneity of all this civilized morality, they have recourse to a great number of subterfuges, sometimes relegating to the rank of exceptions, importations or survivals, everything which embarrasses them, sometimes drowning reality in an ocean of vague phrases and, most often, employing both methods the better to confuse the question. I believe, on the contrary, that *any group of ideas in the history of thought is best understood if all the contradictions are brought into sharp relief*. I shall adopt this method and take for a starting point the celebrated opposition which Nietzsche[h] has established between two groups of moral values, an opposition about

1914) was one of the heroes of the Dreyfus affair. As head of the intelligence service it was Picquart who was the first to discover the guilt of Esterhazy and thus to establish the innocence of Dreyfus. This earned him public disgrace and a posting overseas. In 1906, with the triumph of the Dreyfusard cause, he was appointed minister of war, a post he held until 1909. It is this that Sorel is referring to when he speaks of Picquart being subject to 'exceptional favours'.]

[h] Friedrich Nietzsche (1844–1900). This is Sorel's only extended discussion of Nietzsche's ideas and is drawn entirely from *On the Genealogy of Morality*. Indeed, there are only three other references to Nietzsche in Sorel's entire work and thus there is general agreement that Sorel should not be placed amongst the numerous French Nietzscheans. Nietzsche, however, was very much in vogue in the first decade of the twentieth century. Daniel Halévy, for example, published his *La Vie de Frédéric Nietzsche* (1909), whilst Sorel's closest intellectual associate, Edouard Berth, made frequent reference to Nietzsche's ideas, regarding him as an indispensable aid to the syndicalist movement in its attempts to unmask the 'intellectualist' philosophy. Significantly, Berth was able to publish these views in Lagardelle's *Le Mouvement socialiste*, the principal mouthpiece of the *new school*.

which much has been written but which has never been properly studied.

A. – We know with what force Nietzsche praised the values constructed by the *masters*, by a superior class of warriors who, in their expeditions, enjoying to the full freedom from all social constraint, return to the simplicity of mind of a wild beast, become once more triumphant monsters who continually bring to mind 'the superb blond beast, prowling in search of prey and bloodshed' in whom 'a basis of hidden bestiality needs from time to time an outlet'. To understand this thesis properly, we must not attach too much importance to formulas which have at times been intentionally exaggerated, but should examine the historical facts; the author tells us that he has in mind 'the aristocracy of Rome, Arabia, Germany and Japan, the *Homeric heroes*, the Scandinavian Vikings'.

It is chiefly the Homeric heroes that we must have in mind in order to understand what Nietzsche wished to make clear to his contemporaries. We must remember that he had been professor of Greek at the University of Basle and that his reputation began with a book devoted to the glorification of the Hellenic genius (*L'Origine de la tragédie*). He observes that, even at the period of their highest culture, the Greeks still preserved a memory of their former character as *masters*: 'Our daring', said Pericles, 'has traced a path over earth and sea, raising everywhere imperishable monuments both of good and evil.' It was of the heroes of Greek legend and history that Nietzsche was thinking when he speaks of 'that audacity of noble races, that mad, absurd and spontaneous audacity ... their indifference and contempt for all security of the body, for life, for comfort'. Does not 'the terrible gaiety and the profound joy which [the heroes] tasted in destruction, in all the pleasures of victory and of cruelty' apply particularly to Achilles?[33]

It was certainly to the model of classical Greece that Nietzsche alluded when he writes: 'The moral judgements of the warrior aristocracy are founded on a powerful bodily constitution, a flourishing health, without forgetting what is necessary to the maintenance of

[33] Friedrich Nietzsche, [*La*] *Généalogie de la morale*, French trans. [Paris, Mercure de France, 1900], pp. 58–9. [See *On the Genealogy of Morality* (Cambridge, Cambridge University Press, 1994), p. 25.]

that overflowing vigour: war, adventure, hunting, dancing, games and physical exercises and, in general, everything implied by a robust, free and joyful activity.'[34]

That very ancient figure, the Achaean ideal celebrated by Homer, is not simply a memory; it has reappeared several times in the world. 'During the Renaissance there was a superb reawakening of the classical ideal, of the aristocratic valuation of things'; and, after the Revolution, 'the most prodigious and unexpected event came to pass: the antique ideal stood *in person* and with unwonted splendour before the eyes and the conscience of humanity . . . [Then] appeared Napoleon, a unique and belated example though he was.'[35]

I believe that if Nietzsche had not been so dominated by his memories of being a professor of philology, he would have perceived that the *master* type still exists under our own eyes, and that it is this type which, at the present time, creates the extraordinary greatness of the United States; he would have been struck by the singular analogies that exist between the Yankee, ready for any kind of enterprise, and the ancient Greek sailor, sometimes a pirate, sometimes a colonist or a merchant; above all, he would have established a parallel between the ancient heroes and the man who sets out to conquer the Far West.[36] P[aul] de Rousiers has described the *master* type admirably: 'To become and to remain an American, one must consider life *as a struggle and not as a pleasure*, and seek in it victorious effort, energetic and efficient action, rather than pleasure, than leisure embellished by the cultivation of the arts and the refinements proper to other societies. Everywhere . . . we have seen what makes the American succeed, what constitutes his type . . . it is moral character, personal energy, energy in action, creative energy.'[37] The profound contempt which the Greek had for the barbarian is matched by that of the Yankee for the foreign worker who makes

---

[34] *Ibid.*, p. 43. [See *On the Genealogy of Morality*, p. 18.]

[35] *Ibid.*, pp. 78–80. [See *On the Genealogy of Morality*, pp. 35–6.]

[36] P[aul] de Rousiers observes that everywhere in America approximately the same social environment is found, the same type of men at the head of big businesses; but 'it is in the West that the qualities and the defects of this extraordinary people manifest themselves with the greatest energy; . . . *it is there that the key to the whole social system is to be found*' (*La Vie américaine: ranches, fermes, et usines*, [Paris, Fermin-Didot, 1899], pp. 8–9; cf. p. 261).

[37] [Paul] de Rousiers, *La Vie américaine: l'éducation et la société* [Paris, Fermin-Didot, 1899], p. 325.

no effort to become truly American. 'Many of these people would be better if we took them in hand', an old colonel of the War of Secession said to a French traveller, 'but we are a proud race'; a shopkeeper from Pottsville spoke of the Pennsylvania miners as 'the senseless populace'.[38] J[ean] Bourdeau has drawn attention to the strange likeness which exists between the ideas of A[ndrew] Carnegie and [Theodore] Roosevelt and those of Nietzsche, the first deploring the waste of money in maintaining the incapable, the second urging the Americans to become conquerors, a race of prey.[39]

I am not among those who consider Homer's Achaen type, the indomitable hero, confident in his strength and putting himself above rules, as necessarily disappearing in the future. If this has often been believed, it is because the Homeric values were imagined to be irreconcilable with other values which spring from an entirely different principle; Nietzsche committed this error, which all those who believe in the necessity of unity in thought are bound to make. It is quite evident that liberty would be seriously compromised if men came to regard the Homeric values (which are approximately the same as the values of Corneille)[i] as suitable only to barbaric peoples. Many moral evils would prevent humanity from progressing if some hero of revolt did not force the people to examine its conscience; and art, which is after all of some value, would lose the finest jewel in its crown.

The philosophers are little disposed to admit the right of art to support the cult of the 'will to power'; it seems to them that they ought to give lessons to artists, instead of receiving lessons from them; they believe that only those sentiments which have received the stamp of the universities have the right to manifest themselves in poetry. Art, like industry, has never adapted itself to the demands

---

[38] De Rousiers, *La Vie américaine: ranches, fermes et usines*, pp. 303–5.
[39] J[ean] Bourdeau, *Les Maîtres de la pensée contemporaine* [Paris, Alcan, 1904], p. 145. The author informs us on the other hand that 'Jaurès greatly astonished the people of Geneva by revealing to them that the hero of Nietzsche, the *superman*, was nothing else but the proletariat' (p. 139). I have not been able to get any information about this lecture of Jaurès; let us hope that he will some day publish it, for our amusement.

[i] Pierre Corneille (1606–84); one of the great dramatists of French classical theatre. In general, Corneille exalts the possibility of man rising above his tragic destiny, with his characters possessed of almost superhuman will and strength.

of the theorists; it always upsets their plans of social harmony; humanity has found the freedom of art far too satisfying ever to think of allowing it to be controlled by the creators of dull systems of sociology. The Marxists are accustomed to seeing the ideologists look at things the wrong way round and so, in contrast to their enemies, they should look upon art as a reality which begets ideas and not as an application of ideas.

B. – To the values created by the *masters*, Nietzsche opposes the system created by sacerdotal castes, the ascetic ideal against which he has piled up so much invective. The history of these values is much more obscure and complicated than that of the preceding ones; the German author tries to connect the origin of asceticism with psychological reasons that I will not examine here. He certainly makes a mistake in attributing a preponderant part to the Jews; it is not at all evident that antique Judaism had an ascetic character; doubtless, like the other Semitic religions, it attached importance to pilgrimages, fasts and prayers recited in ragged clothes; the Hebrew poets sang the hope of revenge that existed in the heart of the persecuted; but, until the second century of our era, the Jews looked to be revenged by arms;[40] – on the other hand, with them family life was too strong for the monkish ideal ever to become important.

As imbued with Christianity as our modern civilization may be, it is none the less evident that, even in the Middle Ages, it submitted to influences foreign to the Church, with the result that the old ascetic ideals were gradually transformed. The values to which the contemporary world clings most closely, and which it considers the true *values of virtue*, are not realized in convents, but in the family; respect for the human person, sexual fidelity and devotion to the weak constitute the elements of morality of which all high-minded men are proud; – indeed, very often morality is made to consist of these alone.

When we examine in a critical spirit the numerous writings which today discuss marriage, we see that the serious reformers propose to improve family relations in such a way as to assure the better

---

[40] It is always necessary to remember that the resigned Jew of the Middle Ages was more like the Christians than his ancestors.

realization of these ethical values; thus, they demand that the scandals of conjugal life shall not be exposed in the law courts, that unions shall not be maintained when fidelity no longer exists, and that the authority of the head of the family shall not be diverted from its moral purpose to become mere exploitation, etc.

On the other hand, it is curious to observe to what extent the modern Church misunderstands the values that classico-Christian civilization has produced: it sees in marriage, above all, a contract directed by financial and worldly interests; it is extremely indulgent towards love affairs; it is unwilling to allow that the union be dissolved when the household is a hell, and takes no account of the obligation of devotion. The priests are wonderfully skilful in procuring rich dowries for impoverished nobles, so much so that the Church has been accused of considering marriage as a coupling of noblemen living as *pimps* with bourgeois women reduced to the role of *prostitutes*. When it is heavily recompensed, the Church finds unexpected reasons for divorce and finds means of annulling inconvenient unions for ridiculous motives: 'Is it possible', asks Proudhon ironically, 'for a responsible man of a serious turn of mind, a true Christian, to care for the love of his wife? . . . If the husband seeking divorce or the wife seeking separation, alleges the refusal of the *debitum*, then there is a legitimate reason for a rupture, for the service for which the marriage is granted has not been carried out.'[41]

Our civilization, having come to consider nearly all morality as consisting of values derived from those observed in the normally constituted family, produces from this two very serious consequences: 1) it has been asked if, instead of considering the family as an application of moral theories, it would not be more exact to say that it is the base of these theories; 2) it seems that the Church, having become incompetent on matters connected with sexual union, must also be incompetent as regards morality. These are precisely the conclusions to which Proudhon came: 'Sexual duality was created by Nature to be the instrument of Justice . . . To produce Justice is the higher aim of the bisexual division: generation, and what follows from it, only figure here as accessory.'[42] –

---

[41] Proudhon, [*De la Justice*], IV, p. 99. We know that the theologians do not like curious people to consult ecclesiastical writings about *conjugal duty* and the legitimate method of fulfilling it.

[42] *Ibid.*, p. 212.

'Marriage, both in principle and in purpose, being *the very instrument of human right*, the living negation of the divine right is thus in formal contradiction with theology and the Church.'[43]

Love, by the enthusiasm it begets, can produce that sublimity without which there would be no effective morality. At the end of his book on Justice, Proudhon has written pages on the role of women which will never be surpassed.

C. – Finally we have to examine the values which escape Nietzsche's classification and which deal with *civil relations*. Originally, magic was much mixed up in the evaluation of these values; among the Jews, until recent times, one finds a mixture of hygienic principles, rules about sexual relationships, precepts about honesty, benevolence and national solidarity, the whole wrapped up in magical superstitions; this mixture, which seems strange to the philosopher, had the happiest influence on their morality as long as they maintained their traditional way of life; and one notices among them even now a particular exactitude in the carrying out of contracts.

The ideas held by modern moralists are drawn mainly from those of Greece in its time of decadence; Aristotle, living in a period of transition, combined ancient values with values that, as time went on, were to prevail; wars and production had ceased to occupy the attention of the most distinguished men of the towns, who sought to secure an easy existence for themselves; the most important thing was the establishment of friendly relations between the well brought up men of the community, and the fundamental maxim therefore was that of always remaining within a happy medium; the new morality was to be acquired principally by means of the habits which the young Greek would pick up in mixing with cultivated people. It may be said that here we are on the level of an ethic adapted to consumers; it is not surprising then that Catholic theologians still find Aristotle's ethics an excellent one, for they themselves take the consumer's point of view.

In the civilization of antiquity, the ethics of the producers could hardly be any other than that of slave-owners and it did not seem

---

[43] Proudhon, *Oeuvres* [Paris, Lacroix, 1868], XX, p. 169. This is extracted from the memoir he wrote in his own defence before the Paris High Court after he had been condemned to three years in prison for his book on Justice. – It is worthwhile noting that Proudhon was accused of attacking marriage! This affair is one of the shameful acts which dishonoured the Church in the reign of Napoleon III.

worth developing at length at the time when philosophy made an inventory of Greek customs. Aristotle says that no sophisticated and far-reaching science was needed to employ slaves: 'It consists only in knowing *how to order what the slaves must carry out.* So, as soon as a man can save himself this trouble, he leaves it in charge of a steward, so as to be himself free for a political or philosophical life.'[44] A little farther on he writes: 'It is manifest, then, that the master ought to be the source of excellence in the slave; but not merely because he possesses the art which *trains him in his duties.*'[45] This clearly expresses the preoccupations of the urban consumer who finds it very tiresome to be obliged to pay any attention whatever to the conditions of production.[46]

As to the slave, he needs very limited virtues: 'He needs only enough to prevent him from neglecting his work through intemperance or idleness.' He should be treated with 'more indulgence even than children', although certain people consider that slaves are deprived of reason and are only fit to receive orders.[47]

It is quite easy to see that for a considerable period the moderns did not think that there was anything more to be said about the workers than Aristotle had said: they must be given orders; they should be corrected with gentleness like children; they ought to be treated like passive instruments who do not need to think. Revol-

---

[44] Aristotle, *Politique*, bk I, chap. II, 23. [Aristotle, *The Politics*, bk I, chap. VII.]
[45] *Ibid.*, bk I, chap. V, 11. [Aristotle, *The Politics*, bk I, chap. XIII.]
[46] Xenophon, who represents in everything a conception of Greek life very much earlier than the time in which he lived, discusses the proper method of training an overseer for a farm (*Oeconomicus*, [sections] 12–14). [For a fuller discussion of Xenophon in Sorel's writings, see Sorel, *Le Procès de Socrate* (Paris, Alcan, 1889)]. Marx remarks that Xenophon speaks of the division of labour in the workshop and that appears to him to show a bourgeois instinct ([*Le*] *Capital* [Paris, Librairie du Progrès, 1875], I, p. 159, col. 1 [see *Capital* (New York, Charles H. Kerr, 1906), p. 402]); I myself think that it characterizes an observer who understood the importance of production, an importance of which Plato had no comprehension. In *Memorabilia* (book II, 7) Socrates advises a citizen, who had to look after a large family, to set up a workshop with his family; J[acques] Flach supposes that this was something new (*Leçon du 19e avril 1907*); it seems to me to be a return to more ancient customs. The historians of philosophy appear to me to have been very hostile to Xenophon because he is too much of an *old Greek*; Plato suits them better since he is more of an *aristocrat* and consequently more detached from production. [Jacques Flach (1846–1919) held the post of chair of comparative law. In addition to those of Bergson, Sorel regularly attended his lectures.]
[47] Aristotle, [*Politique*], bk I, chap. V, 9 and 11.

utionary syndicalism would be impossible if the world of the workers were under the influence of such a *morality of the weak*; state socialism, on the contrary, could accommodate itself perfectly to this morality, since it is based on the idea of a society divided into a class of producers and a class of thinkers applying the results of scientific investigation to the work of production. The only difference which would exist between this sham socialism and capitalism would consist in the employment of more ingenious methods of procuring discipline in the workshop.

At the present moment, the official moralists of the Bloc are working to create a kind of ethical discipline which will replace the vague religion that G[ustave] de Molinari thinks necessary for the successful working of capitalism. It is very clear, in fact, that religion is daily losing its efficacy with the people; something else must be found, if the Intellectuals are to be provided with the means of continuing to live off the production of others.

IV

The problem which we shall now try to solve is the most difficult of all those which a socialist writer can touch upon; we are about to ask how it is possible to conceive of the transformation of the men of today into the free producers of tomorrow working in workshops where there are no masters. The question must be expressed accurately; we pose it not for a world that has already arrived at socialism, but solely for our own time and for the preparation of the transition from one world to the other; if we do not limit the question in this way, we shall find ourselves straying into utopias.

Kautsky has given a great deal of attention to the question of the conditions immediately following a social revolution; the solution he proposes seems to me to be quite as feeble as that of G[ustave] de Molinari. If the *syndicats* are strong enough to induce the workers of today to abandon their workshops and to submit to great sacrifices during strikes kept up against the capitalists, they will doubtless be strong enough to bring the workers back to the workshops and to obtain excellent work from them, when once they see that this work is necessary for the general good.[48] Kautsky, however,

[48] Karl Kautsky, *La Révolution sociale*, French trans. [Paris, Rivière, 1901], p. 153.

does not seem to feel much confidence in the excellence of his solution.

Evidently no comparison can be made between the kind of discipline which forces a general stoppage of work on workers and that which will induce them to handle machinery with greater skill. The error springs from the fact that Kautsky is more of an ideologue than he is a disciple of Marx; he loves to reason about abstractions and believes that he has brought a question nearer to solution when he manages to produce a phrase with a scientific appearance; the underlying reality interests him less than its academic presentation. Many others have committed the same error, led astray by the different meanings of the word 'discipline', which may be applied both to regular conduct founded on the deepest feelings of the soul or to a merely external restraint.

The history of ancient corporations furnishes us with no really useful information on the subject; they do not seem to have had any effect whatever in promoting any progressive movement; it would seem rather that they served to protect routine. If we examine English trade unionism closely, we find that it also is strongly imbued with this industrial routine springing from the corporative spirit.

Nor can the example of democracy throw any light on the question. Work conducted democratically would be regulated by resolutions, inspected by police and subject to the sanction of tribunals dealing out penalties or imprisonment. Discipline would be an exterior constraint closely analogous to that which now exists in capitalist workshops; but it would probably be still more arbitrary because of the electoral calculations of the various committees. When one thinks of the peculiarities found in judgements in penal cases, one feels easily convinced that repression would be exercised in a very unsatisfactory manner. It seems to be generally agreed that light offences cannot be properly dealt with in law courts, when hampered by the rules of a strict legal system; the establishment of administrative councils to decide on the future of children has often been suggested; in Belgium, begging is subject to an administrative arbitration which may be compared to the policing of morals; it is well known that this sort of policing, in spite of innumerable complaints, continues to be almost supreme in France. It is very noticeable that administrative intervention in the case of important crimes is continually increasing, since the power of mitigating or even of suppressing penalties is being more and more handed over to the heads of penal establishments; doctors and sociologists speak loudly in favour of this system, which tends to give the police as important a function as they had under the *ancien régime*. Experience shows that the discipline of the capitalist workshops is greatly superior to that maintained by the police, so that it cannot be seen how it would be possible to improve capitalist discipline by means of the methods that democracy would have at its disposal.[49]

I think, however, that there is one good point in Kautsky's hypothesis: he seems to have been aware that the motive force of the revolutionary movement must also be the motive force of the ethic of the producers; this is a view quite in conformity with Marxist principles, but the idea must be applied in quite a different way from that in which the German author applied it. It must not be thought that the action of the *syndicat* on work is direct, as he supposes; the influence will result from complex and distant causes.

A satisfactory result can be arrived at by starting from the curious analogies that exist between the most remarkable qualities of the soldiers who took part in the wars of Liberty, those that engender the propaganda in favour of the general strike, and those that will be required of a free worker in a highly progressive state of society. I believe that these analogies constitute a new (and perhaps decisive) proof in favour of revolutionary syndicalism.

In the wars of Liberty each soldier considered himself as an *individual* having something of importance to do in the battle, instead of looking upon himself as simply one part of the military mechanism entrusted to the supreme direction of a leader. In the literature of those times one is struck by the frequency with which the *free men* of the republican armies are contrasted with the *automatons* of the royal armies; this was no mere figure of rhetoric employed by the French writers; I have convinced myself, as a result of a thorough personal study of one of the wars of this period, that these terms corresponded perfectly to the actual sentiments of the soldier.

Battles, therefore, could no longer be likened to games of chess in which each man is comparable to a pawn; they became collections

---

[49] We might ask if the ideal of the relatively honest and enlightened democrats is not at the present moment the discipline of the capitalist workshop. The increase in the power given to the mayors and State governors in America seems to me to be a sign of this tendency.

of heroic exploits accomplished by individuals who drew the
motives of their conduct from their enthusiasm. Revolutionary literature is not entirely false when it reports so many grandiloquent
phrases said to have been uttered by the combatants; doubtless none
of these words were spoken by the people to whom they are attributed; their form is due to men of letters used to manipulating
classical declamation; but the content is real, in the sense that we
have, thanks to the falsehoods of revolutionary rhetoric, a perfectly
exact representation of the angle through which the combatants
looked on war, a true expression of the sentiments that it provoked
and the *very tone of the truly Homeric conflicts* which took place at
the time. I do not think that any of the actors in these dramas ever
protested against the words attributed to them; that is because each
rediscovered his own intimate soul beneath the fantastic detail.[50]

Until the moment when Napoleon appeared, the war had none of
the scientific character which later theorists of strategy have sometimes believed should be attributed to it; misled by the analogy which
they discovered between the triumphs of the revolutionary armies and
those of the Napoleonic armies, historians imagined that the generals
prior to Napoleon had made great plans of campaign; such plans never
existed or had but very little influence on the course of operations.
The best officers of that time fully realized that their talent consisted
in furnishing their troops with the material means of expressing their
enthusiasm; victory was assured each time that the soldiers could give
free rein to all their spirit, unfettered by the poor administration of
supplies or by the stupidity of the representatives of the people looking upon themselves as strategists. On the field of battle, those in
charge gave an example of the most audacious courage and were
merely the first combatants, like true Homeric kings: it is this which,
amongst the young troops, explains the enormous prestige immediately gained by so many non-commissioned officers of the *ancien
régime* who were borne to the highest rank by the unanimous accla-
mations of the soldiers at the outset of the war.

If we wished to find, in these first armies, what it was that took
the place of the later idea of discipline, we might say that the soldier
was convinced that the slightest failure of the most lowly soldier

---

[50] This history has also been burdened by a great number of adventures which have
been fabricated by imitating real adventures and which have an obvious likeness
to those which later on were rendered popular by *Les Trois Mousquetaires*.

might compromise the success of the whole and the life of all his comrades – and that the soldier acted accordingly. This presupposes that no account is taken of the relative values of the different factors that go to make up victory, so that all things are considered from a *qualitative and individualistic* point of view. One is, indeed, struck by the individualistic characters which are met in these armies and one finds nothing which resembles the obedience spoken of by our contemporary authors. There is therefore some truth in saying that the incredible French victories were due to intelligent bayonets.[51]

The same spirit is found in the working-class groups who are enthusiastic about the general strike; these groups, in fact, picture the revolution as an immense uprising which can again be defined as individualistic: each one marching with as much fervour as possible, each acting on his own account, and hardly troubling to subordinate his conduct to a carefully drawn up overall plan. This character of the proletarian general strike has often been pointed out and it has the effect of frightening the greedy politicians who understand perfectly well that a revolution of this kind would do away with all their chances of seizing the government.

Jaurès, whom nobody would dream of classing with any but the most circumspect of men, has clearly recognized the danger that threatens him; he accuses the supporters of the general strike of *fragmenting life* and thus going against the revolution.[52] This nonsense should be translated thus: the revolutionary syndicalists wish to extol the individuality of the life of the producer; they therefore go against the interests of the politicians, who want to direct the

---

[51] In a pamphlet that caused some uproar, General Donop denounced the ridiculous effects of contemporary discipline, which gives officers 'habits of servility'; like Bugeaud and Dragomiroff, he would like every participant in the battle to know the plan of his leaders in detail; he finds it absurd that 'acts of war are frowned on and proscribed, since they call into play and put to the test the noblest faculties of man, under the most difficult and the most tragic of circumstances, thought, the human soul, in the fullness of all the power that God, the God of armies, has given to them for the defence and for the triumph of noble causes': *Commandement et obéissance* [Paris, Nouvelle librairie nationale, 1907], pp. 14–19 and p. 37. [Sorel reviewed this text in *Le Mouvement socialiste* 188 (July 1907), pp. 92–3, commenting that 'the pamphlet has been written above all to defend the officers who have been pursued through the application of political–ecclesiastical laws'.] This general was one of the most eminent leaders of our cavalry; this branch of the army seems to have preserved a conception of war much superior to those which remain in the other branches.

[52] [Jean] Jaurès, *Etudes socialistes* [Paris, Ollendorf, 1902], pp. 117–18.

revolution in such a way as to transmit power to a new minority; they undermine the foundations of the State. We entirely agree with all of this; and it is precisely this character (which so terrifies the parliamentary socialists, financiers and theorists) which gives such extraordinary moral weight to the notion of the general strike.

The adherents of the general strike are accused of anarchical tendencies; and, indeed, it has been observed that anarchists have entered the *syndicats* in significant numbers during the last few years and that they have worked hard to develop tendencies favourable to the general strike.

This movement becomes understandable when we bear in mind the preceding explanations; for the general strike, like the wars of Liberty, is the most striking manifestation of *individualistic force in the rebellious masses*. It seems to me, in addition, that the official socialists would do well not to insist too much on this point, because they run the risk of inspiring reflections that would not be to their advantage. We might, in fact, be led to ask if our official socialists, with their passion for discipline and their infinite confidence in the genius of their leaders, are not the authentic heirs to the royal armies while the anarchists and the adherents of the general strike represent today the spirit of the revolutionary armies who, against all the rules of the art of war, so thoroughly thrashed the fine armies of the coalition. I can understand that the socialists endorsed, controlled and duly patented by the administrators of *L'Humanité*, have not much sympathy for the heroes of Fleurus,[i] who were very badly dressed and who would have cut sorry figures in the drawing-rooms of the great financiers; but not everybody adapts his convictions to suit the convenience of the business partners of Jaurès.

V

We are now going to try to point out the analogies that will show how revolutionary syndicalism is the great educative force that contemporary society has at its disposal for preparing the work of the future.

---

[i] From 1792 onwards, the French were obliged to undertake a major restructuring of the armed forces, producing an army of over 1,169,000 men by September 1794. The battle of Fleurus, on 26 June 1794, was the major fruit of this reorganization, opening the way for a renewed invasion of Belgium and putting an end to the threat of invasion by Austria.

A. – The free producer in a highly progressive workshop must never measure his efforts by an external standard; he finds all the models presented to him to be mediocre and wants to surpass everything that has been done before him. Production is thus assured of constant improvement in both quality and quantity; the idea of indefinite progress is realized in such a workshop.

The early socialists had had an intuition of this law when they asked that each should produce according to his abilities; but they did not know how to explain this principle which, in their utopias, seemed made more for a convent or for a family than for a modern society. Sometimes, however, they pictured the men of their utopias as possessed by a fervour similar to that which we find in the lives of certain great artists: this last point of view is not unimportant, although the early socialists hardly understood the value of this comparison.

Every time that we approach a question relating to industrial progress we are led to regard art as an *anticipation* of the highest form of production – even though the artist, with his capricious character, often seems to be the very opposite of the modern worker.[53] This analogy is justified by the fact that the artist does not like to reproduce standard models; the *infinite nature of his will* distinguishes him from the ordinary artisan, who is mainly successful in the unending reproduction of models which are not his own. The inventor is an artist who exhausts himself in pursuit of the realization of ends that ordinary people generally regard as absurd and who, if he has made an important discovery, is often thought to be mad; – practical people resemble artisans. In every industry one could cite significant advances which originated in small changes made by workers endowed with the artist's taste for innovation.

[53] When we speak of the educative value of art, we often forget that the patterns of behaviour of modern artists, founded on an imitation of those of a jovial aristocracy, are in no way necessary and are derived from a tradition which has been fatal to many fine talents. – Lafargue appears to believe that a Parisian jeweller might find it necessary to dress elegantly, to eat oysters and to run after women in order 'to keep up the artistic quality of his work': ['La théorie de la plus-valeur de Karl Marx et la critique de M. Paul Leroy-Beaulieu',] *Journal des économistes* [27] (September 1884), p. 386. He gives no reasons to support this paradox; we might, moreover, point out that Marx's son-in-law is always obsessed by aristocratic concerns.

This state of mind is, moreover, exactly that which was found in the first armies that fought in the wars of Liberty and that which is possessed by the propagandists of the general strike. This passionate individualism is totally lacking in the working classes who have been educated by politicians; all they are fit for is to change their masters. These *bad shepherds*[k] sincerely hope that it will be so; and the people of the Stock Exchange would not provide them with money if they were not convinced that parliamentary socialism is quite compatible with financial robbery.

B. – Modern industry is characterized by an ever-increasing concern for exactitude; to the extent that tools become more scientific it is demanded that the product will have fewer hidden faults and that its quality shall be as good in use as in appearance.

If Germany has not yet taken the place in the economic world which the mineral resources of its soil, the energy of its manufacturers and the technological expertise of its technicians ought to give it, it is because for a long time its producers believed that it was smart to flood the market with cheap goods; although German production has greatly improved during the last few years, it is not yet held in very high esteem.

Here again it is possible to draw a comparison between highly perfected industry and art. There have been periods when the public appreciated above all the tricks by which the artist created an illusion; but these methods have never been accepted in the great schools and they are universally condemned by authors who are accepted as authorities in questions of aesthetics.[54]

This integrity, which now seems to us as necessary in industry as in art, was hardly suspected by the utopians;[55] Fourier,[l] at the

---

[54] See the chapter in [John] Ruskin's *Les Sept Lampes de l'architecture* [Paris, Société d'édition artistique, 1900], entitled 'Lampe de vérité'. [*The Seven Lamps of Architecture* (London, Smith Elder & Co., 1849), 'The lamp of truth', pp. 27–62.]

[55] It must not be forgotten that there are two ways of discussing art; Nietzsche attacks Kant for having, 'like all the philosophers, meditated on art and the beautiful as a *spectator* instead of looking at the aesthetic problem from the point of view of the artist, the *creator*': [*La Généalogie de la morale*,] p. 178. [See *On the Genealogy of Morality*, p. 78.] In the time of the utopians, aesthetics was nothing but

[k] This is a reference to a play by Octave Mirbeau (1848–1917), *Les mauvaises bergers*, first performed on 14 December 1898.

[l] Charles Fournier (1772–1837); utopian socialist and author of *Le Nouveau monde industriel et sociétaire* (1829–30).

245

beginning of the new era, believed that fraud in the quality of merchandise was a characteristic trait of the relations between civilized people; he turned his back on progress and showed himself to be incapable of understanding the world which was being formed around him; like nearly all professional prophets, this would-be oracle confused the future with the past. Marx, on the contrary, said that 'deception in merchandise in the capitalist system of production is unjust' because it no longer corresponds to the modern system of business.[56]

The soldier of the wars of Liberty attached an almost superstitious importance to the carrying out of the smallest order. As a result, he felt no pity for the generals or the officers whom he saw guillotined after a defeat on the charge of the dereliction of duty; he did not look at these events as a historian would judge them today; he had no means of knowing if the condemned had committed an act of treason. In his eyes, failure could only be explained by some grave error on the part of his leaders. The high sense of responsibility that the soldier had towards his own duty, and the excessive integrity he brought to the execution of the least order, made him approve of the rigorous measures taken against men who seemed to him to have brought about the defeat of the army and caused it to lose the fruit of so much heroism.

It is not difficult to see that the same spirit is met with during strikes; the defeated workers are convinced that their lack of success is due to the base conduct of a few comrades who have not done all that might be expected of them; numerous accusations of treason are brought forward because, for the vanquished masses, treason alone can explain the defeat of heroic troops; the sentiment, felt by all, of the integrity that must be brought to the accomplishment of responsibilities will therefore be accompanied by many acts of violence. I do not think that the authors who have written on the events that follow strikes have sufficiently reflected on the analogy which exists between strikes and the wars of Liberty and, consequently, between these acts of violence and the executions of generals accused of treason.[57]

the gossip of amateurs, who were delighted with the cleverness with which the artist had been able to deceive the public.

[56] Marx, *Le Capital*, French trans., III, first part, p. 375.

[57] P[aul] Bureau has devoted a chapter of his book on *Le Contrat de travail* [Paris, Alcan, 1902] to an explanation of the reasons which justify the boycotting of

C. – There would never have been any great acts of valour in war if each soldier, while acting as an heroic individual, claimed to receive a reward equal to his merit. When a column sets forth on an assault the men who march at its head know that they are sent to their death and that glory will fall upon those who, passing over their dead bodies, enter the enemy's position; however, they do not reflect upon this great injustice but march forward.

When in an army the need for rewards is strongly felt, it may be said that its value is on the decline. Officers who served in the campaigns of the Revolution and of the Empire, but who only served under the direct orders of Napoleon in the last years of their career, were amazed at the fuss made about feats of arms which, at the time of their youth, would have passed unnoticed: 'I have been overwhelmed with praise', said General Duhesne, 'for things which would not have been noticed in the army of Sambre-et-Meuse.'[58] The showing off was carried by Murat[m] to a grotesque level, and historians have not taken enough notice of the responsibility of Napoleon for this degeneracy of the true martial spirit. The great enthusiasm which had been the cause of so many marvellous deeds on the part of the men of 1794 was entirely foreign to him; he believed that it belonged to him to measure all abilities and to give to each a reward exactly proportionate to what he had accomplished; this was the Saint-Simonian principle already coming into practice[59] and every officer was encouraged to push himself forward. Charlatanism exhausted the moral forces of the nation whilst its material forces were still very considerable; Napoleon formed very few

workers who did not follow their comrades in a strike; he thinks that these people merit their treatment because they are manifestly of inferior worth, both professionally and morally. This seems to me to be very inadequate as an account of the reasons which, in the eyes of the working masses, explain these acts of violence. The author takes up a far too intellectualist point of view.

[58] [Gabriel] Laffaille, *Mémoires sur les campagnes de Catalogne de 1808 à 1814*, [Paris, Anselin et Pochard, 1826], p. 336.

[59] The charlatanism of the Saint-Simonians was as disgusting as that of Murat; moreover, the history of this school is unintelligible if we do not compare it with its Napoleonic models.

[m] In 1793 the title of marshall or *maréchal* was abolished, but it was revived by Napoleon in 1804, when eighteen *maréchaux* were created. One of these was Joachim Murat (1771–1815). A brilliant soldier who was promoted to general on the battlefield of Aboukir in 1799, he subsequently married Napoleon's sister Caroline, was created a prince in 1805 and then king of Naples in 1808. He was subsequently shot by royalists in 1815.

distinguished general officers and carried on the war principally
with those that the Revolution had left him; this impotence is the
most absolute condemnation of the system.[60]

The poverty of the information that we possess about the great
Gothic artists has often been pointed out. Among the stone-carvers
who sculptured the statues in the cathedrals there were men of great
talent who seem always to have remained hidden amongst the mass of
their companions; nevertheless they produced masterpieces: Viollet-
le-Duc[n] found it strange that the archives of Notre-Dame had preserved for us no detailed information about the construction of this
gigantic public building and that, as a general rule, the documents of
the Middle Ages say very little about the architects; he adds that
'genius can develop itself in obscurity and that it is its very nature to
seek silence and obscurity'.[61] We might even go further and ask ourselves whether their contemporaries suspected that these artists of
genius were erecting buildings of an imperishable glory; it seems very
probable to me that the cathedrals were only admired by the artists.

This striving towards excellence, which exists in the absence of
any personal, immediate or proportional reward, constitutes the
secret virtue that assures the continued progress of the world. What
would become of modern industry if inventors could only be found
for those things which would procure them an almost certain
remuneration? The occupation of inventor is the most miserable of
all and yet there is no lack of them. How many times in workshops
have little modifications introduced by ingenious workers into their

---

[60] General Donop insists strongly on the deficiency of Napoleon's lieutenants who
passively obeyed instructions that they did not try to understand and whose
execution was minutely overlooked by the master ([*Commandement et obéissance*],
pp. 28–9 and 32–3). In such an army all merit was theoretically equalized and
constituted standards of recompense; but in practice errors of evaluation were
innumerable.

[61] [Eugène-Emmanuel] Viollet-le-Duc, *Dictionnaire raisonné de l'architecture française*
[Paris, Bance, 1854–68], IV, pp. 42–3. This is not in contradiction with what he
says in the article 'Architect'; here we learn that the builders often inscribed their
names in the cathedrals (I, pp. 109–11); from that it has to be concluded that
these works were not anonymous (L[ouis] Bréhier, *Les Eglises gothiques* [Paris,
Bloud, 1905], p. 17); but what meaning did these inscriptions have for the people
of the town? They could only be of interest to artists who came later on to work
on the same edifice and who were familiar with the traditions of the schools.

[n] Eugène-Emmanuel Viollet-le-Duc (1814–79); architect and restorer of medieval
buildings, and especially of Notre-Dame.

work become, by accumulation, fundamental improvements, without the innovators ever getting any permanent and appreciable benefit for their ingenuity? And has not even simple piece-work brought about a gradual but uninterrupted progress in production which, after having temporarily improved the position of a few workers and especially that of their employers, has proved finally of benefit to the consumer?

Renan asked what it was that moved the heroes of the great wars: 'The soldier of Napoleon was well aware that he would always be a poor man; but he felt that the epic in which he participated would be eternal, that he would live on in the glory of France.' The Greeks had fought for glory; the Russians and the Turks seek death because they expect a chimerical paradise. 'One does not become a soldier through promises of temporal rewards. He must have immortality. For want of paradise, there is glory which is itself a kind of immortality.'[62]

Economic progress has implications far beyond us as individuals and profits future generations more than those who create it; but does it give glory? Is there an economic epic capable of stimulating the enthusiasm of the workers? The inspiration of immortality, which Renan considered to be so powerful, is obviously without force here because we have never seen artists produce masterpieces under the influence of the idea that their work would secure them a place in paradise (as the Turks seek death that they may enjoy the happiness promised by Mahomet). The workers are not entirely mistaken when they look upon religion as a bourgeois luxury since, in truth, religion does not have the resources to improve machines and to provide the means of working more rapidly.

The question must be posed differently from the way in which Renan put it; we need to know if there exist, in the world of the producers, forces of enthusiasm capable of combining with the ethics of good work in such a way that, in our days of crisis, this ethic may acquire all the authority necessary to lead society along the path of economic progress.

We must be careful that the keen sentiment that we have of the necessity of such a morality and our ardent desire to see it realized

---

[62] Renan, *Histoire du peuple d'Israël*, IV, p. 191. Renan seems to me to have identified too easily glory and immortality; he was a victim of figures of speech.

does not induce us to mistake phantoms for forces capable of moving the world. The abundant idyllic literature of the professors of rhetoric is evidently a total conceit. Equally vain are the efforts attempted by so many scholars to find institutions of the past that can be imitated and which might serve as means of disciplining their contemporaries; imitation has never produced much of worth and has often bred disappointment. How absurd then is the idea of borrowing from some previous social structure a suitable means for controlling a system of production whose principal characteristic is that every day it must become more and more opposed to all preceding economic systems? Is there then nothing to hope for?

Morality is not doomed to perish because the motive forces behind it will change; it is not condemned to become a simple collection of maxims as long as it can ally itself with an enthusiasm capable of overcoming all the obstacles posed by routine, prejudices and the need for immediate pleasures. But it is certain that this sovereign force will not be found by following the paths along which contemporary philosophers, experts in social science and the inventors of *far-reaching reforms* would make us go. There is today only one force which can produce the enthusiasm without whose cooperation no morality is possible, and that is the force resulting from propaganda in favour of the general strike.

The preceding explanations have shown that the idea of the general strike, constantly rejuvenated by the sentiments provoked by proletarian violence, produces an entirely epic state of mind and, at the same time, bends all the energies of the mind towards the conditions that allow the realization of a freely functioning and prodigiously progressive workshop; we have thus recognized that there is a strong relationship between the sentiments aroused by the general strike and those which are necessary to bring about a continued progress in production. We have then the right to maintain that the modern world possesses the essential motivating power which *can* ensure the existence of the morality of the producers.

I shall stop here, because it seems to me that I have accomplished the task that I imposed upon myself; I have, in fact, established that proletarian violence has an entirely different historical significance from that attributed to it by superficial thinkers and by politicians; in the total ruin of institutions and of morals there remains something which is powerful, new and intact, and it is this, properly speaking, which constitutes the soul of the revolutionary proletariat; nor will this be swept away in the general decline of moral values if the workers have enough energy to bar the road to the bourgeois corrupters by responding to their advances with the plainest brutality.

I believe that I have made an important contribution to discussions on socialism; henceforth these discussions must deal with the conditions which allow the development of specifically proletarian forces, that is to say, with *violence enlightened by the idea of the general strike*. All the old abstract dissertations on the socialist system of the future become useless; we pass to the domain of real history, to the interpretation of facts, to the ethical evaluations of the revolutionary movement.

The connection, which I pointed out at the beginning of this enquiry, between socialism and proletarian violence, now appears to us in all its force. It is to violence that socialism owes those high ethical ideals by means of which it brings salvation to the modern world.

Appendix I: Unity and multiplicity

I. Biological images which foster the idea of unity; their origin.
II. Ancient unity and its exceptions. – Christian mysticism. – The rights of man; their consequences and their criticism. – Utility of the conception of *ahistoric* man.
III. The ecclesiastical monarchy. – Harmony of powers. – Abandonment of the theory of harmony; idea of absoluteness better understood today.
IV. Current preference of Catholics for accommodation. – Indifference of the State. – Current conflicts.
V. Contemporary experiments provided by the Church: parliamentarianism; the selection of fighting groups; multiplicity of forms.

I

This new edition of *Reflections on Violence* is a republication of the one that appeared in 1908; I have thought it necessary to add this chapter in order to show how mistaken are those people who believe that they raise an irrefutable argument against the doctrines based upon the class struggle by saying that, according to the evidence of common sense, the notion of society is completely permeated with the idea of unity.

That in many circumstances, and especially in those which are most related to acting on the everyday constructions of the mind which we attribute to common sense, the unity of society must be taken into very serious consideration is something that no reasonable person will dream of disputing. One may say, in effect, that social unity presses upon us from all sides, as it were, in the ordinary course of life; because we feel, almost all the time, the force of the effects of a hierarchical authority which imposes uniform rules upon the citizens of the same country. It must not be forgotten, on the other hand, that if common sense is perfectly adapted to the conditions of ordinary relations it almost always ignores the most serious events in life, those in which the value of profound intentions reveal themselves; it must not therefore be regarded as certain that the idea of unity imposes itself upon every social philosophy.

Certain habits of language that are prevalent today have contributed more than all arguments to popularizing the prejudices in favour of unity. Very often it has been found convenient to employ formulas in which human organizations are assimilated to a higher order of organisms; sociologists have derived enormous advantages from these ways of speaking, allowing them to give the impression that they possessed a very serious science based upon biology; since, during the nineteenth century, naturalists had made many resounding discoveries, sociology profited from the prestige that natural history had acquired. Such socio-biological analogies present the idea of unity with a singular insistence; one cannot, indeed, study the higher animals without being struck by the state of extreme dependence of the parts in relation to the whole living body. This connection is in fact so strong that many scientists believed for a long time that it would be impossible to apply to physiology the methods which had been so successful in physics; natural unity, they thought, would find itself jeopardized by the mechanism of experimentation, in such a way that one would observe a sick being in an analogous way to those who are destroyed by neoplasms.[1]

It is not necessary to be a very profound philosopher to recognize that language deceives us constantly as to the true nature of the relationships that exist between things. Before commencing a systematic critique of a system, there would often be a very real advantage in finding out the origin of the images which are frequently encountered in it. In the present case, it is evident that the socio-biological analogies indicate the reverse of reality. It is sufficient, for example, to read the famous book of Edmond Perrier entitled

---

[1] Physiologists arrange things such that their experiments do not disturb the regular course of phenomena to the extent that the animal may be said to be sick.

Les Colonies animales: this scholar succeeds in rendering quite intelligible the mysterious phenomena that he wishes to describe by employing concepts borrowed from the very varied groupings that humans form amongst themselves; he thus follows a very good method, because he employs the relatively clear areas of knowledge in order to make understood the organization of the extremely obscure parts;[2] but he does not doubt for a moment the nature of the task that he sets himself. Misled by the doctrine of the sociologists who claim to teach something more advanced than biology, he thinks that his researches on animal colonies are capable of providing the basis of a social science designed 'to enable us to foresee the future of our societies, to regulate their organization and to explain the contracts on which they are based'.[3]

After having utilized the abundant evidence provided by human groups in order to obtain sound biological descriptions, does one have the right to transfer into social philosophy, as do the sociologists, formulas which have been constructed by means of observations made upon men but which, in the course of their adaptation to the demands of natural history, have not escaped some modifications? In order to be suitably applied to organisms, they have singularly distorted the notion of human activity by disregarding what everyone regards as being the most noble prerogatives of our nature.

When one compares animal colonies, they may be arranged on a scale of evolution culminating in that perfect unity of all the partial activities that reveal to us the normal psychology of man; it may be said of those which are least controlled by a directing centre that they already possess a potential unity; the diverse levels are distinguishable, one from the other, only by the greater or lesser concentration that they present; because there is nowhere any element reducible to unification. On the other hand, it has often been said that our Western societies, due to their Christian culture, offer the

---

[2] Cournot observes, in opposition to Comte, that there 'is nothing clearer to the human intellect, nothing which less imposes the extra burden of a new mystery, of a new irreducible problem, than the explanation of the social mechanism. Who does not see that, in passing from the phenomena of life to social facts, one is in the process of passing from a relatively obscure region to a relatively clear one?' (A[ntoine Augustin] Cournot, *Matérialisme, vitalisme, rationalisme. [Etudes sur l'emploi des données de la science en philosophie*, Paris, Hachette, 1875], p. 172.

[3] Edmond Perrier, *Les Colonies animales* [Paris, Masson, 1881], p. XXXII.

spectacle of consciences which achieve a full moral life only on condition that they understand the infinity of their value;[4] such societies are therefore irreconcilable with the unity which animal colonies reveal to us. By relocating in sociology the social images that biology has developed for its needs, one exposes oneself therefore to committing serious misinterpretations.

II

Historians have often pointed out that the societies of antiquity were very much more unitary than are ours.[5] In reading in the second book of the *Politics* the arguments that Aristotle opposes to the Platonic theories, one becomes readily aware that the spirit of the Greek philosophers was generally dominated by the idea that the most absolute unity is the greatest good that one could wish for a city;[6] one is even led to doubt if Aristotle would have dared to present his anti-unitary conceptions with so much assurance if, in his day, the cities had not been infected by an irremediable decadence, such that the restoration of the old discipline must have appeared strangely utopian to his readers.

In probably all periods there have existed anarchical elements in the world: but these elements were confined to the *limits of society*, which did not protect them; the people succeeded in understanding their existence only by assuming the existence of mysterious protectors who defended these isolated groups from the dangers which threatened them; such anomalies could not influence the outlook of men who sought to found the science of politics in Greece through the observation of things which most commonly occurred.

Beggars, certain itinerant artists and especially singers, and bandits have provided examples of the most significant isolated characters; their adventures were able to give birth to the legends that charmed the masses; this charm arose especially from what these

---

[4] [Hippolyte] Taine, *Le Gouvernement révolutionnaire*, [Paris, Hachette, 1885] p. 126. Cf. [Georg Wilhelm Friedrich] Hegel, *Philosophie de l'esprit*, French trans. [Paris, Baillière, 1867–9], II, p. 254.

[5] Dom Leclercq says that the regime of the Spanish Church, at the time of the Visigoths, provides us with an example in which the unitary conception of the classical City survived in Christianity ([Dom Henri Leclercq], *L'Espagne chrétienne* [Paris, Lecoffre, 1906], pp. XXXII–XXXIII).

[6] Aristotle, *Politique*, bk II, chap. I, 7. [Aristotle, *The Politics*, bk II, chaps. II, III.]

adventures contained of the extraordinary; the extraordinary could not enter into the classical philosophy of the Greeks.

I seriously believe, however, that despite this rule Aristotle was thinking of the Greek hero, who had occupied such a prominent place in the national traditions, when he spoke of the destiny reserved for the man of genius. The latter may not be subjected to ordinary laws; he could not be suppressed by death or by exile; the city-state therefore had no other alternative than that of submitting to his authority. It must be observed that these celebrated reflections occupy only a few lines in the *Politics* and, especially, that Aristotle seems to regard the hypothesis of the reappearance of such demi-gods as highly unlikely.[7]

The ascetics were called upon to have a history of very different importance from that of the other isolated individuals. The men who submit themselves to bodily ordeals sufficient to strike the imagination of the people with amazement are regarded throughout the Orient as being placed above the conditions that limit human powers; as a consequence, they appear to be capable of achieving in nature things as extraordinary as the tortures which they inflict on their flesh; the more powerful, therefore, are they as miracle work-ers, the more extravagant their acts. In India they easily become divine incarnations when, because of the numerous marvels being accomplished around their tombs, the Brahmins find it advan-tageous to deify them.[8]

The Greeks had no taste for this kind of life; but they were influenced a little by Stoic literature which had derived its most curious paradoxes on pain from the practices of Oriental asceticism. Saint Nilus, who, in the fifth century, adapted the maxims of Epic-tetus to the teachings of the spiritual life, did no more than recog-nize the true nature of this doctrine.

Western Christianity profoundly transformed asceticism in its mon-asteries; it brought forth this multitude of mystical persons who, instead of fleeing from the world, were devoured by the desire to spread their reforming activities all around them and to whom the

[7] *Ibid.*, bk III, chap. VIII, 1 and chap. XI, 12. [Aristotle, *The Politics*, bk III, chaps. XIII, XV, XVI. This is a reference to Aristotle's doctrine of *pambasileia*, the absolute Kingship of one man.]

[8] [Sir Alfred Comyns] Lyall, *Etudes sur les moeurs religieuses et sociales de l'Extrême-Orient*, French trans. [Paris, Thorin, 1885], pp. 42–8. [See *Asian Studies, Religious and Social* (London, J. Murray, 1882).]

religious experience gave superhuman strength. To universalize these gifts of grace, until then almost exclusively reserved for monks, was the principal objective of the Reformation: instead of saying, as is normally done, that Luther wanted to make a priest of every Christian, it would be more accurate to say that he *attributes* to each of the convinced faithful some of the mystical faculties which the mystical life develops in the monasteries. The disciple of Luther who reads the Bible in the religious disposition that his master calls 'faith' believes he enters into regular contact with the Holy Spirit, exactly as the members of a religious order embarked on the road to mysticism believe they receive revelations from Christ, from the Virgin Mary or from the saints.

This postulate of the Reformation is manifestly false; it is not easy for men drawn along by all the currents of everyday life to undergo this experience of the Holy Spirit which Luther, as a fanatical monk, found so simple. For the great majority of present-day Protestants, the reading of the Bible is only a form of educational study; ascertaining consequently that they do not receive, in the presence of the sacred texts, the supernatural light that had been promised them, they question the teaching of their ministers: some go as far as complete unbelief whilst others convert to Catholicism because they wish at any price to remain Christians. By not relating the mystical faculties to the conditions of an exceptional life that could sustain them, the theoreticians of the Reformation committed a very major error which, in the long run, must lead to the failure of their Churches; we will only concern ourselves here with the consequences which this error has had for philosophy.

It has often been observed that there have almost always existed two divergent tendencies in the work of human reflection; for want of better terms, one may distinguish them by names borrowed from the history of the Middle Ages and say that thinkers divide themselves into *scholastics* and *mystics*. The writers of the first group believe that our intelligence, starting from the evidence of the senses, may discover how things really are, express the relations that exist between essences, in a language that commands the assent of every reasonable man, and thus arrive at a science of the external world. The others are preoccupied with personal convictions; they have an absolute confidence in the decisions of their conscience; they wish to have their way of seeing the world shared by those

who will listen to them; but they have no scientific proof to vindi-
cate them.

Properly to distinguish these two tendencies ought to be the most
important objective proposed for philosophy; it does not seem to me
that this undertaking would be too difficult; the frequently imposing
obscurity which the doctrine of Kant presents arises from the fact
that these two tendencies are mixed up within it in a particularly
complicated way. Catholic writers constantly reproach Kant for
having taught a subjectivism which may easily lead to scepticism;
he did not think that he merited such criticism, accustomed as he
was to accepting that religious experience provides us with all the
expression of truth compatible with our human frailty.[9]

The errors of Kant must make us indulgent towards men who did
not have his philosophical genius and who derived from a mysticism
corrupted and vulgarized by Protestantism such highly defective
political theories. Protestantism was to lead people ignorant of every
historical consideration to a strange hypothesis: they supposed that,
in order to arrive at the social principles of prime importance, it
was necessary for them to imagine they had consciences sufficiently
like that of the monk who lives constantly in the presence of God.
Such a hypothesis, which cuts all connections between the citizen
and the economic, familial and political bases of life, has been introduced into juridical constructions, the importance of which has been
enormous.

It is easily understood why the earliest American societies should
have regulated their public law in accordance with the paradoxical
principles of the mystical; their constitutions were to embrace something of the monastic, considering that the Puritans strongly
resembled monks intoxicated with the spiritual life; their formulas
survived in the United States, by virtue of the religious respect that
has not ceased to be attached to the memory of these illustrious
ancestors. This literature came to be mixed in our country with that
of Rousseau; he had dreamed of a city inhabited by Swiss artisans
and based on an *ahistoric* man, in accordance with his impressions

---

[9] In the second edition there was a passage relative to the antinomies of Kant that
I have removed, because I have treated this question more fully in the *Revue de
métaphysique et de morale* (September 1910) and because I expect to return to it
again elsewhere. [See 'Vues sur les problèmes de la philosophie', *Revue de métaphysique et de morale* 18, pp. 581–613.]

of life as a nomad wanderer. The legislators of the Revolution, great admirers of Americans and of Jean-Jacques, believed they had produced a masterpiece by proclaiming the rights of absolute man.

The jests made by Joseph de Maistre in 1796 on the subject of the work of our constituent assemblies have often been cited; they wanted to make laws 'for *man*; but there is no such thing as *man* in the world. I have seen Frenchmen, Italians, Russians, etc.; but as for *man* I declare that I have never in my life met him; if he exists, he is unknown to me ... A constitution that is made for all nations is made for none: it is a pure abstraction, an academic exercise made according to some hypothetical ideal, which should be addressed to *man* in his imaginary dwelling place. What is a constitution? Is it not merely the solution to the following problem? Given the population, the religion, the geographical situation, the political circumstances, the wealth, the good and bad qualities of a particular nation, to find the laws that suit it.'[10]

The formulas of this too-clever writer amount to saying that legislators must be of their country and of their time; moreover, it does not seem that the men of the Revolution had forgotten this truth as much as Joseph de Maistre said; it has often been commented that, even in those cases where they proclaimed their intention to reason about an *ahistoric* man, they had usually worked to satisfy the needs, the aspirations or the rancour of the contemporary middle classes; so many of the rules relating to civil law or administration would not have survived the Revolution if their authors had always navigated in imaginary space, in pursuit of absolute man.

What is especially worthy of being closely examined in the heritage which they have left us, is the coexistence of a law formulated for real people of that time and the *ahistorical* arguments. The history of modern France allows us to determine with precision what disadvantages result from the introduction of theses of this kind into the juridical system. The principles of [17]89 were regarded as forming the philosophical foundation of our codes; professors believed themselves obliged to prove that these principles could

[10] Joseph de Maistre, *Considérations sur la France* [Paris, Nouvelle Librairie Nationale, 1907], chap. IV *ad finem.* – There is a great similarity between the formula cited here and the subtitle of [Montesquieu's] *Esprit des lois*: 'Concerning the relation which laws must have to the constitution of each government, to mores, to climate, to religion and to commerce.'

serve to substantiate the general rules of the *juridical science* which they taught: they succeeded in this because, by means of subtlety, the mind may complete the most difficult undertakings; but other clever writers set other sophisms against these conservative sophisms, either in order to establish the necessity for furthering the progress of law or even to establish the absurdity of the present social order.

In Rome something very similar occurred when the jurists of the Antonian period wanted to utilize Stoic philosophy to clarify their doctrines. This philosophy, derived from Oriental asceticism, could only reason about a man removed from the conditions of real life; as a consequence, the dissolution of the ancient juridical order occurred. Historians have generally been so bedazzled by the prestige possessed, in the traditions of the schools [medieval universities], by the texts which the Pandects have preserved for us,[11] that they have not normally seen the social consequences of this great work of renovation. They have extolled the fine *progress* accomplished by jurisprudence but they have not recognized that, at the same time, the respect that the ancient Romans had had for the law was disappearing.[12] Similarly with us, juridical *progress*[13] engendered by the introduction of the principles of [17]89 into our legislation has certainly contributed to the debasement of the idea of law.

In the course of the nineteenth century many detailed criticisms were directed at the doctrine of the *ahistoric* man; it was shown on many occasions that, if we started from laws suitable to this scholastic being, it was impossible to construct a society which resembled those that we know. If the theoreticians of democracy have believed

---

[11] Cf. [Ernest] Renan, *Marc-Aurèle et la fin du monde antique* [Paris, Calmann-Lévy, 1892], pp. 22–9. [The Pandects were a compendium in fifty books of the Roman civil law made by order of Justinian in the sixth century.]

[12] The history of the persecutions provides evidence of considerable value; the ancient Romans, so cruel, would not have dreamed of condemning virgins to the *lupanar* [brothel] (Edmond Le Blant, *Les Persécuteurs et les Martyrs* [Paris, Leroux, 1893], chap. XVIII). The decision taken by Marcus Aurelius against the martyrs of Lyon seems to me to mark a regression towards barbarism. (G[eorges] Sorel, *Le Système historique de Renan* [Paris, Jacques, 1906], p. 335).

[13] I use the word *progress* because I find it in current usage for speaking of changes which are not always very desirable.

that this undertaking was possible, it was because they had – without always being aware of the hoax that they employed – greatly restricted the field upon which this absolute man may extend the action of his free will.

A philosophy established upon postulates borrowed from the mystical life can apply only to isolated persons or to people who have left their isolation by joining a group where exactly the same convictions as theirs predominate. In order to find a true and normal application of the principles proclaimed by modern democracy, one will therefore be led to study what happens in monasteries; this is what Taine said in an excellent manner: 'At the base of this [religious] republic may be found the corner stone designed by Rousseau ... a *social contract*, a pact proposed by the legislator and accepted by the citizens; it is only in a monastic pact that the will of the consenting parties is unanimous, sincere, serious, deliberate and permanent, whilst in the political pact it is not so; thus, whereas the second contract is a theoretical fiction, the first contract is an actual fact.'[14]

One would be tempted to conclude from this criticism that we must abandon every consideration of the *ahistoric* man to the professors of rhetoric; but such a conclusion would arouse protestations from the majority of moralists; for more than a century, the latter have been accustomed to proposing an idea of absolute duty,[15] which presupposes, obviously, that man can detach himself from the ties that bind him to historical conditions. On the other hand, many of the great things of history have been accomplished by the human masses who, during a fairly lengthy period of time, were dominated by convictions analogous to religious forces in that they are sufficiently absolute to make them forget many of the material circumstances which are habitually taken into consideration in choosing the direction to be taken. If one wishes to express this fact in a language appropriate to the procedures which are called scientific, juridical or logical, it is necessary to formulate principles which

[14] [Hippolyte] Taine, *Le Régime moderne* [Paris, Hachette, 1894], II, p. 108.
[15] Cf. [Ferdinand] Brunetière, *Questions actuelles* [Paris, Hachette, 1907], p. 33. This idea has been expressed in the celebrated saying of Jesus: 'Be ye therefore perfect, even as your Father which is in heaven is perfect.' (Matthew V:48); the evangelical life was confined to the monasteries after the triumph of the Church (Renan, [*Marc-Aurèle*], p. 558); modern philosophy is inspired by the Reformation, which aspired to unify the entire Christian world on the monastic model.

will be considered as having been those of *ahistoric* men, more or less thrust on the road of the absolute. The abstract man is not, therefore, as Joseph de Maistre thought, a useless person for philosophy; he constitutes an artifice of our understanding; – many artifices are necessary in the work that we undertake to adapt reality to our intelligence.

The fundamental difference that exists between the methods of social philosophy and those of physiology now appears to us more clearly. The latter can never consider the functioning of an organ without relating it to the whole of the living being; one could say that this whole determines the type of activity into which this element enters. Social philosophy, in order to study the most significant phenomena of history, is obliged to proceed to a *diremption*, to examine certain parts without taking into account all of the ties which connect them to the whole, to determine in some manner the character of their activity by pushing them towards independence. When it has thus arrived at the most perfect understanding it can no longer attempt to reconstitute the broken unity.

We are going to apply these principles to the history of the Church, and their value can then be better understood.

III

It cannot be doubted that at the beginning of our era and, very probably, immediately after the death of Jesus, the Christian communities, by taking Oriental monarchies for models, organized themselves very solidly: their leaders were not, therefore, popular magistrates, as the Protestants have written, but kings acting by virtue of divine delegation.[16] Thanks to this theocratic administration, the Church was able to render the greatest services to the faithful while the Roman State was beginning to disintegrate:[17] it assured them a more uniform justice than that of the official tribunals; it bought the good will of the imperial police so as to avoid harassment;[18] it supported bands of the poor who might be of great

---

[16] Sorel, [*Le Système historique*], p. 421.
[17] Renan compares the bishop of the third century to the Greek or Armenian bishops of contemporary Turkey (Renan, [*Marc-Aurèle*], p. 586).
[18] Tertullien was indignant that the Church could thus mitigate the persecutions (Tertullien, *De fuga*, 13).

help in defending the peaceful bourgeoisie against the agitators of the cities.

The Empire, after the conversion of Constantine, ended by giving the episcopal authority a prestige which enabled it to impose itself upon the Germanic conquerors. For several centuries the Church protected, in a very efficient manner, those privileged groups in which was maintained a very large part of the Roman tradition; our Western civilization owes to Catholicism much more than the preservation of classical literature; above all it owes to it what it has retained of the Roman spirit; and we can comprehend the immense value of this inheritance by comparing the peoples who have shared in it with the Orientals, who have so much difficulty in understanding our institutions.[19]

Ecclesiastical theoreticians have constructed their doctrines by idealizing the glorious past of the Church; she is, according to them, the sole monarchy that can claim to derive its authority directly from God; against the Protestant jurists, who defended the divine right of kings, the Catholic theologians consider that there is something popular in the origins of temporal powers,[20] which puts them in an inferior position in relation to the Papacy. The Church could not, therefore, be controlled by a sovereign; but, in practice, it is not in as independent a position as a kingdom, because it does not have a territory which is distinct from that of the States; it is inserted into civil societies; its supporters are citizens at the same time. Two crowns may easily remain entirely without relations, whereas the Church cannot perform everything it judges necessary for the accomplishment of its mission without meeting, at every step, some of the social relations on which secular law has, rather generally, formulated rules; it is, therefore, necessary that the State

---

[19] The Germans seem to have particularly profited from the lessons provided by the Church. When we examine the resignation with which they accept inequality, the strict discipline that they observe in their associations, such as the army and the factory, the tenacity that they display in their undertakings, we cannot but compare them to the ancient Romans. The Lutheran Reformation has protected them for a long time against the invasion of Renaissance ideas and has therefore prolonged for them the influence of Roman education.

[20] Some contemporary Catholics go into ecstasies about the democratic spirit of the Church; the theologians have only followed the doctrine of the imperial jurists who attributed a delegation of authority from the Roman people to the emperors (Taine, [*Le Régime moderne*], p. 133).

come to an understanding with the Church or that it abstain from legislating on certain matters.

Christianity has a tradition which prevents it from becoming a military power analogous to that of the Muslim caliphate; this derives not only from the doctrines of the very earliest Fathers,[21] but also from a system of government created by Theodosius which remained 'the eternal dream of the Christian conscience, at least in the Roman countries'; Renan is correct in saying that the Christian Empire has been 'the thing which the Church, in its long life, has loved the most'.[22] During the Middle Ages the Papacy tried to carry out great projects which would have been easy with the collaboration of a Theodosius and which presented extraordinary difficulties through the use of forces accidentally grouped together under its patronage; the Crusades, the Inquisition, the Italian wars show us very mediocre results obtained by means of desperate efforts; this experience presented the best evidence one could wish for in favour of the Theodosian system.

The theologians, therefore, arrive neither at unity nor a perfect independence of the two powers; they dream of a harmony which does not seem to them to be very difficult to obtain, because they trust too much to arguments that allow them to say what ought to exist rather than to the observation of facts. Men would have some right, in the judgement of these learned men, to accuse Providence of lacking wisdom if it did not normally assure them the means of enjoying all the advantages which the Church and State must procure; these advantages could only be obtained if a perfect harmony existed between the two powers. From these premises it is concluded that harmony will exist whenever the true order of things, as discovered by reasoning, is not troubled by abuses.

During the time following the Counter-Reformation and the consolidation of the monarchies, this felicitous harmony had been regarded as deriving naturally from institutions. Monarchy was then

---

[21] Gregory VII was inspired by very old Christian ideas when he denounced the power of the princes as having at its origin the character of brigandage, which permitted associating it with the action of the devil, 'the prince of darkness'. ([Jacques] Flach, *Les Origines de l'ancienne France* [Paris, Larose et Forcel, 1904], III, p. 297).

[22] Renan, [*Marc-Aurèle*], p. 621 and pp. 624–5.

the normal government of civilized societies;[23] harmony could not fail to produce these benefits if the kings had, to the same degree as the heads of the Christian hierarchy, a clear knowledge of the heavy responsibility which would weigh on them in the case of conflict. It was sufficient, they thought, that the men called upon to educate the princes should apply themselves to instilling in them feelings for the episcopacy similar to those that Theodosius had felt for Saint Ambrose.

The history of the Church during the nineteenth century has not been promising for the doctrine of harmony; there have been, almost constantly, grave difficulties between the ecclesiastical authorities and successive governments in France; the preoccupations of the present time have led to an examination of the past from a position very different to that adopted by the earlier theoreticians; it has been seen that, in all periods, conflicts were too frequent for it to be possible to regard them as aberrant facts; it was more appropriate to compare them to wars that broke out so frequently between independent powers, which disputed the hegemony of a part of Europe.

The ecclesiastical writers, attributing a major importance to the education of princely consciences as a means of securing harmony, formerly ascribed the conflicts to moral origins: the pride of sovereigns, the cupidity of the great, the mean, nasty and sometimes impious jealousy of the legists. The scholars of the nineteenth century introduced the rule of explaining great things only by great causes; since then the old controversies of the casuist-historians have been found ridiculous; the politico-ecclesiastical struggles have been regarded as having been motivated by the same type of reasons as those which permit an understanding of the great European wars.

The work carried out on the Middle Ages by the apologists of the Papacy has greatly contributed to confirming this interpretation. Wishing to defend the popes from the people who had so often denounced their insatiable ambitions, many Catholics began to write the history of the quarrels of the priesthood and of the Empire in

---

[23] In the first half of the eighteenth century Vico believed that England was destined to become a pure monarchy ([Jules] Michelet, *Oeuvres choisies de Vico* [Paris, Flammarion, 1894], p. 629).

the spirit of the *Guelphs*.[a] They maintained that the sovereign pontiffs had rendered immense services to civilization in defending Italian liberties against Germanic despotism. This entire political manner of presenting the greatest conflicts that have ever existed between the Church and the State entails a comparison of the normal relations that exist between the two powers with those that exist between two independent crowns.

The old doctrine of harmony has therefore become as chimerical in the eyes of modern historians as perhaps that of a United States of Europe; they are two conceptions of the same kind, intended to replace the fact of *accidental peace* with the theory of *normal union*. Now and then people hold forth on the United States of Europe after drinks at the congresses of jokers; but no serious person occupies himself with these children's games.

For a long time, secular authors have examined the assertions of papal power, formulated during the quarrels of the priesthood and of the Empire, more from a juridical point of view than a historical one. French jurists had found absurd the theses that would have rendered impossible the royal order of which they were the principal representatives; they had put forward Gallican principles with a view to restraining Ultramontane pretensions within limits compatible with the principles of civil administration;[b] the historians were disposed to regarding as extravagant paradoxes the things which the jurists condemned with so much rigour. But today we no longer concern ourselves with knowing to what extent the popes were legally right and how their theories could have been applied in practice; we want to know what relations exist between these assertions of ecclesiastical authority and the development of conflicts; it is beyond doubt that they constitute a very convenient ideological translation of the struggle in which the Church was engaged.

When one has properly understood the implications of these old documents, one better comprehends the claims which caused such a great scandal in liberal circles at the time of the publication in

[a] The Guelphs were members of one of the great factions in Italian medieval politics, siding with the pope in the long struggle between the Papacy and the Holy Roman Empire.
[b] The supporters of Gallicanism acknowledged the authority of the French State over the Church; whilst the supporters of Ultramontanism (literally, 'over the Alps') recognized the superior authority of the Vatican.

1864 of the Syllabus of Pius IX.[c] The Church has almost always had a clear awareness that, in order to fill the role which was assigned to it by its founder, it is obliged to affirm an absolute right, although in practice, in order to facilitate the working of the civil societies into which it is inserted, it is disposed to accept many limitations upon its authority. *Diremption* alone makes possible the recognition of this internal law of the Church; in the periods when the struggle is intense, Catholics claim for the Church an independence conforming to this internal law and incompatible with the general order established by the State; most often, ecclesiastical diplomacy arranges agreements which, for the superficial observer, dissimulate the absoluteness of its principles. Harmony is only a dream of the theoreticians, which corresponds neither to the internal law of the Church nor to practical arrangements, and which serves to explain nothing in history.

With each renaissance of the Church, history has been thrown into confusion by manifestations of the absolute independence claimed by Catholics; it is these periods of renaissance that reveal what constitutes the *essential nature* of the Church; and thus fully justifies the method of *diremption* outlined at the end of section II.

IV

In the eyes of a great many French Catholics the Church should abandon its old absolute *theses* to the spare-time activities of college pedants. The latter, who only know the world through what is said about it in old books, will never be able to understand how modern society functions; it is therefore necessary that men devoid of scholastic prejudices apply themselves to observing with care the phenomena of contemporary life; the Church would gain much from listening to the advice of people who have a sense of the suitable and the possible. It should resolve to replace *thesis* by *hypothesis*, by making all the concessions which are necessary in order to suffer least from the detestable conditions in the midst of which Catholicism must henceforth live.

We are assured that this policy of extreme prudence is based upon the highest considerations of scientific philosophy. The

[c] In 1864 the encyclical *Quanta cura* and the *Syllabus errorum* sharply criticized all liberal Catholic groups and what were taken to be associated modern errors.

Catholic public is nearly always far behind the secular public;[24] it adopts as very important novelties fashions which are beginning to disappear; the clergy, for example, has for some years become passionately enthusiastic about *Science*, to the point that it could give advice to M[onsieur] Homais himself.[d] The clerical party, which prides itself on being up to scratch on present-day questions, has discovered transformism and loves to intoxicate itself with discussions about development; but there are many ways of understanding these words; it cannot be doubted that for the modern priests – to a greater or lesser extent tinged with modernism – evolution, adaptation and relativity correspond to a single current of ideas. In proclaiming themselves transformists, Catholics wish to combat the former *fanaticism for truth*, to content themselves with the most convenient theories, and to have on all matters only those opinions likely to win the favour of people indifferent to religious matters. They are *pragmatists* of a rather low type.

There exists a very great difference between the doctrine of harmony and the transformist nonsenses which so please today's Catholics. The first was suited to an active and powerful Church, infused with the idea of the absolute, which often deigned to limit its demands in order not to obstruct overmuch the operation of the State, but which imposed on it, as often as it could, the obligation of recognizing the infinite rights that it derived from God. The second system is appropriate to those people whose weakness has been put to the test by numerous defeats, who live constantly in the fear of receiving new blows, and who are overjoyed when they secure a delay sufficient to allow them to develop habits of a new servility, consistent with the demands of their masters.

This clever tactic has not been very successful for the Church: Leo XIII was frequently celebrated by the republicans and considered by them to be a *great pope* because he counselled Catholics to submit to the necessities of the age; the crowning achievement

---

[24] Huysmans assures us that from the 'point of view of an understanding of art, the Catholic public is well below the secular public': [Joris K. Huysmans,] *La Cathédrale* [Paris, C. Pirot, 1898], p. 19. This inferiority is not limited to art!

[d] Monsieur Homais is a character in Flaubert's *Madame Bovary*: a self-satisfied country apothecary, he had an opinion on all things.

of his policy was the dissolution of the religious orders;[25] Drumont was able on several occasions to make him responsible for the disasters which had overwhelmed the Church in France (for example, *La Libre parole*, 30 March 1903); but it might also be said that the Catholics reaped the bitter fruits of their cowardice and that never were misfortunes more merited than theirs. Such an experience must not be lost on the syndicalists, who are advised so often to abandon the absolute in order to confine themselves to a policy which is wise and prudent and completely focused on immediate results; the syndicalists do not want to adapt themselves to circumstances, and they are certainly right since they have the courage to bear the inconveniences of the struggle.

There is no lack of Catholics who feel that peace might be obtained in contemporary society without submitting to an accommodation and without seeking to achieve the impossible harmony of the earlier theologians. The difficulties presented by the coexistence of two powers might be reduced, in effect, to almost nothing if and when the number of matters over which the competition of the two sovereigns has been further reduced.

In barbaric times, the excessive extension of ecclesiastical jurisdiction could be beneficial, even though there did not yet exist any very well-organized tribunals; this regime had to disappear to the extent that the State performed its functions more completely; secular institutions were rightly preferred because they were better adapted to the economy: no one dreams any more, for example, of treating wills as religious acts; many centuries ago, we stopped completing contracts with promissory oaths the consequences of which were examined by ecclesiastical courts; priests have finished up by being judged like other citizens. Whilst the theologians continue to assert, with the same force as previously, that the Church alone may bring true marriages into existence, the constitution of

---

[25] It was observed in France that the protest contained in the letter of 29 June 1901 against the law of associations was particularly petty. Compare this vague literature to the dispatches of 1 and 8 June 1903, relative to the journey of [Emile] Loubet to Rome; Leo XIII was very conscious of the significance of the *Italian action*, which wounded his pride, after having believed that the *French actions* had no great significance, because he based his strange hopes on the consequences that ought to have followed from his general diplomacy.

the family escapes the Church completely; the clergy are no longer even able to limit, however slightly, the respectability enjoyed in society by people who have civil marriages after divorce. The wealth that had been accumulated by previous generations to support works of Catholic charity has been confiscated and these activities have, in large part, been secularized.

The fundamental prescriptions for the purpose of which the religious monarchy was instituted could, in the opinion of many people, be faithfully executed if the Church contented itself with governing public worship, the schools of theological instruction and the monastic institutions. Should the common law be sufficiently permeated with liberty, it might suffice to let Catholicism accomplish this mission. An understanding would no longer be necessary between the heads of the spiritual power and those of the temporal power; instead of the harmony which was only a dream of the theorists, there would reign the most complete indifference. One could not say that the State would ignore the Church totally; because the first duty of the legislator is fully to understand the conditions in which each of the juridical persons carries out his activity. It would then be necessary for the laws to be so framed that they did not hinder the free expansion of the Church.

This regime of indifference would not be without similarities to that experienced by Judaism after the destruction of the kingdom of Judea.[26] The Jews wanted to restore Jerusalem, but solely to make of it a kind of great monastery consecrated to the rites of the Temple; of the administration of Nehemiah, Renan writes: 'It is a Church which is being founded and not a city. A crowd that one amuses with entertainments, nobles whose vanity is flattered by the honours of processions, are not the components of a homeland: a military aristocracy is necessary. The Jew will not be a citizen; he will remain in the towns of the others. But, let us hasten to say, there are in the world other things than the homeland.'[27] It was precisely when they no longer had a homeland that the Jews came

[26] The juridical causes would not be the same, even though the results might be similar; Renan does, in fact, point out that 'liberty is definitely a creation of the modern age. It is the consequence of an idea that Antiquity did not possess, the State guaranteeing the most diverse forms of human activity and remaining neutral in matters of conscience, tastes and sentiment': *Histoire du peuple d'Israël* [Paris, Calmann-Lévy, 1887–93], IV, p. 82.

[27] *Ibid.*, p. 81.

to give their religion a definitive character; during the time of their national independence they were very inclined towards a syncretism that was odious to the prophets; they became fanatic worshippers of Jehovah when they were subject to the pagans. The development of the priestly code, the Psalms (whose theological importance came to be so great), the second part of the book of Isaiah,[28] date from this period.[c] Thus, the most intense religious life may exist in a Church which lives under a regime of indifference.[29]

The Catholicism that exists in Protestant countries is very happy with this system: its hierarchy, its professors and its monasteries have little substance; it is something as politically insignificant as Judaism was in the Persian world. It is very different for French Catholicism whose leaders, until recently, were mixed up in too many matters to be able easily to accept the transformation of their activity in line with the plan which I indicated above. The right to open educational institutions appears to them to be especially important to preserve; they are persuaded, in effect, that primary and secondary schools must be directed with the object of implanting in the instruction of the faithful the theological formulations which they judge appropriate to secure the guidance of souls by the clergy; from that derives the ardent competition between the Church and the State.

For some thirty years or more the republican government has been driven by a sort of Antichurch, which pursues an underhand policy[30] which is sometimes brutal and always fanatical and which

[28] Renan places this book before the second Temple; I agree with the opinion of Isidore Loëb, which seems to me more credible.

[29] Judaism displays, in the literature that postdates the fall from independence, such a marked indifference towards the State that Renan marvels at it as a paradox: 'All the monastic conditions are there,' he says; 'The Catholic Church, so scornful of the State, could not live without the State' (*[Histoire du peuple d'Israël]*, III, p. 427).

[30] For example, the famous academic neutrality has only been a strategy designed to lull the vigilance of Catholics; today the official representatives of the government declare that the great object to be pursued in the primary schools is the eradication of religious faith. (Cf. the speech delivered by Aristide Briand before the Ligue de l'Enseignement in 1906 at Angers.)

[c] It is generally agreed that the Book of Isaiah has at least two authors, with everything after chapter 36 referred to as Deutero-Isaiah. Sorel here once more shows his detailed knowledge of the nineteenth-century Biblical scholarship. The main theme of this part of the Book is that of Israel's Redemption and her Mission in the world.

seeks to destroy Christian faiths in France. This Antichurch, today triumphant, wishes to profit from the unexpected success that it has enjoyed since the Dreyfusard revolution; it believes that the regime of indifference is only a fraud as long as the Church retains considerable influence; its great preoccupation is completely to suppress the religious orders, its leaders believing, with reason, that the priests would not be sufficient to preserve Catholicism.

V

The present situation of Catholicism in France offers sufficient remarkable parallels with that of the proletariat engaged upon the class struggle for the syndicalists to have a real interest in following closely contemporary ecclesiastical history. In the same way that in the world of the workers we find many *reformists* who regard themselves as being great experts in social science, the Catholic world abounds with men of distinction, very up-to-date with modern knowledge and knowing the needs of their century, who dream of religious peace, the moral unity of the nation, compromise with the enemy. The Church does not have the same facilities as the *syndicats* for brushing aside bad counsellors.

Renan points out that the renewal of the Roman persecutions provoked a renewal of ideas about the advent of the Antichrist,[31] and, as a consequence, of all the apocalyptic hopes relative to the reign of Christ; we can therefore compare these persecutions to the great violent strikes which give such an extraordinary importance to catastrophic conceptions. We will no longer see in our day the atrocities which were committed during the first centuries of our era; but Renan has, again quite correctly, seen the monasteries as able to replace the martyr.[32] It is beyond doubt that certain religious orders have been very effective educators for heroism; unhappily, for a good number of years the monastic institutions seem to have made serious efforts to embrace the secular spirit, with the object of better getting on with people of the world. From this new situation it results that the Church today lacks the conditions which for so long generated the advent, sustained the energy and popularized

[31] Renan, *Marc-Aurèle*, p. 337.
[32] *Ibid.*, p. 558.

the guidance of heroic leaders; the compromisers no longer have much to fear from these nuisances.

The *wise* men of Catholicism, like the *wise* men of the world of the workers, believe that, in order to improve a difficult situation, the best method to follow consists in winning the support of political powers; the ecclesiastical colleges have greatly contributed to developing this spirit of intrigue amongst their clientele. The Church was greatly surprised when it tested at its own expense the value of its *wisdom*; parliament voted against it a whole set of laws that were clearly dictated to it by Freemasonry; judgements based upon bizarre considerations were multiplied against the religious congregations; the public, with extreme indifference, welcomed the most arbitrary measures; all recourse against the activities of the Antichurch was therefore closed. The Catholics were happy to hear at least a few eloquent voices condemn these unjust laws; but their indignation flowed out in the form of literature; the only heroic response that they were capable of taking was that of soliciting a few votes in favour of the Sganarelles who represent the Church in parliament in such a comic fashion.[33]

The practice of strikes has led the workers to entertain more virile thoughts; they scarcely respect all the sheets of paper on which imbecilic legislators inscribe marvellous formulas designed to ensure social peace; for discussions about laws[34] they substitute acts of war; they no longer allow socialist deputies to come to give them advice; the *reformists* are almost always obliged to go to ground while the energetic work to impose their victorious will upon the bosses.

Many people are of the opinion that if the *syndicats* were rich enough to occupy themselves largely with mutual aid work, their spirit would change; the majority of the union members would be afraid to see their social funds threatened by financial penalties imposed as a result of the illegal acts of the revolutionaries; the

[33] In the discussion which occurred on 21 December 1906 in the Chamber on the circumstances in which Cardinal Richard had been expelled from his palace, Denys Cochin performed the role of *dupe* of the comedy with great authority. [Sganarelle was a comic figure in Molière's *Le Médecin malgré lui* (1666).]

[34] On 9 November 1906, Aristide Briand declared to the Chamber that if the Catholic deputies had refused to concern themselves with the laws of Separation, he would not have succeeded in working out the project. The utility of parliamentarians clearly appears here!

tactics of trickery would thus become necessary and leadership would pass into the hands of those swindlers with whom the republican statesmen have always got on. The clergy are driven by other economic considerations; without too much cost to themselves, they has been able to give up the control of church property, because the generosity of the faithful will permit them to live from day to day; but they are afraid that they will not be able to celebrate the act of worship with the extravagant material which they habitually use; not having a secure right to the churches, they could not guarantee to the pious that their gifts would always be assigned to increase the splendour of the ritual. It is for this reason that intriguing Catholics do not cease to propose schemes of conciliation to the Papacy.

The meetings of the bishops held after the vote on the law of Separation showed that the *moderate* party would have prevailed in the Church of France if the parliamentary regime had been able to function. The prelates were not sparing in their solemn declarations affirming the absolute rights of the religious monarchy;[35] but they very much desired not to embarrass Aristide Briand;[f] many facts allow us to conclude that episcopal parliamentarianism would have even had as a result the giving, under the regime of Separation, of more influence to ministers of the Republic over the Church than the ministers of Napoleon III had ever had. The Papacy ended by adopting the only reasonable course that it could take; it suppressed the general assemblies, in order that the energetic should not be hindered by the clever; one day French Catholics will bless Pius X who saved the honour of their Church.

This experience of parliamentarianism is worth studying; the *syndicats* also must be wary of great solemn meetings in which it is so easy for the government to prevent every virile resolution from securing support; war is not made under the leadership of talking assemblies.[36]

---

[35] Nor are the socialist congresses sparing in declarations devoted to the execration of the bourgeoisie.

[36] The republicans do not appear to be disposed to forgive Pius X for having frustrated their manoeuvres: Aristide Briand has complained on many occasions in the Chamber about the conduct of the pope; he has even insinuated that it may

[f] Aristide Briand (1862–1932); socialist deputy and later prime minister; one of the first advocates of the general strike, after the Dreyfus affair Briand became an

Catholicism has always reserved the functions of combat to a limited number of bodies whose members have been rigidly selected by means of tests designed to authenticate their commitment; the clergy therefore accept this rule, very often forgotten by revolutionary writers but one that a trade union leader once stated before P[aul] de Rousiers: 'One weakens oneself by assimilating weak elements.'[37] It is with elite troops, perfectly trained through monastic life, ready to face all obstacles and filled with an absolute confidence in victory, that Catholicism has until now been able to triumph over its enemies. Every time that a formidable peril has confronted the Church, men particularly adept, like great captains, at discerning the weak points in the opposing army have created new religious orders appropriate to the tactics demanded by the new struggle. If today the religious tradition appears so threatened, it is because it has not organized institutions capable of leading the struggle against the Antichurch; the faithful still preserve perhaps a great deal of piety; but they form an inert mass.

It would be extremely dangerous if the proletariat were not to practise a division of functions which has so well served Catholicism during its long history; it would be no more than an inert mass destined to fall, as with democracy,[38] under the control of politicians who live off the subordination of their electors; the *syndicats* must search less for the greatest number of adherents than for the organization of vigorous elements; revolutionary strikes are excellent as a means of selection as they estrange the pacifists who would spoil the elite troops.

have been instigated by Germany: 'We were disposed to accept the law. What happened? I do not know. Has a related situation influenced the decisions of the Holy See? Does the current situation in this country become *the ransom for a better situation in another country?* . . . It is a problem which poses itself and which I have the right and the duty to place before your consciences': session of 9 November 1906. Joseph Reinach consoles himself for the wickedness of Pius X by proclaiming that the latter only has 'the education of a country priest' and that he does not understand the importance of the outcome of the Reformation, the *Encyclopedia* and the Revolution: *Histoire de l'affaire Dreyfus* [Paris, Editions de la Revue Blanche, 1901–11], VI, p. 427.

[37] [Paul] de Rousiers, *Le Trade-unionisme en Angleterre* [Paris, Colin, 1897], p. 93.

[38] The socialist party has become a democratic mob since it contains 'officers, the decorated, the rich, great investors and big businessmen' (cf. an article of Lucien Rolland in *Le Socialiste* of 29 August 1909).

apostle of conciliation towards the Church and one of the architects of the law on the separation of Church and State.

This division of functions has enabled Catholicism to be very diverse: from the groups whose life is drowned by the general unity to the orders who are dedicated to the absolute. Because of its religious specializations, Catholicism finds itself in much better conditions than Protestantism: a true Christian, following the principles of the Reformation, would have to be able to pass, at will, from an economic standard to a monastic standard; this transition is considerably more difficult to achieve by an individual than the exact discipline of a monastic order. Renan has compared the small Anglo-Saxon congregations to monasteries;[39] these groups show us that the principle of the Reformation is applicable to those of an exceptional nature; but the action of these societies is generally less fruitful than that of the regular clergy, because it is supported less by the great Christian public. It has often been observed that the Church has adopted with extreme ease the new systems designed to strengthen spiritual life that were put into practice by the founders of orders; by contrast, the Protestant pastors have been, almost always, hostile to sects; in this way, Anglicanism has much to be sorry for in having allowed Methodism to escape from its control.[40]

The majority of Catholics have thus been able to remain remote from the pursuit of the absolute and yet collaborate very effectively in the work of those who, through struggle, were maintaining or perfecting their doctrines; the elite, which led the assault on the enemy positions, received the material and moral support of the masses who saw in it the reality of Christianity. According to the position one adopts, one will have the right to consider society as either a unity or as a multiplicity of antagonistic forces: there is an approximation of economico-juridical uniformity which is generally sufficiently developed for one to be able, in a great number of cases, not to concern ourselves with the religious absolute represented by the monk; on the other hand, there are many important questions that one could not comprehend without picturing the activity of institutions of combat as being preponderant.

[39] Renan, *Marc-Aurèle*, p. 627.
[40] A sentence of Macaulay has often been cited on this subject, to the effect that if Wesley had been Catholic he would no doubt have founded a great religious order ([Thomas Babington] Macaulay, *Essais [politiques et] philosophiques*, French trans. [Paris, Michel-Lévy, 1862], p. 275 [the majority of these essays are taken from Macaulay's *Critical and Historical Essays* (1848)]; Brunetière, [*Questions actuelles*],

Similar observations could be made with regard to workers' organizations; they seem under an obligation to vary themselves to infinity, to the extent that the proletariat feels itself more capable of taking its place in the world; the socialist parties believe themselves charged with providing ideas to these organizations,[41] advising them and grouping them into a class unit, at the same time as their parliamentary activity would establish a connection between the workers' movement and the bourgeoisie; and we know that the socialist parties have taken from democracy their great love of unity. In order properly to understand the revolutionary movement, we must place ourselves in a position diametrically opposed to that of the politicians. A large number of organizations are merged, to a greater or lesser extent, into the economico-juridical life of the whole of society, to the extent that whatever unity is required in society is produced automatically; others, less numerous but well selected, lead the class struggle; it is these that discipline proletarian thought by creating the ideological unity which the proletariat needs in order to accomplish its revolutionary work; – and the guides ask for no recompense and in this, as in so many other things, are very different from the Intellectuals, who insist upon being maintained in a joyous way of life by the poor devils before whom they consent to hold forth.

pp. 37–8). – America appears to have better used the zeal of her sectarians than has England.
[41] A pretension all the more absurd when these parties are lacking in ideas of their own.

Appendix II: Apology for violence

Men who address revolutionary words to the people are bound to submit themselves to high standards of sincerity, because the workers understand these words in their exact and literal sense and never indulge in any symbolic interpretation. When in 1905 I ventured to write in some detail on proletarian violence I was fully aware of the grave responsibility I assumed in trying to show the historic bearing of acts that our parliamentary socialists try to cover up with so much skill. Today I do not hesitate to declare that socialism could not continue to exist without an apology for violence.

It is through strikes that the proletariat asserts its existence. I cannot be persuaded to see in strikes something analogous to the temporary rupture of commercial relations which is brought about when a grocer and his supplier of prunes cannot agree about the price. The strike is a phenomenon of war; it is therefore a serious misrepresentation to say that violence is an accidental feature destined to disappear from strikes.

The social revolution is an extension of this war in which each great strike is an episode; this is why the syndicalists speak of this revolution in the language of strikes; for them socialism is reduced to the conception, the expectation of and the preparation for the general strike, which, like the Napoleonic battle, is to annihilate completely a condemned regime.

Such a conception allows none of the subtle exegeses in which Jaurès excels. It is a question here of an overthrow in the course of which both employers and the State will be removed by the organized producers. Our Intellectuals, who hope to obtain the highest positions from democracy, would be sent back to their literature; the parliamentary socialists, who find in the organizations created by the bourgeoisie the means of exercising a certain amount of power, would become useless.

The analogy that exists between violent strikes and war is rich in consequences. No one doubts (except d'Estournelles de Constant)[a] that it was war that provided the republics of antiquity with the ideas which form the ornament of our modern culture. The social war, for which the proletariat ceaselessly prepares itself in the *syndicats*, may engender the elements of a new civilization suited to a people of producers. I continually call the attention of my young friends to the problems presented by socialism when considered from the point of view of a civilization of producers; I assert that today a philosophy is being elaborated according to this plan which would hardly have been imagined a few years ago; this philosophy is closely bound to the apology of violence.

I have never had for *creative hatred* the admiration that Jaurès has devoted to it; I do not feel the same indulgence towards the guillotiners as he does; I have a horror of any measure which strikes the vanquished under a judicial disguise. War, carried on in broad daylight, without any hypocritical attenuation, for the purpose of ruining an irreconcilable enemy, excludes all the abominations which dishonoured the bourgeois revolution of the eighteenth century. The apology for violence in this case is particularly easy.

It would serve no great purpose to explain to the poor that they are mistaken to feel sentiments of jealousy and vengeance against their masters; these sentiments are too powerful to be repressed by exhortations; it is upon their widespread prevalence that democracy chiefly founds its strength. Social war, by making an appeal to the honour which develops so naturally in all organized armies, can eliminate these evil feelings against which morality would remain powerless. If this were the only reason we had for attributing a high civilizing value to revolutionary syndicalism, this reason alone

---

[a] Paul d'Estournelles de Constant (1852–1924); politician and diplomat; he devoted himself to furthering international conciliation, for which he was awarded the Nobel peace prize in 1909.

would seem to me to be decisive in favour of the apologists of violence.

The idea of the general strike, engendered by the practice of violent strikes, entails the conception of an irrevocable overthrow. There is something terrifying in this – which will appear more and more terrifying as violence takes a greater place in the mind of the proletarians. But, in undertaking a serious, formidable and sublime work, the socialists raise themselves above our frivolous society and make themselves worthy of pointing out new roads to the world.

The parliamentary socialists may be compared to the officials whom Napoleon made into a nobility and who worked to strengthen the State bequeathed by the *ancien régime*. Revolutionary syndicalism corresponds well enough to the Napoleonic armies whose soldiers accomplished so many acts of valour, knowing all the time that they would remain poor. What remains of the Empire? Nothing but the epic of the *Grande Armée*; what will remain of the present socialist movement will be the epic of the strikes.

Le Matin, 18 May 1908

Appendix III:[1] In defence of Lenin

On 4 February 1918 *Le Journal de Genève* published under the title 'The other danger' an article the greater part of which I reproduce below.

'The great revolutionary wave, which originated in the East, is spreading in Europe, is passing over the German plains and is already breaking against the rocks at the foot of the Alps. We must expect that our country will have to undergo a supreme test before having definitely won its right to exist in the new world to which the war will give birth. Our banal and vain quarrels between the French Swiss and the German Swiss are a turned page, a sad page to which we must not return. Another ditch has been dug that it will be more difficult to refill.

It is becoming more and more evident that an internationalist agitation, which is both planned and methodical, is spreading in our large towns. It seeks to incite, by violence, a revolution which, from Switzerland, would advance step by step to neighbouring countries.

... Before the war there was propagated a doctrine of Force in syndicalist circles which had an obvious affinity with that of the German imperialists. In his *Reflections on Violence* Georges Sorel preached this new gospel: "The role of violence", he said, "appears to us as singularly great in history, provided that it is the brutal and

---

[1] The appendix was written in September 1919 for the fourth edition of *Réflexions sur la violence*.

283

direct expression of the class struggle."[2] Nothing can be done except by violence. It is only necessary that it no longer be exercised from the top down, as formerly, but from the bottom up. There is no intention of putting an end to the abuse of Force. They want Force to change hands and the oppressed of yesterday to become the tyrant of tomorrow,[3] whilst waiting for the inevitable tip of the scale which will put things back to their original state.

During their stay in Switzerland, Lenin and Trotsky must have thought over the book of Georges Sorel at their leisure. They are applying its principles with the most dangerous logic . . . They must have an army in order to impose the tyrannical domination of a minority upon a great people that is amorphous and has been trained for centuries for servitude . . . If they want to put an end to foreign war, it is in order to pursue the class war at their ease. These Jacobin militarists aspire to establish a tsarism in reverse to their own benefit. And this is the ideal which is being proposed today to the European nations.

In Germany socialism has become impregnated with the same despotic spirit. Marxism is the enemy-brother of Prussian militarism. It has the same outlook, the same methods, the same worship of automatic discipline, the same sovereign contempt for individual independence.[4]

. . . Let us not worry. Switzerland is still a country where each citizen has the old habit of discharging his function and duty at the post which he occupies. He does it voluntarily and freely, because

[2] On page 130 we read: 'Proletarian violence, exercised as a pure and simple manifestation of the feeling of class struggle, appears as a very beautiful and heroic thing.' It is likely that the contributor to *Le Journal de Genève* used an old edition; I have not verified the reference.

[3] I have, however, very strongly criticized in my book the frequently bloody tyranny of the French Revolution.

[4] It is not fair to impute to Marxism all the practices of German social democracy, which was far more under the influence of Lassalle than under that of Marx. In 1897 Charles Andler said of Lassalle: 'It is in order to give strength to ideal justice that he demands universal suffrage for the job of the emancipation of the proletariat. But immediately he is seized with mistrust and, as if he sensed his own error, he appeals to the existing State, though military and monarchical, to introduce his practical reforms. From the oscillation between the two systems was born a curious constitutional conception: a military monarchy, tied to universal suffrage and working with it, in a collaboration fraught with conflict, to achieve social emancipation. That is really the German Empire of today': *Les Origines du socialisme d'Etat en Allemagne* [Paris, Alcan, 1897], pp. 60–1.

that is his function and duty and not because he has been made into an automaton . . . All despotism is odious to him, whether it comes from above or below. It is because of this that the Swiss citizen, heir to a long tradition of healthy and normal public life, will not allow himself to be subjected to doctrines coming from a neighbour- ing empire whose subjects are still held in a condition of political minority or from a republic which is only a few months old[5] whose impoverished citizens have no political education whatsoever and most of whom neither know how to read nor how to write.

Let those *Papierlischweizer*,[6] who are beginning to speak among us as masters and who, before our excessively docile assemblies, permit themselves to dictate ultimatums addressed to our authorit- ies, remember this: we will not allow them to sabotage the country which has sheltered them. If they imagine that the Swiss nation may be used as a culture for the bacteria of disorder, they are greatly mistaken. We will know how to protect ourselves from civil strife as from foreign war, knowing moreover that the one would only be a prelude to the other and that the least crack in the walls of our house could become a breach open to invasion.'[7]

Although, more than once, the friends of *Le Journal du Genève* have been accused of being agents of the secret diplomacy of the Entente, I am inclined to believe that Professor Paul Seippel, in writing this article, did not have the charitable desire of calling the attention of the suspicious French police to me. I need not point out to my readers that this eminent representative of the liberal bourgeoisie understood nothing of my book. His case shows, once again, how

---

[5] The *bolshevik* revolution occurred on 7 November 1917.
[6] In the same way the *zionists* call the Jews who naturalize themselves in our country 'stamped paper Frenchman'.
[7] The author is obviously threatening his compatriots with the intervention of the Entente. Under the regime of the peaceful Louis-Philippe, the Swiss were twice threatened with a French invasion: in 1838, because it would not expel the future Napoleon III, who was a burgher of the canton of Thurgau, and in 1848, because after the affair of the *Sonderbund* it wanted to reform its constitution in a more unitary direction. During the last war, the engagements which the Entente made in support of Swiss neutrality were hardly unequivocal; General Brialmont had written that France would probably invade Germany through Switzerland; the Swiss general staff was frequently attacked with violence by the press supporting the Entente, because the general staff took the ideas of the great Belgian engineer seriously.

the polemicists who undertake the defence of Latin civilization against Nordic barbarism, take an approach bordering upon stupidity.

* * *

I do not intend meriting the indulgence of the innumerable Paul Seippels which the *literature of Victory* contains by cursing the *bolsheviks* whom the bourgeoisie fear so greatly.[8] I have no reason to believe that Lenin made use of some of the ideas in my books; but were it so, I would be immoderately proud of having contributed to the intellectual formation of a man who seems to me to be, at one and the same time, the greatest theoretician that socialism has had since Marx and a head of State whose genius recalls that of Peter the Great.

At the moment when the Paris Commune was falling, Marx wrote a manifesto for the Internationale in which present-day socialists are accustomed to look for the most complete expression of the political doctrines of their master. The speech pronounced by Lenin in May 1918 on the problems of the power of the *soviets* has no less importance than the study by Marx of the civil war in 1871. It may be that the *bolsheviks* will end by succumbing, in the long run, under the blows of the mercenaries engaged by the plutocracies of the Entente; but the ideology of the new form of proletarian State will not perish; it will survive by merging with the myths which will take their substance from the popular accounts of the struggle undertaken by the Republic of *soviets* against the coalition of great capitalist powers.

When Peter the Great ascended to the throne, Russia did not differ greatly from Merovingian Gaul: he wanted it to be transformed from top to bottom, in such a way that his empire might be worthy

---

[8] The advocates of the *Union sacrée* are more afraid of the *bolsheviks* than of the Germans – and that is saying a great deal! – because, oddly enough, a defeated Germany, humiliated and crushed with the cost of the war, frightens many of our patriotic *propagandists*. In order to give some courage to their clientele, the editors of the great newspapers ordinarily speak of Russian revolutionaries with a boasting tone, the impudence of which is matched by the terror that convulses their entrails.

of figuring amongst the civilized states of the day; all those who could be called the *ruling class* (court nobility, civil servants, officers) were obliged to apply themselves to imitating the persons who held analogous positions in France. His work was completed by Catherine the Great, whom the *philosophes* of the Voltairian period exalted, with just cause, as a prodigious creator of order – as order was understood in the eighteenth century.

It could be said of Lenin that, like Peter the Great, he wants to force history.[9] He intends, in effect, to introduce into his country the socialism which, according to the most authoritative representatives of social democracy, could only follow a highly developed capitalism; now, Russian industry, subjected for such a long time to a regime of heavy governmental direction, of interfering regulation and technical negligence, finds itself in a very backward condition; there is no lack of distinguished socialists who regard Lenin's enterprise as chimerical. Good manufacturing practices had succeeded in imposing themselves upon capitalists through the play of half-blind mechanisms; the role of intelligence, limiting itself to an analysis which pointed out what each practice contained of advantage or harm, had been rather mediocre; if the socialist economy followed a capitalist economy in the conditions that Marx, inspired by observations made in England,[10] had foreseen, then the transmission of these good practices would operate in an almost automatic manner – intelligence being at most required to protect the

---

[9] The words 'to force' are used here in a sense close to that employed by gardeners.

[10] In 1888 the Russian *Moniteur juridique* published a note found among the papers of Marx, according to which the author of *Capital* was very far from believing that all economies must follow the same lines of development. He did not believe that Russia, in order to arrive at socialism, was obliged to begin by destroying its ancient communal agriculture, in order to turn its peasants into proletarians; it seemed possible to him that Russia could, 'without experiencing the tortures of the [capitalist] regime, appropriate all of its fruits while developing its own historic situation'. This note of Marx is reproduced by Nicolas-On in his *Histoire du développement économique de la Russie depuis l'affranchissement des serfs*, French trans. [Paris, Giard et Brière, 1902], pp. 507–9. – In a preface written in 1882 for a Russian translation of the *Communist Manifesto*, Marx expressed the following hypothetical opinion: 'If it should happen that the Russian revolution should give the signal for a workers' revolution in the West, in such a manner that the two revolutions complement each other, the agrarian communism of Russia, the present-day *mir*, will become the point of departure for a communist development' (*Le Manifeste communiste*, trans. Charles Andler [Paris, Jacques, n.d.], I, p. 12). These texts are sufficient to show that true Marxism is not as absolute in its predictions as the enemies of Lenin would very much like to have it.

acquisitions of the bourgeois past from the illusions of revolutionary simpletons. In order to give to Russian socialism a foundation that a Marxist (such as Lenin) may regard as secure, a prodigious effort of intelligence is required: the latter must be in a position to demonstrate to the directors of production the value of certain rules derived from the experience of a highly developed capitalism; it is necessary to have them accepted by the masses, by virtue of the moral authority enjoyed by men who, through their services, have secured the confidence of the people; at every instant, the people who lead the revolution are obliged to defend it against the instincts which always push humanity towards the lowest levels of civilization.

When Lenin asserts that the campaign undertaken to establish the socialist regime in Russia upon a permanent basis is a thousand times more difficult than the most difficult military campaign, he is not guilty of exaggeration. He is right to say that never have revolutionaries found themselves confronted with a task similar to his; formerly the innovators had only to destroy certain reputedly harmful institutions, while the reconstruction was left to the initiatives of those whom the search for extra profits led to throw themselves into such enterprises; but the *bolsheviks* are obliged to destroy and to reconstruct, in such a way that the capitalists will no longer come to interpose themselves between society and the workers. No substantial progress can be made in industry without passing through various stages; the directors of production must stop in time when they are following the wrong track and see if there is not a better chance of succeeding by another method; this is what is called 'learning by experience'. Lenin is not one of those theorists who believes that their genius puts themselves above the evidence of reality; he is, therefore, very careful to note the lessons provided by practical experience since the Revolution.

For Russian socialism to succeed in establishing a stable economy, it is necessary therefore that the intelligence of the revolutionaries should be very alert, very well informed and very free from prejudices. Even though Lenin might not carry out his whole programme he could leave to the world very important lessons from which European society could draw profit.[11] Lenin may, justifiably,

---

[11] See the speech by Lenin translated in *L'Humanité*, 4 September 1919.

be proud of what his comrades are doing; the Russian workers are acquiring an immortal glory by approaching the realization of what until now has only been an abstract idea.

* * *

Despite the predictions of the great men of the Entente, *bolshevism* does not seem easy to suppress; the English and French governments should begin to recognize that they were mistaken in bending an obliging ear to wealthy Russians who live in the capitals of the West; this entire world is completely alien to the ideas that have taken hold among the workers and the peasants of their country. Although he has lived for a long time outside Russia, Lenin has remained a true Muscovite. When the time arrives which allows the evaluation of present-day events with historical impartiality, it will be recognized that *bolshevism* owed a great part of its strength to the fact that the masses saw it as a protest against an oligarchy whose greatest concern was not to appear Russian; at the end of 1917, the former mouthpiece of the *Black Hundreds* said that the *bolsheviks* had 'proved that they were more Russian than the rebels Laledin, Roussky,[12] etc., who had betrayed the tsar and the homeland' (*Le Journal de Genève*, 20 December 1917); Russia patiently endures much suffering because she feels herself finally governed by a true Muscovite.

For the last two centuries, one tsar alone had wanted to be Russian: this was Nicholas I. 'I love my country', he said to Custine in 1839, 'and I believe that I have understood it; I assure you that when I am weary of all the troubles of our time I try to forget the rest of Europe by retiring to the interior of Russia. No one is more Russian than I.'[13] Custine considered that Nicholas wanted to return 'to its own nature a nation led astray for over a century along paths of servile imitation'; the emperor demanded especially that Russian be spoken at court, although most of the women did not know the national language.[14] He regretted that Nicholas, 'despite his strong

---

[12] Very probably in the pay of the Entente.
[13] [Astolphe de] Custine, *La Russie en 1839* [Paris, Librairie d'Aymot, 1843], 2nd edn, II, p. 46. On page 41 this author calls him 'the Louis XIV of the Slavs'.
[14] *Ibid.*, pp. 209–11.

practical sense and his profound sagacity', did not have the courage to abandon Saint Petersburg for Moscow: 'By this return, he might have repaired the error of Tsar Peter who, instead of training his boyars in the play-house he built for them on the shores of the Baltic, might have been able and should have civilized them at home, taking advantage of the admirable elements that nature had put at his disposal, elements which he ignored with disdain, with a levity of spirit unworthy of a superior man, which he was in certain respects . . . Either Russia will not fulfil what appears to us to be its destiny or Moscow will again become one day the capital of the empire. If ever I were to see the throne of Russia majestically restored to its true home, I would say: the Slav nation, triumphing through a just pride over the vanity of its leaders, finally lives its own life.'[15]

The accidents of war have led the *bolsheviks* to effect this transfer: if it came to pass that they were to succumb under the blows of their enemies, it is not likely that a government of reaction would dare to remove from old Moscow its status as capital;[16] thus, admitting that the new regime may not last, it would have contributed to the reinforcement of Muscovitism in a society whose rulers had for a long time oriented their minds towards the West.

It is by reference to the Muscovite characteristics of *bolshevism* that as a historian one may speak of the process of revolutionary repression in Russia.[17] There are certainly many lies in the accusations that the press of the Entente direct against the *bolsheviks*,[18] but properly to evaluate the painful episodes of the Russian Revolution one must ask oneself what would the great tsars have done had they been threatened by revolts similar to those which the

---

[15] *Ibid.*, III, pp. 271-3.

[16] If Finland and Estonia remain separated from Russia the capital would find itself poorly placed at the mouth of the Neva.

[17] *Le Journal de Genève* of 27 September 1917 reports a speech of Lenin in which he opposes the measures of general proscription decreed following the attempt to assassinate him at the beginning of the month. It seems that it was the Jews who had entered the revolutionary movement who are primarily responsible for the terroristic measures blamed upon the *bolsheviks*. This hypothesis appears to me to be all the more reasonable given that the intervention of the Jews in the Hungarian Soviet Republic has not been a happy one.

[18] Our compatriots, who believe themselves to be the most clever men in the world, have accepted, like fools, the most absurd calumnies invented by impudent journalists with the express purpose of dishonouring the *bolsheviks*.

Republic of *soviets* is obliged to defeat quickly if it does not wish to commit suicide; they would certainly have recoiled from the most terrifying severities in order to wipe out conspiracies supported from abroad and swarming with assassins.[19] On the other hand, the national traditions provided the *Red Guards* with innumerable precedents which they believed they had the right to imitate in order to defend the Revolution;[20] after a war of frightening bloodshed, in the course of which we have seen General Kornilov massacre entire regiments (*Le Journal de Genève*, 16 October 1917), human life cannot be respected in Russia;[21] the number of people shot by the *bolsheviks* is, in any case, considerably less that the number of victims of the blockade organized by the official representatives of democratic *Justice*.

Lenin is not, after all, a candidate for the prize of virtue awarded by the Académie Française; he is answerable only to *Russian history*; the only truly important question that the philosopher should address is that of knowing whether he is contributing to the orientation of Russia towards the construction of a republic of the producers, capable of encompassing an economy as progressive as that of our capitalist democracies.

* * *

By way of conclusion, let us return to the moral complicity which, according to *Le Journal de Genève*, links me with Lenin. I do not believe that, in any of my writings, I have presented an apology for proscriptions; it is therefore absurd to imagine, as Professor Paul

---

[19] On 3 September 1918 *Le Petit Parisien*, an organ dear to our Joseph Prudhommes, published an article of wild enthusiasm in honour of Dora Kaplan, who had just attempted to assassinate Lenin.

[20] A correspondent of *Le Journal de Genève* asks if the Russian counter-revolutionaries did not count greatly on the assistance of criminal elements, because they had distributed proclamations calling upon 'the population to massacre the *youpins* and the revolutionaries' (14 October 1917). In many cases the *Red Guards* could believe that, by suppressing the enemies most determined to exterminate them in the case of victory, they were engaging in legitimate defence.

[21] The politicians who maintain with Clemenceau that the French Revolution forms a bloc have little justification in their displays of severity towards the *bolsheviks*; the bloc admired by Clemenceau was responsible for the death of at least ten times as many people as the *bolsheviks*, denounced by the friends of Clemenceau as abominable barbarians.

Seippel does, that Lenin may have found in *Reflections on Violence*
any incitement to terrorism; but if he had really pondered on them
during his stay in Switzerland they could have exercised upon his
genius an entirely different influence than that of which my accuser
speaks. It would not have been impossible that this book, so Proud-
honian in inspiration, had led Lenin to adopt the doctrines set out
by Proudhon in *La Guerre et la paix*. If this hypothesis were correct,
he might have been led to believe, with all the energy of his passionate soul, that violations of the laws of war have infallible historical
sanctions. His indomitable resistance could then be easily
explained.[22]

This is a statement that I would willingly attribute to Lenin. The
war of starvation that the capitalist democracies are directing against
the Republic of the *soviets* is a war of cowardice; it leads to nothing
less than the denial of the true laws of war defined by Proudhon;
accepting the possibility that the *Red Guards* were obliged to capitulate, the fraudulent victory of the Entente would only produce
ephemeral results. By contrast, the heroic efforts of the Russian
proletariat warrant history's reward for bringing about the triumph
of institutions in whose defence so many sacrifices have been made
by the worker and peasant masses of Russia. History, according to
Renan, rewarded the military virtues by giving Rome the Mediter-
ranean empire; despite the innumerable abuses of the conquest, the
legions accomplished what he called 'the work of God';[23] if we are
grateful to the Roman soldiers for having replaced aborted, strayed
and impotent civilizations by a civilization whose pupils we still are
in law, literature and monuments, how grateful will not the future
have to be towards the Russian soldiers of socialism! How lightly
will the historians weigh the criticisms of the rhetoricians charged
by democracy with denouncing the excesses of the *bolsheviks*! New
Carthages must not triumph over what is now the Rome of the
proletariat.

And this finally is what I permit myself to add on my own
account: Cursed be the plutocratic democracies that are starving

[22] A French writer, who has seen the *bolsheviks* at work, speaks of the 'stubborn and
inspired mysticism' of Lenin (Etienne Antonelli, *La Russie bolcheviste* [Paris, Grasset, 1919], p. 272). This expression is not clear.
[23] [Ernest] Renan, *Histoire du peuple d'Israël* [Paris, Calmann-Lévy, 1887–93], IV,
p. 267.

Russia; I am only an old man whose life is at the mercy of trifling accidents; but may I, before descending into my grave, see the humilation of the arrogant bourgeois democracies, today shamelessly triumphant![24]

---

[24] In closing *Reflections on Violence*, I pay a final tribute to the memory of the one to whom this book is dedicated; it was in thinking of a past filled with labour that I wrote: 'Happy is the man who has known a devoted wife, strong and proud in her love, who will always keep ever present his youth, who will prevent his soul from ever being satisfied, who will always remind him of the obligations of his task and who, at times, will even reveal to him his genius.' [These remarks are taken from Sorel's earlier essay 'Jean-Jacques Rousseau', *Le Mouvement socialiste* 21 (1907), p. 513.]

INDEX

Index

Cambridge Texts in the History of Political Thought

Titles published in the series thus far

Aristotle *The Politics* and *The Constitution of Athens* (edited by Stephen Everson)
 0 521 48400 6 paperback
Arnold *Culture and Anarchy and other Writings* (edited by Stefan Collini)
 0 521 37796 x paperback
Astell *Political Writings* (edited by Patricia Springborg)
 0 521 42845 9 paperback
Augustine *The City of God against the Pagans* (edited by R. W. Dyson)
 0 521 46843 4 paperback
Austin *The Province of Jurisprudence Determined* (edited by Wilfrid E. Rumble)
 0 521 44756 9 paperback
Bacon *The History of the Reign of King Henry VII* (edited by Brian Vickers)
 0 521 58663 1 paperback
Bakunin *Statism and Anarchy* (edited by Marshall Shatz)
 0 521 36973 8 paperback
Baxter *A Holy Commonwealth* (edited by William Lamont)
 0 521 40580 7 paperback
Bayle *Political Writings* (edited by Sally L. Jenkinson)
 0 521 47677 1 paperback
Beccaria *On Crimes and Punishments and other Writings* (edited by Richard Bellamy)
 0 521 47982 7 paperback
Bentham *A Fragment on Government* (introduction by Ross Harrison)
 0 521 35929 5 paperback
Bernstein *The Preconditions of Socialism* (edited by Henry Tudor)
 0 521 39808 8 paperback
Bodin *On Sovereignty* (edited by Julian H. Franklin)
 0 521 34992 3 paperback
Bolingbroke *Political Writings* (edited by David Armitage)
 0 521 58697 6 paperback
Bossuet *Politics Drawn from the Very Words of Holy Scripture* (edited by Patrick Riley)
 0 521 36807 3 paperback

The British Idealists (edited by David Boucher)
    0 521 45951 6 paperback
Burke *Pre-Revolutionary Writings* (edited by Ian Harris)
    0 521 36800 6 paperback
Christine de Pizan *The Book of the Body Politic* (edited by Kate
    Langdon Forhan)
    0 521 42259 0 paperback
Cicero *On Duties* (edited by M. T. Griffin and E. M. Atkins)
    0 521 34835 8 paperback
Cicero *On the Commonwealth* and *On Laws* (edited by James E. G.
    Zetzel)
    0 521 45959 1 paperback
Comte *Early Political Writings* (edited by H. S. Jones)
    0 521 46923 6 paperback
Conciliarism and Papalism (edited by J. H. Burns and Thomas M.
    Izbicki)
    0 521 47674 7 paperback
Constant *Political Writings* (edited by Biancamaria Fontana)
    0 521 31632 4 paperback
Dante *Monarchy* (edited by Prue Shaw)
    0 521 56781 5 paperback
Diderot *Political Writings* (edited by John Hope Mason and Robert
    Wokler)
    0 521 36911 8 paperback
The Dutch Revolt (edited by Martin van Gelderen)
    0 521 39809 6 paperback
The Early Political Writings of the German Romantics (edited by Frederick
    C. Beiser)
    0 521 44951 0 paperback
Early Greek Political Thought from Homer to the Sophists (edited by
    Michael Gagarin and Paul Woodruff)
    0 521 43768 7 paperback
The English Levellers (edited by Andrew Sharp)
    0 521 62511 4 paperback
Erasmus *The Education of a Christian Prince* (edited by Lisa Jardine)
    0 521 58811 1 paperback
Fenelon *Telemachus* (edited by (Patrick Riley)
    0 521 45662 2 paperback
Ferguson *An Essay on the History of Civil Society* (edited by Fania
    Oz-Salzberger)
    0 521 44736 4 paperback

Filmer *Patriarcha and Other Writings* (edited by Johann P. Sommerville)
  0 521 39903 3 paperback
Fletcher *Political Works* (edited by John Robertson)
  0 521 43994 9 paperback
Sir John Fortescue *On the Laws and Governance of England* (edited by
  Shelley Lockwood)
  0 521 58996 7 paperback
Fourier *The Theory of the Four Movements* (edited by Gareth Stedman
  Jones and Ian Patterson)
  0 521 35693 8 paperback
Gramsci *Pre-Prison Writings* (edited by Richard Bellamy)
  0 521 42307 4 paperback
Guicciardini *Dialogue on the Government of Florence* (edited by Alison
  Brown)
  0 521 45623 1 paperback
Harrington *A Commonwealth of Oceana* and *A System of Politics* (edited
  by J. G. A. Pocock)
  0 521 42329 5 paperback
Hegel *Elements of the Philosophy of Right* (edited by Allen W. Wood
  and H. B. Nisbet)
  0 521 34888 9paperback
Hegel *Political Writings* (edited by Laurence Dickey and H. B. Nisbet)
  0 521 45975 3 paperback
Hobbes *Leviathan* (edited by Richard Tuck)
  0 521 56797 1 paperback
Hobbes *On the Citizen* (edited by Michael Silverthorne and Richard Tuck)
  0 521 43780 6 paperback
Hobhouse *Liberalism and Other Writings* (edited by James
  Meadowcroft)
  0 521 43726 1 paperback
Hooker *Of the Laws of Ecclesiastical Polity* (edited by A. S. McGrade)
  0 521 37908 3 paperback
Hume *Political Essays* (edited by Knud Haakonssen)
  0 521 46639 3 paperback
King James VI and I *Political Writings* (edited by Johann P.
  Sommerville)
  0 521 44729 1 paperback
Jefferson *Political Writings* (edited by Joyce Appleby and Terence Ball)
  0 521 64841 6 paperback
John of Salisbury *Policraticus* (edited by Cary Nederman)
  0 521 36701 8 paperback

Kant *Political Writings* (edited by H. S. Reiss and H. B. Nisbet)
   o 521 39837 1 paperback
Knox *On Rebellion* (edited by Roger A. Mason)
   o 521 39988 2 paperback
Kropotkin *The Conquest of Bread and other Writings* (edited by Marshall
   Shatz)
   o 521 45990 7 paperback
Lawson *Politica sacra et civilis* (edited by Conal Condren)
   o 521 39248 9 paperback
Leibniz *Political Writings* (edited by Patrick Riley)
   o 521 35899 X paperback
Locke *Political Essays* (edited by Mark Goldie)
   o 521 47861 8 paperback
Locke *Two Treatises of Government* (edited by Peter Laslett)
   o 521 35730 6 paperback
Loyseau *A Treatise of Orders and Plain Dignities* (edited by Howell A.
   Lloyd)
   o 521 45624 X paperback
Luther and Calvin on Secular Authority (edited by Harro Höpfl)
   o 521 34986 9 paperback
Machiavelli *The Prince* (edited by Quentin Skinner and Russell Price)
   o 521 34993 1 paperback
de Maistre *Considerations on France* (edited by Isaiah Berlin and Richard
   Lebrun)
   o 521 46628 8 paperback
Malthus *An Essay on the Principle of Population* (edited by Donald
   Winch)
   o 521 42972 2 paperback
Marsiglio of Padua *Defensor minor* and *De translatione Imperii* (edited by
   Cary Nederman)
   o 521 40846 6 paperback
Marx *Early Political Writings* (edited by Joseph O'Malley)
   o 521 34994 X paperback
Marx *Later Political Writings* (edited by Terrell Carver)
   o 521 36739 5 paperback
James Mill *Political Writings* (edited by Terence Ball)
   o 521 38748 5 paperback
J. S. Mill *On Liberty*, with *The Subjection of Women* and *Chapters on
   Socialism* (edited by Stefan Collini)
   o 521 37917 2 paperback

Milton *Political Writings* (edited by Martin Dzelzainis)
0 521 34866 8 paperback
Montesquieu *The Spirit of the Laws* (edited by Anne M. Cohler,
Basia Carolyn Miller and Harold Samuel Stone)
0 521 36974 6 paperback
More *Utopia* (edited by George M. Logan and Robert M. Adams)
0 521 40318 9 paperback
Morris *News from Nowhere* (edited by Krishan Kumar)
0 521 42233 7 paperback
Nicholas of Cusa *The Catholic Concordance* (edited by Paul E. Sigmund)
0 521 56773 4 paperback
Nietzsche *On the Genealogy of Morality* (edited by Keith Ansell-Pearson)
0 521 40610 2 paperback
Paine *Political Writings* (edited by Bruce Kuklick)
0 521 36678 x paperback
Plato *Statesman* (edited by Julia Annas and Robin Waterfield)
0 521 44778 x paperback
Price *Political Writings* (edited by D. O. Thomas)
0 521 40969 1 paperback
Priestley *Political Writings* (edited by Peter Miller)
0 521 42561 1 paperback
Proudhon *What Is Property?* (edited by Donald R. Kelley and Bonnie G.
Smith)
0 521 40556 4 paperback
Pufendorf *On the Duty of Man and Citizen according to Natural Law*
(edited by James Tully)
0 521 35980 5 paperback
The Radical Reformation (edited by Michael G. Baylor)
0 521 37948 2 paperback
Rousseau *The Discourses and other Early Political Writings* (edited by
Victor Gourevitch)
0 521 42445 3 paperback
Rousseau *The Social Contract and other Later Political Writings* (edited by
Victor Gourevitch)
0 521 42446 1 paperback
Seneca *Moral and Political Essays* (edited by John Cooper and John
Procope)
0 521 34818 8 paperback
Sidney *Court Maxims* (edited by Hans W. Blom, Eco Haitsma Mulier
and Ronald Janse)
0 521 46736 5 paperback